Beginning PHP 5 and MySQL E-Commerce: From Novice to Professional

CRISTIAN DARIE AND MIHAI BUCICA

Beginning PHP 5 and MySQL E-Commerce: From Novice to Professional
Copyright © 2005 by Cristian Darie and Mihai Bucica

ISBN (pbk): 1-59059-392-8

Printed and bound in the United States of America 9 8 7 6 5 4 3

Trademarked names may appear in this book. Rather than use a trademark symbol with every occurrence of a trademarked name, we use the names only in an editorial fashion and to the benefit of the trademark owner, with no intention of infringement of the trademark.

Contributing Authors: Emilian Balanescu, Radu Calauz, Lucian Gheorghe, Karli Watson
Lead Editor: Jason Gilmore
Technical Reviewers: Mark Evans, Radu Calauz
Editorial Board: Steve Anglin, Dan Appleman, Ewan Buckingham, Gary Cornell, Tony Davis, John Franklin, Jason Gilmore, Chris Mills, Dominic Shakeshaft, Jim Sumser
Project Manager: Tracy Brown Collins
Copy Edit Manager: Nicole LeClerc
Copy Editor: Julie McNamee
Production Manager: Kari Brooks-Copony
Production Editor: Janet Vail
Compositor and Artist: Diana Van Winkle
Proofreader: Patrick Vincent
Indexer: John Collin
Interior Designer: Diana Van Winkle
Cover Designer: Kurt Krames
Manufacturing Manager: Tom Debolski

Distributed to the book trade in the United States by Springer-Verlag New York, Inc., 233 Spring Street, 6th Floor, New York, NY 10013, and outside the United States by Springer-Verlag GmbH & Co. KG, Tiergarten-str. 17, 69112 Heidelberg, Germany.

In the United States: phone 1-800-SPRINGER, fax 201-348-4505, e-mail orders@springer-ny.com, or visit http://www.springer-ny.com. Outside the United States: fax +49 6221 345229, e-mail orders@springer.de, or visit http://www.springer.de.

For information on translations, please contact Apress directly at 2560 Ninth Street, Suite 219, Berkeley, CA 94710. Phone 510-549-5930, fax 510-549-5939, e-mail info@apress.com, or visit http://www.apress.com.

The source code for this book is available to readers at http://www.apress.com in the Downloads section.

Contents at a Glance

PART 1 ▪▪▪ Phase I of Development

PART 2 ▪▪▪ Phase II of Development

PART 3 ▪▪▪ Phase III of Development

PART 4 ▪▪▪ Appendixes

Contents

PART 1 ▪▪▪ Phase I of Development

PART 2 ▪▪▪ Phase II of Development

PART 3 ▪▪▪ Phase III of Development

PART 4 ■■■ Appendixes

About the Authors

CRISTIAN DARIE, currently the technical lead for the Better Business Bureau Romania, is an experienced programmer specializing in open source and Microsoft technologies, and relational database management systems. Having worked with computers since he was old enough to reach the keyboard, he initially tasted programming success with a first prize in his first programming contest at the age of 13, and from there moved onto many other similar achievements in the following years. In the past five years he has designed, deployed, and optimized many data-oriented software applications while working as a consultant for a wide variety of companies, and now he is studying advanced distributed application architectures for his PhD degree. Cristian co-authored several programming books for Apress, Wrox, and Packt Publishing, including *Beginning ASP.NET 1.1 E-Commerce: From Novice to Professional* and *The Programmer's Guide to SQL*. Cristian can be contacted through his personal web site, http://www.CristianDarie.ro.

MIHAI BUCICA started programming at the age of 12, when he also started competing in programming contests (and winning many of them). With a bachelor's degree in computer science from the Automatic Control and Computers Faculty of the University Politehnica of Bucharest, Mihai is working as an Outsourcing Project Manager for Galaxy Soft SRL (http://www.galaxysoft.ro). Even after working with a multitude of languages and technologies, his programming language of choice remained C++, and he loves the LGPL word.

About the Technical Reviewers

MARK EVANS is an IT Consultant residing in Almeria, Spain. Mark has been developing applications based on PHP and MySQL for more than five years and is a member of the osCommerce Development team developing an Open Source E-Commerce application released under the GPL license. Mark has also published articles on PHP/MySQL development and Open Source Development in a number of magazines. He can be contacted via his web site at http://www.smarkit.com or via email at mark@smarkit.com.

RADU CALAUZ, a former component of the Romanian national chess juniors team, holds a Bachelor's degree in computer science, and a Master's degree in "Database in Internet and electronic trade" with a paper disquisition on "PHP in electronic trade." Radu is presently a Senior Web Programmer and Project Manager at Ecommerce Corporation (http://www.ecommerce.com), and has more than four years experience with PHP, MySQL, PostgreSQL, Apache, XHTML, CSS, JavaScript, and related technologies under both Windows and Unix platforms. He can be contacted via email at radu@ecommerce.com or through his personal web site at http://www.tackesoft.com.

Acknowledgments

I'd like to say a big "Thank you!" to our wonderful team at Apress that worked so hard to produce this book. Special thanks go to the project manager, Tracy Brown Collins (see, Tracy, we managed to do the book on time!); the copy editor, Julie McNamee; the production manager, Janet Vail; and the lead editor, Jason Gilmore.

—Cristian Darie

I wish to thank my parents, all my real friends, and Miruna.

— Mihai Bucica

Introduction

Welcome to *Beginning PHP 5 and MySQL E-Commerce: From Novice to Professional!* The explosive growth of retail over the Internet is encouraging more small- to medium-sized businesses to consider the benefits of setting up e-commerce web sites. While there are great and obvious advantages to online retail, there are also many hidden pitfalls that you might encounter when developing a retail web site. This book provides you with a practical, step-by-step guide to setting up an e-commerce web site. Guiding you through every step of the design and build process, this book will have you building high quality, extendable e-commerce web sites quickly and easily.

Over the course of the book, you will develop all the skills necessary to get your business up on the web and available to a worldwide audience. We present this information in a book-long case study, the complexity of which develops as your knowledge increases through the book.

The case study is presented in three phases. The first phase focuses on getting the site up and running as quickly as possible, and at a low cost. Although not yet full-featured, at the conclusion of this phase, your site will be capable of accepting PayPal payments, enabling you to begin generating revenue immediately.

Phase two concentrates on increasing revenue by improving the shopping experience. In this phase, you'll learn how to proactively encourage customers to buy more by implementing product recommendations. We'll also begin laying the groundwork for handling credit card transactions by developing and integrating custom shopping cart functionality.

In the third phase, we'll show you how to increase your profit margins by reducing costs through automating and streamlining order processing and administration, and by handling credit card transactions yourself. You also learn how to integrate external functionality through web services, and improve your customer's shopping experience by adding product reviews functionality.

Who Is This Book For?

Beginning PHP 5 and MySQL E-Commerce: From Novice to Professional is aimed at developers looking for a tutorial approach to building a full e-commerce web site from design to deployment. However, it's assumed that you have some knowledge of building web sites with PHP and MySQL. W. Jason Gilmore's *Beginning PHP 5 and MySQL: From Novice to Professional* (Apress, 2004) can provide this foundation knowledge for you.

The book will also prove valuable for PHP 4 developers who learn best by example, and want to experience PHP 5 development techniques first hand.

What Does This Book Cover?

This book is divided into three parts consisting of 16 chapters and 3 Appendixes. We cover a wide variety of topics, showing you how to

- Build an online product catalog that can be browsed and searched

- Implement the catalog administration pages that allow adding, modifying, and removing products, categories, and departments

- Create your own shopping basket and check out in PHP

- Increase sales by implementing product recommendations and product reviews

- Handle payments using PayPal, DataCash, and VeriSign Payflow Pro

- Implement a customer accounts system

- Integrate external functionality through web services

The following brief roadmap highlights how we'll take you from novice to professional regarding each of the topics in the previous list.

Phase I of Development

Chapter 1: Starting an E-Commerce Site

In this chapter, we'll introduce some of the principles of e-commerce in the real world. You see the importance of focusing on short-term revenue and keeping risks down. We look at the three basic ways in which an e-commerce site can make money. We then apply those principles to a three-phase plan that provides a deliverable, usable site at each phase of this book.

Chapter 2: Laying Out the Foundations

The first chapter offered an overview of e-commerce in the real world. Now that you've decided to develop a web site, we start to look in more detail at laying down the foundations for its future. We'll talk about what technologies and tools you'll use, and even more importantly, how you'll use them.

Chapter 3: Creating the Product Catalog: Part I

After learning about the three-tier architecture and implementing a bit of your web site's main page, it's time to continue your work by starting to create the TShirtShop product catalog. Because the product catalog is composed of many components, you'll create it over two chapters. In Chapter 3, you'll create the first database table, and implement the data access code. By the end of this chapter, you'll have something dynamically generated on your web page.

Chapter 4: Creating the Product Catalog: Part II

The fun isn't over yet! In the previous chapter, you created a selectable list of departments for TShirtShop. However, a product catalog is much more than a list of departments. In Chapter 4, you'll add the rest of the product catalog features.

Chapter 5: Searching the Catalog

In the preceding two chapters, you will have implemented a functional product catalog for TShirtShop. However, the site still lacks the all-important search feature. The goal in this chapter is to allow the visitor to search the site for products by entering one or more keywords. You'll learn how to implement search results rankings, and how to browse through the search results page by page. You'll see how easy it is to add new functionality to a working site by integrating the new components into the existing architecture.

Chapter 6: Receiving Payments Using PayPal

Let's make some money! Your e-commerce web site needs a way to receive payments from customers. The preferred solution for established companies is to open a merchant account, but many small businesses choose to start with a solution that's simpler to implement, where they don't have to process credit card or payment information themselves.

A number of companies and web sites exist to help individuals or small businesses that don't have the resources to process credit card and wire transactions, and can be used to process the payment between companies and their customers. In this chapter, we'll demonstrate some of the functionality provided by one such company, PayPal, as we use it on the TShirtShop web site in the first two stages of development.

Chapter 7: Catalog Administration

The final detail to take care of before launching a web site is to create its administrative interface. Although this is a part visitors will never see, it's still key to delivering a quality web site to your client.

Phase II of Development

Chapter 8: The Shopping Basket

With this chapter you enter the second phase of development, where you start improving and adding new features to the already existing, fully functional e-commerce site. In Chapter 8, you'll implement the custom shopping basket, which stores its data in the local database. This provides you with more flexibility than the PayPal shopping basket, over which you have no control and which you can't save into your database for further processing and analysis.

Chapter 9: Dealing with Customer Orders

The good news is that the brand new shopping cart implemented in Chapter 8 looks good and is fully functional. The bad news is that it doesn't allow the visitor to actually place an order, making it totally useless in the context of a production system. As you have probably already guessed, you'll deal with that problem in this chapter, in two separate stages. In the first part of the chapter, you'll implement the client-side part of the order-placing mechanism. In the second part of the chapter, you'll implement a simple orders administration page where the site administrator can view and handle pending orders.

Chapter 10: Product Recommendations

One of the best advantages of an Internet store compared to a brick-and-mortar store is the capability to customize the web site for each visitor based on his or her preferences, or based on data gathered from other visitors with similar preferences. If your web site knows how to suggest additional products to your visitor in a clever way, he or she might end up buying more than initially planned. In Chapter 10, you'll learn how to implement a dynamic product recommendation system.

Phase III of Development

Chapter 11: Customer Details

In the first two stages of development, you've built a basic (but functional) site, and have hooked it into PayPal for taking payments and confirming orders. In the third section of the book, you'll take things a little further. By cutting out PayPal from the ordering process, you can gain better control as well as reduce overhead. This isn't as complicated as you might think, but you must be careful to do things right. Chapter 11 lays the groundwork by implementing a customer account system, as well as looking into the security aspects of exchanging and storing customer and credit card details.

Chapter 12: Implementing the Order Pipeline: Part I

The TShirtShop e-commerce application is shaping up nicely. You've added customer account functionality, and you're keeping track of customer addresses and credit card information, which is stored in a secure way. However, you're not currently using this information—you're delegating responsibility for this to PayPal. In this and the next chapter, you'll build your own order-processing pipeline that deals with authorizing credit cards, stock checking, shipping, providing email notifications, and so on. We'll leave the credit card processing specifics until Chapter 14, but we'll show you where this process fits in before then.

Chapter 13: Implementing the Order Pipeline: Part II

In this chapter, you'll add the required pipeline sections so that you can process orders from start to finish, although you won't be adding full credit card transaction functionality until the next chapter. We'll also look at the web administration of orders by modifying the order admin pages added earlier in the book to take into account the new order-processing system.

Chapter 14: Credit Card Transactions

The last thing you need to do before launching the e-commerce site is enable credit card processing. In this chapter, we'll look at how you can build this into the pipeline you created in Chapters 12 and 13. You'll see how to use two popular credit card gateways to do this, DataCash and VeriSign Payflow Pro. By the end of this chapter, TShirtShop will be a fully functioning, secure, and usable e-commerce application.

Chapter 15: Product Reviews

At this point, you have a complete and functional e-commerce web site. However, this doesn't stop you from adding even more features to it, making it more useful and pleasant for visitors. By adding a product reviews system to your web site, you increase the chances that visitors will get back to your site, either to write a review for a product they bought, or to see what other people think about that product.

Chapter 16: Connecting to Web Services

In the dynamic world of the Internet, sometimes it isn't enough to just have an important web presence; you also need to interact with functionality provided by third parties to achieve your goals. So far in this book, you already saw how to integrate external functionality to process payments from your customers. In Chapter 16, you'll learn how to use Amazon.com functionality from and through web services. A *web service* is a piece of functionality that is exposed through a web interface using standard Internet protocols such as HTTP. The messages exchanged by the client and the server are encoded using an XML-based protocol named SOAP (Simple Object Access Protocol), or by using REST (Representational State Transfer). These messages are sent over HTTP. You'll learn more about these technologies in this chapter.

What You Need to Use This Book

The examples in this book are designed to be run with PHP 5 and MySQL 4. Appendix A contains complete installation instructions for all the software you need to follow the examples in this book.

The complete source code for the sample TShirtShop web site is available in the Downloads section of the Apress web site (http://www.apress.com), and at the author's web site at http://www.cristiandarie.ro.

PART 1

Phase I
of Development

CHAPTER 1

Starting an E-Commerce Site

The word "e-commerce" has had a remarkable fall from grace in the past few years. Just the idea of having an e-commerce web site was enough to get many businessmen salivating with anticipation. Now it's no longer good enough to just say, "e-commerce is the future—get online or get out of business." You now need compelling, realistic, and specific reasons to take your business online.

This book focuses on programming and associated disciplines, such as creating, accessing, and manipulating databases. But before we jump into that, we need to understand the business decisions that lead to the creation of an e-commerce site in the first place.

If you want to build an e-commerce site today, you must answer some tough questions. The good news is these questions do have answers, and we're going to have a go at answering them in this chapter:

- So many big e-commerce sites have failed. What can e-commerce possibly offer me in today's tougher environment?

- Most e-commerce companies seemed to need massive investment. How can I produce a site on my limited budget?

- Even successful e-commerce sites expect to take years before they turn a profit. My business can't wait that long. How can I make money now?

Deciding Whether to Go Online

Although there are hundreds of possible reasons to go online, they tend to fall into the following groups:

- Get more customers

- Make existing customers spend more

- Reduce the costs of fulfilling orders

We'll look at each of these in the following sections.

Get More Customers

Getting more customers is immediately the most attractive reason. With an e-commerce site, even small businesses can reach customers all over the world. This reason can also be the most dangerous, however, because many people set up e-commerce sites assuming that the site will reach customers immediately. It won't. In the offline world, you need to know a shop exists before you can go into it. This is still true in the world of e-commerce—people must know your site exists before you can hope to get a single order.

Addressing this issue is largely a question of advertising, rather than the site itself. Popular methods of getting more customers include registering the web site with the popular search engines and directory listings, optimizing the site for search engine ranking, creating forums, sending newsletters, and so on. A simple web search for "web site advertising tutorial" will point you to many useful resources.

We don't cover these aspects of e-commerce in this book. However, because an e-commerce site is always available, some people might stumble across it. It's certainly easier for customers to tell their friends about a particular web address than to give them a catalog, mailing address, or directions to their favorite offline store.

Make Customers Spend More

Assuming your company already has customers, you probably wish that they bought more. What stops them? If the customers don't want any more of a certain product, there's not a lot that e-commerce can do, but chances are there are other reasons, too:

- Getting to the shop/placing an order by mail is a hassle.

- Some of the things you sell can be bought from more convenient places.

- You're mostly open while your customers are at work.

- It's harder to implement an efficient product recommendations system in a physical store.

A quality e-commerce site (because there are so many buggy, insecure, or hard-to-use web sites out there) can fix those problems. People with Internet access will find placing an order online far easier than any other method—meaning that when the temptation to buy strikes, it's much easier for them to give in. Of course, the convenience of being online also means that people are more likely to choose you over other local suppliers.

Because your site is online 24 hours a day, rather than the usual 9 to 5, your customers can shop with you outside of their working hours. Having an online store brings a double blessing to you if your customers work in offices because they can indulge in retail therapy directly from their desks.

Skillful e-commerce design can encourage your customers to buy things they wouldn't usually think of. You can easily update your site to suggest items of particular seasonal interest, to announce interesting new products, or to recommend products similar to what they have already bought.

Many of the large e-commerce sites encourage customers to buy useful accessories along with the main product, or to buy a more expensive alternative to the one they're considering. Others give special offers to regular shoppers, or suggest impulse purchases during checkout.

You'll learn how to use some of these methods in later chapters, and by the end of the book, you'll have a good idea of how to add more features for yourself.

Finally, it's much easier to learn about your customers via e-commerce than in face-to-face shops, or even mail order. Even if you just gather email addresses, you can use these to send out updates and news. More sophisticated sites can automatically analyze a customer's buying habits to make suggestions on other products the customer might like to buy.

Another related benefit of e-commerce is that there's no real cost in having people browse without buying. In fact, getting people to visit the site as often as possible can be valuable. You should consider building features into the site that are designed purely to make people visit regularly; for example, you might include community features such as forums or free content related to the products you're selling.

Reduce the Costs of Fulfilling Orders

A well-built e-commerce site will be much cheaper to run than a comparable offline business. Under conventional business models, a staff member must feed an order into the company's order-processing system. With e-commerce, the customer can do this for you—the gateway between the site and the order processing can be seamless.

Of course, after your e-commerce site is up and running, the cost of actually taking orders gets close to zero—you don't need to pay for checkout staff, assistants, security guards, or rent in a busy shopping mall.

If you have a sound business idea, and you execute the site well, you can receive these benefits without a massive investment. What's important is to always focus on the almighty dollar: Will your site, or any particular feature of it, really help you get more customers, get customers to spend more, or reduce the costs and therefore increase your margins?

Now it's time to introduce the site we'll be using as the example in this book, and see just how all of these principles relate to our own shop.

Let's Make Money

We're going to build an e-commerce store that sells T-shirts with postage stamp themes. On all the e-commerce sites we've worked on, there's always been a trade-off to make between building an amazing site that everybody will love and creating a site on a limited budget that will make money. Usually, I'm on the trigger-happy, really amazing site side, but I'm always grateful that my ambitions are reined in by the actual business demands. If you're designing and building the site for yourself, and you are the client, then you have a challenge—keeping your view realistic while maintaining your enthusiasm for the project.

This book shows you a logical way to build an e-commerce site that will deliver what it needs to be profitable. However, when designing your own site, you need to think carefully about exactly who your customers are, what they need, how they want to place orders, and what they are most likely to buy. Most important, you need to think about how they will come to your site in the first place. You should consider the following points before you start to visualize or design the site, and certainly before you start programming:

- *Getting customers*: How will you get visitors to the site in the first place?

- *Offering products*: What you will offer, and how will you expect customers to buy? Will they buy in bulk? Will they make a lot of repeat orders? Will they know what they want before they visit, or will they want to be inspired? These factors will influence how you arrange your catalog and searching, as well as what order process you use. A shopping basket is great if people want to browse. If people know exactly what they want, then they might prefer something more like an order form.

- *Processing orders*: How will you turn a customer order into a parcel ready for mailing? Your main consideration here is finding an efficient way to process payments and deliver orders to whoever manages your stocks or warehouse. How will you give your customers confidence in your ability to protect their data and deliver their purchases on time?

- *Serving customers*: Will customers require additional help with products that they buy from you? Do you need to offer warranties, service contracts, or other support services?

- *Bringing customers back*: How will you entice customers back to the site? Are they likely to only visit the site to make a purchase, or will there be e-window shoppers? Are your products consumables and can you predict when your customers will need something new?

After you've answered these questions, you can start designing your site, knowing that you're designing for your customers—not just doing what seems like a good idea at the time. Determining the answers to these questions will also help ensure that your design covers all the important areas, without massive omissions that will be a nightmare to fix later.

The example site presented in this book has taken a deliberate generic approach to show you the most common e-commerce techniques. To really lift yourself above the competition, however, you don't need fancy features or Flash movies—you just need to understand, attract, and serve your customers better than anybody else. Think about this before you launch into designing and building the site itself.

Risks and Threats

All this might make it sound as if your e-commerce business can't possibly fail. Well, it's time to take a cold shower and realize that even the best-laid plans often go wrong. Some risks are particularly relevant to e-commerce companies, such as

- Hacking

- Credit card scams

- Hardware failures

- Unreliable shipping services

- Software errors

- Changing laws

You can't get rid of these risks, but you can try to understand them and defend yourself from them. The software developed in this book goes some way to meeting these issues, but many of the risks have little to do with the site itself.

An important way to defend your site from many risks is to keep backups. You already know backups are important. But if you're anything like me, when it gets to the end of the day, saving five minutes and going home earlier seems even more important. When you have a live web site, this simply isn't an option.

We haven't talked much about the legal side of e-commerce in this book, because we are programmers, not lawyers. However if you are setting up an e-commerce site that goes much beyond an online garage sale, you will need to look into these issues before putting your business online.

While we're on the subject of risks and threats, one issue that can really damage your e-commerce site is unreliable order fulfillment. This is a programming book, and focuses on offering products to customers, and communicating their orders to the site's owner. An essential part of the processes is delivering the products, and to do this you need a good logistics network set up before launching your shop. If your store doesn't deliver the goods, customers won't come back or refer their friends.

Tip Webmonkey provides an excellent general e-commerce tutorial, which covers taxation, shipping, and many of the issues you'll face when designing your site, at `http://hotwired.lycos.com/webmonkey/e-business/building/tutorials/tutorial3.html`. Check this out before you start designing your site.

Designing for Business

Building an e-commerce site requires a significant investment. If you design the site in phases, you can reduce the initial investment, and therefore cut your losses if the idea proves unsuccessful. You can use the results from an early phase to assess whether it's worthwhile to add extra features, and even use revenue from the site to fund future development. If nothing else, planning to build the site in phases means that you can get your site online and receiving orders much earlier than if you build every possible feature into the first release.

Even after you've completed your initial planned phases, things might not end there. Whenever planning a large software project, it's important to design in a way that makes unplanned future growth easy. In Chapter 2, where we'll start dealing with the technical details of building e-commerce sites, you'll learn how to design the web site architecture to allow for long-term development flexibility.

If you're building sites for clients, they will like to think their options are open. Planning the site, or any other software, in phases will help your clients feel comfortable doing business with you. They will be able to see that you are getting the job done, and can decide to end the project at the end of any phase if they feel—for whatever reason—that they don't want to continue to invest in development.

Phase I: Getting a Site Up

Chapters 2 through 7 concentrate on establishing the basic framework for the site, and putting a product catalog online. We'll start by putting together the basic site architecture, deciding how the different parts of the application will work together. We'll then build the product catalog into this architecture. You'll learn how to

- Design a database for storing the product catalog, containing departments, categories, and products

- Write the SQL (Structured Query Language) and PHP code for accessing that data and making the product catalog functional

- Provide a product search engine

- Receive payments through PayPal

- Give the site's administrators a private section of the site where they can administer the catalog online

After you've built this catalog, you'll see how to offer the products for sale by integrating it with PayPal's shopping cart and order-processing system, which will handle credit card transactions for you and email you with details of orders. These orders will be processed manually, but in the early stages of an e-commerce site, the time you lose processing orders will be less than the time it would have taken to develop an automated system.

Phase II: Creating Your Own Shopping Cart

Using PayPal's shopping cart is okay, and really easy, but it does mean you lose a lot of advantages. For example, you can't control the look and feel of PayPal's shopping cart, whereas if you use your own, you can make it an integral part of the site.

This is a significant advantage, but it's superficial compared to some of the others. For example, with your own shopping cart, you can store complete orders in the database as part of the order process, and use that data to learn about the customers. With additional work, you also can use the shopping basket and checkout as a platform for selling more products. How often have you been tempted by impulse purchases near the checkout of your local store? Well, this also works with e-commerce. Having your own shopping cart and checkout gives you the option of later offering low-cost special offers from there. You can even analyze the contents of the cart, and make suggestions based on this.

Chapters 8 through 10 show you how to

- Build your own shopping cart

- Pass a complete order through to PayPal for credit card processing

- Create an orders administration page

- Implement a product recommendations system

Once again, at the end of Phase II, our site will be fully operational. If you want, you can leave it as it is or add features within the existing PayPal-based payment system. But when the site gets serious, you'll want to start processing orders and credit cards yourself. This is the part where things get complicated, and you need to be serious and careful about your site's security.

Phase III: Processing Orders and Adding Features

The core of e-commerce—and the bit that really separates it from other web-development projects—is handling orders and credit cards. PayPal has helped us put this off, but there are many good reasons why—eventually—you'll want to part company with PayPal:

- *Cost*: PayPal is not expensive, but the extra services it offers must be paid for somehow. Moving to a simpler credit-card processing service will mean lower transaction costs, although developing your own system will obviously incur upfront costs.

- *Freedom*: PayPal has a fairly strict set of terms and conditions, and is designed for residents of a limited number of countries. By taking on more of the credit card processing responsibility yourself, you can better control the way your site works. As an obvious example, you can accept payment using regional methods such as the Switch debit cards common in the United Kingdom.

- *Integration*: If you deal with transactions and orders using your own system, you can integrate your store and your warehouse to whatever extent you require. You could even automatically contact a third-party supplier and have them ship the goods straight to the customer.

- *Information*: When you handle the whole order yourself, you can record and collate all the information involved in the transaction—and then use it for marketing and research purposes.

By integrating the order processing with the warehouse, fulfillment center, or suppliers, you can reduce costs significantly. This might reduce the need for staff in the fulfillment center or allow the business to grow without requiring additional staff.

Acquiring information about customers can feed back into the whole process, giving you valuable information about how to sell more. At its simplest, you could email customers with special offers or just keep in touch with a newsletter. You also could analyze buying patterns and use that data to formulate targeted marketing campaigns.

During Phase III, you will learn how to

- Build a customer accounts module, so that customers can log in and retrieve their details every time they make an order

- Allow customers to add product reviews

- Integrate Amazon.com products into your web site using XML Web Services

- Establish secure connections using SSL (Secure Socket Layer), so that data sent by users is encrypted on its travels across the Internet

- Authenticate and charge credit cards using third-party companies, such as DataCash and VeriSign

- Store credit card numbers securely in a database

This third phase is the most involved of all of them, and requires some hard and careful work. By the end of Phase III, however, you will have an e-commerce site with a searchable product catalog, shopping cart, secure check out, and complete order-processing system.

TShirtShop

As we said earlier, we're going to build an online shop called TShirtShop (which will sell, surprisingly enough, T-shirts). Figure 1-1 shows the way TShirtShop will look at some point during the first stage of development.

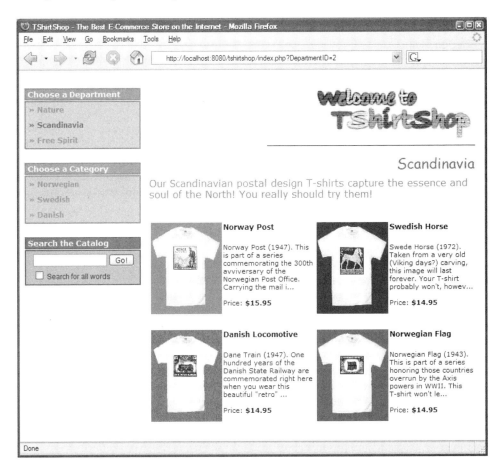

Figure 1-1. *TShirtShop during Phase I of development*

Tip You can find a link to an online version of TShirtShop at `http://www.CristianDarie.ro/books.html`. Many thanks go to David Ryan and `http://www.goingpostal.cc` who allowed us to use some of their products to populate our virtual TShirtShop store.

For the purposes of this book, we'll assume that the client already exists as a mail-order company, and has a good network of customers. The company is not completely new to the business, and wants the site to make it easier and more enjoyable for its existing customers to buy—with the goal that they'll end up buying more.

Knowing this, I suggest the phased development because

- The company is unlikely to get massive orders initially—we should keep the initial cost of building the web site down as much as possible.

- The company is accustomed to manually processing mail orders, so manually processing orders emailed by PayPal will not introduce many new problems.

- The company doesn't want to invest all of its money in a massive e-commerce site, only to find that people actually prefer mail order after all! Or it might find that, after Phase I, the site does exactly what it wants and there's no point in expanding it further. Either way, I hope that offering a lower initial cost gives my bid the edge. (It might also mean I can get away with a higher total price.)

Because this company is already a mail-order business, it probably already has a merchant account, and can process credit cards. Therefore, moving on to Phase III as soon as possible would be best for this company so it can benefit from the preferential card-processing rates.

Summary

In this chapter we've seen some of the principles of e-commerce in the real, hostile world where it's important to focus on short-term revenue and keeping risks down. We've looked at the three basic reasons an e-commerce site can make money:

- Acquiring more customers

- Making customers spend more

- Reducing the costs of fulfilling orders

We've applied those principles to a three-phase plan that provides a deliverable, usable site at each stage and continues to expand throughout the book.

At this point, you've presented your plan to the owners of the T-shirt shop. In the next chapter you'll put on your programming hat and start to design and build the web site (assuming you get the contract, of course).

■ ■ ■

CHAPTER 2

Laying Out the Foundations

Now that you've convinced the client that you can create a cool web site to complement his or her activity, it's time to stop celebrating and start thinking about how to put into practice all the promises you've made. As usual, when you lay down on paper the technical requirements you must meet, everything starts to seem a bit more complicated than initially anticipated.

To ensure this project's success, you need to come up with a smart way to implement what you have signed the contract for. You want to develop the project smoothly and quickly, but the ultimate goal is to make sure the client is satisfied with your work. Consequently, you should aim to provide your site's increasing number of visitors with a positive web experience by creating a pleasant, functional, and responsive web site.

The requirements are high, but this is normal for an e-commerce site today. To maximize the chances of success, we'll analyze and anticipate as many of the technical requirements as possible, and implement solutions in a way that supports changes and additions with minimal effort.

This chapter lays down the foundations for the future TShirtShop web site. We will talk about the technologies and tools you'll use, and even more importantly, how you'll use them. Your goals for this chapter are to

- Analyze the project from a technical point of view

- Analyze and choose an architecture for your application

- Decide which technologies, programming languages, and tools to use

- Discuss naming and coding conventions

- Create the basic structure of the web site and set up the database

Designing for Growth

The word *design* in the context of a web application can mean many things. Its most popular usage probably refers to the visual and user interface design of a web site.

This aspect is crucial because, let's face it, the visitor is often more impressed with how a site looks and how easy it is to use than about which technologies and techniques are used behind the scenes, or what operating system the web server is running. If the site is slow, hard to use, or easy to forget, it just doesn't matter what rocket science was used to create it.

Unfortunately, this truth makes many inexperienced programmers underestimate the importance of the way the invisible part of the site is implemented—the code, the database, and so on. The visual part of a site gets visitors interested to begin with, but its functionality makes them come back. A web site can sometimes be implemented very quickly based on certain initial requirements, but if not properly architected, it can become difficult, if not impossible, to change.

For any project of any size, some preparation must be done before starting to code. Still, no matter how much preparation and design work is done, the unexpected does happen and hidden catches, new requirements, and changing rules always seem to work against deadlines. Even without these unexpected factors, site designers are often asked to change or add new functionality many times after the project is finished and deployed. This will also be the case for TShirtShop, which will be implemented in three separate stages, as discussed in Chapter 1.

You will learn how to create the web site so that the site (or you) will not fall apart when functionality is extended or updates are made. Because this is a programming book, instead of focusing on how to design the user interface or on marketing techniques, we'll pay close attention to designing the code that makes them work.

The phrase, *designing the code*, can have different meanings; for example, we'll need to have a short talk about naming conventions. Still, the most important aspect that we need to take a look at is the application architecture. The architecture refers to the way you split the code for a simple piece of functionality (for example, the product search feature) into smaller components. Although it might be easier to implement that functionality as quickly and as simply as possible, in a single component, you gain great long-term advantages by creating more components that work together to achieve the desired result.

Before talking about the architecture itself, you must determine what you want from this architecture.

Meeting Long-Term Requirements with Minimal Effort

Apart from the fact that you want a fast web site, each of the phases of development we talked about in Chapter 1 brings new requirements that must be met.

Every time you proceed to a new stage, you want to be able to **reuse** most of the already existing solution. It would be very inefficient to redesign the whole site (not just the visual part, but the code as well!) just because you need to add a new feature. You can make it easier to reuse the solution by planning ahead, so any new functionality that needs to be added can slot in with ease, rather than each change causing a new headache.

When building the web site, implementing a **flexible architecture** composed of pluggable components allows you to add new features—such as the shopping cart, the departments list, or the product search feature—by coding them as separate components and plugging them into the existing application. Achieving a good level of flexibility is one of the goals regarding the application's architecture, and this chapter shows how you can put this into practice. You'll see that the flexibility level is proportional to the amount of time required to design and implement it, so we'll try to find a compromise that will provide the best gains without complicating the code too much.

Another major requirement that is common to all online applications is having a **scalable architecture**. Scalability is defined as the capability to increase resources to yield a linear increase in service capacity. In other words, ideally, in a scalable system the ratio (proportion) between the number of client requests and the hardware resources required to handle those requests is constant, even when the number of clients increases. An unscalable system can't deal with an increasing number of clients, no matter how many hardware resources are provided. Because we're optimistic about the number of customers, we must be sure that the site will be able to deliver its functionality to a large number of clients without throwing out errors or performing sluggishly.

Reliability is also a critical aspect for an e-commerce application. With the help of a coherent error-handling strategy and a powerful relational database, you can ensure data integrity and ensure that noncritical errors are properly handled without bringing the site to its knees.

The Magic of the Three-Tier Architecture

Generally, the architecture refers to splitting each piece of the application's functionality into separate components based on what they do, and grouping each kind of component into a single logical tier.

Almost every module that you'll create for your site will have components in these three tiers from the application server:

- The **presentation tier**

- The **business tier**

- The **data tier**

The **presentation tier** contains the user interface elements of the site, and includes all the logic that manages the interaction between the visitor and the client's business. This tier makes the whole site feel alive, and the way you design it has a crucial importance for the site's success. Because your application is a web site, its presentation tier is composed of dynamic web pages.

The **business tier** (also called the *middle tier*) receives requests from the presentation tier and returns a result to the presentation tier depending on the business logic it contains. Almost any event that happens in the presentation tier usually results in the business tier being called (except events that can be handled locally by the presentation tier, such as simple input data validation, and so on). For example, if the visitor is doing a product search, the presentation tier calls the business tier and says, "Please send me back the products that match this search criterion." Almost always, the business tier needs to call the data tier for information to be able to respond to the presentation tier's request.

The **data tier** (sometimes referred to as the *database tier*) is responsible for managing the application's data and sending it to the business tier when requested. For the TShirtShop e-commerce site, you'll need to store data about products (including their categories and their departments), users, shopping carts, and so on. Almost every client request finally results in the data tier being interrogated for information (excepting when previously retrieved data has been cached at the business tier or presentation tier levels), so it's important to have a fast database system. In Chapters 3 and 4, you'll learn how to design the database for optimum performance.

These tiers are purely logical—there is no constraint on the physical location of each tier. In theory, you are free to place all of the application, and implicitly all of its tiers, on a single server machine, or you can place each tier on a separate machine if the application permits this. In practice, PHP is not very suited to build applications that you want to split on different machines, but this is expected to change in the future. Chapter 16 explains how to integrate functionality from other web sites using XML Web Services. XML Web Services permit easy integration of functionality across multiple servers.

An important constraint in the three-layered architecture model is that information must flow in sequential order between tiers. The presentation tier is only allowed to access the business tier, and never directly the data tier. The business tier is the "brain" in the middle that communicates with the other tiers and processes and coordinates all the information flow. If the presentation tier directly accessed the data tier, the rules of three-tier architecture programming would be broken. When you implement a three-tier architecture, you must be consistent and obey its rules to reap the benefits.

Figure 2-1 is a simple representation of the way data is passed in an application that implements the three-tier architecture.

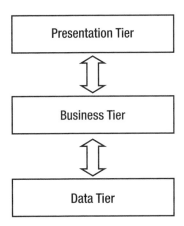

Figure 2-1. *Simple representation of the three-tier architecture*

A Simple Example

It's easier to understand how data is passed and transformed between tiers if you take a closer look at a simple example. To make the example even more relevant to our project, let's analyze a situation that will actually happen in TShirtShop. This scenario is typical for three-tier applications.

Like most e-commerce sites, TShirtShop will have a shopping cart, which we will discuss later in the book. For now, it's enough to know that the visitor will add products to the shopping cart by clicking an "Add to Cart" button. Figure 2-2 shows how the information flows through the application when that button is clicked.

When the user clicks on the "Add to Cart" button for a specific product (Step 1), the presentation tier (which contains the button) forwards the request to the business tier—"Hey, I want this product added to my shopping cart!" (Step 2). The business tier receives the request, understands that the user wants a specific product added to the shopping cart, and handles the request by telling the data tier to update the visitor's shopping cart by adding the selected product (Step 3). The data tier needs to be called because it stores and manages the entire web site's data, including users' shopping cart information.

The data tier updates the database (Step 4) and eventually returns a success code to the business tier. The business tier (Step 5) handles the return code and any errors that might have occurred in the data tier while updating the database, and then returns the output to the presentation tier.

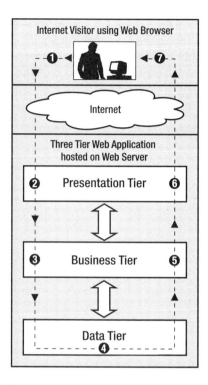

Figure 2-2. *Internet visitor interacting with a three-tier application*

Finally, the presentation tier generates an updated view of the shopping cart (Step 6). The results of the execution are wrapped up by generating an HTML (Hypertext Markup Language) web page that is returned to the visitor (Step 7), where the updated shopping cart can be seen in the visitor's web browser.

Note that in this simple example, the business tier doesn't do a lot of processing and its business logic isn't very complex. However, if new business rules appear for your application, you would change the business tier. If, for example, the business logic specified that a product could only be added to the shopping cart if its quantity in stock was greater than zero, an additional data tier call would have been made to determine the quantity. The data tier would only be requested to update the shopping cart if products are in stock. In any case, the presentation tier is informed about the status and provides human-readable feedback to the visitor.

What's in a Number?

It's interesting to note how each tier interprets the same piece of information differently. For the data tier, the numbers and information it stores have no significance because this tier is an engine that saves, manages, and retrieves numbers, strings, or other data types—not product quantities or product names. In the context of the previous example, a product quantity of 0 represents a simple, plain number without any meaning to the data tier (it is simply 0, a 32-bit integer).

The data gains significance when the business tier reads it. When the business tier asks the data tier for a product quantity and gets a "0" result, this is interpreted by the business tier as "Hey, no products in stock!" This data is finally wrapped in a nice, visual form by the presentation tier, such as a label reading, "Sorry, at the moment the product cannot be ordered."

Even if it's unlikely that you want to forbid a customer from adding a product to the shopping cart if the product is not in stock, the example (described in Figure 2-3) is good enough to present in yet another way how each of the three tiers has a different purpose.

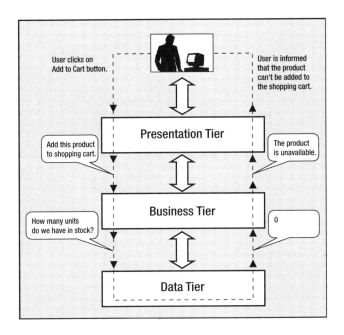

Figure 2-3. *Internet visitor interacting with a three-tier application*

The Right Logic for the Right Tier

Because each layer contains its own logic, sometimes it can be tricky to decide where exactly to draw the line between the tiers. In the previous scenario, instead of reading the product's quantity in the business tier and deciding whether the product is available based on that number (resulting in two data tier, and implicitly database, calls), you could have a single data tier method named AddProductIfAvailable that adds the product to the shopping cart only if it's available in stock.

In this scenario some logic is transferred from the business tier to the data tier. In many other circumstances, you might have the option to place same logic in one tier or another, or maybe in both. In most cases, there is no single best way to implement the three-tier architecture, and you'll need to make a compromise or a choice based on personal preference or external constraints.

Furthermore, there are occasions in which even though you know the *right* way (in respect to the architecture) to implement something, you might choose to break the rules to get a performance gain. As a general rule, if performance can be improved this way, it is okay to break the strict limits between tiers *just a little bit* (for example, add some of the business rules to the data tier or vice versa), *if* these rules are not likely to change in time. Otherwise, keeping all the business rules in the middle tier is preferable because it generates a "cleaner" application that is easier to maintain.

Finally, don't be tempted to access the data tier directly from the presentation tier. This is a common mistake that is the shortest path to a complicated, hard-to-maintain, and inflexible system. In many data access tutorials or introductory materials, you'll be shown how to perform simple database operations using a simple user interface application. In these kinds of programs, all the logic is probably written in a short, single file, instead of separate tiers. Although the materials might be very good, keep in mind that most of these texts are meant to teach you how to do different individual tasks (for example, access a database), and not how to correctly create a flexible and scalable application.

A Three-Tier Architecture for TShirtShop

Implementing a three-tiered architecture for the TShirtShop web site will help achieve the goals listed at the beginning of the chapter. The coding discipline imposed by a system that might seem rigid at first sight allows for excellent levels of flexibility and extensibility in the long run.

Splitting major parts of the application into separate smaller components encourages reusability. More than once when adding new features to the site, you'll see that you can reuse some of the already existing bits. Adding a new feature without needing to change much of what already exists is, in itself, a good example of reusability.

Another advantage of the three-tiered architecture is that, if properly implemented, the overall system is resistant to changes. When bits in one of the tiers change, the other tiers usually remain unaffected, sometimes even in extreme cases. For example, if for some reason the backend database system is changed (say, the manager decides to use Oracle instead of MySQL), you only need to update the data tier and maybe just a little bit of the business tier.

Why Not Use More Tiers?

The three-tier architecture we've been talking about so far is a particular (and the most popular) version of the n-Tier Architecture, which is a commonly used buzzword these days. n-Tier Architecture refers to splitting the solution into a number (n) of logical tiers. In complex projects, sometimes it makes sense to split the business layer into more than one layer, thus resulting in architecture with more than three layers. However, for our web site, it makes the most sense to stick with the three-layered design, which offers most of the benefits while not requiring too many hours of design or a complex hierarchy of framework code to support the architecture.

Maybe with a more involved and complex architecture, you could achieve even higher levels of flexibility and scalability for the application, but you would need much more time for design before starting to implement anything. As with any programming project, you must find a fair balance between the time required to design the architecture and the time spent to implement it. The three-tier architecture is best suited to projects with average complexity, like the TShirtShop web site.

You also might be asking the opposite question, "Why not use fewer tiers?" A two-tier architecture, also called *client-server* architecture, can be appropriate for less-complex projects. In short, a two-tier architecture requires less time for planning and allows quicker development in the beginning, although it generates an application that's harder to maintain and extend in the long run. Because we're expecting to have to extend the application in the future, the client-server architecture is not appropriate for our application, so it won't be discussed further in this book.

Now that the general architecture is known, let's see what technologies and tools you will use to implement it. After a brief discussion of the technologies, you'll create the foundation of the presentation and data tiers by creating the first page of the site and the backend database. You'll start implementing some real functionality in each of the three tiers in Chapter 3 when you start creating the web site's product catalog.

Choosing Technologies and Tools

No matter which architecture is chosen, a major question that arises in every development project is which technologies, programming languages, and tools are going to be used, bearing in mind that external requirements can seriously limit your options.

■**Note** In this book we're creating a web site using PHP, MySQL, and related technologies. We really like these technologies, but it doesn't necessarily mean they're the best choice for any kind of project, in any circumstances. Additionally, there are many situations in which you must use specific technologies because of client requirements. The System Requirements and Software Requirements stages in the software development process will determine which technologies you must use for creating the application. See Appendix C for more details.

In this book, we'll work with PHP 5.0 and MySQL 4.x, the most popular combination for creating data-driven web sites on the planet. Although the book assumes some previous experience with each of these, we'll take a quick look at them and see how they fit into our project and into the three-tier architecture.

■**Note** We included complete environment installation instructions (including Apache 2, PHP 5, and MySQL 4) in Appendix A.

Using PHP to Generate Dynamic Web Content

PHP is an open-source technology for building dynamic, interactive web content. Its short description (on the official PHP web site, http://www.php.net) is: "PHP is a widely-used general-purpose scripting language that is especially suited for Web development and can be embedded into HTML."

PHP stands for PHP: Hypertext Preprocessor (yes, it's a recursive acronym), and is available for free download at its official web site. We included complete installation instructions for PHP in Appendix A. Because we're using PHP to build a dynamic web site, you'll also learn how to install Apache and how to integrate PHP with it in Appendix A.

The story of PHP, having its roots somewhere in 1994, is a successful one. Among the factors that led to its success are the following:

- PHP is free; especially when combined with Linux server software, PHP can prove to be a very cost-efficient technology to build dynamic web content.

- PHP has a shorter learning curve than other scripting languages.

- The PHP community is agile, many useful helper libraries or new versions of the existing libraries are being developed (such as PEAR and Smarty), and new features are added frequently.

- PHP works very well on a variety of web servers and operating systems (Unix-like platforms, Windows, Mac OS X).

However, PHP is not the only server-side scripting language around for creating dynamic web pages. Among its most popular competitors are JSP (Java Server Pages), Perl, ColdFusion, and ASP.NET. Between these technologies are many differences, but also some fundamental similarities. For example, pages written with any of these technologies are composed of basic HTML, which draws the static part of the page (the template), and code that generates the dynamic part.

▨Note You might want to check out *Beginning ASP.NET 1.1 E-Commerce* (Apress, 2004) or *Beginning ASP.NET 2.0 E-Commerce* (Apress, 2005), which explain how to build e-commerce web sites with ASP.NET, Visual Basic .NET, and SQL Server.

Working Smart with Smarty

Because PHP is simple and easy to start with, it has always been tempting to start coding without properly designing an architecture and framework that would be beneficial in the long run.

What makes things even worse is that the straightforward method of building PHP pages is to mix PHP instructions with HTML, because PHP doesn't have by default an obvious technique of separating the PHP code from the HTML layout information.

Mixing the PHP logic with HTML has two important disadvantages:

- This technique often leads to long, complicated, and hard-to-manage code. Maybe you have seen those kilometric source files with an unpleasant mixture of PHP and HTML, hard to bear by the eye and impossible to understand after a week.

- These mixed files are the subject of both designers' and programmers' work, complicating the collaboration more than necessary. This also increases the chances of the designer creating bugs in the code logic while working on cosmetic changes.

These kinds of problems led to the development of template engines, which offer frameworks of separating the presentation logic from the static HTML layout. Smarty (http://smarty.php.net)

is the most popular and powerful template engine for PHP. Its main purpose is to offer you a simple way to separate application logic (PHP code) from its presentation code (HTML).

This separation permits the programmer and the template designer to work independently on the same application. The programmer can change the PHP logic without needing to change the template files, and the designer can change the templates without caring how the code that makes them alive works.

Figure 2-4 shows the relationship between the Smarty Design Template file and its Smarty plugin file.

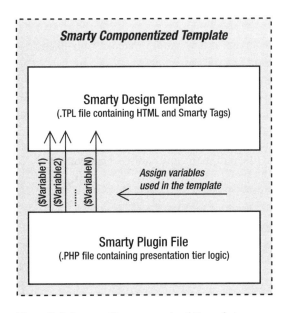

Figure 2-4. *Smarty Componentized Template*

The Smarty Design Template (a .tpl file containing the HTML layout and Smarty-specific tags and code) and its Smarty plugin file (a .php file containing the associated code for the template) form a **Smarty Componentized Template**. You'll learn more about how Smarty works while you're building the e-commerce web site. For a fast introduction to Smarty, read the Smarty Crash Course at `http://smarty.php.net/crashcourse.php`.

What About the Alternatives?

Smarty is not the only template engine available for PHP. Other popular template engines are

- Yapter (`http://yapter.sourceforge.net/`)

- EasyTemplate (`http://www.onlinetools.org/tools/easytemplate/index.php`)

- phpLib (`http://phplib.sourceforge.net/`)

- TemplatePower (`http://templatepower.codocad.com/`)

- FastTemplate (`http://www.thewebmasters.net/php/FastTemplate.phtml`)

Although all template engines follow the same basic principles, we chose to use Smarty in the PHP e-commerce project for this book because of its very good performance results, powerful features (such as template compilation and caching), and wide acceptance in the industry.

Storing Web Site Data in MySQL Databases

Most of the data your visitors will see while browsing the web site will be retrieved from a relational database. A Relational Database Management System (RDBMS) is a complex software program, the purpose of which is to store, manage, and retrieve data as quickly and reliably as possible. For the TShirtShop web site, it will store all data regarding the products, departments, users, shopping carts, and so on.

Many RDBMSs are available for you to use with PHP, including MySQL, PostgreSQL, Oracle, and so on. A 2003 survey of Zend (http://www.zend.com/zend/php_survey_results.php), with more than 10,000 respondents, revealed that the preferred database for PHP development is MySQL (see Figure 2-5).

What databases are currently being used in your organization in relation to PHP development? (Choose as many as apply)	Number of Responses	Response Ratio
MySQL	3220	93%
PostgreSQL	773	22%
Oracle	500	14%
Microsoft SQL Server	565	16%
Sybase	74	2%
LDAP	309	9%
SAP	33	1%
None	50	1%
Other, Please Specify	204	6%

Figure 2-5. *Survey results show that MySQL is popular among PHP developers.*

MySQL is the world's most popular open-source database, and it's a free (for noncommercial use), fast, and reliable database. Another important advantage is that many web hosting providers offer access to a MySQL database, which makes your life easier when going live with your newly created e-commerce web site. We'll use MySQL as the backend database when developing the TShirtShop e-commerce web site.

The language used to communicate with a relational database is SQL (Structured Query Language). However, each database engine recognizes a particular dialect of this language. If you decide to use a different RDBMS than MySQL, you'll probably need to update some of the SQL queries.

■ **Note** If you're using more database systems, we recommend you read *The Programmer's Guide to SQL* (Apress, 2003), which teaches the SQL standard with practical examples for SQL Server, Oracle, MySQL, DB2, and Access.

Getting in Touch with MySQL

You talk with the database server by formulating an SQL query, sending it to the database engine, and retrieving the results. The SQL query can say anything related to the web site data, or its data structures, such as "give me the list of departments," "remove product no. 223," "create a data table," or "search the catalog for yellow T-shirts."

No matter what the SQL query says, we need a way to send it to MySQL. MySQL ships with a simple, text-based interface, that permits executing SQL queries and getting back the results. The command-line interface isn't particularly easy to use, but it is functional. However, there are alternatives.

A number of free, third-party database administration tools allow you to manipulate data structures and execute SQL queries via an easy-to-use graphical interface. In this book we'll show you how to use phpMyAdmin, which is the most widely used MySQL admin tool in the PHP world (its interface is a PHP web interface). Many web-hosting companies offer database access through phpMyAdmin, which is another good reason for you to be familiar with this tool. However, you can use the visual client of your choice. You can find complete installation instructions for phpMyAdmin in Appendix A.

Apart from needing to interact with MySQL with a direct interface to its engine, you also need to learn how to access MySQL programmatically, from PHP code. This requirement is obvious, because the e-commerce web site will need to query the database to retrieve catalog information (departments, categories, products, and so on), when building pages for the visitors.

As for querying MySQL databases through PHP code, the tool you'll rely on here is PEAR DB.

Implementing Database Integration Using PEAR DB

PEAR (PHP Extension and Application Repository) represents a structured library of open-source code for PHP users. PEAR DB is the database abstraction layer package in PEAR, and offers a very flexible and powerful means to interact with database servers.

PEAR DB layers itself on top of PHP's existing database functionality, offering a uniform way to access a variety of data sources. Using PEAR DB increases your application's portability and flexibility because if the backend database changes, the effects on your data access code are kept to a minimum (in many cases, all that needs to change is the connection string for the new database).

After you become familiar with the PEAR DB database abstraction layer, you can use the same programming techniques on other projects that might require a different database solution.

To demonstrate the difference between accessing the database using native PHP functions and PEAR DB, let's take a quick look at two short PHP code snippets. If you aren't familiar with how the code works, don't worry—we'll analyze everything in greater detail in the next chapter.

- Database access using PHP native (MySQL-specific) functions:

```
/* Connecting to MySQL */
$link = mysql_connect("mysql_host", "mysql_user", "mysql_password")
            or die("Could not connect: " . mysql_error());
/* Connect to database */
mysql_select_db("my_database") or die("Could not select database");
/* Execute SQL query */
$query = "SELECT * FROM product";
$result = mysql_query($query) or die("Query failed : " . mysql_error());
/* Close connection */
mysql_close($link);
```

- The same action, this time using PEAR DB:

```
/* reference PEAR DB library */
require_once 'DB.php';
/* Data Source Name */
$dsn = "mysql://user:pass@host/db_name";
/* Connect to database */
$db = DB::connect($dsn);
/* Test if we have a valid connection */
if (DB::isError($db)) die ($db->getMessage());
/* Execute SQL query */
$sql = "SELECT * FROM product";
$result = $db->query($sql);
/* Check if the SQL query executed successfully */
if (DB::isError($result)) die ($result->getMessage());
/* Closing connection */
$db->disconnect();
```

When using PEAR DB, you won't need to change the data access code if, for example, you decide to use PostgreSQL instead of MySQL. On the other hand, the first code snippet, which uses MySQL-specific functions, would need to change completely (use pg_connect and pg_query instead of mysql_connect and mysql_query, and so on). Also, some PostgreSQL-specific functions have different parameters than the similar MySQL functions.

When using a database abstraction layer (like PEAR DB), you'll probably only need to change the connection string when changing the database backend. Note that here we're only talking about the PHP code that interacts with the database. In practice, you might also need to update some SQL queries if the database engines support different dialects of SQL.

■**Note** To keep your SQL queries as portable as possible, keep their syntax as close as possible to the SQL-92 standard. You'll learn more about SQL details in Chapter 3.

MySQL and the Three-Tier Architecture

The code presented in this book was designed to work with MySQL 4.0 (the most recent stable version at the time of writing), and MySQL 4.1. MySQL consists of the data store in the e-commerce software project. Data access logic (the SQL queries) will be centralized in a number of PHP classes consisting of the data tier of the application.

■**Note** MySQL 5 will support stored procedures. Stored procedures contain SQL code and are managed and stored by the MySQL database itself, and provide more clarity and improved performance over the traditional method of storing the SQL logic in PHP code.

When using MySQL 4.0 (or MySQL 4.1), we are going to compensate for the lack of stored procedures by keeping all the data logic in our data tier classes. We design this tier to make the eventual transition to MySQL 5 stored procedures as easy as possible, without needing to change any code in the presentation and business tiers. Figure 2-6 shows the technologies used in each tier, using MySQL 4.0 (or 4.1) and MySQL 5.

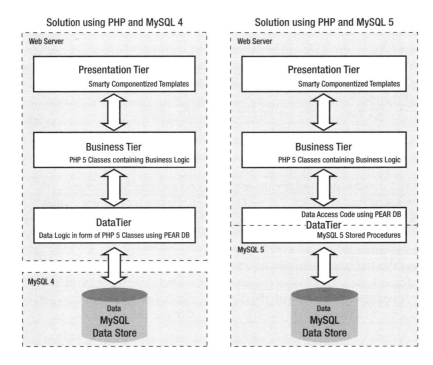

Figure 2-6. *The technologies you'll use to develop TShirtShop.*

Choosing Naming and Coding Standards

Although coding and naming standards might not seem that important at first, they definitely shouldn't be overlooked. Not following a set of rules for your code will almost always result in code that's hard to read, understand, and maintain. On the other hand, when you follow a consistent way of coding, you can almost say your code is already half documented, which is an important contribution toward the project's maintainability, especially when more people are working on the same project at the same time.

Tip Some companies have their own policies regarding coding and naming standards, whereas in other cases, you'll have the flexibility to use your own preferences. In either case, the golden rule to follow is *be consistent in the way you code*. Commenting your code is another good practice that improves the long-term maintainability of your code.

Naming conventions refer to many elements within a project, simply because almost all of a project's elements have names: the project itself, files, classes, variables, methods, method parameters, database tables, database columns, and so on. Without some discipline when naming all those elements, after a week of coding you won't understand a single line of what you've written.

When developing TShirtShop, we followed the naming conventions described at http://www.phpinfo.net/articles/article_php-coding-standard.html. These standards are followed by many professional PHP programmers and we'll try to keep our code close to it. Some of the most important rules are summarized here on the following piece of code:

```
class WarZone
{
   public $mSomeSoldier;
   public $mAnotherSoldier;

   function SearchAndDestroy($someEnemy,$anotherEnemy)
   {
     $master_of_war="Soldier";
     $this->mSomeSoldier = $someEnemy;
     $this->mAnotherSoldier = $anotherEnemy;
   }
}
```

- Class names and method names should be written using Pascal casing (uppercase letters for the first letter in every word), such as in GetHtmlOuput or IsDataValid.

- Class attribute names follow the same rules as class names, but should be prepended with the character "m". So, valid attribute names look like this: $mGetData,$mWriteData.

- Method argument names should use camel casing (uppercase letters for the first letter in every word except the first one), such as $someEnemy, $anotherEnemy.

- Variable names should be written in lowercase, with an underscore as the word separator, such as $master_of_war.

- Database objects use the same conventions as variable names (the department_id column).

- Try to indent your code using a fixed number of spaces (say, four) for each level. This book uses fewer spaces because of physical space limitations.

Starting the TShirtShop Project

So far, we have dealt with theory regarding the application you're going to create. It was fun, but it's going to be even more interesting to put into practice what you've learned up until now. Start your engines!

Installing the Required Software

The code in this book has been tested with

- PHP 5.0

- Apache 2.0

- MySQL 4.0 and 4.1

The project should work with other web servers as well, as long as they're compatible with PHP 5.0 (see http://www.php.net/manual/en/installation.php). However, Apache is the web server of choice for the vast majority of PHP projects.

There are places where MySQL 4.1's capability to handle subqueries offers more possibilities to implement the same query. We'll try to highlight these situations, while keeping the main code compatible with MySQL 4.0.

See Appendix A for detailed installation instructions for PHP, Apache, and MySQL.

Getting a Code Editor

Before writing the first line of code, you'll need to install a code editor, if you don't already have one. A good choice is the freely available and cross-platform SciTe text editor that you can download at http://scintilla.sourceforge.net/SciTEDownload.html.

Alternatively, you can choose a professional commercial PHP IDE such as Zend Studio, or a simple text editor like Notepad. It's a matter of taste and money. You can find a list of PHP editors at http://www.php-editors.com.

Preparing the tshirtshop Virtual Folder

One of the advantages of working with open-source, platform-independent technologies is that you can choose the operating system to use for development. You should be able to develop and run TShirtShop on Windows, Unix, Linux, Mac, and others.

When setting up the project's virtual folder, a few details differ depending on the operating system (mostly because of the different file paths), so we'll cover them separately for Windows and for Unix systems in the following pages. However, the main steps are the same:

1. Create a folder in the file system named `tshirtshop` (we use lowercase for folder names), which will contain the TShirtShop project's files (such as PHP code, image files, and so on).

2. Edit Apache's configuration file (`httpd.conf`) to create a virtual folder named `tshirtshop` that points to the `tshirtshop` physical folder created earlier. This way, when pointing a web browser to `http://localhost/tshirtshop`, the project in the `tshirtshop` physical folder will be loaded. This functionality is implemented in Apache using aliases, which are configured through the `httpd.conf` configuration file. The syntax of an alias entry is as follows:

```
Alias virtual_folder_name real_folder_name
```

■**Tip** The `httpd.conf` configuration file is well documented, but you can also check the Apache 2 documentation available at `http://httpd.apache.org/docs-2.0/`.

If you're working on Windows, follow the steps in the following exercise. The steps for Unix systems will follow after this exercise.

Exercise: Preparing the tshirtshop Virtual Folder on Windows

Follow the steps in this exercise to set up the `tshirtshop` folder.

1. Create a new folder named `tshirtshop`, which will be used for all the work you'll do in this book. You might find it easiest to create it in the root folder (`C:\`), but because we'll use relative paths in the project, feel free to create it in any location.

2. The default place used by Apache to serve client requests from is usually something like `C:\Program Files\Apache Group\Apache2\htdocs`. This location is defined by the `DocumentRoot` directive in the Apache configuration file, which is located in the `APACHE_BASE/conf/httpd.conf` file (where `APACHE_BASE` is the Apache installation folder).

   Because we want to use our folder instead of the default folder mentioned by `DocumentRoot`, we need to create a virtual folder named `tshirtshop` that points to the `tshirtshop` physical folder you created in Step 1. Open the Apache configuration file (`httpd.conf`), find the Aliases section, and add the following lines:

   ```
   Alias /tshirtshop/ "c:/tshirtshop/"
   Alias /tshirtshop "c:/tshirtshop"
   ```

   After adding these lines, a request for `http://localhost/tshirtshop` or `http://localhost/tshirtshop/` will result in the application in the `tshirtshop` folder (if it existed) being executed.

> **Note** If the web server is not running on the default port (80), you need to manually supply the port number if you need to reach it using a web browser. So if you installed Apache to run on port 8080, you'll need to browse to `http://localhost:8080/tshirtshop` instead of `http://localhost/tshirtshop`. Also, keep in mind that instead of `localhost`, you can always use `127.0.0.1` (the computer's loopback address), or the network name of your machine.

3. Create a file named `test.php` in the `tshirtshop` folder, with the following line inside:

   ```
   <?php phpinfo();?>
   ```

4. Restart the Apache web server, and load `http://localhost/tshirtshop/test.php` (or `http://localhost:8080/tshirtshop/test.php` if Apache works on port 8080) in a web browser.

Exercise: Preparing the tshirtshop Virtual Folder on Unix Systems

Follow the steps in this exercise to set up the `tshirtshop` folder.

1. Create a new folder named `tshirtshop`, which will be used for all the work you'll do in this book. You might find it easiest to create it in your home directory (in which case the complete path to your `tshirtshop` folder will be something like `/home/username/tshirtshop`), but because we'll use relative paths in the project, feel free to create it in any location.

2. The default place used by Apache to serve client requests from is usually something like `/var/www/html`. This location is defined by the `DocumentRoot` directive in the Apache configuration file, whose complete path is usually `/etc/httpd/conf/httpd.conf`

   Because we want to use our folder instead of the default folder mentioned by `DocumentRoot`, we need to create a virtual folder named `tshirtshop` that points to the tshirtshop physical folder you created in Step 1. Open the Apache configuration file (`httpd.conf`), find the Aliases section, and add the following lines:

   ```
   Alias /tshirtshop/ "/home/username/tshirtshop/"
   Alias /tshirtshop "/home/username/tshirtshop"
   ```

   After adding these lines, a request for `http://localhost/tshirtshop` or `http://localhost/tshirtshop/` will result in the application in the `tshirtshop` folder (if it existed) being executed.

> **Note** If the web server is not running on the default port (80), you need to manually supply the port number if you need to reach it using a web browser. So if you installed Apache to run on port 8080, you'll need to browse to `http://localhost:8080/tshirtshop` instead of `http://localhost/tshirtshop`. Also, keep in mind that instead of `localhost`, you can always use `127.0.0.1` (the computer's loopback address), or the network name of your machine.

3. Create a file named `test.php` in the `tshirtshop` folder, with the following line inside:

```
<?php phpinfo();?>
```

4. The last step in this exercise has to do with setting security options. You need to ensure that Apache has access to the `tshirtshop` folder.

   In a default Windows installation, Apache runs as the SYSTEM user so it has wide privileges locally (including write access to the `templates_c` directory, where the Smarty engine needs to save its compiled template files).

   If you're building your project under a Unix system, you should execute the following commands to ensure your Apache server can access your project's files, and has write permissions to the `templates_c` directory:

```
chmod a+rx /home/mylinuxuser
chmod -R a+rx  /home/mylinuxuser/tshirtshop
chmod a+w /home/mylinuxuser/templates_c
```

■**Note** Setting permissions on Unix systems as shown here allows any user with a shell account on your Unix box to view the source code of any files in your folder, including PHP code and other data (which might include sensitive information such as database passwords, keys used to encrypt/ decrypt credit card information, and so on). Running PHP in safe mode with a good configuration file solves the problem of the "custom PHP scripts," but if you have shell accounts on your box, you should go the suexec way, which is the most secure although not easy to configure. Setting up PHP for a shared server web hosting or for a Unix box with multiple shell accounts is beyond the scope of this book.

---

5. Restart the Apache web server, and load `http://localhost/tshirtshop/test.php` (or `http://localhost:8080/tshirtshop/test.php` if Apache works on port 8080) in a web browser.

How It Works: The Virtual Folder

This first step toward building the TShirtShop e-commerce site is a small, but important, one because it allows you to test that Apache, PHP, and the `tshirtshop` alias work okay. If you have problems running the test page, make sure you followed the installation steps in Appendix A correctly.

No matter whether you're working on Windows or a Unix flavor, loading `test.php` in a web browser should give you the PHP information returned by the `phpinfo` function as shown in Figure 2-7.

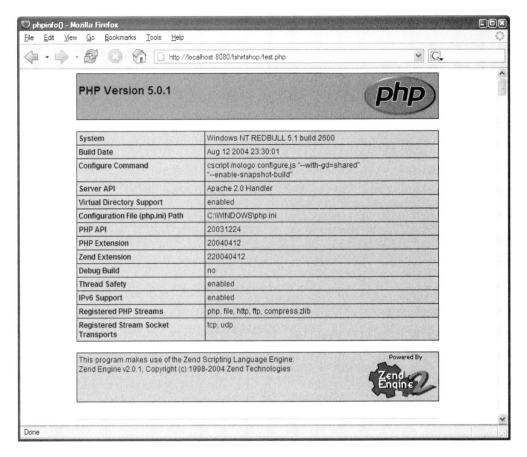

Figure 2-7. *Testing PHP and the* tshirtshop *virtual folder*

■**Tip** In case you were wondering, we use the FireFox web browser for taking our screenshots. Have a look at it at http://www.mozilla.org/products/firefox/.

Installing Smarty and PEAR

The Smarty and PEAR libraries are PHP classes you can simply install in your project's folder and use from there. Many web-hosting companies provide these for you, but it's better to have your own installation for two reasons:

- It's always preferable to make your project independent of the server's settings, when possible.

- Even if the hosting system has PEAR and Smarty installed, that company's version might be changed in time, perhaps without notice, possibly affecting your web site's functionality.

You'll install PEAR and Smarty into a subfolder of the `tshirtshop` folder named libs in the following exercise. The steps should work the same no matter what operating system you're running on.

Exercise: Installing Smarty and PEAR

Follow the steps to have Smarty and PEAR working in your project's folder:

1. Create a folder named `libs` inside the `tshirtshop` folder, and then a folder named `smarty` inside the `libs` folder. Download the latest version of Smarty from `http://smarty.php.net/download.php`, and copy the contents of the `Smarty-2.x.x/libs` directory from the archive to the folder you created earlier (`tshirtshop/libs/smarty`).

2. To operate correctly, Smarty requires you to create three folders: `templates`, `templates_c`, and `configs`. Create these folders in your `tshirtshop` folder.

3. Now you can install PEAR. Use a web browser to navigate to `http://pear.php.net/go-pear`. This page contains the source code for a page. Save that code as a file named `go-pear.php` in your `tshirtshop/libs` folder, and then run it by loading it (`http://localhost/tshirtshop/libs/go-pear.php`) into a web browser (see Figure 2-8).

   Click Next, and then in the next screen, click Install. Clicking on the `Start Web Frontend of the PEAR Installer >>` link in the final screen forwards you to `http://localhost/index.php`, which might not exist on your system.

   After following these steps, you'll find the PEAR subdirectory in your `tshirtshop/libs` directory.

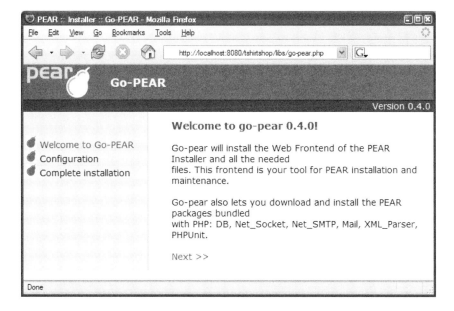

Figure 2-8. *Installing PEAR*

How It Works: The Smarty and PEAR installation

In this exercise you created these three folders used by Smarty:

- The `templates` folder will contain the Smarty templates for your web site (.tpl files).

- The `templates_c` folder will contain the compiled Smarty templates (generated automatically by the Smarty engine).

- The `configs` folder will contain configuration files you might need for templates.

After adding these folders and installing PEAR, your folder structure should look like this:

```
tshirtshop/
    configs/
    libs/
        PEAR/
        smarty/
    templates/
    templates_c/
```

You also ensured that the `tshirtshop` directory and all its contents can be accessed properly by the web server.

Implementing the Site Skeleton

The visual design of the site is usually agreed upon after a discussion with the client, and in collaboration with a professional web designer. Alternatively, you can buy a web site template from one of the many companies that offer this kind of service for a reasonable price.

Because this is a programming book, we won't focus on web design issues. Furthermore, we want to have a pretty simple design that allows you to focus on the technical details of the site. Having a simplistic design also makes your life easier if you'll need to apply your layout on top of the one we're creating here.

All pages in TShirtShop, including the first page, will have the structure shown in Figure 2-9.

Although the detailed structure of the product catalog is covered in the next chapter, right now we know that a main list of departments needs to be displayed on every page of the site. When the visitor clicks on a department, the list of categories for that department will appear below the departments list. The site also has the search box that will allow visitors to perform product searches. At the top of the page, the site header will be visible in any page the visitor browses to.

To implement this structure as simply as possible, we'll use Smarty Componentized Templates (or simple Smarty Design Templates) to create the separate parts of the page as shown in Figure 2-10.

As Figure 2-10 suggests, you will create a Smarty componentized template named `departments_list`, and a simple Smarty design template file named `header.tpl`, which will help you populate the first page.

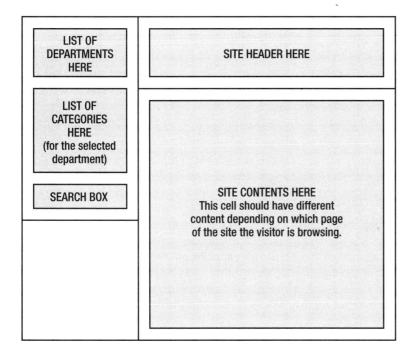

Figure 2-9. *Structure of web pages in TShirtShop*

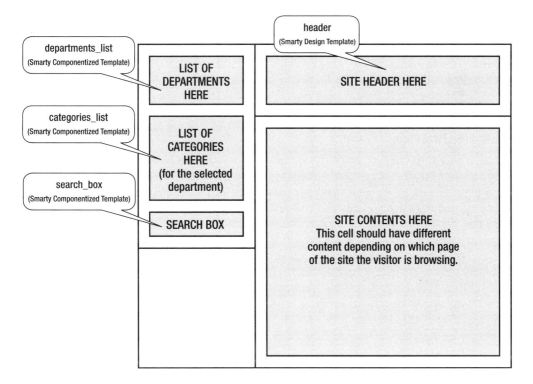

Figure 2-10. *Using Smarty to generate content*

▪Note We call **Smarty Componentized Template** the combination of a **Smarty Design Template** (the .tpl file) and its associated **Smarty Plugin file** which contains the presentation tier logic (a .php file). In cases of simple pages that don't need an associated .php code file, such as the header, we'll use just a Smarty Design Template file. You'll meet Smarty plugins in Chapter 3, and you can learn more about them at `http://smarty.php.net/manual/en/plugins.php`.

Using Smarty templates to implement different pieces of functionality provides benefits discussed earlier in the chapter. Having different, unrelated pieces of functionality logically separated from one another gives you the flexibility to modify them independently, and even reuse them in other pages without having to write their code again. It's also extremely easy to change the place in the parent web page of a feature implemented as a Smarty template.

The list of departments, the search box, and the site header are elements that will be present in every page of the site. The list of categories appears only when the visitor selects a department from the list. The most dynamic part of the web site that changes while browsing through the site will be the contents cell, which will update itself depending on the site location requested by the visitor. There are two main options for implementing that cell: add a componentized template that changes itself depending on the location or use different componentized templates to populate the cell depending on the location being browsed. There is no rule of thumb about which method to use, because it mainly depends on the specifics of the project. For TShirtShop, you will create a number of componentized templates that will fill that location.

In the remainder of this chapter, you will

- Create the main web page and the header componentized template.

- Implement the foundations of the error-handling system in TShirtShop.

- Create the TShirtShop database.

Building the First Page

The main page in TShirtShop will be generated by index.php and index.tpl.

You'll write the index.tpl Smarty template with placeholders for the three major parts of the site—the header, the table of departments, and the page contents cell. Implement the main page in the following exercise, and we'll discuss the details in the "How it Works" section thereafter.

Exercise: Implementing the First Page and Its Header

Follow these steps:

1. Create a new folder named images inside the tshirtshop folder.

2. Copy the files in image folders/images from the code download of the book (which you can find at `http://www.apress.com` or `http://www.CristianDarie.ro`) to tshirtshop/images (the folder you just created).

3. Create a file named `site.conf` in the `tshirtshop/configs` folder (used by the Smarty templates engine), and add the following line to it:

```
sitetitle = "TShirtShop - The Best E-Commerce Store on the Internet"
```

4. Create a file named `index.tpl` in tshirtshop/templates, and add the following code to it:

```
{* smarty *}
{config_load file="site.conf"}
<!DOCTYPE html
PUBLIC "-//W3C//DTD XHTML 1.0 Transitional//EN"
"http://www.w3.org/TR/xhtml1/DTD/xhtml1-transitional.dtd">
<html>
  <head>
    <title>{#sitetitle#}</title>
  </head>
  <body>
    <table cellspacing="0" cellpadding="0" width="750" border="0">
      <tr>
        <td width="200" height="100%" valign="top">
          <table  width="100%" cellspacing="0" cellpadding="0">
            <tr>
              <td valign="top" height="100%">
                Place list of departments here
              </td>
            </tr>
          </table>
        </td>
        <td>   </td>
        <td valign="top" width="550"><br />
          {include file="header.tpl"}
          Place contents here
        </td>
      </tr>
    </table>
  </body>
</html>
```

5. Create a template file named `header.tpl` in tshirtshop/templates and add the following contents to it.

```
<table border="0" width="550" cellspacing="0" cellpadding="0">
  <tr align="right">
    <td>
     <a href="index.php">
      <img src="images/title.png" border="0" alt="site title" />
     </a>
    </td>
  </tr>
  <tr align="right">
```

```
        <td>
          <img src="images/1n.gif" border="0" width="350" height="1"
               alt="line here" />
        </td>
      </tr>
    </table>
```

6. Create a folder named tshirtshop/include and add a file named config.inc.php to it with the following contents:

```php
<?php
// SITE_ROOT contains the full path to the tshirtshop folder
define("SITE_ROOT", dirname(dirname(__FILE__)));
// Settings needed to configure the Smarty template engine
define("SMARTY_DIR", SITE_ROOT."/libs/smarty/");
define("TEMPLATE_DIR", SITE_ROOT."/templates");
define("COMPILE_DIR", SITE_ROOT."/templates_c");
define("CONFIG_DIR", SITE_ROOT."/configs");
?>
```

Before moving on, let's see what happens here. dirname(__FILE__) returns the parent directory of the current file; naturally, dirname(dirname(__FILE__)) returns the parent of the current file's directory. This way our SITE_ROOT constant will be set to the full path of tshirtshop. With the help of the SITE_ROOT constant, we set up absolute paths of Smarty folders.

7. Create a file named setup_smarty.php in the tshirtshop/include folder, and add the following contents to it:

```php
<?php
// Reference Smarty library
require_once SMARTY_DIR.'Smarty.class.php';
// Reference our configuration file
require_once 'config.inc.php';

// Class that extends Smarty, used to process and display Smarty files
class Page extends Smarty
{
  // constructor
  function __construct()
  {
    // Call Smarty's constructor
    $this->Smarty();
    // Change the default template directories
    $this->template_dir = TEMPLATE_DIR;
    $this->compile_dir = COMPILE_DIR;
    $this->config_dir = CONFIG_DIR;
  }
}
?>
```

In setup_smarty.php, you extend the Smarty class with a wrapper class named Page, which changes Smarty's default behavior. The Page class configures in its constructor the Smart folders you created earlier.

Tip As mentioned earlier, Smarty requires three folders to operate: templates, templates_c, and configs. In the constructor of the Page class, we set a separate set of these directories for our application. If you want to turn on caching, then Smarty also needs a directory named cache. We will not be using Smarty caching for TShirtShop, but you can read more details about this in the Smarty manual at http://smarty.php.net/manual/en/caching.php.

---

8. Create the tshirtshop/include/app_top.php file, and add the following contents to it:

```php
<?php
// include utility files
require_once 'config.inc.php';
require_once 'setup_smarty.php';
?>
```

This file (app_top.php) will be included at the top of the main web pages to perform the necessary initializations.

9. Add the index.php file to the tshirtshop folder. The role of this file is to load the index.tpl template by using the Page class you created earlier. Here's the code for index.php:

```php
<?php
// load Smarty library and config files
require_once 'include/app_top.php';
// Load Smarty template file
$page = new Page();
$page->display('index.tpl');
?>
```

10. Now it's time to see some output from this thing. Load http://localhost/tshirtshop/ in your favorite web browser and admire the results as shown in Figure 2-11.

Figure 2-11. *Running TShirtShop*

How It Works: The First Page of TShirtShop

The main web page contains three major sections. There are two table cells that you'll fill with componentized templates—one for the list of departments and one for the page contents—in the following chapters.

Notice the departments list placed on the left side, the header at the top, and the contents cell filled with information regarding the first page. As previously mentioned, this contents cell is the only one that changes while browsing the site; the other two cells will look exactly the same no matter what page is visited. This implementation eases your life as a programmer and keeps a consistent look and feel of the web site.

Before you move on, it's important to understand how the Smarty template works. Everything starts from index.php, so you need to take a close look at it. Here's the code again:

```php
<?php
// load Smarty library and config files
require_once 'include/app_top.php';
// Load Smarty template file
$page = new Page();
$page->display('index.tpl');
?>
```

At this moment, this file has very simple functionality. First it loads app_top.php, which sets some global variables, and then it loads the Smarty template file, which will generate the actual HTML content when a client requests index.php.

The standard way to create and configure a Smarty page is shown in the following code snippet:

```php
<?php
// Load the Smarty library
require("smarty/Smarty.class.php");
// Create a new instance of the Smarty class.
$smarty = new Smarty();
$smarty->template_dir= TEMPLATE_DIR;
$smarty->compile_dir= COMPILE_DIR;
$smarty->config_dir= CONFIG_DIR;
?>
```

In TShirtShop, we created a class named Page that inherits Smarty, which contains the initialization procedure in its constructor. This makes working with Smarty templates easier. Here's again the code of the Page class:

```php
class Page extends Smarty
{
  // constructor
  function __construct()
  {
    // Call Smarty's constructor
    $this->Smarty();
    // Change the default template directories
```

```
    $this->template_dir = TEMPLATE_DIR;
    $this->compile_dir = COMPILE_DIR;
    $this->config_dir = CONFIG_DIR;
  }
}
```

Note The notion of constructor is specific to object-oriented programming terminology. The constructor of a class is a special method that executes automatically when an instance of that class is created. In PHP, the constructor of a class is called __construct(). Writing that code in the constructor of the Page class guarantees that it gets executed automatically when a new instance of Page is created.

The Smarty template file (index.tpl), except for a few details, contains simple HTML code. Those details are worth analyzing. In index.tpl, before the HTML code begins, the configuration file site.conf is loaded.

```
{* smarty *}
{config_load file="site.conf"}
```

Tip Smarty comments are enclosed between {* and *} marks.

At this moment, the only variable set in site.conf is sitetitle, which contains the name of the web site. The value of this variable is used to generate the title of the page in the HTML code:

```
<!DOCTYPE html
PUBLIC "-//W3C//DTD XHTML 1.0 Transitional//EN"
"http://www.w3.org/TR/xhtml1/DTD/xhtml1-transitional.dtd">
<html>
  <head>
    <title>{#sitetitle#}</title>
  </head>
```

Variables that are loaded from the config files are referenced by enclosing them within hash marks (#), or with the smarty variable $smarty.config, as in:

```
  <head>
    <title>{$smarty.config.sitetitle}</title>
  </head>
```

We loaded the site.conf config file using {config_load file="site.conf"} and accessed the sitetitle variable with {#sitetitle#}, which you'll use whenever you need to obtain the site title. If you want to change the site title, all you have to do is to edit site.conf.

Finally, it's important to notice how to include a Smarty template in another Smarty template. index.tpl references header.tpl, which will also be reused in a number of other pages:

```
<td valign="top" width="550"><br/>
  {include file="header.tpl"}
  Place contents here
</td>
```

Handling and Reporting Errors

Although the code will be written to run without any unpleasant surprises, there's always a possibility that something might go wrong when processing client requests. The best strategy to deal with these unexpected problems is to find a centralized way to handle these errors and perform certain actions when they do happen.

PHP is known for its confusing error messages. If you've worked with other programming languages, you probably appreciate the information you can get from displaying the stack trace when you have an error. Tracing information is not displayed by default when you have a PHP error, so you'll want to change this behavior. In the development stage, tracing information will help you debug the application, and in a release version, the error message must be reported to the site administrator. Another problem is the tricky E_WARNING error message, because it's hard to tell whether it's fatal or not for the application.

Tip If you don't remember or don't know what a PHP error message looks like, try adding the following line in your include/app_top.php file:

require_once 'inexistent_file.php';

Load the web site in your favorite browser, and notice the error message you get.

In the context of a live web application, errors can happen unexpectedly for various reasons, such as software failures (operating system or database server crashes, viruses, and so on) and hardware failures. It's important to be able to log these errors, and eventually inform the web site administrator (perhaps by sending an email message), so the error can be taken care of as fast as possible.

For these reasons, we'll start establishing an efficient error handling and reporting strategy. You'll create a user-defined error handler function named tss_error_handler, which will get executed anytime a PHP error happens during runtime. Serious error types (E_ERROR, E_PARSE, E_CORE_ERROR, E_CORE_WARNING, E_COMPILE_ERROR, and E_COMPILE_WARNING) cannot be intercepted and handled by tss_error_handler, but the other types of PHP errors (E_WARNING for example) can be.

Note You can find more info about PHP errors and logging in the PHP manual at http://www.php.net/manual/en/ref.errorfunc.php.

The error-handling method, tss_error_handler, will behave like this:

- It creates a detailed error message.

- If configured to do so, the error is emailed to the site administrator.

- If configured to do so, the error is logged to an errors log file.

- If configured to do so, the error is shown in the response web page.

- Serious errors will halt the execution of the page. The other ones will allow the page to continue processing normally.

Let's implement tss_error_handler in the next exercise.

Exercise: Implementing tss_error_handler

Follow these steps:

1. Add the following error-handling related configuration variables to config.inc.php:

```
// these should be true while developing the web site
define("IS_WARNING_FATAL", true);
define("DEBUGGING", true);
// settings about mailing the error messages to admin
define("SEND_ERROR_MAIL", false);
define("ADMIN_ERROR_MAIL", "admin_mail@localhost");
define("SENDMAIL_FROM", "errors@tshirtshop.com");
ini_set("sendmail_from", SENDMAIL_FROM);
// by default we don't log errors to a file
define("LOG_ERRORS", false);
define("LOG_ERRORS_FILE", "c:\\tshirtshop\\errors_log.txt"); // Windows
// define("LOG_ERRORS_FILE", "/var/tmp/tshirtshop_errors.log"); // Unix
// Generic error message to be diplayed instead of debug info
// (when DEBUGGING is false)
define("SITE_GENERIC_ERROR_MESSAGE", "<h2>TShirtShop Error!</h2>");
```

2. Add the include/tss_error_handler.php file:

```
<?php
// set the user error handler method to be tss_error_handler
set_error_handler("tss_error_handler", E_ALL);

// error handler function
function tss_error_handler($errNo, $errStr, $errFile, $errLine)
{
  /* the first two elements of the backtrace array are irrelevant:
     -DBG_Backtrace
     -outErrorHandler */
  $backtrace = dbg_get_backtrace(2);
  // error message to be displayed, logged or mailed
```

```
      $error_message = "\nERRNO: $errNo \nTEXT: " . $errStr . " \n" .
                "LOCATION: " . $errFile . ", line " . $errLine . ", at " .
                date("F j, Y, g:i a") . "\nShowing backtrace:\n" .
                $backtrace . "\n\n";
  // email the error details, in case SEND_ERROR_MAIL is true
  if (SEND_ERROR_MAIL == true)
    error_log($error_message, 1, ADMIN_ERROR_MAIL, "From: " .
              SENDMAIL_FROM . "\r\nTo: " . ADMIN_ERROR_MAIL);
  // log the error, in case LOG_ERRORS is true
  if (LOG_ERRORS == true)
    error_log($error_message, 3, LOG_ERRORS_FILE);
  // warnings don't abort execution if IS_WARNING_FATAL is false
  // E_NOTICE and E_USER_NOTICE errors don't abort execution
  if (($errNo == E_WARNING && IS_WARNING_FATAL == false) ||
     ($errNo == E_NOTICE || $errNo == E_USER_NOTICE))
    // if the error is non-fatal ...
  {
    // show message only if DEBUGGING is true
    if (DEBUGGING == true)
      echo "<pre>" . $error_message . "</pre>";
  }
  else
  // if error is fatal ...
  {
    // show error message
    if (DEBUGGING == true)
      echo "<pre>" . $error_message . "</pre>";
    else
      echo SITE_GENERIC_ERROR_MESSAGE;
    // stop processing the request
    exit;
  }
}
}
?>
```

3. Add the dbg_get_backtrace function at the end of tss_error_handler.php:

```
// builds backtrace message
function dbg_get_backtrace($irrelevantFirstEntries)
{
  $s = '';
  $MAXSTRLEN = 64;
  $traceArr = debug_backtrace();
  for ($i = 0; $i < $irrelevantFirstEntries; $i++)
    array_shift($traceArr);
  $tabs = sizeof($traceArr) - 1;
  foreach($traceArr as $arr)
  {
```

```php
    $tabs -= 1;
    if (isset($arr['class']))
      $s .= $arr['class'] . '.';
    $args = array();
    if (!empty($arr['args']))
    foreach($arr['args']as $v)
    {
      if (is_null($v))
        $args[] = 'null';
      else if (is_array($v))
        $args[] = 'Array[' . sizeof($v).']';
      else if (is_object($v))
        $args[] = 'Object:' . get_class($v);
      else if (is_bool($v))
        $args[] = $v ? 'true' : 'false';
      else
      {
        $v = (string)@$v;
        $str = htmlspecialchars(substr($v, 0, $MAXSTRLEN));
        if (strlen($v) > $MAXSTRLEN)
          $str .= '...';
        $args[] = "\"" . $str . "\"";
      }
    }
    $s .= $arr['function'] . '(' . implode(', ', $args) . ')';
    $Line = (isset($arr['line']) ? $arr['line']: "unknown");
    $File = (isset($arr['file']) ? $arr['file']: "unknown");
    $s .= sprintf(" # line %4d, file: %s", $Line, $File, $File);
    $s .= "\n";
  }
  return $s;
}
```

4. Modify the include/app_top.php file to include the newly created
   tss_error_handler.php file:

```php
<?php
require_once 'config.inc.php';
require_once 'tss_error_handler.php';
require_once 'setup_smarty.php';
?>
```

5. Great! You just finished writing the new error-handling code. Let's test it. First, load
   the web site in your browser to see that you typed in everything correctly. If you get
   no errors, test the new error handling system by adding the following line to include/
   app_top.php:

```php
<?php
require_once 'config.inc.php';
```

```
require_once 'tss_error_handler.php';
require_once 'setup_smarty.php';
require_once 'inexistent_file.php';
?>
```

Now load again index.php in your browser, and admire your brand new error message as shown in Figure 2-12.

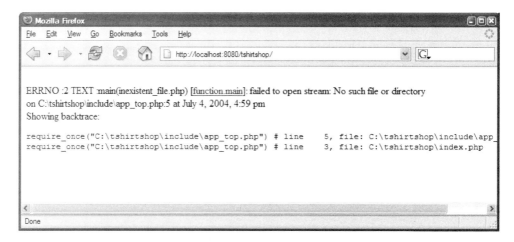

Figure 2-12. *Error message showing backtrace information*

■**Note** Due to a bug in the PHP 5 engine (which is reported at http://bugs.php.net/bug.php?id=28054), this "improved" error message might be incorrect sometimes.

Don't forget to remove the buggy line from app_top.php before moving on.

How It Works: Error Handling

The method that intercepts web site errors and deals with them is tss_error_handler (located in tss_error_handler.php). The code that registers the tss_error_handler function to be the one that handles errors in your site is at the beginning of tss_error_handler.php:

```
// set the user error handler method to be tss_error_handler
set_error_handler("tss_error_handler", E_ALL);
```

■**Note** The second parameter of set_error_handler specifies the range of errors that should be inter-cepted. E_ALL specifies all types of errors, including E_NOTICE errors, which should be reported during web site development.

When called, `tss_error_handler()` constructs the error message with the help of a method named `dbg_get_backtrace`, and forwards the error message to the client's browser, to a log file, to the administrator (by email), or a combination of these, which can be configured by editing `config.inc.php`.

`dbg_get_backtrace()` gets the backtrace information from the `debug_backtrace` function (which was introduced in PHP 4.3.0), and changes its output format to generate an HTML error message similar to a Java error. It isn't important to understand every line in `dbg_get_backtrace` unless you want to personalize the backtrace displayed in case of an error. The 2 parameter sent to `dbg_get_backtrace` specifies that the backtrace results should omit the first two entries (the calls to `tss_error_handler` and `dbg_get_backtrace`).

You build the detailed error string in tss_error_handler, including the backtrace information:

```
$backtrace = dbg_get_backtrace(2);
// error message to be displayed, logged or mailed
$error_message = "\nERRNO: $errNo \nTEXT: " . $errStr . " \n" .
          "LOCATION: " . $errFile . ", line " . $errLine . ", at " .
          date("F j, Y, g:i a") . "\nShowing backtrace:\n" .
          $backtrace . "\n\n";
```

Depending on the configuration options from the `config.inc.php` file, you decide whether to display, log, and/or email the error. Here we use PHP's `error_log` method, which knows how to email or write the error's details to a log file:

```
// email the error details, in case SEND_ERROR_MAIL is true
if (SEND_ERROR_MAIL == true)
   error_log($error_message, 1, ADMIN_ERROR_MAIL, "From: " .
            SENDMAIL_FROM . "\r\nTo: " . ADMIN_ERROR_MAIL);
// log the error, in case LOG_ERRORS is true
if (LOG_ERRORS == true)
   error_log($error_message, 3, LOG_ERRORS_FILE);
```

■**Note** If you want to be able to send an error mail to a localhost mail account (your_name@locahost), then you should have an SMTP (Simple Mail Transfer Protocol) server started on your machine. On a Red Hat (or Fedora) Linux distribution, you can start an SMTP server with the following command:

```
service sendmail start
```

On Windows systems, you should check in IIS (Internet Information Services) Manager for Default SMTP Virtual Server and make sure it's started.

While you are developing the site, the DEBUGGING constant should be set to `true`, but after launching the site in the "wild," you should make it `false`, causing a user-friendly error message to be displayed instead of the debugging information in case of serious errors, and no message shown at all in case of nonfatal errors.

The errors of type E_WARNING are pretty tricky because you don't know which of them should stop the execution of the request. The IS_WARNING_FATAL constant set in config.inc.php decides whether this type of error should be considered fatal for the project. Also, errors of type E_NOTICE and E_USER_NOTICE are not considered fatal:

```
// warnings don't abort execution if IS_WARNING_FATAL is false
// E_NOTICE and E_USER_NOTICE errors don't abort execution
if (($errNo == E_WARNING && IS_WARNING_FATAL == false) ||
    ($errNo == E_NOTICE || $errNo == E_USER_NOTICE))
  // if the error is non-fatal ...
{
  // show message only if DEBUGGING is true
  if (DEBUGGING == true)
    echo "<pre>" . $error_message . "</pre>";
}
else
// if error is fatal ...
{
  // show error message
  if (DEBUGGING == true)
    echo "<pre>" . $error_message . "</pre>";
  else
    echo SITE_GENERIC_ERROR_MESSAGE;
  // stop processing the request
  exit;
}
```

In the following chapters you'll need to manually trigger errors using the trigger_error PHP function, which lets you specify the kind of error to generate. By default, it generates E_USER_NOTICE errors which are not considered fatal, but are logged and reported, by tss_error_handler code.

Preparing the tshirtshop Database

The final step in this chapter is to create the MySQL database, although you won't use it until the next chapter. We will show you the steps to create your database and create a user with full privileges to it using phpMyAdmin, but you can use other visual interfaces such as MySQL Control Center or even the MySQL text-mode console.

Before moving on, make sure you have MySQL 4.0 (or 4.1) and phpMyAdmin installed. Consult Appendix A for installation instructions.

■**Note** For an excellent coverage of phpMyAdmin I recommend you read "Mastering phpMyAdmin for effective MySQL Management" (Packt Publishing, 2004)

Exercise: Creating the tshirtshop Database and a New User Account

1. Load the phpMyAdmin page in your favorite web browser, and type **tshirtshop** in the Create new database text box, as shown in Figure 2-13.

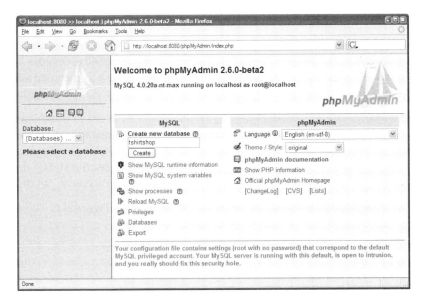

Figure 2-13. *The main phpMyAdmin page*

2. Click the Create button to create the new database. In the screen that follows (see Figure 2-14), you're shown the SQL query phpMyAdmin used to create your database.

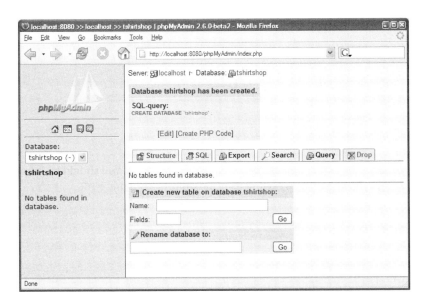

Figure 2-14. *Editing your database using phpMyAdmin*

Note You'll learn more about SQL queries in Chapter 3. SQL is the language used to interact with the database. However, you can accomplish many tasks, such as creating databases and data tables, using a visual interface such as phpMyAdmin, which generates the SQL queries for you.

---

3. Now add a new user to the database. Our data tier access code will access the TShirtShop database using this user's credentials. You'll create a user named admin (with the password "admin"), who will have full access inside the TShirtShop database, but not to any other database.

   Because phpMyAdmin doesn't have visual interface tools to create new users or to manage security, you'll need to create the new user using an SQL query. You have more alternatives to achieve the same results, and for more details, see the MySQL documentation at http://dev.mysql.com/doc/mysql/en/Account_management_SQL.html.

   Now click the SQL tab, and type the SQL query you can see in Figure 2-15.

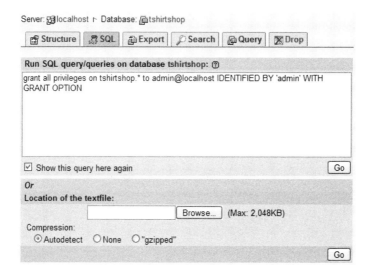

Figure 2-15. *Creating a new database user*

4. After entering the SQL query as shown, click the Go button. You should be informed that the SQL query has been executed successfully (see Figure 2-16).

Your SQL-query has been executed successfully (Query took 0.0644 sec)

SQL-query:
GRANT ALL PRIVILEGES ON tshirtshop .* TO admin@localhostIDENTIFIED BY 'admin' WITH GRANT OPTION

[Edit] [Create PHP Code]

Figure 2-16. *The new user has been successfully created in the database.*

Downloading the Code

You can find the latest code downloads and a link to an online version of TShirtShop at the author's web site, `http://www.CristianDarie.ro`, or in the Downloads section of the Apress web site at `http://www.apress.com`. It should be easy to read through this book and build your solution as you go; however, if you want to check something from our working version, you can. Instructions on loading the chapters are available in the `WELCOME.HTML` document in the download.

Summary

Hey, we covered a lot of ground in this chapter, didn't we? We talked about the three-tier architecture and how it helps you create great flexible and scalable applications. We also saw how each of the technologies used in this book fits into the three-tier architecture.

So far, we have a very flexible and scalable application because it only has a main web page, but you'll feel the real advantages of using a disciplined way of coding in the next chapters. In this chapter you have only coded the basic, static part of the presentation tier, implemented a bit of error-handling code, and created the TShirtShop database, which is the support for the data tier. In the next chapter you'll start implementing the product catalog and learn a lot about how to dynamically generate visual content using data stored in the database with the help of the middle tier and with smart and fast controls and components in the presentation tier.

■ ■ ■

CHAPTER 3

Creating the Product Catalog: Part I

After learning about the three-tier architecture and implementing a bit of your web site's main page, it's time to continue your work by starting to create the TShirtShop product catalog.

Because the product catalog is composed of many components, you'll create it over two chapters. In this chapter, you'll create the first data table, implement access methods in the middle tier, and learn how to deal with the data tier. By the end of this chapter, you'll finally have something dynamically generated on your web page. In Chapter 4, you'll finish building the product catalog by adding support for categories, product lists, a product details page, and more!

The main topics we'll touch on in this chapter are

- Thinking about what you want the catalog to look like and what functionality it should support

- Creating the database structures for the catalog and the data tier of the catalog

- Implementing the business tier objects required to make the catalog run

- Implementing a functional user interface for the product catalog

Showing the Visitor Your Products

One of the essential features required in any e-store is to allow the visitor to easily browse through the products. Just imagine what Amazon.com would be like without its excellent product catalog!

Whether your visitors are looking for something specific or just browsing, it's important to make sure their experience with your site is a pleasant one. When looking for a specific product or product type, you want the visitor to find it as easily as possible. This is why you'll want to add search functionality to the site, and also find a clever way of structuring products into categories so they can be quickly and intuitively accessed.

Depending on the size of the store, it might be enough to group products under a number of categories, but if there are a lot of products, you need to find even more ways to categorize and structure the product catalog.

Determining the structure of the catalog is one of the first tasks to accomplish in this chapter. After this is done, we'll move to the technical details that will make the catalog work.

What Does a Product Catalog Look Like?

Today's web surfers are more demanding than they used to be. They expect to find information quickly on whatever product or service they have in mind, and if they don't find it, they are likely to go to the competition before giving the site a second chance. Of course, you don't want this to happen to *your* visitors, so you need to structure the catalog to make it as intuitive and helpful as possible.

Because the e-store will start with around 100 products and will probably have many more in the future, it's not enough to just group them in categories. The store also has a number of departments and each department will contain a number of categories. Each category can then have any number of products attached to it.

Note   Even if you have a fairly clear idea of the categories, departments, and products, the client wants these to be configurable from the administrative part of the web site. This requirement is not unusual, because it is likely that catalog information will change in time. Of course, one solution would be for you to manually change these in the database whenever needed, but this solution would be highly unprofessional. You'll create the administrative part of the product catalog, which will allow the client to manage the departments, categories, and products, in Chapter 7.

Another particularly important detail that you need to think about is whether a category can exist in more than one department, and whether a product can exist in more than one category. As you might suspect, this is the kind of decision that has implications on the way you code the product catalog, so you need to consult your client on this matter.

For the TShirtShop product catalog, each category can exist in only one department, but a product can exist in more than one category. For example, the product "Danish Locomotive" will appear in both "Danish" and "Train" categories. This decision will have implications in the way you'll design the database, and we'll highlight those implications when we get there.

Finally, apart from having the products grouped in categories, you also want to have featured products. For this web site, a product can be featured either on the front page or in the department pages. The next section shows a few screenshots that explain this.

Previewing the Product Catalog

Although you'll have the fully functional product catalog finished by the end of the next chapter, taking a look at it right now will give you a better idea about where you're heading. In Figure 3-1, you can see the TShirtShop front page and two of its featured products.

Note the departments list in the upper-left corner of the page. The list of departments is dynamically generated with data gathered from the database; you'll implement the list of departments in this chapter.

When site visitors click a department in the departments list, they go to the main page of the specified department. This replaces the store's list of catalog-featured products with a page containing information specific to the selected department—including the list of featured products for that department. In Figure 3-2, you see the page that will appear when the Nature department is clicked.

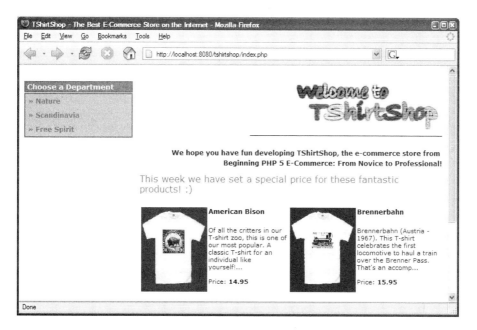

Figure 3-1. *TShirtShop front page and two of its featured products*

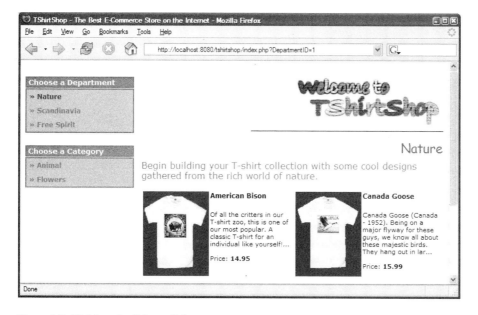

Figure 3-2. *Visiting the "Nature" department*

Under the list of departments, you can now see the list of categories that belong to the selected department. In the right side of the screen, you can see the name of the selected department, its description, and its featured products. We decided to list only the featured products in the department page, in part because the complete list would be too long. The text above the list of featured products is the description for the selected department, which means you'll need to store in the database both a name and a description for each department.

In this page, when a particular category from the categories list is selected, all of its products are listed, along with updated title and description text. In Figure 3-3, you can see the page that appears when selecting the "Flowers" category.

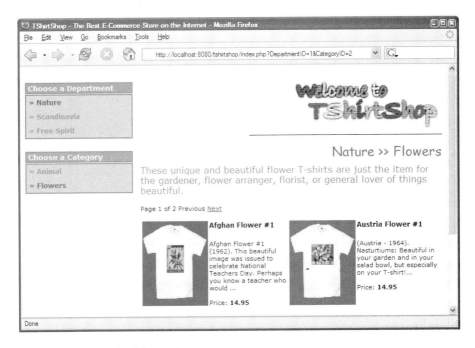

Figure 3-3. *Visiting the "Flowers" category*

When a category is selected, all its products are listed—you no longer see featured products. Note that the description text also changes. This time, this is the description of the selected category.

Planning the Departments List of Your Catalog

As you can see, the product catalog, although not very complicated, has more parts that need to be covered. In this chapter, you'll only create the departments list (see Figure 3-4).

Figure 3-4. *The departments list*

The departments list will be the first dynamically generated data in your site (the names of the departments will be extracted from the database).

In this chapter, you'll implement just the departments list part of the web site. After you understand what happens behind the list of departments, you'll quickly implement the other components of the product catalog in Chapter 4.

In Chapter 2, we discussed the three-tiered architecture that you'll use to implement the web application. The product catalog part of the site makes no exception to the rule, and its components (including the departments list) will be spread over the three logical layers. Figure 3-5 previews what you'll create at each tier in this chapter to achieve a functional departments list.

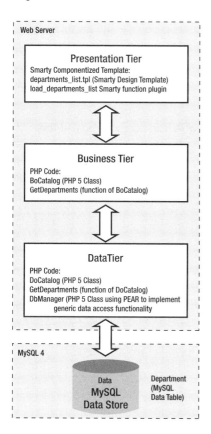

Figure 3-5. *The components of the departments list*

So far, you've only played a bit with the presentation tier in Chapter 2. Now, when building the catalog, you'll finally meet the other two tiers and work further with the tshirtshop database. The database backend itself is not considered an integral part of the three-tiered architecture.

These are the main steps you'll take toward having your own dynamically generated department list. Note that you start with the database, and make your way to the presentation tier:

1. Create the department table in the database. This table will store data regarding the store's departments. Before adding this table, you'll learn the basic concepts of working with relational databases.

2. Create the DbManager class, which is a wrapper class for some PEAR DB functions that will ensure errors are handled in case of database-related errors

3. Create the DoCatalog class and add the GetDepartments method to it. DoCatalog is logically located in the data tier of the application. At this step, you'll learn how to speak with the database using SQL and how to use the PEAR DB database abstraction layer.

4. Create the business tier components of the departments list (BoCatalog class and GetDepartments method). You'll see how to communicate with the data tier objects and return the results to the presentation tier.

5. Implement the departments_list Smarty template, which achieves the goal of this chapter.

So, let's start with the creation of the department table.

Storing Catalog Information

In this book, we assume you have basic knowledge about the Structured Query Language (SQL), the language used to interact with relational databases, including MySQL. However, we'll cover the basic concepts here.

■**Note** If you want to know more about SQL, read *The Programmer's Guide to SQL* (Apress, 2003) or *The Definitive Guide to MySQL*, Second Edition (Apress, 2003).

Essentially, a relational database is made up of **data tables** and the **relationships** that exist between them. Because you'll work with a single data table in this chapter, we'll cover only the database theory that applies to the table as a separate, individual database item. In the next chapter, when you'll add the other tables to the picture, we'll take a closer look at the theory behind relational databases by analyzing how the tables relate to each other.

■**Note** In a real world situation, you would probably design the whole database (or at least all the tables relevant to the feature you build) from the start. In this book, we chose to split the development over two chapters to maintain a better balance of theory and practice.

So, let's start with a little bit of theory, after which you'll create the department data table and the rest of the required components:

Determining What Makes Up a Data Table

This section provides a quick database lesson covering the essential information you need to know to design simple data tables. We'll briefly discuss the main parts that make up a database table:

- Primary keys

- MySQL Server data types

- UNIQUE columns

- NOT NULL columns and default values

- Auto-increment columns

- Indexes

■**Note** If you have enough experience with MySQL, you might want to skip this section and go directly to the "Creating the department table" section.

A data table is made up of columns and rows. Columns are also referred to as **fields**, and rows are sometimes also called **records**.

Because this chapter only covers the departments list, you'll only need to create one data table: the department table. This table will store your departments' data, and is one of the simplest tables you'll work with.

With the help of tools such as phpMyAdmin, it's easy to create a data table in the database *if* you know for sure what kind of data it will store. When designing a table, you must consider which fields it should contain and which data types should be used for those fields. Besides a field's data type, there are a few more properties to consider, which you'll learn about in the following pages.

To determine which fields you need for the department table, write down a few examples of records that would be stored in that table. Remember from the previous figures that there isn't much information to store about a department—just the name and description for each department. The table containing the departments' data might look like Figure 3-6 (you'll implement the table in the database later, after we discuss the theory).

name	description
Nature	Begin building your T-shirt collection with some cool designs gathered from the rich world of nature.
Scandinavia	Our Scandinavian postal design T-shirts capture the essence and soul of the North! You really should try them!
Free Spirit	Some free spirit T-shirts for the really free people.

Figure 3-6. *Data from the* department *table*

From a table like this, the names would be extracted to populate the list in the upper-left part of the web page, and the descriptions would be used as headers for the featured products list.

Primary Keys

The way you work with data tables in a relational database is a bit different from the way you usually work on paper. A fundamental requirement in relational databases is that each data row in a table must be *uniquely identifiable*. This makes sense because you usually save records into a database so that you can retrieve them later; however, you can't always do that if each table row doesn't have something that makes it unique. For example, suppose you add another record to the departments table shown previously in Figure 3-6, making it look like the table shown in Figure 3-7.

name	description
Nature	Begin building your T-shirt collection with some cool designs gathered from the rich world of nature.
Scandinavia	Our Scandinavian postal design T-shirts capture the essence and soul of the North! You really should try them!
Free Spirit	Some free spirit T-shirts for the really free people.
Free Spirit	Don't try this at home.

Figure 3-7. *Having two departments with the same name*

Please look at this table, and then find the description of the "Free Spirit" department. Yep, we have a problem! The problem arises because there are two departments with the name "Free Spirit" (the name isn't unique). If you queried the table using the name column, you would get two results.

To solve this problem, you use a **primary key**, which allows you to uniquely identify a specific row out of many rows. Technically, the primary key is not a column itself. Instead, the PRIMARY KEY is a **constraint** that when applied on a column guarantees that the column will have unique values across the table.

■**Note** Applying a PRIMARY KEY constraint on a field also generates a unique index created on it by default. Indexes are objects that improve performance of many database operations, dramatically speeding up your web application (you'll learn more about this later).

Constraints are rules that apply to data tables and make up part of the **data integrity** rules of the database. The database takes care of its own integrity and makes sure these rules aren't broken. If, for example, you try to add two identical values for a column that has a PRIMARY KEY constraint, the database refuses the operation and generates an error. We'll do some experiments later in this chapter to show this.

■**Note** Although a primary key is not a column, but a constraint that applies to that column, from now on, for convenience, when referring to the primary key we'll be talking about the column that has the PRIMARY KEY constraint applied to it.

Back to the example, setting the name column as the primary key of the department table would solve the problem because two departments would not be allowed to have the same name. If name is the primary key of the department table, searching for a product with a specific name will always produce exactly one result if the name exists, or no results if no records have the specified name.

■**Tip** This is common sense, but it has to be said: a primary key column will never allow NULL values.

An alternative solution, and usually the preferred one, is to have an additional column in the table, called an ID column, to act as its primary key. With an ID column, the department table would look like Figure 3-8.

department_id	name	description
1	Nature	Begin building your T-shirt collection with some cool designs gathered from the rich world of nature.
2	Scandinavia	Our Scandinavian postal design T-shirts capture the essence and soul of the North! You really should try them!
3	Free Spirit	Some free spirit T-shirts for the really free people.

Figure 3-8. *Adding an* ID *column as the primary key of* department

The primary key column is named department_id. We'll use this naming convention for primary key columns in all data tables we'll create.

There are two main reasons it's better to create a separate numerical primary key column than to use the name (or another existing column) as the primary key:

- *Performance*: The database engine handles sorting and searching operations much faster with numerical values than with strings. This becomes even more relevant in the context of working with multiple related tables that need to be frequently joined (you'll learn more about this in Chapter 4).

- *Department name changes*: If you need to rely on the ID value being stable in time, creating an artificial key solves the problem, because it's unlikely you'll ever want to change the ID.

In Figure 3-8, the primary key is composed of a single column, but this is not a requirement. If the primary key is set on more than one column, the group of primary key columns (taken as a unit) is guaranteed to be unique, but the individual columns that form the primary key can have repeating values in the table. In Chapter 4, you'll see an example of a multi-valued primary key. For now, it's enough to know that they exist.

Unique Columns

UNIQUE is yet another kind of constraint that can be applied to table columns. This constraint is similar to the PRIMARY KEY constraint in that it doesn't allow duplicate data in a column. Still, there are differences:

- Although there is only one PRIMARY KEY constraint per table, you are allowed to have as many UNIQUE constraints as you like.

- A column with the UNIQUE constraint can be set to accept NULL values (in which case, it can accept *any number of* NULL values).

Columns having the UNIQUE constraint are useful when you already have a primary key, but still have columns (or groups of columns) for which you want to have unique values. You can set name to be unique in the department table if you want to forbid repeating values, in the situation where the department_id column is the primary key.

We won't use the UNIQUE constraint in this book, but we mention it here for completeness. We decided to allow identical department names because only site administrators will have the privilege to modify or change department data.

Columns and Data Types

Each column in a table has a particular data type. By looking at the previously shown Figure 3-8 with the department table, department_id has a numeric data type, whereas name and description contain text.

It's important to consider the many data types that MySQL Server supports so that you'll be able to make correct decisions about how to create your tables. Table 3-1 isn't an exhaustive list of MySQL Server data types, but it focuses on the main types you might come across in your project. Refer to the MySQL Manual for a more detailed list at http://dev.mysql.com/doc/mysql/en/Column_types.html.

■**Tip** For more details about any specific detail regarding MySQL or PHP, including MySQL data types, you can always refer to *Beginning PHP 5 and MySQL* by Jason Gilmore (Apress, 2004), which is an excellent reference.

To keep the table short, under the *Data Type* heading we have listed the used types in this project, while similar data types are explained under the "Description and Notes" heading. The list is not exhaustive, but it's meant to offer you a quick guide to MySQL data types. You don't need to memorize the list, but you should get an idea of which data types are available.

Table 3-1. *MySQL Server Data Types for Use in TShirtShop*

Data Type	Size in Bytes	Description and Notes
int	4	Stores integer numbers from -2,147,483,648 to 2,147,483,647. Related types are smallint and tinyint. A bit data type is able to store values of 0 and 1.
decimal (M,N)	M+2 bytes if N > 0	One character for each digit of the value, the decimal point (if the scale is greater than 0), and the "-" sign (for negative numbers)
	M+1 bytes if N = 0	decimal is a numeric data type you'll use to store monetary information because of its exact precision. To preserve the decimal precision of these numbers, MySQL stores decimal values internally as strings. M represents the precision (the number of significant decimal digits that will be stored for values), and N is the scale (the number of digits after the decimal point). If N is 0, decimal will only store integer values.
datetime	8 bytes	Supports date and time data from 1000-01-01 00:00:00 to 9999-12-31 23:59:59.
varchar	Variable	Stores variable-length character data up to 255 characters. The dimension you set represents the maximum length of strings it can accept.
text (blob)	L+2 bytes, where L < 2^16	A column with a maximum length of 65,535 (2^16 − 1) characters.

Keep in mind that data type names are case insensitive; in most database interface programs, data type names aren't capitalized.

Now let's get back to the department table and determine which data types to use. Don't worry that you don't have the table yet in your database; you'll create it a bit later. Figure 3-9 shows the design of department in phpMyAdmin. department_id is an int, and name and description are varchar data types.

Field	Type	Attributes	Null	Default	Extra
department_id	int(10)	UNSIGNED	No		auto_increment
name	varchar(50)		No		
description	varchar(200)		Yes	*NULL*	

Figure 3-9. *Designing the* department *table*

For varchar, the associated dimension—such as in varchar(50)—represents the maximum length of the stored strings. We'll choose to have 50 characters available for the department's name and 200 for the description. For int, the number is less important (it represents the number of padding spaces used when displaying values in the MySQL console). An int record, as shown in the table, always occupies 4 bytes.

The UNSIGNED attribute specifies the column can only accept positive values, double the positive range of values it can accept. For example, the unsigned int can accept values from 0 to 4294967295.

The fact that department_id is underlined specifies that the column is the primary key of the department table.

NOT NULL Columns and Default Values

The best and shortest definition for NULL is "undefined." In your department table, only department_id and name are really required, while description is optional—meaning that you are allowed to add a new department without supplying a description for it. If you add a new row of data without supplying a value for columns that allow nulls, NULL is automatically supplied for them.

Especially for character data, there is a subtle difference between the NULL value and an "empty" value. If you add a product with an empty string for its description, this means that you actually set a value for its description; it's an empty string, not an undefined (NULL) value.

The primary key field never allows NULL values. For the other columns, it's up to you (and your client) as to which fields are required and which are not.

In some cases, instead of allowing NULLs, you'll prefer to specify default values. This way, if the value is unspecified when creating a new row, it will be supplied with the default value. The default value must be a constant and not a function.

Auto-increment Columns

Auto-increment columns are "auto-numbered" columns. When a column is set as an auto-increment column, MySQL automatically provides values for it when inserting new records into the table. Usually if max is the largest value currently in the table for that column, then the next generated value will be max+1.

This way, the generated values are always unique, which makes them especially useful when used in conjunction with the PRIMARY KEY constraint. You already know that primary keys are used on columns that uniquely identify each row of a table. If you set a primary key column to also be an auto-increment column, MySQL Server automatically fills that column with values when adding new rows (in other words, it generates new IDs), ensuring that the values are unique.

When setting an auto-increment column, the first value that MySQL Server provides for that column is 1, but you can change this before adding data to your table with an SQL statement like the following:

```
ALTER TABLE YourTableName AUTO_INCREMENT=1234;
```

This way, your MySQL server will start generating values with 1234.

Although it wasn't shown in the earlier Figure 3-9, department_id in your department table is an auto-increment column. You'll learn how to set auto-increment columns when creating the department table.

■**Note** Unlike other database servers, MySQL still allows you to manually specify for an auto-numbered field when adding new rows, if you want.

Indexes

Indexes are related to MySQL Server performance tuning, so we'll mention them only briefly here.

Indexes are database objects meant to increase the overall speed of database operations. Indexes work on the presumption that the vast majority of database operations are read operations. Indexes increase the speed of search operations, but slow down insert, delete, and update operations. Usually, the gains of using indexes considerably outweigh the drawbacks.

On a table, you can create one or more indexes, with each index working on one column or on a set of columns. When a table is indexed on a specific column, its rows are either indexed or physically arranged based on the values of that column and the type of index. This makes search operations on that column very fast. If, for example, an index exists on `department_id` and then you do a search for the department with the `ID` value 934, the search would be performed very quickly.

The drawback of indexes is that they can slow down database operations that add new rows or update existing ones because the index must be actualized (or the table rows rearranged) each time these operations occur.

You should keep the following in mind about indexes:

- Indexes greatly increase search operations on the database, but they slow down operations that change the database (delete, update, and insert operations).

- Having too many indexes can slow down the general performance of the database. The general rule is to set indexes on columns frequently used in `WHERE`, `ORDER BY`, and `GROUP BY` clauses or used in table joins.

- By default, unique indexes are automatically created on primary key table columns.

You can use dedicated tools to test the performance of a database under stress conditions with and without particular indexes; in fact, a serious database administrator will want to make some of these tests before deciding on a winning combination for indexes.

Creating the department table

You created the `tshirtshop` database in Chapter 2. In the following exercise, you'll add the `department` table to it using phpMyAdmin. Alternatively, you can use the SQL scripts from the code download to create and populate the `department` table (you can also execute them through phpMyAdmin)

Note You can find the database creation scripts for this book in the Downloads section of the Apress web site (`http://www.apress.com`) or at `http://www.CristianDarie.ro`. The script file that creates and populates the `department` table is named `create_department.sql`.

Exercise: Creating the department table

Follow these steps to create the department table using phpMyAdmin:

1. Point your web browser to your phpMyAdmin installation, like you did in Chapter 2 when creating the tshirtshop database (it should be something like http://localhost/ phpMyAdmin/index.php.

2. Select the tshirtshop database from the Database combo box in the left side of the window. Type **department** in the Name text box under the Create a New Table on database tshirtshop, and **3** in the Fields text box, as shown in Figure 3-10.

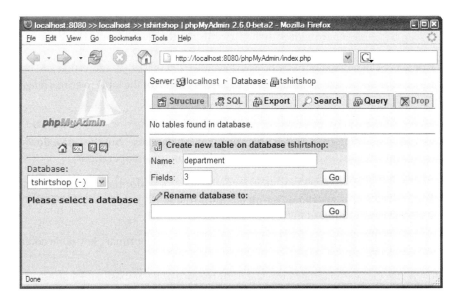

Figure 3-10. *Adding the* department *table to the database*

3. Click Go. You'll be presented with a screen where you need to specify the details for each of the three table columns as shown in Figure 3-11.

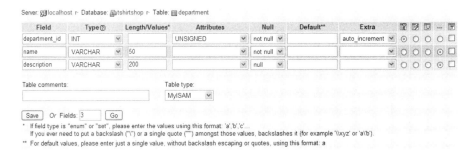

Figure 3-11. *Designing the* department *table*

■**Note** You learned about some data table properties in the previous pages. For more details about each of them, including details about the different table types (here we manually specified MyISAM although this is the default anyway), review the MySQL online manual at http://dev.mysql.com/doc/ or Jason Gilmore's *Beginning PHP 5 and MySQL* book (Apress, 2004). For more details about working with phpMyAdmin, you can refer to *Mastering phpMyAdmin for Effective MySQL Management* (Packt Publishing, 2004). In the phpMyAdmin form, keeping the mouse over various elements will show you a simple explanation of their meaning.

4. Click Save. You'll be shown a page with many details about the table you just created. There you can see the SQL code that was generated to create it, and you can see various other details such as confirmation that an index was indeed created automatically for the primary key field.

5. Now, you can add some data in the department table as shown in Table 3-2.

Table 3-2. *Three records for the* department *table*

department_id	name	description
1	Nature	Begin building your T-shirt collection with some cool designs gathered from the rich world of nature.
2	Scandinavia	Our Scandinavian postal design T-shirts capture the essence and soul of the North! You really should try them!
3	Free Spirit	Some free spirit T-shirts for the really free people.

■**Tip** If you need to change or delete existing records, you can either execute an SQL command in the SQL tab, or use the Browse tab in phpMyAdmin.

How It Works: Creating Data Tables Using phpMyAdmin

You have just created your first database table! You also set a primary key, set an auto_increment column, and filled it with some data.

As you can see, as soon as you have a clear idea about the structure of a table, phpMyAdmin makes it very easy to implement with its user-friendly interface. Let's move on!

Implementing the Data Tier

Now that you have a table filled with data, let's do something useful with it. The ultimate goal with this table is to get the list of department names from a PHP page and populate the Smarty design template with that list.

First, you'll learn about SQL (Structured Query Language). This is the language MySQL understands. You'll also learn how to create database connections, how to execute SQL instructions, and how to retrieve the results from PHP code using the PEAR DB.

Speaking with the Database

SQL is the language used to speak with relational databases, including MySQL. However, we haven't seen a database system yet that supports exactly the SQL-92 or SQL-99 standards. Instead, each database system supports a particular dialect of SQL, such as PL/SQL (Procedural Language extensions to SQL) for Oracle, T-SQL (Transact-SQL) for SQL Server, and so on. This means that in many cases, the SQL code that works with one database, will not work with the other.

Currently, MySQL supports most of SQL 92, and in version 5.0, it's expected to support an important part of SQL 99.

■**Tip** If you are interested in entering the world of SQL, we recommend another book we've authored called *The Programmer's Guide to SQL* (Apress, 2003). It covers the SQL standard and its dialects implemented in SQL Server, Oracle, DB2, MySQL, and Access. To get more information about this book, visit `http://www.CristianDarie.ro`.

The most commonly used SQL commands are `SELECT`, `INSERT`, `UPDATE`, and `DELETE`. These commands allow you to perform the most basic operations on the database.

The basic syntax of these commands is very simple, as you'll see in the following pages. However, keep in mind that SQL is a very flexible and powerful language, and can be used to create much more complicated and powerful queries than what you see here. You'll learn more while building the web site, but for now let's take a quick look at the basic syntax. For more details about any of these commands, you can always refer to their official documentation at

- `http://dev.mysql.com/doc/mysql/en/SELECT.html`

- `http://dev.mysql.com/doc/mysql/en/INSERT.html`

- `http://dev.mysql.com/doc/mysql/en/UPDATE.html`

- `http://dev.mysql.com/doc/mysql/en/DELETE.html`

SELECT

The SELECT statement is used to query the database and retrieve selected data that match the criteria you specify. Its basic structure is

```
SELECT <column list>
FROM <table name(s)>
[WHERE <restrictive condition(s)>]
```

> ■**Note** In this book, the SQL commands and queries appear in uppercase for consistency and clarity although SQL is not case sensitive. The WHERE clause appears in brackets because it is optional.

The following command returns the name of the department that has the DepartmentID of 1. In your case, the returned value is "Nature," but you would receive no results if there was no department with an ID of 1.

```
SELECT name FROM department WHERE department_id = 1
```

> ■**Tip** You can easily test these queries to make sure they actually work by using the SQL tab in phpMyAdmin, after opening the tshirtshop database.

If you want more columns to be returned, you simply list them, separated by commas. Alternatively, you can use *, which means "all columns." However, for performance reasons, if you need only certain specific columns, you should list them separately instead of asking for them all. With your current department table, the following two statements return the same results:

```
SELECT department_id, name, description
FROM department
WHERE department_id = 1

SELECT * FROM department WHERE department_id = 1
```

> ■**Tip** You can split an SQL query on more lines, if you prefer—MySQL won't mind.

If you don't want to place any condition on the query, simply remove the WHERE clause, and you'll get all. The following SELECT statement returns all rows and all columns from the product table:

```
SELECT * FROM product
```

INSERT

The INSERT statement is used to insert a row of data into the table. Its syntax is as follows:

```
INSERT INTO <table name> [(column list)] VALUES (column values)
```

Tip Although the column list is optional (in case you don't include it, column values are assigned to columns in the order in which they appear in the table's definition), you should always include it. This ensures that changing the table definition doesn't break the existing INSERT statements.

The following INSERT statement adds a department named "Weapons Department" to the department table:

```
INSERT INTO department (name) VALUES ('Weapons Department')
```

No value was specified for the description field because it was marked to allow NULLs in the department table. This is why you can omit specifying a value, if you want to. Also, you're allowed to omit specifying a department ID, because the department_id column was created with the AUTO_INCREMENT option, which means the database takes care of automatically generating a value for it when adding new records. However, you're allowed to manually specify a value, if you prefer.

Tip Because department_id is the primary key column, trying to add more records with the same ID would cause the database to generate an error. The database doesn't permit having duplicate values in the primary key field.

When letting MySQL generate values for AUTO_INCREMENT columns, you can obtain the last generated value using the LAST_INSERT_ID() function. Here's an example of how this works:

```
INSERT INTO department (name) VALUES ('Some New Department');
SELECT LAST_INSERT_ID();
```

Tip In MySQL, ";" is the delimiter between more SQL commands.

UPDATE

The UPDATE statement is used to modify existing data, and has the following syntax:

```
UPDATE  <table name>
SET <column name> = <new value> [, <column name> = <new value> ... ]
[WHERE <restrictive condition>]
```

The following query changes the name of the department with the ID of 43 to "Cool Department". If there were more departments with that ID, all of them would have been modified, but because department_id is the primary key, you can't have more departments with the same ID.

```
UPDATE department SET name='Cool Department' WHERE department_id = 43
```

Be careful with the UPDATE statement, because it makes it easy to mess up an entire table. If the WHERE clause is omitted, the change is applied to every record of the table, which you usually don't want to happen. MySQL will be happy to change all of your records; even if all departments in the table would have the same name and description, they would still be perceived as different entities because they have different department_id values.

DELETE

The syntax of the DELETE command is actually very simple:

```
DELETE FROM <table name>
[WHERE <restrictive condition>]
```

Most times, you'll want to use the WHERE clause to delete a single row:

```
DELETE FROM department
WHERE department_id = 43
```

As with UPDATE, be careful with this command, because if you forget to specify a WHERE clause, you'll end up deleting all of the rows in the table. The following query deletes all the records in department. The table itself isn't deleted by the DELETE command.

```
DELETE FROM department
```

Accessing MySQL Using PEAR DB

The SQL queries you write must be sent somehow to the database engine for execution. As you learned in Chapter 2, you'll use PEAR DB instead of the native PHP functionality to access the MySQL server.

Before writing the data tier code, you need to analyze and understand the possibilities for implementation. The important questions to answer before writing any code include the following:

- What strategy should you adopt for opening and closing database connections, when you need to execute a SQL query?

- How should you execute the SQL queries and which methods of PEAR DB should you use for this?

- How should you handle possible errors and integrate the error-handling solution with the error-handling code you wrote in Chapter 2?

Let's have a look at each of these questions one by one, and then we'll start writing some code.

Opening and Closing Connections to the MySQL Server

There are two main possible approaches you can take for this. The first is illustrated by the following sequence of actions:

1. *Open* a connection to the database exactly before you need to execute a command on the database.

2. *Execute* the SQL query on the database, and get back the results. At this stage, you also need to handle any possible errors.

3. *Close* the database connection immediately after executing the command.

This method has the advantage that you don't keep database connections for a long time (which is good because database connections consume server resources), and is also encouraged for servers that don't allow many simultaneous database connections. The disadvantage is the overhead implied by opening and closing the database connection all the time, which can be partially reduced by using persistent connections.

Note Persistent connections is a technology that is meant to improve the efficiency of opening and closing database connections, while not having impact on functionality. You can learn more about this technology at `http://www.php.net/manual/en/features.persistent-connections.php`.

The alternative solution, and the one you'll use when implementing tshirtshop, can be described like this:

1. *Open* a connection to the database when `index.php` starts being processed as a result of a client request.

2. *Execute* all SQL queries using that connection, without closing it. Here you also need to handle any possible errors.

3. *Close* the database connection when the client request finishes processing.

Using this method, all database operations that happen for a single client request (such as asking for the list of departments, the list of categories, the products to be listed on the page, and so on) will go through a single database connection, avoiding opening and closing the connection each time you need something from the database. You'll still use persistent connections to improve efficiency of opening a new database connection for each client request.

This is the approach you'll use for data access in the TShirtShop project.

Using PEAR DB for Database Operations

Now you should learn the theory about how to put this in practice using PEAR DB. You'll effectively write the code a bit later, when building the added functionality into the web site.

As explained in Chapter 2, you won't access MySQL through PHP's native database functions, but through a database abstraction layer (PEAR DB). The PEAR DB classes permit accessing various data sources using the same API (Application Programming Interface), so you won't need to change the PHP data access code or learn different data access techniques when working with other database systems than MySQL (but you might need to change the SQL code if the database you migrate to uses a different dialect). Using PEAR DB makes your life as a programmer easier in the long run.

The important PEAR DB classes you'll work with are

- DB is the main class in PEAR DB that provides static methods for creating DB objects.

- DB_Error is usually the type of the object returned by all the PEAR DB functions in case of error. It contains information about the error.

■**Note** In this book, you'll learn about the PEAR DB functionality as used in TShirtShop. For more details about PEAR DB, see its official documentation at http://pear.php.net/manual/en/package.database.php.

The DB class provides the functionality to connect to the MySQL server and execute SQL queries. The function that opens a database connection is DB::connect, and receives as parameters the connection string to the database server, and an optional parameter that specifies whether the connection is a persistent connection:

```
$db = DB::connect("mysql://$db_user:$db_pass@$db_host/$db_name",$persistent);
```

■**Note** DB::connect returns an initialized database connection object (which is specific to the type of database you're connecting to, such as DB_mysql) in case the connection is successful, or a DB_Error instance otherwise.

The **connection string** contains the data required to connect to the database server. The previous code snippet shows the standard data you need to supply when connecting to a MySQL server:

- $db_user represents the username.

- $db_pass represents the user's password.

- $db_host is the hostname of your MySQL server.

- $db_name is the name of the database you're connecting to.

The optional parameter ($persistent) has a default value of false and decides whether the database connection is persistent.

To disconnect from the database, you need to call the disconnect() function on the database connection object that is returned by DB::connect().

The following code snippet demonstrates how to create, open, and then close a MySQL database connection:

```
// create and open a database connection
$db = DB::connect("mysql://myusername:mypassword@localhost/tshirtshop");
// close the connection
$db->disconnect();
```

Issuing Commands Using the Connection

After opening the connection, you're now at the stage we've been aiming for from the start: executing SQL commands through the connection.

You can execute the command in many ways, depending on the specifics. Does it return any information? If so, what kind of information, and in which format? The PEAR DB methods you'll use when executing commands are

- query() can be used to execute any kind of SQL statements. If the query executes without errors, query() simply returns DB_OK, and on failure it returns a DB_Error object. You'll use this method for operations that insert, delete, or update information in the database. When you need to retrieve data from the database, you'll use GetAll(), which is discussed next.

- GetAll() is a method that allows retrieving all the information from a query without using fetchRow() and looping through results, as is needed when using query(). You'll use this method for every SELECT command you issue from your code. As with all the other PEAR DB functions, getAll() returns a DB_Error object on errors.

- GetRow() returns only the first row of data from the query result. You'll use this method when your SELECT query returns only one row. The method returns a DB_Error object on errors.

- GetOne() returns the data from the first cell of the result set (the first column of the first row). You'll use this method when your SELECT statement returns a single value.

Handling Errors

This is the last detail you need to consider before you start writing some code. In Chapter 2, you implemented the code that intercepts and handles (and eventually reports) errors that happen in the TShirtShop site.

Now let's see how to integrate the data access code into the already existing error-handling code.

Although it doesn't do it by default, PEAR DB can be instructed to generate errors in case something goes wrong when executing an SQL command, or opening a database connection, and so on. In this case, the error would be intercepted by our existing error-handling code, but the error message won't be as helpful as possible for the developer, because the error would appear as originating somewhere from inside the PEAR DB classes (which most probably aren't the actual cause of the error).

In the code for TShirtShop, you'll let PEAR DB tell whether an error happened through the DB::isError method, without letting PEAR DB generate errors. If you discover something bad happened, you manually generate an error using the PHP trigger_error function. The following code snippet shows a short function with this functionality implemented:

```
public function DbGetRow($queryString)
{
  $result = $this->db->getRow($queryString);
  if(DB::isError($result)) trigger_error($result->getMessage(), E_USER_ERROR);
  return $result;
}
```

This method generates an error (using the trigger_error function) in case the database command didn't execute successfully. The error is captured by the error-handling mechanism you implemented in Chapter 2.

Because of the way you implemented the error-handling code in Chapter 2, generating an E_USER_ERROR error freezes the execution of the request, eventually logging and/or emailing the error data, and showing the visitor a nice "Please come back later" message (if there is such thing as a nice "Please come back later" message, anyway).

By default, if you don't specify to trigger_error the kind of error to generate, by default an E_USER_NOTICE message is generated, which doesn't interfere with the normal execution of the request (the error is eventually logged, but execution continues normally afterwards).

Preparing the Ground for the Data Access Code

Okay, let's write some code! You'll start by writing the DbManager class, which will be the support class, containing generic functionality needed in the other data tier methods. You'll then complete another exercise in which you'll implement the functionality that opens a database connection when the main page starts processing, and closes the connection in the end. Finally, you'll implement the core data tier functionality in a separate exercise.

Exercise: Creating the DbManager Class

To make your life easy when implementing the data tier, you'll first create DbManager, a support class that will be used from all the other data tier methods. This class implements the error-handling integration code, so after you write it, you won't have to bother with this detail ever again.

Each method in DbManager is in fact a wrapper method for the main PEAR DB methods required for data access—the methods that we discussed in the previous pages. Follow the steps to do the magic:

1. Modify config.inc.php to define the include_path configuration option, so that the PEAR DB classes will be accessible from the TShirtShop project. You change the include_path configuration option by using the ini_set PHP function, taking care to have a path separator compatible to your operating system.

   Add the following code at the end of your config.inc.php file:

   ```
   // Change the include_path configuration option to enable PEAR DB access
   if ((substr(strtoupper(PHP_OS), 0, 3)) == "WIN")
     define("PATH_SEPARATOR", ";");
   else
     define("PATH_SEPARATOR", ":");
   ini_set('include_path', SITE_ROOT . '/libs/PEAR' .
           PATH_SEPARATOR . ini_get('include_path'));
   ```

2. Add the database login information at the end of tshirtshop/include/config.inc.php, modifying the constants' values to fit your server's configuration. The following code assumes you created the admin user account as instructed in Chapter 2:

   ```
   // database login info
   define("USE_PERSISTENT_CONNECTIONS", "true");
   define("DB_SERVER", "localhost");
   define("DB_USERNAME", "admin");
   define("DB_PASSWORD", "admin");
   define("DB_DATABASE", "tshirtshop");
   define("MYSQL_CONNECTION_STRING", "mysql://" . DB_USERNAME . ":" .
           DB_PASSWORD . "@" . DB_SERVER . "/" . DB_DATABASE);
   ```

3. Create a new file named database.php in the tshirtshop/include folder, and create the DbManager class as shown in the following code. At this moment, we only included its constructor, which receives as a parameter the database connection string and automatically initiates a database connection. You add a reference to the PEAR DB library by including DB.php.

   ```
   <?php
   // reference the PEAR DB library
   require_once 'DB.php';

   // class providing generic data access functionality
   class DbManager
   {
     public $db;
   ```

```
  // open database connection in the constructor
  function __construct($connectionString)
  {
    $this->db = DB::connect($connectionString,
                            USE_PERSISTENT_CONNECTIONS);
    if (DB::isError($this->db))
      trigger_error($this->db->getMessage(), E_USER_ERROR);
    $this->db->setFetchMode(DB_FETCHMODE_ASSOC);
  }
}
?>
```

4. Add the DbDisconnect method to the DbManager class, which will be called to close the database connection:

```
  // close the connection
  public function DbDisconnect()
  {
    $this->db->disconnect();
  }
```

5. Add the DbQuery method to DbManager. This method uses PEAR DB's query method, and you'll use it for executing INSERT, DELETE, or UPDATE queries:

```
  // wrapper class for PEAR DB's query() method
  public function DbQuery($queryString)
  {
    $result = $this->db->query($queryString);
    if (DB::isError($result))
      trigger_error($result->getMessage(), E_USER_ERROR);
    return $result;
  }
```

6. Add the DbGetAll function, the wrapper class for getAll. You'll call this function for retrieving a complete result set from a SELECT query.

```
  // wrapper class for PEAR DB's getAll() method
  public function DbGetAll($queryString)
  {
    $result = $this->db->getAll($queryString);
    if (DB::isError($result))
      trigger_error($result->getMessage(), E_USER_ERROR);
    return $result;
  }
```

7. Add the DbGetRow function, the wrapper class for getRow, as shown. This will be used to get a row of data resulted from a SELECT query.

```
// wrapper class for PEAR DB's getRow() method
public function DbGetRow($queryString)
{
  $result = $this->db->getRow($queryString);
  if (DB::isError($result))
    trigger_error($result->getMessage(), E_USER_ERROR);
  return $result;
}
```

8. Add the DbGetOne function, the wrapper class for getOne, as shown. This will be used to get a single value resulted from a SELECT query.

```
// wrapper class for PEAR DB's getOne() method
public function DbGetOne($queryString)
{
  $result = $this->db->getOne($queryString);
  if (DB::isError($result))
    trigger_error($result->getMessage(), E_USER_ERROR);
  return $result;
}
```

How It Works: The DbManager class

In Chapter 2, you installed the PEAR library in tshirtshop/libs/PEAR. For the PEAR library to be accessible from the TShirtShop project, you had to include its path in the include_path configuration option using ini_set:

```
if ((substr(strtoupper(PHP_OS), 0, 3)) == "WIN")
  define("PATH_SEPARATOR", ";");
else
  define("PATH_SEPARATOR", ":");
ini_set('include_path', SITE_ROOT . '/libs/PEAR' .
        PATH_SEPARATOR . ini_get('include_path'));
```

To correctly create the include_path configuration option, you had to check whether the site was running on Windows (where the path separator is ";") or Unix (where the path separator is ":"). You got this information by checking the value of the PHP_OS system variable, which returns something that starts with WIN (such as WINNT) for Windows operating systems.

Also in config.inc.php, you set the database connection string.

The DbManager class contains a number of wrapper methods that access at their turn PEAR DB functions, and provide the functionality needed for the rest of the data tier methods.

The methods in DbManager generate an error using trigger_error in case the database command didn't execute successfully. The error is captured (and eventually reported) by the error-handling mechanism you implemented in Chapter 2.

Note PEAR DB can be instructed to generate errors instead of simply returning an error code, in which case, you wouldn't need to manually generate errors using `trigger_error`. However, as also explained earlier, it's preferable to generate your own errors to have more control of the error-handling and reporting mechanism.

Exercise: Opening and Closing the Database Connection

In this exercise, you'll write the code that opens the database connection at the beginning of `index.php`, and closes the connection in the end. This connection will be used for all database operations needed during the client's request.

1. The ideal place to open the database connection is `tshirtshop/include/app_top.php`, which is the file included at the start of `index.php`. Update `app_top.php` as shown in the following code snippet:

```php
<?php
// include utility files
require_once 'config.inc.php';
require_once 'tss_error_handler.php';
require_once 'setup_smarty.php';
require_once 'database.php';

// global DbManager instance
$gDbManager = new DbManager(MYSQL_CONNECTION_STRING);
?>
```

2. Create the `tshirtshop/include/app_bottom.php` file and add the following in it:

```php
<?php
$GLOBALS['gDbManager']->DbDisconnect();
?>
```

3. This file must be included at the end of the main page `index.php` to close the connection. Modify your `index.php` file as follows:

```php
<?php
// Load Smarty library and config files
require_once 'include/app_top.php';
// Load Smarty template file
$page = new Page();
$page->display('index.tpl');
// Load app_bottom which closes the database connection
require_once 'include/app_bottom.php';
?>
```

How It Works: Opening and Closing the Database Connection

Right now, the database connection is opened when index.php starts processing, and is closed at the end. All database operations that happen in one iteration of this file will be done through this connection.

Exercise: Implementing the DoCatalog Class

The DoCatalog class will contain the actual data tier code, which will provide the functionality needed for the business tier. Almost all methods of the DoCatalog class will have a one-to-one relationship with the methods that you'll create in the business tier.

Because in this chapter we only implement the departments list, you'll only create the GetDepartments method of the Catalog class, which will populate the departments_list.tpl componentized template. In the next chapter, you'll keep adding methods to this class to support new pieces of functionality, such as retrieving categories and products from the database.

Follow these steps:

1. Create a folder named data_objects in your site root (the tshirtshop folder).

2. Create a file named do_catalog.php in the newly created data_objects directory, and add the following code to it:

```php
<?php
// data tier class
class DoCatalog
{
  // class constructor
  function __construct()
  {
    // get the global DbManager instance (created in app_top.php)
    $this->dbManager = $GLOBALS['gDbManager'];
  }

  // retrieves all departments
  public function GetDepartments()
  {
    $query_string = "SELECT department_id, name FROM department";
    $result = $this->dbManager->DbGetAll($query_string);
    return $result;
  }
} //end DoCatalog
?>
```

How It Works: DoCatalog and GetDepartments

For the moment the only method in the newly created DoCatalog class is GetDepartments(), which will read the department's information from the department table. This function is part of the data tier and is accessed from the business tier. The final goal is to have the departments list in the upper-left corner of the page.

The SQL query needs to ask for the name and department_id for each department. You need the department_id because you'll use it later when you need to get more data about a specific department—for example, when the visitor clicks on a department to see its categories. The next SELECT statement fulfills this need:

```
SELECT department_id, name
FROM department
```

The functionality is performed via the DbGetAll() static method of the DbManager class, which executes the SELECT query:

```
$result = $this->dbManager->DbGetAll($query_string);
```

Because the default fetch mode was set to DB_FETCHMODE_ASSOC in DbManager's constructor, the $result variable contains an associative array, with a structure such as the following:

```
Array ( [0] => Array ( [department_id] => 1, [name] => Nature )
        [1] => Array ( [department_id] => 2, [name] => Scandinavia )
        [2] => Array ( [department_id] => 3, [name] => Free Spirit )
      )
```

Using an associative array (setting the fetch mode to DB_FETCHMODE_ASSOC) allows you to access the elements of the inner arrays using the column names instead of numbers, such as in $result[1]['name'] (which would return "Scandinavia" because arrays in PHP are zero-based) instead of $result[1][1].

Implementing the Business Tier

The business tier part of the product catalog will consist of a file named bo_catalog.php, which holds the BoCatalog class. In the following exercise, you'll implement the middle tier code that gets department data by calling the earlier implemented GetDepartments method of the data tier.

Exercise: Implementing the BoCatalog Class

Follow these steps to implement the business tier part of your departments list:

1. Create a folder named business_objects in the tshirtshop directory.

2. Create a file named bo_catalog.php file inside business_objects. Add the following code into this file:

```php
<?php
// reference the data tier
require_once SITE_ROOT.'/data_objects/do_catalog.php';

// business tier class for reading product catalog information
class BoCatalog
{
  /* private stuff */
  private $mDoCatalog;
```

```
    // class constructor initializes the data tier object
    function __construct()
    {
      $this->mDoCatalog = new DoCatalog();
    }

    // retrieves all departments
    public function GetDepartments()
    {
      $result = $this->mDoCatalog->GetDepartments();
      return $result;
    }
  } //end BoCatalog
  ?>
```

How It Works: BoCatalog and GetDepartments

For the moment, you might be a little confused about this class because the GetDepartments() method does nothing but call the GetDepartments() method from the data tier. When developing other parts of the site, the business tier code will have an important role, but here we're just implementing it in order to follow the rules of the three-tier architecture so we can reap its benefits in the long run.

Implementing the Presentation Tier

Now that everything is in place in the other tiers, all you have to do is create the presentation tier part—this is the final goal that we've been aiming toward from the beginning. As shown at the beginning of this chapter, the departments list needs to look something like Figure 3-12, when the site is loaded in the browser.

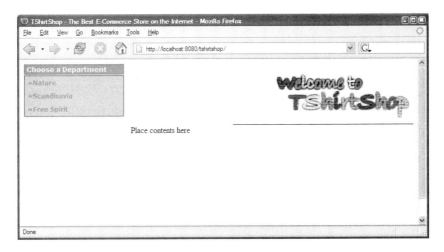

Figure 3-12. *TShirtShop with a dynamically generated list of departments*

You implement this as a separate componentized template named `departments_list` made up of two files: the Smarty design template (`templates/departments_list.tpl`) and the Smarty plugin file (`smarty_plugins/function.load_departments_list.php`). You'll then just include this componentized template in the main Smarty template (`templates/index.tpl`).

Using Smarty Plugins

The Smarty plugin is the Smarty technology we'll use to implement the logic behind Smarty design template files (with the .tpl extension). This is not the only way to store the logic behind a Smarty design template, but it's the way the Smarty documentation recommends at `http://smarty.php.net/manual/en/tips.componentized.templates.php`.

For the departments list, the Smarty plugin file is `function.load_departments_list.php`, which contains the `smarty_function_load_departments_list` function that loads the list of departments from the database. The list is loaded into Smarty variables that are read from the Smarty design template file (`departments_list.tpl`) that generates the HTML output.

Smarty plugin files and functions must follow strict naming conventions to be located by Smarty. Smarty plugin files must be named as `type.name.php` (in our case, `function.load_departments_list.php`), and the functions inside them as `smarty_type_name` (in our case, `smarty_function_load_departments_list`). The official page for Smarty plugins naming conventions is `http://smarty.php.net/manual/en/plugins.naming.conventions.php`. You can learn more about Smarty plugins at `http://smarty.php.net/manual/en/plugins.php`.

After the Smarty plugin file is in place, you can reference it from the Smarty design template file (`departments_list.tpl`) with a line like this:

```
{load_departments_list assign="departments_list"}
```

Given the correct naming conventions where used, this line is enough to get Smarty to load the plugin file and execute the function that loads the departments list. The Smarty design template file can then access the variables populated by the plugin function like this:

```
{$departments_list->mDepartments[i].name}
```

Before actually writing the componentized template, it's one more little detail to learn about.

Presenting with Style

CSS (Cascading Style Sheets) files are used to store font and formatting information that can be easily applied to various parts of a site. Instead of setting fonts, colors, and dimensions for an HTML link, you can simply set its class to one of the existing styles. You might want to read one of the many dedicated books that exist for CSS. You can find many free tutorials on the Internet by searching, for example, for "css tutorial" with a web search engine.

Now you'll create the CSS file for the TShirtShop site, and then add some styles that will be used in the `department_list.tpl` Smarty template.

Exercise: Creating the departments_list Componentized Template

Right now everything is in place, the only missing part is the Smarty template:

1. Open `templates/index.tpl` and modify it like this:

```
{config_load file="site.conf"}
<!DOCTYPE html
PUBLIC "-//W3C//DTD XHTML 1.0 Transitional//EN"
"http://www.w3.org/TR/xhtml1/DTD/xhtml1-transitional.dtd">
<html>
  <head>
    <title>{#sitetitle#}</title>
    <link href="tshirtshop.css" type="text/css" rel="stylesheet"/>
  </head>
```

2. Create the `tshirtshop.css` file in the tshirtshop folder and add the styles shown in the following code listing. Having a central place to store style information helps you easily change the look of the site in certain situations without changing a line of code.

The following styles refer to the way department names should look inside the departments list when they are unselected, unselected but with the mouse hovering over them, or selected.

```
.DepartmentListHead
{
  border-right: #01a647 2px solid;
  border-top: #01a647 2px solid;
  border-left: #01a647 2px solid;
  border-bottom: #01a647 2px solid;
  background-color: #30b86e;
  font-family: Verdana, Arial;
  font-weight: bold;
  font-size: 10pt;
  color: #f5f5dc;
  padding-left: 3px
}
.DepartmentListContent
{
  border-right: #01a647 2px solid;
  border-top: #01a647 2px solid;
  border-left: #01a647 2px solid;
  border-bottom: #01a647 2px solid;
  background-color: #9fe1bb
}
a.DepartmentUnselected
{
  font-family: Verdana, Arial;
  font-weight: bold;
  font-size: 9pt;
```

```
  color: #5f9ea0;
  line-height: 25px;
  padding-left: 5px;
  text-decoration: none
}
a.DepartmentUnselected:hover
{
  padding-left: 5px;
  color: #2e8b57
}
a.DepartmentSelected
{
  font-family: Verdana, Arial;
  font-weight: bold;
  font-size: 9pt;
  color: #556b2f;
  line-height: 25px;
  padding-left: 5px;
  text-decoration: none
}
```

3. Edit the setup_smarty.php file and add the following two lines to the constructor of the page class. These lines configure the plugin folders used by Smarty. The first one is for the internal Smarty plugins, and the second specifies the smarty_plugins folder you'll create to hold the plugins you'll write for TShirtShop.

```
// Class that extends Smarty, used to process and display Smarty files
class Page extends Smarty
{
  // constructor
  function __construct()
  {
    // Call Smarty's constructor
    $this->Smarty();
    // Change the default template directories
    $this->template_dir = TEMPLATE_DIR;
    $this->compile_dir = COMPILE_DIR;
    $this->config_dir = CONFIG_DIR;
    $this->plugins_dir[0] = SMARTY_DIR . 'plugins';
    $this->plugins_dir[1] = SITE_ROOT . "/smarty_plugins";
  }
}
```

4. Now create the Smarty template file for the departments_list componentized template. Write the following lines in templates/departments_list.tpl:

```
{* departments_list.tpl *}
{load_departments_list assign="departments_list"}
```

```
{* start departments list *}
<table border="0" cellpadding="0" cellspacing="1" width="200">
  <tr>
    <td class="DepartmentListHead"> Choose a Department </td>
  </tr>
  <tr>
    <td class="DepartmentListContent">
      {* loop through the list of departments *}
      {section name=i loop=$departments_list->mDepartments}
        {* verify if the department is selected
           to decide what CSS style to use *}
        {if ($departments_list->mSelectedDepartment ==
            $departments_list->mDepartments[i].department_id)}
          {assign var=class_d value="DepartmentSelected"}
        {else}
          {assign var=class_d value="DepartmentUnselected"}
        {/if}
        {* generate a link for a new department in the list *}
        <a class="{$class_d}"
           href="{$departments_list->mDepartments[i].onclick}">
           &raquo; {$departments_list->mDepartments[i].name}
        </a>
        <br/>
      {/section}
    </td>
  </tr>
</table>
{* end departments list *}
```

5. Create a folder named smarty_plugins in your project's home (the tshirtshop folder).
   This will contain the Smarty plugin files.

6. Inside the smarty_plugins folder, create a file named
   function.load_departments_list.php and add the following code to it:

```php
<?php
// plugin functions inside plugin files must be named: smarty_type_name
function smarty_function_load_departments_list($params, $smarty)
{
  $departments_list = new DepartmentsList();
  $departments_list->init();
  // assign template variable
  $smarty->assign($params['assign'], $departments_list);
}

// Manages the departments list
class DepartmentsList
{
```

```
  /* public variables available in departments_list.tpl Smarty template */
  public $mDepartments;
  public $mSelectedDepartment;
  /* private members */
  private $mBoCatalog;

  // constructor initializes business tier object
  // and reads query string parameter
  function __construct()
  {
    // creating the middle tier object
    $this->mBoCatalog = new BoCatalog();
    // if DepartmentID exists in the query string, we're visiting a department
    if (isset($_GET['DepartmentID']))
      $this->mSelectedDepartment = (int)$_GET['DepartmentID'];
    else
      $this->mSelectedDepartment = -1;
  }

  // calls business tier method to read departments list
  // and create their links
  function init()
  {
    // get the list of departments from the business tier
    $this->mDepartments = $this->mBoCatalog->GetDepartments();
    // create the department links
    for ($i = 0; $i < count($this->mDepartments); $i++)
      $this->mDepartments[$i]['onclick'] = "index.php?DepartmentID=" .
                          $this->mDepartments[$i]['department_id'];
  }
} //end class
?>
```

7. Modify the index.php file to include a reference to your business tier class:

```
<?php
// Load Smarty library and config files
require_once 'include/app_top.php';
// Load Business Tier
require_once SITE_ROOT.'/business_objects/bo_catalog.php';
// Load Smarty template file
$page = new Page();
$page->display('index.tpl');
// Load app_bottom which closes the database connection
require_once 'include/app_bottom.php';
?>
```

8. Make the following modification in `templates/index.tpl` to load the newly created `departments_list` componentized template. Search for the string "Place the list of departments here" and replace it with this:

```
<br/>
{include file="departments_list.tpl"}
```

9. Examine the result of your work with your favorite browser by loading `http://localhost/tshirtshop/index.php` (see Figure 3.13).

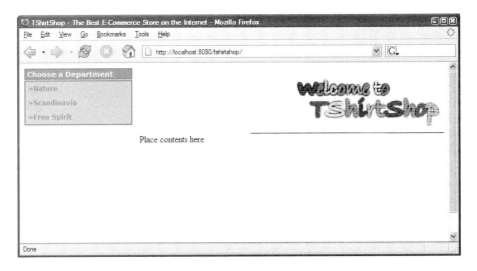

Figure 3-13. *TShirtShop with a dynamically generated list of departments*

Play a little with the page and see what happens when you click on a department or place the mouse over a link.

How It works: The departments_list Smarty Template

The Smarty template generated the fabulous list of departments. Each department name in the list is a link to the department's page, which in fact is a link to the `index.php` page with a `DepartmentID` parameter in the query string that specifies which department was selected. Here's an example of such a link:

```
http://localhost:8080/tshirtshop/index.php?DepartmentID=3
```

When clicking a department's link, the selected department will be displayed using a different CSS style in the list (see Figure 3-14).

Figure 3-14. *Selecting a department*

It is important to understand how the Smarty template file (departments_list.tpl) and its associated plugin file (function.load_departments_list.php) work together to generate the list of departments, and use the correct style for the currently selected one.

The processing starts at function.load_departments_list.php, which is included in the index.tpl file. The first line in departments_list.tpl loads the plugin:

```
{load_departments_list assign="departments_list"}
```

The load_departments_list plugin function creates and initializes a DepartmentsList object (this class is also defined in function.load_departments_list.php), which is then assigned to a variable accessible from the Smarty design template file:

```
function smarty_function_load_departments_list($params, $smarty)
{
  $departments_list = new DepartmentsList();
  $departments_list->init();
  // assign template variable
  $smarty->assign($params['assign'], $departments_list);
}
```

The init() method in DepartmentsList populates a public member of the class ($mDepartments) with an array containing the list of departments, and another public member containing the index of the currently selected department ($mSelectedDepartment).

Back to the Smarty code now. Inside the HTML code that forms the layout of the Smarty template (departments_list.tpl), you can see the Smarty tags that do the magic:

```
{* loop through the list of departments *}
{section name=i loop=$departments_list->mDepartments}
  {* verify if the department is selected decide what CSS style to use *}
  {if ($departments_list->mSelectedDepartment ==
      $departments_list->mDepartments[i].department_id)}
    {assign var=class_d value="DepartmentSelected"}
  {else}
    {assign var=class_d value="DepartmentUnselected"}
  {/if}
  {* generate a link for a new department in the list *}
  <a class="{$class_d}"
    href="{$departments_list->mDepartments[i].onclick}">
    &raquo;{$departments_list->mDepartments[i].name}
  </a>
  <br/>
{/section}
```

Smarty template sections are used for looping over arrays of data. In this case, you want to loop over the departments array kept in $departmentsList->mDepartments:

```
{section name=i loop=$departments_list->mDepartments}
  ...
{/section}
```

Inside the loop, you verify whether the current department in the loop ($departments_list->mDepartments[i].department_id) has the ID that was mentioned in the query string ($departments_list->mSelectedDepartment). Depending on this, you decide what style to apply to the name by saving the style name (DepartmentSelected or DepartmentUnselected) to a variable named class_d.

This variable is then used to generate the link:

```
<a class="{$class_d}"
   href="{$departments_list->mDepartments[i].onclick}">
   &raquo;{$departments_list->mDepartments[i].name}
</a>
```

Summary

This long chapter was well worth the effort, when you consider how much theory you've learned and applied to the TShirtShop project! In this chapter, you accomplished the following:

- Created the department table and populated it with data

- Learned how to access this data from the data tier using PEAR DB, and then how to access the data tier method from the business tier

- Finally, you implemented the user interface using a Smarty template

In the next chapter, you will finish creating the product catalog by displaying the site's categories and products!

■ ■ ■

CHAPTER 4

Creating the Product Catalog: Part II

The fun isn't over yet! In the previous chapter, you implemented a selectable list of departments for the TShirtShop web site. However, a product catalog means much more than that list of departments. In this chapter, you continue your way toward a fully functional product catalog.

In this chapter you'll

- Finish creating the product catalog by displaying categories, products, and the product details page.

- Learn about relational data and the types of relationships that occur between tables.

- Learn how to join related data tables using the SQL JOIN clause.

- Create data tier functions keeping in mind the relationships between the tables in your database.

- Work on finishing the business tier and presentation tier part for the product catalog.

What Is the New Functionality?

In Chapter 2, we decided the general structure of the TShirtShop web site. We established that each page would have the list of departments in the upper-left side and the header in the upper-right part of the page. We managed to do this part in Chapters 2 and 3, and for the moment TShirtShop site looks like Figure 4-1.

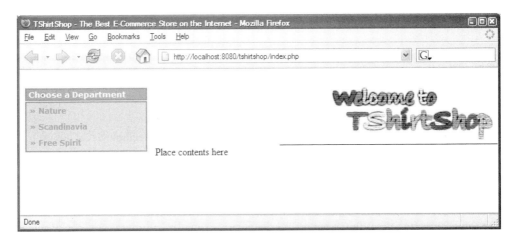

Figure 4-1. *TShirtShop with a dynamically generated list of departments*

Depending on the page being visited, the dynamic part of the site will change. To make things clearer, take another look at what we want to achieve. After implementing the full product catalog functionality in this chapter, the first page will look like Figure 4-2.

When selecting a department, it is highlighted in the list of departments and the new dynamically generated part of the site looks like Figure 4-3. In the left part of the page, you can now see the categories that belong to the selected department. In the contents area, you can see the name of the department, its description, and a list of products that are featured for that department.

When you finally select a category, you'll get the full list of products for that category, the name of the selected category in the title, and the category's description.

All product lists have a paging feature that allows the visitor to browse long lists of products easily by splitting them into multiple subpages. This feature applies to the main page, the department pages, category pages, and the search results pages, but the paging text ("Page 1 of 2") and the page navigation links only appear for lists of products that contain more than an established number of products.

The name and picture of any product in the list will be links to product details pages, which will show the full product's description (in product lists, only a fixed number of characters from each product's description is shown). The product's details page that you'll create in this chapter looks like Figure 4-4. In the later chapters, you'll add more features, such as product recommendations and product reviews.

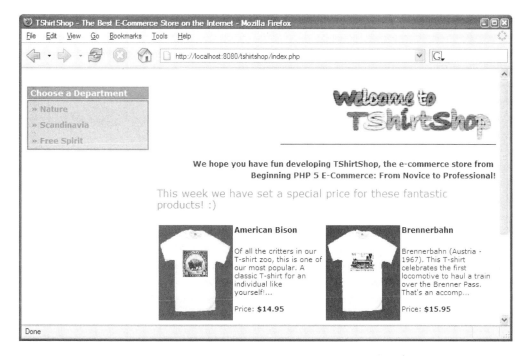

Figure 4-2. *The main page in TShirtShop*

Figure 4-3. *Visiting the Nature department*

Figure 4-4. *Product details page*

So this is the new functionality you will implement in this chapter. You'll start the usual way by creating the new data structures to hold the necessary data. As you can see from the figures, now there's more information to store than just the list of departments. You'll learn about some interesting new theory issues. The data tier will come with some new tricks of its own. You'll finally implement the presentation tier, which has some new surprises as well.

Okay, enough talking. Here we go . . .

Storing the New Data

Given the new functionality you are adding in this chapter, it's not surprising that you need to add more data tables to the database. However, this isn't just about adding new data tables. You also need to learn about relational data and the relationships that you can implement between the data tables, so that you can obtain more significant information from your database.

What Makes a Relational Database

It's no mystery that a database is something that stores data. However, today's modern **Relational Database Management Systems (RDBMS)**, such as MySQL, PostgreSQL, SQL Server, Oracle, DB2, and others, have extended this basic role by adding the capability to store and manage **relational data**. This is a concept that needs some attention.

So what does *relational data* mean? It's easy to see that every piece of data ever written in a real-world database is somehow related to some already existing information. Products are related to categories and departments, orders are related to products and customers, and so on. A relational database keeps its information stored in data tables, but is also aware of the relations between them.

These related tables form the *relational database*, which becomes an object with a significance of its own, rather than simply being a group of unrelated data tables. It is said that *data* becomes *information* only when we give significance to it, and establishing relations with other pieces of data is a good means of doing that.

Look at the product catalog to see what pieces of data it needs, and how you can transform this data into information. For the product catalog, you'll need at least three data tables: one for departments, one for categories, and one for products. It's important to note that physically each data table is an independent database object, even if logically it's part of a larger entity—in other words, even though we say that a category *contains* products, the table that contains the products is not inside the table that contains categories. This is not in contradiction with the relational character of the database. Figure 4.5 shows a simple representation of three data tables, including some selected sample data.

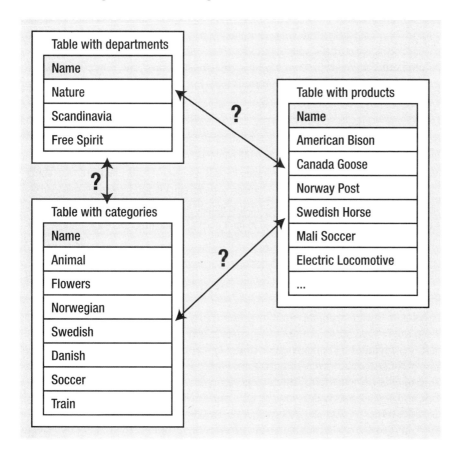

Figure 4-5. *Unrelated departments, categories, and products*

When two tables are said to be related, this more specifically means that the *records* of those tables are related. So, if the products table is related to the categories table, this translates into each product record being somehow related to one of the records in the categories table.

Figure 4-5 doesn't show the physical representation of the database, so we didn't list the table names there. Diagrams like this are used to decide *what* needs to be stored in the database. After you know *what* to store, the next step is to decide *how* the listed data is related, which leads to the physical structure for the database. Figure 4-5 shows three kinds of data that you want to store, but as you'll learn later, to implement this structure in the database, you'll use four tables, not three.

So, now that you know the data you want to store, let's think about how the three parts relate to each other. Apart from knowing that the records of two tables are related *somehow*, we also need to know *the kind of relationship* between them. Let's now take a closer look at the different ways in which two tables can be related.

Relational Data and Table Relationships

To continue exploring the world of relational databases, let's further analyze the three logical tables we've been looking at so far. To make life easier, let's give them names now: the table containing products is `product`, the table containing categories is `category`, and the last one is our old friend, `department`. No surprises here! Luckily, these tables implement the most common kinds of relationships that exist between tables, the **One-to-Many** and **Many-to-Many** relationships, so you have the chance to learn about them.

■**Note** Some variations of these two relationship types exist, as well as the less popular *One-to-One* relationship. In the One-to-One relationship, each row in one table matches exactly one row in the other. For example, in a database that allowed patients to be assigned to beds, you would hope that there would be a one-to-one relationship between patients and beds! Database systems don't support enforcing this kind of relationship, because you would have to add matching records in both tables at the same time. Moreover, two tables with a One-to-One relationship can be joined to form a single table. No One-to-One relationships are used in this book.

One-to-Many Relationships

The One-to-Many relationship happens when one record in a table can be associated with multiple records in the related table, but not vice-versa. In our case, this happens for the `department` – `category` relation. A specific department can contain any number of categories, but each category belongs to *exactly one* department. Figure 4-6 better represents the One-to-Many relationship between departments and categories.

Another common scenario in which you see the One-to-Many relationship is with the `order` – `order_details` tables, where `order` contains general details about the order (such as date, total amount, and so on) and `order_details` contains the products related to the order.

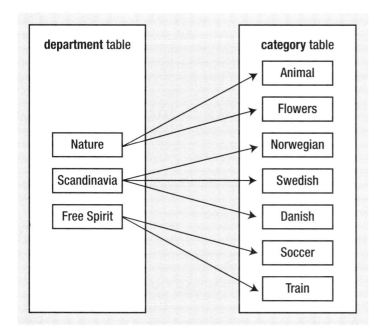

Figure 4-6. *A One-to-Many relationship between departments and categories*

The One-to-Many relationship is implemented in the database by adding an extra column in the table at the *many* side of the relationship, which references the ID column of the table in the *one* side of the relationship. Simply said, in the category table you'll have an extra column (called department_id), which will hold the ID of the department the category belongs to. You'll implement this in your database a bit later, after you learn about the Many-to-Many relationships and the FOREIGN KEY constraint.

Many-to-Many Relationships

The other common type of relationship is the Many-to-Many relationship. This kind of relationship is implemented when records in both tables of the relationship can have multiple matching records in the other. In our scenario, this happens for the product and category tables, because we know that a product can exist in more than one category (*one* product – *many* categories), and also a category can have more than one product (*one* category – *many* products).

This happens because we decided earlier that a product could be in more than one category. If a product could only belong to a single category, you would have another One-to-Many relationship, just like the one that exists between departments and categories (where a category can't belong to more than one department).

If you represent this relationship with a picture as shown previously in Figure 4-6, but with generic names this time, you get something like what is shown in Figure 4-7.

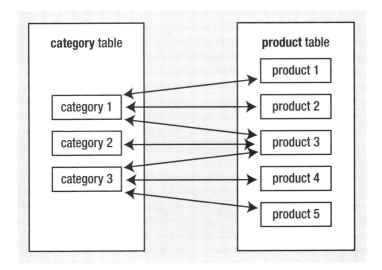

Figure 4-7. *The Many-to-Many relationship between categories and products*

Although logically the Many-to-Many relationship happens between two tables, databases (including MySQL databases) don't have the means to physically implement this kind of relationship by using just two tables, so we cheat by adding a third table to the mix. This third table, called a **junction table** (also known as a *linking table* or *associate table*) and two One-to-Many relationships will help achieve the Many-to-Many relationship. Let's show you what we mean.

The junction table is used to associate products and categories, with no restriction on how many products can exist for a category, or how many categories a product can be added to. Figure 4-8 shows the role of the junction table.

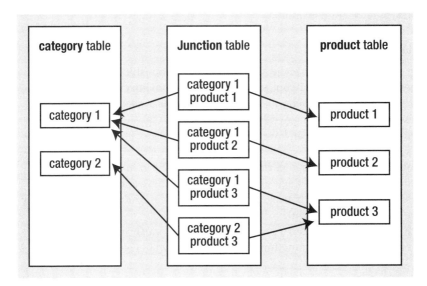

Figure 4-8. *The Many-to-Many relationship between categories and products*

Note that each record in the junction table links one category with one product. You can have as many records as you like in the junction table, linking any category to any product. The linking table contains two fields, each one referencing the primary key of one of the two linked tables. In our case, the junction table will contain two fields: a `category_id` field and a `product_id` field.

Each record in the junction table will consist of a (`product_id`, `category_id`) pair, which will be used to associate a particular product with a particular category. By adding more records to the `product_category` table, you can associate a product with more categories or a category with more products, effectively implementing the Many-to-Many relationship.

Because the Many-to-Many relationship is implemented using a third table that makes the connection between the linked tables, there is no need to add additional fields to the related tables in the way that we added the `department_id` to the `category` table for implementing the One-to-Many relationship.

There's no definitive naming convention to use for the junction table. Most of the time it's okay to just join the names of the two linked tables—in this case, the junction table is named `product_category`.

Enforcing Table Relationships with the FOREIGN KEY Constraint

Relationships between tables can be physically enforced in the database using `FOREIGN KEY` constraints, or simply *foreign keys*.

You learned in the previous chapter about the *primary key* and *unique* constraints. We covered them there because they apply to the table as an individual entity. Foreign keys, on the other hand, occur between two tables: the table in which the foreign key is defined (the *referencing table*) and the table the foreign key references (the *referenced table*).

■**Tip** Actually, the referencing table and the referenced table can be one and the same. This isn't seen too often in practice, but it's not unusual either. For example, you can have a table with employees, where each employee references the employee that is his or her boss (in this scenario the big boss would probably reference itself).

A foreign key is a column or combination of columns used to enforce a link between data in two tables (usually representing a One-to-Many relationship). Foreign keys are used both as a method of ensuring data integrity and to establish a relationship between tables.

To enforce database integrity, the foreign keys, like the other types of constraints, apply certain restrictions. Unlike primary-key and unique constraints that apply restrictions to a single table, the `FOREIGN KEY` constraint applies restrictions on both the referencing and referenced tables. For example, if you enforce the One-to-Many relationship between the `department` and `category` tables by using a `FOREIGN KEY` constraint, the database will include this relationship as part of its integrity. It will not allow you to add a category to a nonexistent department, nor will it allow you to delete a department if there are categories that belong to it.

There's good news and bad news about the FOREIGN KEY constraint and MySQL. The bad news is that the default table type in MySQL—MyISAM—doesn't support enforcing FOREIGN KEY constraints. The alternative to MyISAM is the InnoDB table type, but InnoDB tables don't support full-text searching, which will be useful when implementing the search feature (in Chapter 5).

The good news is that you can have different types of tables inside a single database, so you can use MyISAM for tables that don't need free-text searching and/or primary keys, and InnoDB for the others. You must be extra careful when manipulating data from MyISAM tables, however, because you can't rely on the database to take care of its integrity on its own.

■**Tip** The MySQL documentation says that support of the FOREIGN KEY constraint for all table types is planned for MySQL 5.1 (which, at the time of writing, is at least a couple years away).

Before implementing the rest of the product catalog tables, we need to explain more about the various types of MySQL table types.

MySQL Table Types

MySQL supports six data table types. When creating a new data table, if not specified otherwise, the default table type (MyISAM) is used. We'll have a quick look at them here.

Following are the four important table types supported by MySQL:

MyISAM is the default table type in MySQL since version 3.23 (when it replaced its older version, **ISAM**). It is the fastest table type in MySQL, at the cost of not supporting foreign keys, CHECK constraints, transactions, and some other advanced features. However, unlike the other table types, it supports full-text searching, which is very helpful when implementing the searching capability in the web site.

InnoDB is a very powerful database engine that is developed independently of MySQL (its home page is http://www.innodb.com). It supports transactions, has great capability to handle many simultaneous update operations, and can enforce FOREIGN KEY constraints.

BDB was the first database engine to support transactions. However, InnoDB is usually the preferred choice when needing a powerful database engine under MySQL. BDB was created by Sleepycat Software (http://www.sleepycat.com).

HEAP is a special kind of table type in that it is constructed in system memory. It cannot be used to reliably store data (in case of a system failure, all data is lost and cannot be recovered), but it can be a good choice when working with tables that need to be very fast with data that can be easily reconstructed if accidentally lost.

For the TShirtShop product catalog, you'll be using MyISAM tables, mainly because you need their full-text search feature. In other cases, you'll use InnoDB because of the support for foreign keys. If you change your mind about the type of a table, you can easily change it with the `ALTER TABLE` command. The following line of code would make the `department` table an InnoDB table:

```
ALTER TABLE department TYPE=InnoDB;
```

Creating and Populating the New Data Tables

Now, it's time to create the three required tables in the database:

- `category`

- `product`

- `product_category`

Exercise: Creating the category Table

The process of creating the `category` table is pretty much the same as for the `department` table you created in Chapter 2. The table will have four fields:

- *category_id*: An unsigned integer that represents the unique ID for the category.

- *department_id*: An unsigned integer that represents the department the category belongs to.

- *name*: Represents the category name.

- *description*: Represents the category description.

There are two ways to create the category table and populate it. Either execute the SQL scripts from the code download section of the Apress web site (`http://www.apress.com`) or follow these steps:

1. Using phpMyAdmin, navigate to your tshirtshop database and create a new table named `category` with four fields. Complete the form as shown in Figure 4-9 and click Go.

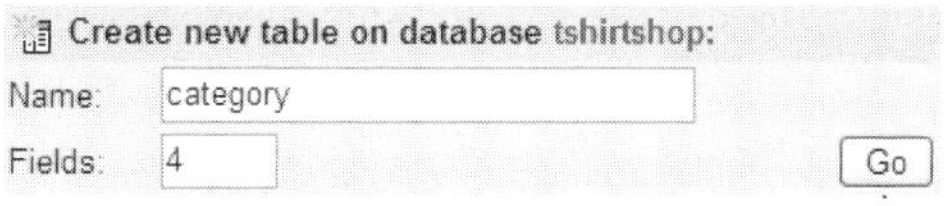

Figure 4-9. *Creating a new data table using phpMyAdmin*

2. Add columns as shown in Figure 4-10 and then click Save.

Figure 4-10. *Creating a new data table in phpMyAdmin*

■**Note**   Leaving Table type set to Default means you're creating a MyISAM table.

---

3. Now you'll populate the table with some data, as shown in Figure 4-11. You use the Insert tab in phpMyAdmin to add new records to the table. Remember that if you add the records in this order, you don't need to supply the category_id value because it'll be automatically generated in sequence.

category_id	department_id	name	description
1	1	Animal	Our ever-growing selection of beautiful animal T-shirts represents critters from everywhere, both wild and domestic.
2	1	Flowers	These unique and beautiful flower T-shirts are just the item for the gardener, flower arranger, florist, or general lover of things beautiful.
3	2	Norwegian	You don't have to be a Norwegian to wear one.
4	2	Swedish	These beautiful and descriptive T-shirts are not only hugely popular among our Scandinavian friends, but also with almost everyone else.
5	2	Danish	Browse through all the cool and unique Danish T-shirts to find the ones you like best.
6	3	Soccer	Soccer is the most popular sport in the world. Now you can wear some of the most unique and soon-to-be popular soccer T-shirts in the world.
7	3	Train	You can sport your favorite train lore and history all over your chest, from Casey Jones to a country's first locomotive.

Figure 4-11. *Creating the* category *data table in phpMyAdmin*

Exercise: Creating the product Table

Most fields in product are self-explanatory, but for completeness, let's take a short look at their descriptions:

- product_id is used to uniquely identify a product. It is the primary key of the table.

- name contains the product's name.

- description contains a description of the product.

- price contains the product's price.

- `image_file_1` stores the name of the product's picture file (or eventually the complete path), which gets displayed when showing lists of products. You could keep the picture in the table (as a `blob` field), but in most cases it's much more efficient to store the picture files in the file system and have only their names stored into the database. If you have a high-traffic web site, you might even want to have the image files placed on a separate physical location (for example, another hard disk) to increase site performance.

- `image_file_2` stores the name of the secondary image file of the product. This image gets displayed when displaying the product details page.

- `on_catalog_promotion` is a `bool` field (can be set to either 0 or 1) that specifies whether the product is featured on the web site front page. When initially loading the site, the first page will always list the products that have this bit set to 1.

- `on_department_promotion` is a `bool` field that specifies whether the product is featured on the department pages. When a visitor selects a department, he is shown only the featured products of that department.

Note The `bool`, `bit`, and (as of MySQL 4.1) `boolean` column types are synonyms for `TINYINT(1)`. Zero is considered false and nonzero values are considered true.

With the help of those `bool` fields, the site administrators can highlight a set of products that will be of particular interest to visitors at a specific time. For example, long before the soccer World Cup, you will want the soccer T-shirts to appear prominently on the front page of the site. Follow these steps to create the `product` table:

1. If you choose to create the table manually without using the scripts from the code download (`create_product.sql`), open the `tshirtshop` database using phpMyAdmin and start creating a new data table named `product`, with eight fields, like you did in the previous exercise.

2. Set the details of your fields as shown in Figure 4-12 to create the `product` table.

Field	Type ⑦	Length/Values*	Attributes	Null	Default**	Extra					
product_id	INT		UNSIGNED	not null		auto_increment	⊙	○	○	○	☐
name	VARCHAR	50		not null			○	○	○	⊙	☐
description	VARCHAR	255		not null			○	○	○	⊙	☐
price	DECIMAL	10,2		not null			○	○	○	⊙	☐
image_file_1	VARCHAR	50		null			○	○	○	⊙	☐
image_file_2	VARCHAR	50		null			○	○	○	⊙	☐
on_catalog_prom	TINYINT	1		not null			○	○	○	⊙	☐
on_department_	TINYINT	1		not null			○	○	○	⊙	☐

Figure 4-12. *Creating the* `product` *data table in phpMyAdmin*

3. Click Save. Populate the table using the `populate_product.sql` script from the code download.

Exercise: Creating the product_category Table

The product_category table is the linking table that allows implementing the Many-to-Many relationship between product and category. It has two fields, product_id and category_id, which form the primary key of the table. Create the table like this:

1. Create a new table named product_category with two fields, as shown in Figure 4-13. Don't forget to select the primary key radio button for both fields:

Figure 4-13. *Creating the* product_category *data table in phpMyAdmin*

2. Finally, populate product_category with this data by running the populate_product_category.sql script.

How It Works: Your New Data Tables

In this exercise, you created the product table and the category table, and implemented the Many-to-Many relationship between product and category by creating the junction table.

The junction table contains (product_id, category_id) pairs, and each record in it associates a particular product with a particular category. So, if you see a record such as (1, 4) in product_category, you know that the product with product_id 1 belongs to the category with category_id 4.

This is also the first time that you set a primary key consisting of more than one column. The primary key of product_category is formed by both of its fields, product_id and category_id. This means that you won't be allowed to have two identical (product_id, category_id) pairs in the table—it wouldn't make much sense to associate a product with a category more than once. However, it is perfectly legal to have a product_id or category_id more than once, as long as it is part of a unique (product_id, category_id) pair.

Unfortunately, the table relationships aren't enforced by the database in any way because we used MyISAM tables, which don't support the FOREIGN KEY constraint. You'll learn how to work with foreign keys in Chapter 9, where you'll create some InnoDB tables.

Using Database Diagrams

A number of tools allow you to build database structures visually, and have the capability to implement them physically in the database for you, and generate the necessary SQL script. Although we won't present any particular tool in this book, it's good to know that they exist. You can find a list of the most popular tools at http://www.databaseanswers.com/modelling_tools.htm.

Database diagrams also have the capability to implement the relationships between tables. For example, if you had implemented the relationships between your four tables so far, the database diagram would look something like Figure 4-14.

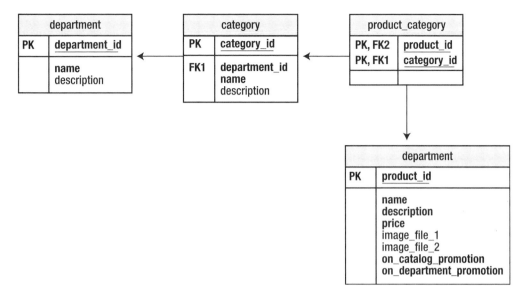

Figure 4-14. *Database diagram representing your four tables*

In the diagram, the primary keys of each table are marked with the PK notation. Foreign keys are marked with FK (because there can be more of them in a table, they're numbered). The arrows between two tables point toward the table in the *one* part of the relationship.

Implementing the Data Tier

You now have a database with a wealth of information just waiting to be read by somebody. Now you'll implement the data-access logic in the `DoCatalog` class.

For this chapter, the data-tier logic is a bit more complicated than in the previous chapter. It must answer queries such as "give me the list of categories for a specific department" or "give me the details for this specific department or category." To accomplish the new requirements, you must get data from multiple data tables.

Filtering SQL Query Results

Remember the SQL Query you used in the previous chapter? It was fairly simple, wasn't it? In that case, you wanted to get the whole list of departments and the query looked like this:

```
SELECT department_id, name FROM department
```

There is a single table involved, the query doesn't have any parameters, and we don't even filter the records with the `WHERE` clause (which we will discuss shortly).

■**Note** Before continuing, you should be aware that almost every SQL query, except maybe for the simplest ones, can be written in a number of alternative ways. Advanced database programming books have entire chapters explaining how you can get the same result using different data interrogation techniques, the performance implications of each of them, and so on. In this book, we employ techniques that are generally recommended as good programming practices, and which work best for TShirtShop.

The first new SQL element to introduce in this chapter is the WHERE clause, which is used to filter the records acted on by SELECT, UPDATE, and DELETE SQL statements. Say you wanted to retrieve the name and description of a particular department. You'll need this query when the visitor clicks on a department and needs to get more data about it. The SQL query that returns the name and description of the department with an ID of 3 is

```
SELECT name, description FROM department
WHERE department_id = 3
```

A similar query can be used to retrieve the list of categories that belong to a particular department:

```
SELECT name, description FROM category
WHERE department_id = 3
```

These two queries were simple enough, as they queried data from a single table. Things get a bit more complicated when you need to gather data from more tables.

Getting Short Descriptions

In the main pages of the catalog, we won't display full product descriptions, but only a portion of them. In MySQL, you can extract a substring from a string using the SUBSTRING function. Alternatively, to extract the left part of the string, you can use the LEFT function.

After extracting a part of the full description, you append "..." at the end using the CONCAT function. The following SELECT returns products' descriptions trimmed at 30 characters with "..." appended:

```
SELECT product.name,
       CONCAT(SUBSTRING(description,1,30),'...') AS description
FROM product
```

The version that uses LEFT instead of SUBSTRING is

```
SELECT product.name,
       CONCAT(LEFT(description,30),'...') AS description
FROM product
```

These queries will return a list such as

```
name                description
Sambar              Sambar (North Borneo - 1892). ...
American Bison      Of all the critters in our T-s...
Cameroun Monkey     Mustache Monkey (Cameroun - 19...
Ruanda Monkey       Colobus (Ruanda-Urundi - 1959)...
Canada Goose        Canada Goose (Canada - 1952). ...
...                 ...
```

Joining Data Tables

Because your data is stored in several tables, frequently not all of the information you'll need is in one table. Figure 4-15 shows an example in which data needs to be extracted from both the department and category tables.

Department Name	Category Name	Category Description
Nature	Animal	Our ever-growing selection of beautiful animal T-s...
Nature	Flowers	These unique and beautiful flower T-shirts are jus...
Scandinavia	Norvegian	You don't have to be a Norvegian to wear one.
Scandinavia	Swedish	These beautiful and descriptive T-shirts are not o...
Scandinavia	Danish	Browse through all the cool and unique Danish T-sh...
Free Spirit	Soccer	Soccer is the most popular sport in the world. Now...
Free Spirit	Train	You can sport your favorite train lore and history...

Figure 4-15. *Data extracted from* department *and* category *tables*

In other cases, all the information you need is in just one table, but you need to place conditions on it, based on the information in another table. The list in Figure 4-16 contains data extracted from the product table, but is filtered to display only the products that belong to the Flowers category.

Product_ID	Name	Description	Price
6	Afghan Flower #1	Afghan Flower #1 (1962). This beautiful image was ...	14.9500
7	Austria Flower #1	(Austria - 1964). Nasturtiums: Beautiful in your g...	14.9500
8	Bulgaria Flower #1	(Bulgaria - 1962). These beautiful pink roses woul...	18.9900
9	Colombia Flower #1	(Colombia - 1950). Cattleya labiata triande—one ...	22.9900
84	Congo Flower #1	Congo Flower #1 (1952). The Congo is not at a loss...	13.9500
85	Congo Flower #2	Congo Flower #2 (1970). If you've been looking for...	16.9500
86	Costa Rica Flower #1	Costa Rica Flower #1. This national flower of Cost...	17.9500
87	Gabon Flower #1	Gabon Flower #1. The combretum, also known as "jun...	17.9500

Figure 4-16. *Products from the Flowers category*

When extracting the products that belong to a category, the SQL query isn't the same as when extracting the categories that belong to a department. This is because products and categories are linked through the product_category associate table.

To get the list of products in a category, you first need to look in the product_category table and get all the (product_id, category_id) pairs where category_id is the ID of the category you're looking for. That list contains the IDs of the products in that category. Using these IDs, you'll be able to generate the required product list.

Although this sounds pretty complicated, it can be done using a single SQL query. The real power of SQL lies in its capability to perform complex operations on large amounts of data using simple queries.

How to Use JOIN

The results shown in the previous figures are the result of table joins. Where you need a result set that is based on the data from multiple tables is a good indication that you might need to join these tables.

You will learn how to use JOIN by analyzing the product and product_category tables, and the way you can get a list of products that belong to a certain category. Suppose you want to get all the products in the category where category_id = 2. Figure 4-17 shows the records that you want returned.

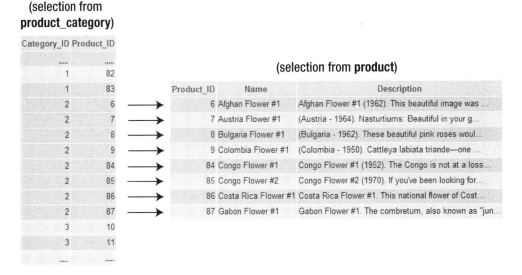

Figure 4-17. *Joining the* product_category *and* product *tables on the* product_id *field*

Tables are joined in SQL using the JOIN clause. Joining one table with another results in the columns (not the rows) of those tables being joined. When joining two tables, there always needs to be a common column on which the join will be made. The query that joins the product and product_category tables is as follows:

```
SELECT *
FROM product_category INNER JOIN product
ON product.product_id = product_category.product_id
```

The result will look something like Figure 4-18 (the figure doesn't include all returned rows and columns).

product_id	category_id	product_id	name	description	price	image_file_1	image_file_2	on_catalog_promotion
1	1	1	Sambar	Sambar (North Borneo - 1892). This handsome Malaya...	14.95	BorneoDeer.gif	BorneoDeer.stamp.jpg	0
2	1	2	American Bison	Of all the critters in our T-shirt zoo, this is on...	14.95	Buffalo.gif	Buffalo.stamp.jpg	1
3	1	3	Cameroun Monkey	Mustache Monkey (Cameroun - 1962). This fellow is ...	12.99	CameroonMonkey.gif	CamerounMonkey.stamp.jpg	0

Figure 4-18. *Results of the table join between* product *and* product_category

The resultant table is composed of the fields from the joined tables, and they are synchronized on the product_id column, which was specified as the column to make the join on. Now if you look at the resultant table, it's easy to see that you need a WHERE clause to obtain just the records that have a category_id of 2. The new query would look like this:

```
SELECT *
FROM product_category INNER JOIN product
ON product.product_id = product_category.product_id
WHERE product_category.category_id = 2
```

When working with multiple tables in the same query, you sometimes need to prefix the column names with the table name so that MySQL Server will know for sure which column you are talking about. This is a requirement in the case of columns that exist in both tables (like product_id); for the other columns, MySQL Server doesn't require you to specify the table, but this is considered good practice anyway. The previous query can also be written as:

```
SELECT *
FROM product_category INNER JOIN product
ON product.product_id = product_category.product_id
WHERE category_id = 2
```

The results are shown in Figure 4-19.

product_id	category_id	product_id	name	description	price	image_file_1	image_file_2
6	2	6	Afghan Flower #1	Afghan Flower #1 (1962). This beautiful image was ...	14.95	AfghanFlower1.gif	AfghanFlower1.stamp.jpg
7	2	7	Austria Flower #1	(Austria - 1964). Nasturtiums: Beautiful in your g...	14.95	AustriaFlower1.gif	AustriaFlower1.stamp.jpg
8	2	8	Bulgaria Flower #1	(Bulgaria - 1962). These beautiful pink roses woul...	18.99	BulgariaFlower1.gif	BulgariaFlower1.stamp.jpg
9	2	9	Colombia Flower #1	(Colombia - 1950). Cattleya labiata triandeùone o...	22.99	ColombiaFlower1.gif	ColombiaFlower1.stamp.jpg
84	2	84	Congo Flower #1	Congo Flower #1 (1952). The Congo is not at a loss...	13.95	CongoFlower1.gif	CongoFlower1.stamp.jpg
85	2	85	Congo Flower #2	Congo Flower #2 (1970). If you've been looking for...	16.95	CongoFlower2.gif	CongoFlower2.stamp.jpg
86	2	86	Costa Rica Flower #1	Costa Rica Flower #1. This national flower of Cost...	17.95	CRFlower1.gif	CRFlower1.stamp.jpg
87	2	87	Gabon Flower #1	Gabon Flower #1. The combretum, also known as "jun...	17.95	Gabon Flower #1	GabonFlower.stamp.gif

Figure 4-19. *Filtered results of the table join between* product *and* product_category

This table has all that you need. The last step is to specify the columns you're interested in. Remember that you aren't required to prefix the columns with the table name:

```
SELECT product.name, product.description
FROM product_category INNER JOIN product
ON product.product_id = product_category.product_id
WHERE product_category.category_id = 2
```

If you want to save a few keystrokes, you can use aliases, which allow you to have shorter queries with identical functionality as their longer versions:

```
SELECT p.name, p.description
FROM product_category pc INNER JOIN product p
ON p.product_id = pc.product_id
WHERE pc.category_id = 2
```

This finally gives the results you were looking for as shown in Figure 4-20.

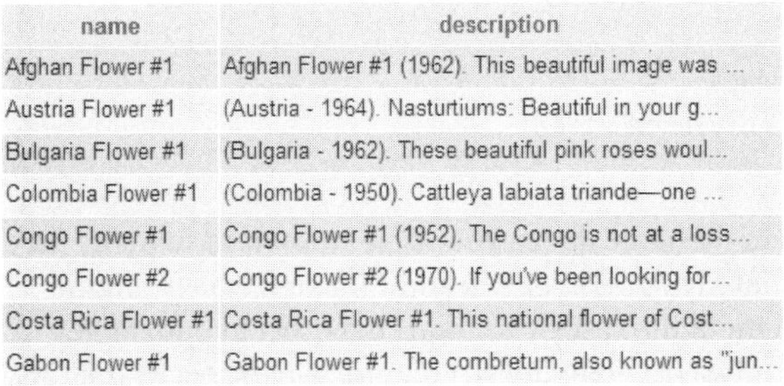

name	description
Afghan Flower #1	Afghan Flower #1 (1962). This beautiful image was …
Austria Flower #1	(Austria - 1964). Nasturtiums: Beautiful in your g…
Bulgaria Flower #1	(Bulgaria - 1962). These beautiful pink roses woul…
Colombia Flower #1	(Colombia - 1950). Cattleya labiata triande—one …
Congo Flower #1	Congo Flower #1 (1952). The Congo is not at a loss…
Congo Flower #2	Congo Flower #2 (1970). If you've been looking for…
Costa Rica Flower #1	Costa Rica Flower #1. This national flower of Cost…
Gabon Flower #1	Gabon Flower #1. The combretum, also known as "jun…

Figure 4-20. *Products of the Flowers category*

Showing Products Page by Page

Here comes the last bit of theory for the data tier. Because showing long lists of products on a single page is annoying for the visitor and inefficient for the web site, you will implement a paging functionality.

With this feature implemented, the visitor can browse through the products in a category (or any other page containing products) using the "Previous" and "Next" navigation controls as shown in Figure 4-21.

Having to display a large number of products on one page would annoy visitors to the site because the information would be cumbersome to read through all at once, plus it would take a long time to display if they have a slow Internet connection. Also the overhead added to your server when processing a large page filled with products might slow it down significantly. Imagine what Google would be like if it tried to display all the results from a search in one page. That's why when a visitor makes a request that causes a large number of products to be returned, you need to display them on separate pages, with a fixed number of products per page, and with navigation links to go from page to page.

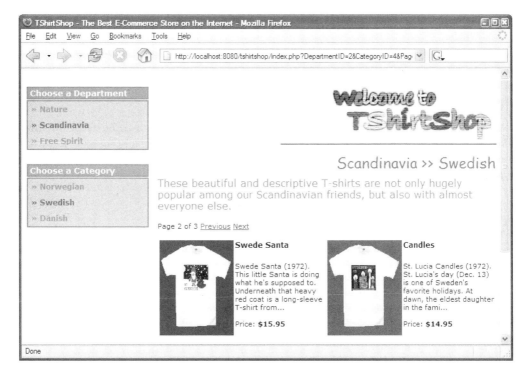

Figure 4-21. *Showing a page of products*

You can get MySQL to retrieve just a portion of a larger result set by using the LIMIT keyword. LIMIT takes two arguments. The first argument specifies the index of the first returned record, and the second specifies how many rows to return. For example, the following SQL query would tell MySQL to return the rows 15, 16, 17, 18, and 19 from the list of alphabetically ordered products:

```
SELECT name
FROM product
ORDER BY name
LIMIT 15, 5;
```

With the current database you should get the products shown in Figure 4-22.

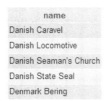

Figure 4-22. *Showing a page of products*

You'll use the LIMIT keyword to specify the range of records you're interested in when retrieving lists of products. In the data tier, you'll implement two generic methods (Create-SubpageQuery and CountQueryRecords), which will assist in implementing paging functionality for all pages that display lists of products.

Implementing the Data Tier Methods

Now you need to start implementing the data tier methods, which retrieve the data from the database. First you'll implement the methods that retrieve department and category information. We'll deal with methods that retrieve products separately, because there we also want to implement paging functionality.

Getting Departments and Categories

The new methods that retrieve departments and categories are

- GetDepartmentDetails

- GetCategoriesInDepartment

- GetCategoryDetails

Let's discuss them one by one.

GetDepartmentDetails

When a user selects a particular department in the product catalog, the name and the description of that particular department must be found. These details are obtained by querying the database again.

GetDepartmentDetails receives the ID of the selected department as a parameter and returns its name and description. Update the DoCatalog class (located in tshirtshop/data_objects/do_catalog.php) by adding the GetDepartmentDetails method:

```
// retrieves all details for the mentioned department
public function GetDepartmentDetails($departmentId)
{
  $query_string = "SELECT name, description
                   FROM department
                   WHERE department_id = $departmentId";
  $result = $this->dbManager->DbGetRow($query_string);
  return $result;
}
```

The WHERE clause (WHERE department_id=$departmentId) is used to request the details of a specific department.

Because the query returns only one row, you use the DbGetRow() method of the DbManager class. Remember that the DbManager class sets the format of the fetched rows to DB_FETCHMODE_ ASSOC, so after the query is performed, you'll have the department name in $result['name'] and its description in $result['description'].

GetCategoriesInDepartment

When a visitor selects a department, the categories that belong to that department should display. This can be done with the help of GetCategoriesInDepartment, which returns the list of categories in a specific department.

All you need now is the ID and the name for each category that belongs to the selected department. Add the GetCategoriesInDepartment method to the DoCatalog class:

```
// retrieves categories that belong to the mentioned department
public function GetCategoriesInDepartment($departmentId)
{
  $query_string = "SELECT category_id, name
                   FROM category
                   WHERE department_id = $departmentId";
  $result = $this->dbManager->DbGetAll($query_string);
  return $result;
}
```

GetCategoryDetails

When the visitor selects a particular category, more information about that category should appear, such as its name and description. Add the GetCategoryDetails method to the DoCatalog class:

```
// retrieves details about the mentioned category
public function GetCategoryDetails($categoryId)
{
  $query_string =
    "SELECT name AS category_name, description AS category_description
     FROM category
     WHERE category_id = $categoryId";
  $result = $this->dbManager->DbGetRow($query_string);
  return $result;
}
```

After the query is performed, you'll have the category name in $result['category_name'] and its description in $result['category_description'].

Getting Products

Only four methods effectively ask for products, but you'll also implement two helper functions (CountQueryRecords and CreateSubpageQuery) to assist in implementing the paging functionality. The complete list of methods you need to implement is

- CountQueryRecords

- CreateSubpageQuery

- GetProductsInCategory

- GetProductsOnDepartmentPromotion

- GetProductsOnCatalogPromotion

- GetProductDetails

You'll also add two constants to the config.inc.php configuration file.

Defining Product List Constants and Activating Session

Before writing the data tier methods, let's first update the include/config.inc.php file by adding these two definitions:

```
// Configure product display options
define("SHORT_PRODUCT_DESCRIPTION_LENGTH",130);
define("PRODUCTS_PER_PAGE",4);
```

Then, modify app_top.php by adding this line to it:

```
<?php
// activate session
session_start();
// include utility files
require_once 'config.inc.php';
require_once 'tss_error_handler.php';
require_once 'setup_smarty.php';
require_once 'database.php';
// global DbManager instance
$gDbManager = new DbManager(MYSQL_CONNECTION_STRING);
?>
```

The SHORT_PRODUCT_DESCRIPTION_LENGTH constant specifies how many characters from the product's description should appear when displaying product lists. The complete definition gets displayed in the product's details page, which you'll implement at the end of this chapter.

PRODUCTS_PER_PAGE specifies the maximum number of products that can be displayed in the catalog page. If the visitor's selection contains more than PRODUCTS_PER_PAGE products, the list of products is split into subpages, accessible through the navigation controls.

The PHP session object is active because you'll need to use it to improve performance when navigating to subpages of products.

■**Note** Session handling is a great PHP feature that allows you to keep track of variables specific to a certain visitor accessing the web site. While the visitor browses various pages of the site, its session variables are persisted by the web server and associated to a unique visitor identifier (which is stored by default in the visitor's browser as a cookie). The visitor's session object stores (*name, value*) pairs that are saved at server-side and are accessible for the entire visitor's session. In this chapter we'll use the session feature for improving performance. When implementing the paging functionality, before requesting the list of products, you first ask the database for the total number of products that are going to be returned, so you can show the visitor how many pages of products are available. This number will be saved in the visitor's session, so in case the visitor browses the subpages of a list of products (in the CountQueryRecords method that you'll implement next), the database wouldn't be queried multiple times for the total number of products— on subsequent calls this number will be directly read from the session. In this chapter, you'll also use the session to implement the Continue Shopping links in product details pages.

CountQueryRecords

CountQueryRecords receives a SELECT query as an argument ($queryString) and returns the number of rows this SQL statement returns. The input parameter of this function is the SELECT query that you need to count the value for. So, if you send a query such as SELECT * FROM product as parameter to CountQueryRecords, the return value will be the total number of products in the catalog.

This method is called from the other data tier methods that need to know how many products are returned for a certain page in a catalog in order to calculate how many subpages to split the list of products into.

Add CountQueryRecords to the DoCatalog class, which is located in do_catalog.php:

```
// counts how many records are returned by a SELECT command
private function CountQueryRecords($queryString)
{
  // test if $queryString is a valid SELECT query
  if (strtoupper(substr($queryString, 0, 6)) != 'SELECT')
    trigger_error("Not a SELECT statement");
  $from_position = stripos($queryString, "FROM ");
  if ($from_position == false)
    trigger_error("Bad SELECT statement");
  // if the previous call to CountQueryRecords had the same SELECT string
  // as parameter, we return directly the cached response
  if (isset($_SESSION['last_count_query']))
    if ($_SESSION['last_count_query'] == $queryString)
      return $_SESSION['last_count'];
  // calculate the number of records the SELECT query returns
  $count_query = "SELECT COUNT(*) ".substr($queryString, $from_position);
  $items_count = $this->dbManager->DbGetOne($count_query);
  // save the query and its record count in the session
  $_SESSION['last_count_query'] = $queryString;
  $_SESSION['last_count'] = $items_count;
```

```
    // return the calculated number of records
    return $items_count;
  }
```

Let's analyze the function to see how it does its job.

The method is private because you won't access it from within other classes—it's a helper class for other methods of DoCatalog. First, it verifies whether the string received as parameter starts with SELECT, and contains FROM. If these conditions aren't met, an error is generated.

Second, the function verifies whether the previous call to it was for the same SELECT query. If it was, the result cached from the previous call is returned. This small trick improves performance when the visitor is browsing subpages of the same list of products, because the actual counting in the database is performed only once.

The previous SELECT statement for which CountQueryRecords calculated the records count is saved in the current visitor's session in a variable named last_count_query. The results are saved in the last_count session variable:

```
    // if the previous call to CountQueryRecords had the same SELECT string
    // as parameter, we return directly the cached response
    if (isset($_SESSION['last_count_query']))
      if ($_SESSION['last_count_query'] == $queryString)
        return $_SESSION['last_count'];
```

If you're not able to use a cached value, you need to ask the database how many records a SELECT query returns. You do this by replacing the first part of the query with SELECT COUNT(*). For example, if the query is SELECT name FROM product (which returns the name of each product in the catalog), you replace it with SELECT COUNT(*) FROM product (which returns the number of products in the catalog).

```
    // calculate the number of records the SELECT query returns
    $count_query = "SELECT COUNT(*) ".substr($queryString, $from_position);
    $items_count = $this->dbManager->DbGetOne($count_query);
```

In the end, the function saves the query and its result to the visitor's session, and returns the calculated number of records to the calling function:

```
    // save the query and its record count in the session
    $_SESSION['last_count_query'] = $queryString;
    $_SESSION['last_count'] = $items_count;
    // return the calculated number of records
    return $items_count;
```

CreateSubpageQuery

CreateSubpageQuery creates the SELECT query that retrieves a subpage of products. It is called from GetProductsInCategory, GetProductsOnDepartmentPromotion, and GetProductsOnCatalog-Promotion, These three functions know the SELECT queries that return lists of products, and they send that query to CreateSubpageQuery, which modifies the query to implement pagination by using LIMIT as shown earlier in this chapter.

CreateSubpageQuery receives three parameters:

- $queryString is a SELECT query that you need to extract the subpage for.

- $pageNo Specifies the page number you want.

- $rTotalPages is a parameter passed by reference; this allows you to set its value in CreateSubpageQuery, and allows its value to be read from the function that called CreateSubpageQuery.

CreateSubpageQuery uses the PRODUCTS_PER_PAGE constant to calculate the number of total pages (it sets this number to rTotalPages) and the list of products that corresponds to the $pageNo page.

Let's write the CreateSubpageQuery method and we'll comment more about it afterwards. Add the method to the DoCatalog class:

```
// alters a SQL query to return only the specified page of products
private function CreateSubpageQuery($queryString, $pageNo, &$rTotalPages)
{
  // calculate number of records returned by the SELECT query
  $items_count = $this->CountQueryRecords($queryString);
  // if we have few products then we don't implement pagination
  if ($items_count <= PRODUCTS_PER_PAGE)
  {
    $pageNo = 1;
    $rTotalPages = 1;
  }
  // else we calculate number of pages and the new SELECT query
  else
  {
    $rTotalPages = ceil($items_count / PRODUCTS_PER_PAGE);
    $start_page = ($pageNo - 1) * PRODUCTS_PER_PAGE;
    $queryString .= " LIMIT " . $start_page . "," . PRODUCTS_PER_PAGE;
  }
  return $queryString;
}
```

Note The ampersand (&) before a function parameter means it is passed by reference. When a variable is passed by reference, an alias of the variable is passed instead of creating a new copy of the value. This way, when a variable is passed by reference and the called function changes its value, its new value will reflect in the caller function, too. Passing by reference is an alternative method to receiving a return value from a called function, and is particularly useful when you need to get multiple return values from the called function. CreateSubpageQuery returns the text of a SELECT query query through its return value, and the total number of subpages through the $rTotalPages parameter that is passed by reference.

The logic of the method is fairly obvious. It calls `CountQueryRecords` to see how many products are returned by the `SELECT` query. If there are more than the number specified by `PRODUCTS_PER_PAGE`, the query that returns the products from the specified page is generated by adding the `LIMIT` option to the original `SELECT` query. The total number of pages is saved to the `rTotalPages` parameter, which is sent by reference, and will be ultimately read from the presentation tier to show it to the visitor.

```
$rTotalPages = ceil($items_count / PRODUCTS_PER_PAGE);
$start_page = ($pageNo - 1) * PRODUCTS_PER_PAGE;
$queryString.= " LIMIT ".$start_page.",".PRODUCTS_PER_PAGE;
```

GetProductsInCategory

This method returns the products that belong to a certain category. To obtain this list of products, you need to join the `product` and `product_category` tables, as explained earlier in this chapter. You also trim the product's description at `SHORT_PRODUCT_DESCRIPTION_LENGTH` characters.

After constructing the query, you pass it to `CreateSubpageQuery` that returns only the subpage of products you're interested in.

Add the following method to the `DoCatalog` class:

```
// retrieves a list of products that belong to the specified category
public function GetProductsInCategory($categoryId, $pageNo, &$rTotalPages)
{
  $query_string =
    "SELECT product.product_id, product.name,
       CONCAT(LEFT(description,".SHORT_PRODUCT_DESCRIPTION_LENGTH."), '...')
         AS description,
       product.price, product.image_file_1,
       product.on_department_promotion, product.on_catalog_promotion
     FROM product INNER JOIN product_category
     ON product.product_id = product_category.product_id
     WHERE product_category.category_id = $categoryId";
  $page_query = $this->CreateSubpageQuery($query_string, $pageNo, $rTotalPages);
  return $this->dbManager->DbGetAll($page_query);
}
```

GetProductsOnDepartmentPromotion

When the visitor selects a particular department, apart from needing to list its name, description, and list of categories (you wrote the necessary code for these tasks earlier), you also want to display the list of featured products for that department.

GetProductsOnDepartmentPromotion needs to return all the products that belong to a specific department and have the on_department_promotion bit set to 1. In GetProductsInCategory,
you needed to make a table join to find out the products that belong to a specific category. Now
that you need to do this for departments, the task is a bit more complicated because you can't
directly know what products belong to what departments.

You know how to find categories that belong to a specific department (you did this in
GetCategoriesInDepartment), and you know how to get the products that belong to a specific
category (you did that in GetProductsInCategory). By combining these pieces of information,
you can generate the list of products in a department. For this, you need two table joins. You
also filter the final result to get only the products that have the on_department_promotion bit
set to 1.

You will also use the DISTINCT clause to filter the results to avoid getting the same record
multiple times. This can happen when a product belongs to more than one category, and these
categories are in the same department. In this situation, you would get the same product
returned for each of the matching categories, unless the results are filtered using DISTINCT.

Add the following method to the DoCatalog class:

```
// retrieves the products that are on promotion for the specified department
public function GetProductsOnDepartmentPromotion($departmentId, $pageNo,
  &$rTotalPages)
{
  $query_string =
      "SELECT DISTINCT product.product_id, product.name,
          CONCAT(LEFT(product.description,".SHORT_PRODUCT_DESCRIPTION_LENGTH."),
            '...') AS description,
          product.price, product.image_file_1
        FROM product
        INNER JOIN product_category
          ON product.product_id = product_category.product_id
        INNER JOIN category
          ON product_category.category_id = category.category_id
        WHERE product.on_department_promotion = 1
          AND category.department_id=$departmentId";
  $page_query = $this->CreateSubpageQuery($query_string, $pageNo, $rTotalPages);
  return $this->dbManager->DbGetAll($page_query);
}
```

■**Tip** If the way table joins work looks too complicated, try to follow them on the diagram shown in
Figure 4-14.

The constructed SQL query is run through CreateSubpageQuery, which adds paging.

GetProductsOnCatalogPromotion

GetProductsOnCatalogPromotion returns the products to be displayed on the catalog's main page. These are the products that have the on_catalog_promotion field set to 1 in the database. You trim the product's description at SHORT_PRODUCT_DESCRIPTION_LENGTH characters.

After constructing the query, it's passed to CreateSubpageQuery, which returns only the subpage of products you're interested in.

Add the GetProductsOnCatalogPromotion method to the DoCatalog class:

```
// retrieves the list of products on catalog promotion
public function GetProductsOnCatalogPromotion($pageNo, &$rTotalPages)
{
  $query_string =
    "SELECT
       product.product_id, product.name,
         CONCAT(LEFT(description,".SHORT_PRODUCT_DESCRIPTION_LENGTH."), '...')
         AS description,
       product.price, product.image_file_1
     FROM product
     WHERE product.on_catalog_promotion = 1";
  $page_query = $this->CreateSubpageQuery($query_string, $pageNo, $rTotalPages);
  return $this->dbManager->DbGetAll($page_query);
}
```

GetProductDetails

GetProductDetails returns complete information about a product (including its secondary image file and the full description), and is called for the product's details page.

```
// retrieves complete product details
public function GetProductDetails($productId)
{
  $query_string =
    "SELECT product_id, name, description,
            price, image_file_1, image_file_2
     FROM product
     WHERE product_id = $productId";
  return $this->dbManager->DbGetRow($query_string);
}
```

Well, that's about it. Right now, your data store is ready to hold and process the product catalog information. It's time to move to the next step: implementing the business tier of the product catalog.

The Business Tier

In the business tier, you'll add some new methods that will call the earlier created methods in the data tier. Remember that you started working on the BoCatalog class (located in the business_objects/bo_catalog.php file) in Chapter 3. The new methods that you'll add here, which correspond to the Get methods of the data tier, are

- GetDepartmentDetails

- GetCategoriesInDepartment

- GetCategoryDetails

- GetProductsInCategory

- GetProductsOnDepartmentPromotion

- GetProductsOnCatalogPromotion

- GetProductDetails

Add these methods to the BoCatalog class, just after the GetDepartments method. Here's the complete code listing of bo_catalog.php:

```php
<?php
// reference the data tier
require_once SITE_ROOT.'/data_objects/do_catalog.php';

// business tier class for reading products catalog information
class BoCatalog
{
  /* private stuff */
  private $mDoCatalog;

  // class constructor initializes the data tier object
  function __construct()
  {
    $this->mDoCatalog = new DoCatalog();
  }

  // retrieves all departments
  public function GetDepartments()
  {
    $result = $this->mDoCatalog->GetDepartments();
    return $result;
  }

  // retrieves complete details for the specified department
  public function GetDepartmentDetails($departmentId)
  {
```

```php
    $result = $this->mDoCatalog->GetDepartmentDetails($departmentId);
    return $result;
  }

  // retrieves list of categories that belong to a department
  public function GetCategoriesInDepartment($departmentId)
  {
    $result = $this->mDoCatalog->GetCategoriesInDepartment($departmentId);
    return $result;
  }

  // retrieves complete details for the specified category
  public function GetCategoryDetails($categoryId)
  {
    $result = $this->mDoCatalog->GetCategoryDetails($categoryId);
    return $result;
  }

  // retrieves list of products that belong to a category
  public function GetProductsInCategory($categoryId, $pageNo, &$rTotalPages)
  {
    // make sure we send a valid page number to data tier
    if (empty($pageNo)) $pageNo=1;
    // call data tier method to obtain the list of products
    $result = $this->mDoCatalog->GetProductsInCategory($categoryId, $pageNo,
      $rTotalPages);
    // return results
    return $result;
  }

  // retrieves list of products that are on promotion for a department
  public function GetProductsOnDepartmentPromotion($departmentId, $pageNo,
    &$rTotalPages)
  {
    // make sure we send a valid page number to data tier
    if (empty($pageNo)) $pageNo=1;
    // call data tier method to obtain the list of products
    $result = $this->mDoCatalog->GetProductsOnDepartmentPromotion
      ($departmentId, $pageNo, $rTotalPages);
    // return results
    return $result;
  }

  // retrieves list of products to be featured in the first page of the catalog
  public function GetProductsOnCatalogPromotion($pageNo, &$rTotalPages)
  {
    // make sure we send a valid page number to data tier
```

```
    if (empty($pageNo)) $pageNo=1;
    // call data tier method to obtain the list of products
    $result = $this->mDoCatalog->GetProductsOnCatalogPromotion($pageNo,
      $rTotalPages);
    // return results
    return $result;
  }

// retrieves complete product details
  public function GetProductDetails($productId)
  {
    $result = $this->mDoCatalog->GetProductDetails($productId);
    return $result;
  }
}
//end BoCatalog
?>
```

The $rTotalPages argument is received by reference from the presentation tier (and passed by reference to the data tier) because the total number of products the data tier calculates needs to get to the presentation tier, which informs the visitor about it.

At the moment, the business tier doesn't have much functionality, but it'll become more useful in the following chapters.

The Presentation Tier

Believe it or not, right now the data and business tiers of the product catalog are complete for this chapter. All you have to do is use their functionality in the presentation tier. In this final section, you'll create a few Smarty templates and integrate them into the existing project.

Execute the TShirtShop project (or load http://localhost/tshirtshop in your favorite web browser) to see once again what happens when the visitor clicks a department. After the page loads, click one of the departments. The main page (index.php) is reloaded, but this time with a query string at the end:

```
http://localhost:8080/tshirtshop/index.php?DepartmentID=1
```

Using this parameter, DepartmentID, you can obtain any information about the selected department, such as its name, description, list of products, and so on. In the following sections, you'll create the controls that display the list of categories associated with the selected department, and the products for the selected department, category, or main web page.

Displaying Data About the Selected Department

The componentized template responsible for showing the contents of a particular department is named department and you'll build it in the exercise that follows. You'll first create the componentized template and then modify index.php and templates/index.tpl to load it when DepartmentID is present in the query string. After this exercise, when clicking a department in the list, you should see a page like the one in Figure 4-23.

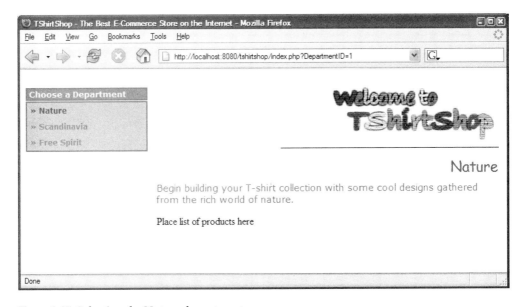

Figure 4-23. *Selecting the Nature department*

Exercise: Creating the department Componentized Template

Let's start with the easy stuff.

1. Add the following two styles to the `tshirtshop.css` file. You'll need them for displaying the department's title and description:

```
.DepartmentTitle
{
  color: red;
  font-family: Comic Sans MS;
  text-decoration: none;
  font-size: 24px;
  line-height: 15px;
  padding-left: 10px
}
.ListDescription
{
  font-family: Verdana;
  font-size: 12pt;
  color: #228aaa;
  padding-right: 3px;
  text-align: left;
}
```

2. Create a new template file named `blank.tpl` in the `templates` folder with the following contents:

```
{* Smarty blank page *}
```

Yes, this is a blank Smarty template file, which contains just a comment. You'll use it a bit later. Make sure you add that comment to the file—otherwise, if you leave it empty, you'll get an error when trying to use it in the PHP code.

3. Create a new template file named `department.tpl` in the `templates` folder and add the following code to it:

```
{* department.tpl *}
{load_department assign="department"}
<br/>
<table cellspacing="0" width="100%">
  <tr>
    <td>
      <p align="right">
        <span class="DepartmentTitle">{$department->mNameLabel}</span>
      </p>
      <p align="left">
        <span class="ListDescription">{$department->mDescriptionLabel}
        </span>
      </p>
      <p align="left">
        Place list of products here
      </p>
    </td>
  </tr>
</table>
```

The two variables, `$department->mNameLabel` and `$department->mDescriptionLabel`, contain the name and description of the selected department, and are populated by the template plugin file, `function.load_department.php`.

4. Let's now create the template plugin file for `department.tpl`. Create the `smarty_plugins/function.load_department.php` file and add the following code to it:

```
<?php
// plugin functions inside plugin files must be named: smarty_type_name
function smarty_function_load_department($params, $smarty)
{
  $department = new Department();
  $department->init();
  // assign template variable
  $smarty->assign($params['assign'], $department);
}
// class that deals with retrieving department details
class Department
{
  /* public variables for the smarty template */
  public $mDescriptionLabel;
  public $mNameLabel;
```

```php
    /* private members */
    private $mBoCatalog;
    private $mDepartmentId;
    private $mCategoryId;
    /* constructor */
    function __construct()
    {
      // create instance of business tier object
      $this->mBoCatalog = new BoCatalog();
      // we need to have DepartmentID in the query string
      if (isset($_GET['DepartmentID']))
        $this->mDepartmentId = (int)$_GET['DepartmentID'];
      else
        trigger_error("DepartmentID not set");
      // if CategoryID is in the query string we save it
      // (casting it to integer to protect against invalid values)
      if (isset($_GET['CategoryID']))
        $this->mCategoryId = (int)$_GET['CategoryID'];
    }
    /* init */
    function init()
    {
      // if visiting a department ...
      $details =
          $this->mBoCatalog->GetDepartmentDetails($this->mDepartmentId);
      $this->mNameLabel = $details['name'];
      $this->mDescriptionLabel = $details['description'];
      // if visiting a category ...
      if (isset($this->mCategoryId))
      {
        $details =
            $this->mBoCatalog->GetCategoryDetails($this->mCategoryId);
        $this->mNameLabel =
            $this->mNameLabel . " >> " . $details['category_name'];
        $this->mDescriptionLabel = $details['category_description'];
      }
    }
  }
?>
```

5. Now let's modify index.tpl and index.php to load the newly created componentized template when DepartmentID appears in the query string. If the visitor is browsing a department, you set the pageContentsCell variable to the componentized template you have just created.

Modify index.php as shown:

```php
<?php
// Load Smarty library and config files
require_once 'include/app_top.php';
// Load Business Tier
require_once SITE_ROOT . '/business_objects/bo_catalog.php';
// Load Smarty template file
$page = new Page();
$pageContentsCell = "blank.tpl";
// load department details if visiting a department
if (isset($_GET['DepartmentID']))
{
  $pageContentsCell = "department.tpl";
}
$page->assign("pageContentsCell", $pageContentsCell);
$page->display('index.tpl');
// Load app_bottom which closes the database connection
require_once 'include/app_bottom.php';
?>
```

6. Open templates/index.tpl and replace the text Place contents here with

```
{include file="$pageContentsCell"}
```

7. Load your web site in a browser and select one of the departments to ensure everything works as expected.

How It Works: The Department Componentized Template

Now that the most important functionality has already been implemented in the data tier, implementing the visual part of the component was an easy task.

After adding the CSS styles and creating the blank template file, you created the Smarty template file department.tpl, which contains the HTML layout for displaying a department's data. This template file is loaded in the page contents cell, just below the header, in index.tpl:

```
<td valign="top" width="550"><br/>
  {include file="header.tpl"}
  {include file="$pageContentsCell"}
</td>
```

The $pageContentsCell variable is populated in index.php, depending on the query string parameters. At the moment, if the DepartmentID parameter is found in the query string, the page contents cell is populated with the department.tpl template file you just wrote. Otherwise (such as when being on the first page), the blank template file is used instead (you'll change this when creating a template to populate the contents cell for the first page). This is the code in index.php that assigns a value to $pageContentsCell:

```
$pageContentsCell="blank.tpl";
if (isset($_GET['DepartmentID']))
{
  $pageContentsCell = "department.tpl";
}
$page->assign("pageContentsCell",$pageContentsCell);
```

The first interesting aspect to know about department.tpl is the way it loads the load_department function plugin.

```
{* department.tpl *}
{load_department assign="department"}
```

This allows you to access the instance of the Department class (that we'll discuss next) and its public members (mNameLabel and mDescriptionLabel), from the template file (department.tpl), like this:

```
        <p align="right">
          <span class="DepartmentTitle">{$department->mNameLabel}</span>
        </p>
        <p align="left">
          <span class="ListDescription">{$department->mDescriptionLabel}</span>
        </p>
        <p align="left">
          Place list of products here
        </p>
```

The next step now is to understand how the template plugin file (function.load_department.php) does its work to obtain the department's name and description. The file begins with a plugin function that is standard in our architecture. It creates a Department instance (the Department class is defined afterwards), initializes it calling its init() method, and then associates the assign plugin parameter with the earlier created Department instance.

```
function smarty_function_load_department($params, $smarty)
{
  $department = new Department();
  $department->init();
  // assign template variable
  $smarty->assign($params['assign'], $department);
}
```

The two public members of Department are the ones you access from the Smarty template (the department's name and description). The final role of this class is to populate these members, which are required to build the output for the visitor:

```
class Department
{
  /* public variables for the smarty template */
  public $mDescriptionLabel;
  public $mNameLabel;
```

There are also three private members that are used for internal purposes. $mBoCatalog will contain an instance of the BoCatalog class of the business tier (which, as you learned in Chapter 2, is the class that provides direct functionality for the presentation tier). $mDepartmentId and $mCategoryId will store the values of the DepartmentID and CategoryID query string parameters:

```
  /* private members */
  private $mBoCatalog;
  private $mDepartmentId;
  private $mCategoryId;
```

And then comes the constructor. In any object-oriented language, the constructor of the class is executed when the class is instantiated, and is used to perform various initialization procedures. In our case, the constructor of Department creates a new business tier object, and then reads the DepartmentID and CategoryID query string parameters into the mDepartmentId and mCategoryId private class members. You need these because if CategoryID actually exists in the query string, then you need to also display the name of the category and the category's description instead of the department's description.

```
  /* constructor */
  function __construct()
  {
    // create instance of business tier object
    $this->mBoCatalog = new BoCatalog();
    // we need to have DepartmentID in the query string
    if (isset($_GET['DepartmentID']))
      $this->mDepartmentId = (int)$_GET['DepartmentID'];
    else
      trigger_error("DepartmentID not set");
    // if CategoryID is in the query string we save it making sure it is integer
    if (isset($_GET['CategoryID']))
      $this->mCategoryId = (int)$_GET['CategoryID'];
  }
```

The real functionality of the class is hidden inside the init() method, which in our case gets executed immediately after the constructor. This method populates the mNameLabel and mDescriptionLabel public members with information from the business tier:

```
/* init */
function init()
{
  // if visiting a department ...
  $details = $this->mBoCatalog->GetDepartmentDetails($this->mDepartmentId);
  $this->mNameLabel = $details['name'];
  $this->mDescriptionLabel = $details['description'];
  // if visiting a category ...
  if (isset($this->mCategoryId))
  {
    $details = $this->mBoCatalog->GetCategoryDetails($this->mCategoryId);
    $this->mNameLabel = $this->mNameLabel." >> ".$details['category_name'];
    $this->mDescriptionLabel = $details['category_description'];
  }
}
```

Displaying the List of Categories

When the visitor selects a department, the categories that belong to that department must appear. For this, you'll implement a new Smarty template named categories_list.

categories_list is very similar to the department_list componentized template. It consists of a template section used for looping over the array of categories data (category name and category ID). This template section will contain links to index.php, but this time their query string will also contain a CategoryID, showing that a category has been clicked, like this:

http://localhost/tshirtshop/index.php?DepartmentID=1&CategoryID=2

The steps in the following exercise are very much like the ones for the departments_list componentized template (created at the end of Chapter 3), so we'll move a bit more quickly this time.

Exercise: Creating the categories_list Componentized Template

Follow the steps to create the categories_list componentized template:

1. First, update tshirtshop.css by adding the following styles, which you'll use for displaying categories:

```
.CategoryListHead
{
  border-right: #ea6d00 2px solid;
  border-top: #ea6d00 2px solid;
  border-left: #ea6d00 2px solid;
  border-bottom: #ea6d00 2px solid;
```

```
  background-color: #ef8d0e;
  font-family: Verdana, Arial;
  font-weight: bold;
  font-size: 10pt;
  color: #f5f5dc;
  padding-left: 3px
}
.CategoryListContent
{
  border-right: #ea6d00 2px solid;
  border-top: #ea6d00 2px solid;
  border-left: #ea6d00 2px solid;
  border-bottom: #ea6d00 2px solid;
  background-color: #f8c78c
}
a.CategoryUnselected
{
  font-family: Verdana, Arial;
  font-weight: bold;
  font-size: 9pt;
  color: #cd853f;
  line-height: 25px;
  padding-right: 5px;
  padding-left: 5px;
  text-decoration: none
}
a.CategoryUnselected:hover
{
  color: #d2691e;
  padding-right: 5px;
  padding-left: 5px
}
a.CategorySelected
{
  font-family: Verdana, Arial;
  font-weight: bold;
  font-size: 9pt;
  color: #a0522d;
  line-height: 25px;
  padding-right: 5px;
  padding-left: 5px;
  text-decoration: none
}
```

2. Create the Smarty template for the `categories_list` componentized template. Write the following lines in `templates/categories_list.tpl`:

```
{* categories_list.tpl *}
{load_categories_list assign="categories_list"}
<br/>
{* start category list *}
<table border="0" cellpadding="0" cellspacing="1" width="200">
  <tr>
    <td class="CategoryListHead"> Choose a Category </td>
  </tr>
  <tr>
    <td class="CategoryListContent">
      {section name=i loop=$categories_list->mCategories}
        {assign var=class_d value="CategoryUnselected"}
        {if ($categories_list->mCategorySelected ==
$categories_list->mCategories[i].category_id)}
          {assign var=class_d value="CategorySelected"}
        {/if}
      <a class="{$class_d}"
          href="{$categories_list->mCategories[i].onclick|escape:"html"}">
        &raquo; {$categories_list->mCategories[i].name}
      </a>
      <br />
      {/section}
    </td>
  </tr>
</table>
{* end category list *}
```

3. Create the `smarty_plugins/function.load_categories_list.php` file and add the following code to it:

```php
<?php
// plugin functions inside plugin files must be named: smarty_type_name
function smarty_function_load_categories_list($params, $smarty)
{
  $categories_list = new CategoriesList();
  $categories_list->init();
  // assign template variable
  $smarty->assign($params['assign'], $categories_list);
}
// class that manages the categories list
class CategoriesList
{
  /* public variables for the smarty template */
  public $mCategorySelected = 0;
  public $mDepartmentSelected = 0;
```

```php
  public $mCategories;
  /* private members */
  private $mBoCatalog;
  /* constructor */
  function __construct()
  {
    $this->mBoCatalog = new BoCatalog();
    if (isset($_GET['DepartmentID']))
      $this->mDepartmentSelected = (int)$_GET['DepartmentID'];
    else
      trigger_error("DepartmentID not set");
    if (isset($_GET['CategoryID']))
      $this->mCategorySelected = (int)$_GET['CategoryID'];
  }
  /* init */
  function init()
  {
    $this->mCategories =
    $this->mBoCatalog->GetCategoriesInDepartment($this->mDepartmentSelected);
// building links for the category pages
    for ($i = 0; $i < count($this->mCategories); $i++)
      $this->mCategories[$i]['onclick'] =
          "index.php?DepartmentID=" .
          $this->mDepartmentSelected . "&CategoryID=" .
          $this->mCategories[$i]['category_id'];
  }
} //end class
?>
```

4. Modify index.php like this:

```php
<?php
// Load Smarty library and config files
require_once 'include/app_top.php';
// Load Business Tier
require_once SITE_ROOT . '/business_objects/bo_catalog.php';
// Load Smarty template file
$page = new Page();
$pageContentsCell = "blank.tpl";
$categoriesCell = "blank.tpl";
// load department details if visiting a department
if (isset($_GET['DepartmentID']))
{
  $pageContentsCell = "department.tpl";
  $categoriesCell = "categories_list.tpl";
}
```

```
$page->assign("pageContentsCell", $pageContentsCell);
$page->assign("categoriesCell", $categoriesCell);
$page->display('index.tpl');
// Load app_bottom which closes the database connection
require_once 'include/app_bottom.php';
?>
```

5. Now include the `categories_list` componentized template to `templates/index.tpl`, just below the list of departments:

```
{include file="departments_list.tpl"}
{include file="$categoriesCell"}
```

6. Load TShirtShop in a web browser. When the page loads, click on one of the departments. You'll see the categories list appear in the chosen place (see Figure 4-24).

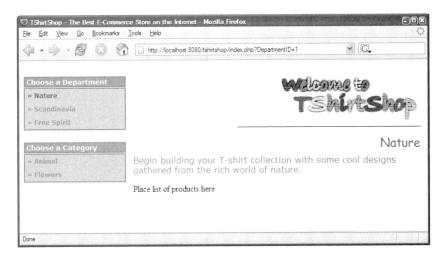

Figure 4-24. *Selecting the Nature department*

How It Works: The categories_list Componentized Template

The `categories_list` componentized template works similarly to the `departments_list`. The `CategoriesList` class (located in the `function.load_categories_list.php` plugin file) has three public members that can be accessed from the template file (`categories_list.tpl`):

```
/* public variables for the Smarty template */
public $mCategorySelected = 0;
public $mDepartmentSelected = 0;
public $mCategories;
```

`$mCategorySelected` retains the category that is selected, which must be displayed with a different style than the other categories in the list. The same is true with `$mDepartmentSelected`. `$mCategories` is the list of categories you populate the categories list with. This list is obtained with a call to the business tier.

The links in the categories list are processed using the escape Smarty command to ensure all characters are transformed to their HTML equivalents (such as & is tranformed to &, and so on).

```
<a class="{$class_d}"
   href="{$categories_list->mCategories[i].onclick|escape:"html"}">
   &raquo; {$categories_list->mCategories[i].name}
</a>
```

Displaying the Products

Whether on the main web page or browsing a category, some products should appear instead of the "Place list of products here" text.

Here you create the products_list componentized template, which is capable of displaying a list containing detailed information about the products. When executed, this componentized template will look like Figure 4-25.

Figure 4-25. *The* products_list *componentized template in action*

When a large number of products are present to be browsed, navigation links will appear (see Figure 4-26).

Figure 4-26. *The* products_list *componentized template with paging*

This componentized template will be used in multiple places within the web site. On the main page, it displays the products on catalog promotion (remember, the ones that have the on_catalog_promotion bit set to 1). When a visitor selects a particular department, the products_list componentized template displays the products featured for the selected department. Finally, when the visitor clicks on a category, the componentized template displays all the products that belong to that category. Due to the way the database is implemented, you can feature a product in the departments it belongs to, but not on the main page, or vice-versa. If a product belongs to more than one department, it will appear on the main page of each these departments.

The componentized template chooses which products to display after analyzing the query string. If both DepartmentID and CategoryID parameters are present in the query string, this means the products of that category should be listed. If only DepartmentID is present, the visitor is visiting a department, so its featured products should appear. If DepartmentID is not present, the visitor is on the main page, so the catalog featured products should appear.

To integrate the products_list componentized template with the first page, you'll need to create an additional template file (first_page_contents.tpl), which you'll implement later. After creating products_list in the following exercise, you'll be able to browse the products by department and by category. Afterwards, you'll see how to add products to the main web page.

Exercise: Creating the products_list Componentized Template

Follow the steps to implement the products list of your catalog:

1. Copy the product_images directory from the code download to your project root.

2. First, create the products_list.tpl Smarty design template. Create a new file in the templates folder named products_list.tpl and add the following code to it:

```
{* products_list.tpl *}
{load_products_list assign="products_list"}
{if $products_list->mrTotalPages > 1}
  <span class="PagingText">
    Page {$products_list->mPageNo} of {$products_list->mrTotalPages}
    {if $products_list->mPreviousLink}
      <a href='{$products_list->mPreviousLink|escape:"html"}'>Previous</a>
    {else}
      Previous
    {/if}
    {if $products_list->mNextLink}
      <a href='{$products_list->mNextLink|escape:"html"}'>Next</a>
    {else}
      Next
    {/if}
    <br /><br />
  </span>
```

```
{/if}
<table cellspacing="0" border="0">
  <tr>
    {section name=k loop=$products_list->mProducts}
    {if  $smarty.section.k.index !=0 && $smarty.section.k.index % 2 == 0}
  </tr>
  <tr>
  {/if}
    <td>
      <table cellPadding="0" align="left">
        <tr>
          <td align="right">
            <a href="{$products_list->mProducts[k].onclick|escape:"html"}">
  <img src='product_images/{$products_list->mProducts[k].image_file_1}'
      height="150" border="0" width="120" alt="product image" />
            </a>
          <br /><br />
          </td>
          <td valign="top" width="200">
            <span class="ProductName">
              <a href="{$products_list->mProducts[k].onclick|escape:"html"}"
                  class="ProductName">
                {$products_list->mProducts[k].name}
              </a>
            </span>
            <br /><br />
            <span class="ProductDescription">
              {$products_list->mProducts[k].description}
              <br /><br />
              Price:
            </span>
            <span class="ProductPrice">
              ${$products_list->mProducts[k].price}
            </span>
          </td>
        </tr>
      </table>
    </td>
    {/section}
  </tr>
</table>
```

3. Add the following code at the beginning of index.php, *after* the reference to app_top.php (app_top.php activates session handling, which is required for the following code to work). This code makes sure to always save the link to the current page if that page is not a product details page. In other words, $_SESSION['PageLink'] will always contain the link to the last visited nonproduct details page. You need to save this value to implement the Continue Shopping link in the product details page, which needs to forward the visitor to the previously visited page.

```php
<?php
// Load Smarty library and config files
require_once 'include/app_top.php';
/* if not visiting a product page, save the link to the current page
   in the PageLink session variable; it will be used to create the
   Continue Shopping link in the product details page and the links
   to product details pages */
if (!isset($_GET['ProductID']))
  $_SESSION['PageLink'] = "http://" . $_SERVER['SERVER_NAME'] .
  ":" . $_SERVER['SERVER_PORT'] . $_SERVER['REQUEST_URI'];
```

4. Now you must create the template plugin file for the products_list.tpl template. Create a new file named function.load_products_list.php in the smarty_plugins folder and add the following code to it:

```php
<?php
// plugin functions inside plugin files must be named: smarty_type_name
function smarty_function_load_products_list($params, $smarty)
{
  $products_list = new ProductsList();
  $products_list->init();
  // assign template variable
  $smarty->assign($params['assign'], $products_list);
}

class ProductsList
{
  /* public variables to be read from Smarty template */
  public $mProducts;
  public $mPageNo;
  public $mrTotalPages;
  public $mNextLink;
  public $mPreviousLink;
  /* private members */
  private $mBoCatalog;
  private $mDepartmentId;
  private $mCategoryId;
  /* constructor */
  function __construct()
  {
```

```
  // create business tier object
  $this->mBoCatalog = new BoCatalog();
  // get DepartmentID from query string casting it to int
  if (isset($_GET['DepartmentID']))
    $this->mDepartmentId = (int)$_GET['DepartmentID'];
  // get CategoryID from query string casting it to int
  if (isset($_GET['CategoryID']))
    $this->mCategoryId = (int)$_GET['CategoryID'];
  // get PageNo from query string casting it to int
  if (isset($_GET['PageNo']))
    $this->mPageNo = (int)$_GET['PageNo'];
  else
    $this->mPageNo = 1;
}
/* init */
function init()
{
  // if browsing a category, get the list of products by calling
  // the GetProductsInCategory business tier method
  if (isset($this->mCategoryId))
    $this->mProducts = $this->mBoCatalog->GetProductsInCategory($this
      ->mCategoryId, $this->mPageNo, $this->mrTotalPages);
  // if browsing a department, get the list of products by calling
  // the GetProductsOnDepartmentPromotion business tier method
  elseif (isset($this->mDepartmentId))
    $this->mProducts =
                $this->mBoCatalog->GetProductsOnDepartmentPromotion
      ($this->mDepartmentId, $this->mPageNo, $this->mrTotalPages);
  // if browsing the first page, get the list of products by calling
  // the GetProductsOnCatalogPromotion business tier method
  else
    $this->mProducts =
      $this->mBoCatalog->GetProductsOnCatalogPromotion($this->mPageNo,
                                          $this->mrTotalPages);
  // if there are subpages of products, display navigation controls
  if ($this->mrTotalPages > 1)
  {
    // read the query string
    $query_string = $_SERVER['QUERY_STRING'];
    // find if we have PageNo in the query string
    $pos = stripos($query_string, "PageNo=");
    // if there is no PageNo in the query string
    // then we're on the first page
    if ($pos == false)
    {
      $query_string .= "&PageNo=1";
      $pos = stripos($query_string, "PageNo=");
```

```
    }
    // read the current page number from the query string
    $temp = substr($query_string, $pos);
    sscanf($temp, "PageNo=%d", $this->mPageNo);
    // build the Next link
    if ($this->mPageNo >= $this->mrTotalPages)
      $this->mNextLink = "";
    else
    {
      $new_query_string = str_replace("PageNo=" . $this->mPageNo,
                    "PageNo=" . ($this->mPageNo + 1), $query_string);
      $this->mNextLink = "index.php?".$new_query_string;
    }
    // build the Previous link
    if ($this->mPageNo == 1)
      $this->mPreviousLink = "";
    else
    {
      $new_query_string = str_replace("PageNo=" . $this->mPageNo,
                    "PageNo=" . ($this->mPageNo - 1), $query_string);
      $this->mPreviousLink = "index.php?".$new_query_string;
    }
  }
  // build links for product details pages
  $url = $_SESSION['PageLink'];
  if (count($_GET) > 0)
    $url = $url . "&ProductID=";
  else
    $url = $url . "?ProductID=";
  for ($i = 0; $i < count($this->mProducts); $i++)
    $this->mProducts[$i]['onclick'] =
                  $url . $this->mProducts[$i]['product_id'];
  }
} //end class
?>
```

5. Add the following styles to the tshirtshop.css file:

```
.ProductName
{
  color: Black;
  font-family: Verdana, Helvetica, sans-serif;
  font-weight: bold;
  font-size: 12px;
}
A.ProductName, A.Link
{
```

```
    color: Black;
    font-family: Verdana, Helvetica, sans-serif;
    font-weight: bold;
    font-size: 12px;
    text-decoration: none;
}
A.ProductName:hover, A.Link:hover
{
    color: Red;
}
.ProductDescription
{
    color: Black;
    font-family: Verdana, Helvetica, sans-serif;
    font-size: 11px;
}
.Price
{
    color: Black;
    font-family: Verdana, Helvetica, sans-serif;
    font-size: 11px;
}
.ProductPrice
{
    color: Black;
    font-family: Verdana, Helvetica, sans-serif;
    font-weight: bold;
    font-size: 11px;
}
.PagingText
{
    font-family: Verdana, Helvetica, sans-serif;
    font-size: 11px;
    color: Black;
}
```

6. Open templates/department.tpl and replace the text

   ```
   Place list of products here
   ```

    with

   ```
   {include file="products_list.tpl"}
   ```

7. Load your project in your favorite browser, navigate to one of departments, and then
   select a category from a department. Also, find a category with more than four products, to test that the paging functionality works.

How It Works: The products_list Componentized Template

Because most functionality regarding the products list has already been implemented in the data and business tiers, this task was fairly simple. The Smarty design template file (products_list.tpl) contains the layout to be used when displaying products, and its template plugin file (function.load_products_list.php) gets the correct list of products to display.

The constructor in function.load_products_list.php (the ProductsList class) creates a new instance of the business tier object (BoCatalog), and retrieves DepartmentID, CategoryID, and PageNo from the query string, casting them to int as a security measure. These values are used to decide which products to display:

```
/* constructor */
function __construct()
{
  // create business tier object
  $this->mBoCatalog = new BoCatalog();
  // get DepartmentID from query string casting it to int
  if (isset($_GET['DepartmentID']))
    $this->mDepartmentId = (int)$_GET['DepartmentID'];
  // get CategoryID from query string casting it to int
  if (isset($_GET['CategoryID']))
    $this->mCategoryId = (int)$_GET['CategoryID'];
  // get PageNo from query string casting it to int
  if (isset($_GET['PageNo']))
    $this->mPageNo = (int)$_GET['PageNo'];
  else
    $this->mPageNo = 1;
}
```

The init() method, which continues the constructor's job, starts by retrieving the requested list of products. It decides what method of the business tier to call by analyzing the mCategoryId and mDepartmentId members (which, thanks to the constructor, represent the values of the CategoryID and DepartmentID query string parameters).

If CategoryID is present in the query string, it means the visitor is browsing a category, so GetProductsInCategory is called to retrieve the products in that category. If only DepartmentID is present, GetProductsOnDepartmentPromotion is called to retrieve the department's featured products. If not even DepartmentID is present, this means the visitor is on the main page, and GetProductsOnCatalogPromotion is called to get the products to be featured on the first page of the site:

```
/* init */
function init()
{
  // if browsing a category, get the list of products by calling
  // the GetProductsInCategory business tier method
  if (isset($this->mCategoryId))
    $this->mProducts = $this->mBoCatalog->GetProductsInCategory($this
      ->mCategoryId, $this->mPageNo, $this->mrTotalPages);
  // if browsing a department, get the list of products by calling
```

```
// the GetProductsOnDepartmentPromotion business tier method
elseif (isset($this->mDepartmentId))
  $this->mProducts =
              $this->mBoCatalog->GetProductsOnDepartmentPromotion
    ($this->mDepartmentId, $this->mPageNo, $this->mrTotalPages);
// if browsing the first page, get the list of products by calling
// the GetProductsOnCatalogPromotion business tier method
else
  $this->mProducts =
    $this->mBoCatalog->GetProductsOnCatalogPromotion($this->mPageNo,
                                     $this->mrTotalPages);
```

The next part of the function takes care of paging. If the business tier call tells you there is more than one page of products (so there are more products than what you specified in the PRODUCTS_PER_PAGE constant), you need to show the visitor the current subpage of products being visited, the total number of subpages, and the Previous and Next page links. The comments in code should make the functionality fairly clear so we won't reiterate the code here.

In the final part of the function, you added the onclick member to each mProducts record, which contains the link to the product's page. These values are used in the template file to create links to the products' pages on the product's name and picture. The links are created using the PageLink session variable, which points to the last loaded page that is not a product details page (which in this case is the current page), and adds ProductID to the query string:

```
$url = $_SESSION['PageLink'];
if (count($_GET) > 0)
  $url = $url . "&ProductID=";
else
  $url = $url . "?ProductID=";
for ($i = 0; $i < count($this->mProducts); $i++)
  $this->mProducts[$i]['onclick'] =
                  $url . $this->mProducts[$i]['product_id'];
```

Displaying Contents on the Main Web Page

Apart from general information about the web site, you also want to show some promotional products on the first page of TShirtShop.

In case the visitor browses a department or a category, the department Smarty template is used to build the output. For the main web page, we'll create the first_page_contents componentized template that will build the output.

Remember in index.tpl you have a cell named pageContentsCell that you fill with different details depending on what part of the site is being visited? When a department or a category is being visited, the department componentized template is loaded and it takes care of filling that space. We still haven't done anything with that cell for the first page, when no department or category has been selected.

In the following exercise, you'll write a template file that contains some information about the web site, and shows the products that have been set up as promotions on the first page. Remember that the product table contains a bit field named on_catalog_promotion. Site administrators will set this bit to 1 for products that need to be featured in the first page.

Exercise: Creating the first_page_contents Componentized Template

Follow the steps to create the first_page_contents componentized template:

1. Start by creating the Smart design template file. The
   templates/first_page_contents.tpl file should have these contents:

```
{* first_page_contents.tpl *}
<p align="right">
  <span class="FirstPageText">
    <br />
   We hope you have fun developing TShirtShop, the e-commerce store from
    <br /><br />
     Beginning PHP 5 and MySQL E-Commerce: From Novice to Professional
  </span>
</p>
<span class="ListDescription">
  This week we have set a special price for these fantastic products! :)
</span>
<br /><br />
{include file="products_list.tpl"}
```

2. Enter the following style into tshirtshop.css:

```
.FirstPageText
{
  color: Navy;
  font-family: Verdana, Helvetica, sans-serif;
  text-decoration: none;
  font-size: 12px;
  font-weight: bold;
  line-height: 9px;
}
```

3. Open the index.php file and replace the line

```
$pageContentsCell = "blank.tpl";
```

   with the line

```
$pageContentsCell = "first_page_contents.tpl";
```

   This way, when no DepartmentID and CategoryID are in the query string, index.php will
   load the first_page_contents componentized template.

4. Load your project in your favorite browser.

How It Works: The first_page_contents Componentized Template

The actual list of products is still displayed using the products_list Smarty componentized template, which you built earlier in this chapter. However, this time it isn't loaded from department.tpl (like it does when browsing a department or a category), but from a new template file named first_page_contents.tpl.

Showing Product Details

The last bit of code you'll implement in this chapter is about displaying product details. When the visitor clicks on any product, he or she will be forwarded to the product's details page, which shows the product's complete description and the secondary product image. In the later chapters, you'll add more features to this page, such as product recommendations or product reviews.

Let's do this in the following exercise.

Exercise: Creating the product Componentized Template

To display full details about a product, you need to build an individual page for each product:

1. Edit index.php to load the product.tpl template using the $pageContentsCell variable if the ProductID parameter exists in the query string. Add two lines to the index.php file as shown in the following code:

```
if (isset($_GET['DepartmentID']))
{
  $pageContentsCell = "department.tpl";
  $categoriesCell = "categories_list.tpl";
}
if (isset($_GET['ProductID']))
  $pageContentsCell = "product.tpl";
```

2. Okay, now create the componentized template for the product details page in which the product with full description and second image will display. Create a file named function.load_product.php in the smarty_plugins folder with the following contents:

```
<?php
// plugin function for the load_product function plugin
function smarty_function_load_product($params, $smarty)
{
  $product = new Product();
  $product->init();
  // assign template variable
  $smarty->assign($params['assign'], $product);
}
// class that handles product details
class Product
{
  // public variables to be used in Smarty template
  public $mProduct;
```

```php
    public $mPageLink = "index.php";
    // private stuff
    private $mBoCatalog;
    private $mProductId;

    // class constructor
    function __construct()
    {
      // create the middle tier object
      $this->mBoCatalog = new BoCatalog();
      // variable initialization
      if (isset($_GET['ProductID']))
        $this->mProductId = (int)$_GET['ProductID'];
      else
        trigger_error("ProductID required in product.php");
    }

    // init
    function init()
    {
      // get product details from business tier
      $this->mProduct =
        $this->mBoCatalog->GetProductDetails($this->mProductId);
      if (isset($_SESSION['PageLink']))
        $this->mPageLink = $_SESSION['PageLink'];
    }
  } //end class
?>
```

3. Now get in touch with your artistic side and spread these variables all over the page in an attempt to make the page more attractive to the visitor. To do that, you need to create a product.tpl file in the templates folder. Feel free to let your artistic side go wild and modify this as you want.

```
{load_product assign="product"}
<br/><br/>
<span class="ListDescription">{$product->mProduct.name}</span><br><br>
<table>
  <tr>
    <td width="250">
      <img src='product_images/{$product->mProduct.image_file_1}'
           height="150" border="0"></a>
    </td>
    <td>
      <img src='product_images/{$product->mProduct.image_file_2}'
           height="150" border="0"></a>
    </td>
```

```
      </tr>
    </table>
    <br/>
    <span class="ProductDescription">{$product->mProduct.description}<br/><br/>
    Price:   </span>
    <span class="ProductPrice">${$product->mProduct.price}</span>
    <br/><br/>
    <a class="Link" href="{$product->mPageLink}">Continue Shopping</a>
```

4. Load the web site and click on the picture or name of any product. You should be forwarded to its details page. Figure 4-27 shows an example details page.

Figure 4-27. *Product details for Electric Locomotive*

How It Works: The product Componentized Template

It all starts in index.php, which loads the product.tpl Smarty template in case ProductID appears in the query string:

```
if (isset($_GET['ProductID']))
  $pageContentsCell = "product.tpl";
```

The Smarty template gets the needed information through the members of the Product class, which is made available to the template by the function plugin it loads:

```
{load_product assign="product"}
```

The Product class gets the necessary data at its turn by calling the GetProductDetails method from the business tier class BoCatalog.

Summary

You've done a lot of work in this chapter. You finished building the product catalog by implementing the necessary logic in the data, business, and presentation tiers. On the way, you learned about many new theory issues, including

- Relational data and the types of relationships that can occur between tables

- How to obtain data from multiple tables in a single result set using JOIN, and how to filter the results using WHERE

- How to display the list of categories and products depending on what page the visitor is browsing

- How to display a product details page, and implement the Continue Shopping functionality

- How to implement paging in the products list, when browsing pages containing many products

Chapter 5 will be at least as exciting as this one, because you'll learn how to add search functionality to your web site!

Searching the Catalog

In the previous chapters, you implemented a functional product catalog for TShirtShop. However, it lacks the all-important search feature. Your goal in this chapter is to allow the visitor to search the site for products by entering one or more keywords.

You'll see how easy it is to add new functionality to a working site by integrating the new components into the existing architecture.

In this chapter, you will

- Learn how to use MySQL to implement database searching

- Implement the data tier part of the search feature, which consists of the `Search` method of the `DoCatalog` class

- Implement the business tier part of the search feature, which consists of the `Search` method of the `BoCatalog` class

- Build the user interface using Smarty componentized templates

Choosing How to Search the Catalog

As always, there are a few things you need to think about before starting to code. When analyzing the technical requirements of a new feature you want to add, it's good to look at that feature from the visitor's perspective.

So what kind of search would be most useful for the visitor? Most of the time, the answer to this comes from the customer for whom you are building the site. For the visual part, the answer is fairly simple—all types of searches require a text box where the visitor can enter one or more words to search for.

In the TShirtShop site, the words entered by the visitor will be searched for in the products' names and descriptions. There are a few ways you can treat the text entered by the visitor:

- *Exact-match search*: If the visitor enters an entire phrase, this would be searched in the database as it is, without splitting the words and searching for them separately.

- *All-words search*: The phrase entered by the visitor is split into words, causing a search for products that contain every word entered by the visitor. This is like the exact-match search in that it still searches for all the entered words, but this time the order of the words is no longer important.

- *Any-words search*: Products must contain at least one of the entered words.

This simple classification isn't by any means complete. The search engine can be as complex as the one offered by Google (http://www.google.com), which provides many options and features and shows a ranked list of results, or as simple as searching the database for the exact string provided by the visitor.

TShirtShop will support the any-words and all-words search modes. This decision leads to the visual design of the search feature (see Figure 5-1).

Figure 5-1. *The design of the search feature*

The text box is there, as expected, along with a check box that allows the visitor to choose between an all-words search and an any-words search.

Another decision you need to make here is the way in which the search results are displayed. How should the search results page look? You want to display, after all, a list of products that match the search criteria.

The simplest solution to display the search results would be to reuse the products_list componentized template you built in the previous chapter. A sample search page will look like Figure 5-2.

Figure 5-2. *Sample search results*

You can also see in the figure that the site employs paging. If there are a lot of search results, you'll only present a fixed (but configurable) number of products per page, and allow the visitor to browse through the pages using Previous and Next links.

Let's begin implementing the functionality, by starting, as usual, with the data tier.

Teaching the Database to Search Itself

You have two main options to implement searching in the database:

- Implement searching using WHERE and LIKE

- Search using the full-text search feature in MySQL

Let's analyze these options.

Searching Using WHERE and LIKE

The straightforward solution, frequently used to implement searching, consists of using LIKE in the WHERE clause of the SELECT statement. Let's take a look at a simple example that will return the products having the word "soccer" somewhere in their description:

```
SELECT name FROM product WHERE description LIKE '%soccer%'
```

The LIKE operator matches parts of strings and the percent wildcard (%) is used to specify any string of zero or more characters. That's why in the previous example, the pattern %soccer% matches all records whose description column has the word "soccer" somewhere in it. This search is case-insensitive.

If you want to retrieve all the products that contain the word "soccer" somewhere in the product's name or description, the query will look like this:

```
SELECT name FROM product
WHERE description LIKE '%soccer%' OR name LIKE '%soccer%'
```

This method of searching has the great advantage that it works on any type of MySQL tables (such as InnoDB table type), but has two important drawbacks:

- *Speed*: Because we need to search for text somewhere inside the description and name fields, the entire database must be searched on each query. This can significantly slow down the overall performance of TShirtShop when database searches are performed, especially if you have a large number of products in the database.

- *Flexibility and quality of search results*: This method doesn't make it easy for you to implement various advanced features, such as returning the matching products sorted by search relevance, or filtering results using Boolean logic.

So how can you do better searches? If you have a large database that needs to be searched frequently, how can you search this database without killing your server?

The answer is MySQL's full-text search capabilities.

Searching Using the MySQL Full-Text Search Feature

MySQL full-text search uses special search indexes called FULLTEXT indexes. These are similar to normal indexes (you learned about them in Chapter 2), but they allow searching for text values that have a certain word *inside* them.

■**Tip** Normal indexes applied on text-based columns (such is `varchar` in this case) only improve searches that look for an exact value or for strings that start with a certain letter or word. They behave like that because they index strings as atomic units, and index their characters from left to right. They are useless when you're looking for strings that contain a certain word (substring).

MySQL full-text search is much faster and smarter than the earlier mentioned method (using the `LIKE` operator). Here are its main advantages:

- Search results are ordered based on search relevance, (which is a decimal number in MySQL)

- Words that aren't at least four characters long—such as "and", "so", and so on—are removed by default from the search query.

- MySQL full-text searches can also be performed in Boolean mode. This mode allows you to search words based on AND/OR criteria, such as "+soccer +mexico", which retrieves all the rows that contain both the words "soccer" and "mexico".

- Because of the use of the special search indexes, the search performs much faster than with the `LIKE` method, which scans every row of the data table to find the matching rows

■**Tip** Learn more about the full-text searching capabilities of MySQL at `http://dev.mysql.com/doc/mysql/en/Fulltext_Search.html`.

As explained in Chapter 3, the main disadvantage of the full-text search feature is that it only works with the MyISAM table type, which is quite primitive. The alternative table type you could use is InnoDB, which is more advanced, and supports features such as foreign keys, ACID transactions, and more, but doesn't support the full-text feature.

■**Note** **ACID** is an acronym that describes the four essential properties for database transactions: **A**tomicity, **C**onsistency, **I**solation, and **D**urability. We won't use database transactions in this book, but you can learn more about them from other sources, such as *The Programmer's Guide to SQL* (Apress, 2003).

Teaching MySQL to Do Any-Words Searches

The general MySQL syntax for performing a full-text search is something like this:

```
SELECT (column list)
FROM (table)
WHERE MATCH (column or list of columns) AGAINST (search criteria)
```

Tip The official documentation for the full-text search feature can be found at `http://dev.mysql.com/doc/mysql/en/Fulltext_Search.html`.

The column or list of columns on which you do the search must be full-text indexed. If there is a list of columns, there must be a full-text index that applies to that group of columns.

Because we want TShirtShop to allow visitors to search for products that contain certain words in their names or descriptions, you need to add a full-text index to the (`name`, `description`) pair of fields of the `product` table. (This is different than having two full-text indexes, one on `name` and one on `description`.)

You'll create this index in an exercise, a bit later. Now let's just assume you have a full-text index on the (`name`, `description`) pair of columns. How can you use this full-text index to perform any-words and all-words searches on your products?

Suppose you want to search for these two words: "soccer" and "mexico". In this case, an any-words search should retrieve the products that contain at least one of these words ("soccer" or "mexico") in their (`name`, `description`) pair. The following SQL statement achieves this:

```
SELECT name, description FROM product
WHERE MATCH (name, description) AGAINST ("soccer mexico");
```

Note When doing full-text searches on the (`name`, `description`) pair, you need to have a single full-text index on both the `name` and `description` columns. This doesn't allow giving more relevance to products that have matching words in their names rather than in their description, but this is the fastest full-text searching implementation.

The query results, shown in Figure 5-3, return the records ordered based on search relevance value, the most relevant results being shown first. For example, products that contain both the words "soccer" and "mexico" (or contain more instances of them) are shown higher in the list than products that contain only one of the words.

name	description
Mexico Soccer #1	Mexico Soccer #1 (1969). The Championship games fo...
Mexico Soccer #2	Mexico Soccer #2 (1969). This is the companion T-s...
Monaco Soccer #1	Monaco #1 (1963). This overhead kick commemorates ...
Ruanda Soccer	Ruanda Soccer (1960). This action-packed stamp was...
Hungary Soccer	Hungary Soccer (1950). Haircuts and uniforms have ...
Tanzania Soccer	(Tanzania - 1993). This guy just saved a goal! Ins...
Mali Soccer	Mali Soccer (1964). This T-shirt remembers the 196...

Figure 5-3. *Sample search results*

■**Note** By default, words that aren't at least four characters long are removed from the search query (and are not indexed), but you can change this behavior if you want. For example, if you want three-character words to be searchable, all you have to do is to set the `ft_min_word_len` variable in your MySQL server config file (usually `/etc/my.cnf` in Unix and `\Windows\my.ini` in Windows) like this:

```
[mysqld]
  ft_min_word_len=3
```

Then restart your MySQL server and rebuild your `FULLTEXT` indexes (you'll learn how to do this in the "Creating a Full-Text Index" exercise that follows shortly).

Teaching MySQL to Do All-Words Searches

For an all-words search, you need to retrieve the products that contain all words you're searching for ("soccer" and "mexico" in this case). For all-words searches, you need to use the Boolean mode of the full-text search feature, which allows using AND/OR logic in the search criteria. The new query would look like this:

```
SELECT name, description FROM product
WHERE MATCH (name, description) AGAINST ("+soccer +mexico" IN BOOLEAN MODE)
```

Because Boolean mode searches do not sort rows in order of decreasing relevance by default, in practice you will also need to use an `ORDER BY` clause to implement search results ranking:

```
SELECT name, description FROM product
WHERE MATCH (name,description)
AGAINST ("+soccer +mexico" IN BOOLEAN MODE)
ORDER BY
MATCH (name, description)
AGAINST ("+soccer +mexico" IN BOOLEAN MODE);
```

The leading plus sign marks the required words, so it needs to be added for every word in an all-words search. The results of this query, with your sample database, should look like Figure 5-4.

Figure 5-4. *Sample search results*

MySQL 4.1 Feature: Full-Text Searches with Query Expansion

The full-text search with query expansion feature was introduced in MySQL 4.1.1 and allows MySQL to find products that match not only the words searched for, but also words that are related to the search string.

When searching with query expansion, MySQL performs the search twice behind the scenes. First, it finds the words that are most relevant to the search string and appends those words to the search string, and then the search is performed again.

This method increases the number of search results, but also increases the chance of getting nonrelevant documents. You can see the official documentation of this feature at http://dev.mysql.com/doc/mysql/en/Fulltext_Query_Expansion.html.

To enable query expansion, you need to add `WITH QUERY EXPANSION` to the search criteria as shown in the following code snippet:

```
SELECT name, description FROM product
WHERE MATCH (name,description)
AGAINST ("+soccer +mexico" IN BOOLEAN MODE WITH QUERY EXPANSION)
ORDER BY
MATCH (name, description)
AGAINST ("+soccer +mexico" IN BOOLEAN MODE WITH QUERY EXPANSION);
```

The data tier code presented in the following pages doesn't include this option. If you have MySQL 4.1.1 or a more recent version, feel free to enable full-text query expansion.

Let's now add the two full-text indexes in the following exercise. Afterwards, when implementing the data tier, you'll write the SQL queries for efficient product searches in the database.

Exercise: Creating a Full-Text Index for the product Table

In this exercise, you will add a full-text index on the (name, description) pair of columns of the product table.

1. Load phpMyAdmin, select the tshirtshop database from the Database box, and click the SQL tab.

2. In the form, type the following command, which adds a new full-text index named NameDescFTIndex:

    ```
    ALTER TABLE product ADD FULLTEXT NameDescFTIndex(name,description)
    ```

    After pressing the Go button, you should be informed that the command executed successfully.

■**Note** When changing full-text searching options, such as modifying the value of the `ft_min_word_len` MySQL server variable, you need to rebuild the full-text search indexes. You can do this by either dropping and recreating the index, or using `REPAIR TABLE` (this latter method is recommended):

```
REPAIR TABLE product QUICK;
```

The commands to drop and recreate the index are

```
ALTER TABLE product DROP INDEX NameDescFTIndex;
ALTER TABLE product ADD FULLTEXT NameDescFTIndex(name,description);
```

How It Works: The Full-Text Index

Creating this full-text index enables you to do full-text searches on the indexed fields. To have phpMyAdmin confirm the existence of the new full-text index, click the Structure tab, and click on the Properties icon for the product table as shown in Figure 5-5.

Server: 🖳localhost ⊢ Database: 🖳tshirtshop

| 🏠 Structure | 🔎 SQL | 🗄 Export | 🔍 Search | 🗄 Query | ✖ Drop |

	Table		Action					Records	Type	Size	Overhead
☐	category	📋	🖼	⅀	🏠	✕	🗑	7	MyISAM	2.9 KB	-
☐	department	📋	🖼	⅀	🏠	✕	🗑	3	MyISAM	2.3 KB	-
☐	product	📋	🖼	⅀	🏠	✕	🗑	57	MyISAM	32.6 KB	-
☐	product_category	📋	🖼	⅀	🏠	✕	🗑	56	MyISAM	2.5 KB	-
	4 table(s)		Sum					123	--	40.3 KB	0 Bytes

 Check All / Uncheck All   With selected: ▾

Figure 5-5. *Editing table properties*

In the new window, under the Indexes section (see Figure 5-6), you can see a new index of type FULLTEXT, for both name and description columns.

Indexes: ⑦

Keyname	Type	Cardinality	Action		Field
PRIMARY	PRIMARY	57	✏	✕	product_id
name	FULLTEXT	None	✏	✕	name description

Create an index on `1` columns `Go`

Figure 5-6. *Visualizing the full-text index in phpMyAdmin*

■**Tip** If you had created separate full-text indexes for name and description, they would have been listed separately in the list. Here, a single index object applies on both columns (name and description).

Implementing the Data Tier

Okay, let's start searching for products. Because you already know the SQL logic that makes MySQL come up with wonderful search results, going through the following exercise will be a piece of cake:

Exercise: Implementing the Search Method

Add the following method in your DoCatalog class, located in data_objects/do_catalog.php. Add it to your class and we'll discuss it in the "How it Works" section.

```
// Search product catalog
public function Search($words, $allWords, $pageNo, &$rTotalPages)
```

```
{
  // if $allWords is "on" then we append a "+" to each word in the $words array
  if (strcmp($allWords, "on") == 0)
    for ($i = 0; $i < count($words); $i++)
      $words[$i] = "+" . $words[$i];
  // join the $words array to create a single search string
  $temp_string = $words[0];
  for ($i = 1; $i < count($words); $i++)
    $temp_string = $temp_string . " $words[$i]";
  // build search query
  if (strcmp($allWords, "on") == 0)
    // build all-words search query
    $query_string = "SELECT product_id, name, CONCAT(LEFT(description,"
                    . SHORT_PRODUCT_DESCRIPTION_LENGTH .
                    "),'...') AS description, price, image_file_1
                    FROM product
                    WHERE MATCH (name,description)
                    AGAINST (\"$temp_string\" IN BOOLEAN MODE)
                    ORDER BY MATCH (name,description)
                    AGAINST (\"$temp_string\" IN BOOLEAN MODE)";
  else
    // built any-words search query
    $query_string = "SELECT product_id, name, CONCAT(LEFT(description,"
                    . SHORT_PRODUCT_DESCRIPTION_LENGTH .
                    "),'...') AS description, price, image_file_1
                    FROM product
                    WHERE MATCH (name,description)
                      AGAINST (\"$temp_string\")";
  // call CreateSubpageQuery to implement paging
  $page_query = $this->CreateSubpageQuery($query_string, $pageNo,
                                          $rTotalPages);
  // execute the query and return the results
  return $this->dbManager->DbGetAll($page_query);
}
```

How It Works: The Data Tier Search Method

The Search method in DoCatalog executes the actual database search. It receives four parameters:

- $words is an array containing the words being searched for.

- $allWords is "on" in case an all-words search is necessary, and has other value otherwise.

- $pageNo represents the page of products being requested.

- $rTotalPages represents the number of pages.

You already know how $pageNo and $rTotalPages work from the examples in Chapter 4.

The query starts by appending a "+" to each word in case it's an any-words search (this is necessary because of the way SQL full-text queries look, as shown earlier in the chapter):

```
// if $allWords is "on" then we append a "+" to each word in the $words array
if (strcmp($allWords, "on") == 0)
  for ($i = 0; $i < count($words); $i++)
    $words[$i] = "+" . $words[$i];
```

You then join all the words back to a single string variable named $temp_string:

```
// join the $words array to create a single search string
$temp_string = $words[0];
for ($i = 1; $i < count($words); $i++)
  $temp_string = $temp_string . " $words[$i]";
```

You use the string containing the words to search for to create the SQL query in a variable named $query_string, which is then parsed by CreateSubpageQuery to implement paging and then executed using the DbGetAll method of the DbManager class:

```
// call CreateSubpageQuery to implement paging
$page_query = $this->CreateSubpageQuery($query_string, $pageNo,
                                        $rTotalPages);
// execute the query and return the results
return $this->dbManager->DbGetAll($page_query);
```

The really important part of the method is the SQL query string that performs the full-text search. After you understand how that works, and the paging feature you learned about in Chapter 4, this method shouldn't be a mystery to you.

Implementing the Business Tier

The business tier of the search feature consists of a method called Search, which at its turn calls the Search method of the data tier. Let's implement it first and discuss how it works afterwards.

Exercise: Implementing the Search Method

Before actually writing the Search method, you need to take care of some details.

1. The full-text search feature automatically removes words that are shorter than a specified length. You need to tell the visitor which words have been removed when doing searches. First, find out the specified length by interrogating the MySQL ft_min_word_len variable. Use phpMyAdmin to execute the following SQL statement in the tshirtshop database:

   ```
   SHOW VARIABLES LIKE 'ft_min_word_len'
   ```

   If you haven't changed the default value, ft_min_word_len should be 4 (see Figure 5-7).

Variable_name	Value
ft_min_word_len	4

Figure 5-7. *Visualizing the full-text index in phpMyAdmin*

2. Now you need to save the value of ft_min_word_len you just found to some place easily accessible from the business tier code. This allows you to easily inform the visitors which words were actually used for searching, and which were omitted. Open config.inc.php and add the following line:

```
// minimum word length for searches; this constant must be kept in sync
// with the ft_min_word_len MySQL variable
define("FT_MIN_WORD_LEN",4);
```

3. Add the following class in bo_catalog.php, but not inside the BoCatalog class (for clarity, preferably just before the BoCatalog class). You'll use this class to wrap the search results information and send it from the business tier to the presentation tier.

```
// Class that stores the results of a product catalog search
class SearchResults
{
  public $mProducts; // list of products
  public $mSearchedWords; // words used for searching
  public $mIgnoredWords; // words that were ignored
}
```

The $mProducts attribute contains the associative array with the products that matched the search. The words that have been accepted for the search are placed in the $mSearchedWords variable and the status of this search will be placed in the $mStatus variable to be used in the presentation tier.

4. Finally, add the Search method to your BoCatalog class:

```
// Search the catalog
public function Search($searchString, $allWords, $pageNo, &$rTotalPages)
{
  // create an instance of SearchResults
  $search_results = new SearchResults();
  // search string delimiters
  $delimiters = ",.; ";
  /* on the first call to strtok you supply the whole search string
  and the list of delimiters. It returns the first word of the string */
  $word = strtok($searchString, $delimiters);
  $accepted_words = array();
  $ignored_words = array();
  // parse the search string word by word until there are no more words
  while ($word)
  {
    // short words are added to the ignored_words lists
```

```
          if (strlen($word) < FT_MIN_WORD_LEN)
            $ignored_words[] = $word;
          else
            $accepted_words[] = $word;
          // get the next word of the search string
          $word = strtok($delimiters);
        }
        // if there are any accepted words...
        if (count($accepted_words))
        {
          // get the search results by calling the data tier Search method
          $search_results->mProducts = $this->mDoCatalog->Search
          ($accepted_words, $allWords, $pageNo, $rTotalPages);
        }
        // save the list of accepted words and ignored words
        if ($accepted_words != null)
          $search_results->mSearchedWords = implode(", ", $accepted_words);
        if ($ignored_words != null)
          $search_results->mIgnoredWords = implode(", ", $ignored_words);
        // return results
        return $search_results;
      }
```

How It Works: The Business Tier Search Method

The main purpose of this method is to analyze which words will and will not be used for searching.

The full-text feature of MySQL automatically filters the words that are less than four letters by default, and you don't interfere with this behavior in the business tier. However, you need to find out which words will be ignored by MySQL so you can inform the visitor.

The Search method of the business tier is called from the presentation tier with the following parameters (notice all of them except the first one are the same as the parameters of the data tier Search method):

- $searchString contains the search string entered by the visitor.

- $allWords is "on" in case an all-words search is necessary, and has other value otherwise.

- $pageNo represents the page of products being requested.

- $rTotalPages represents the number of pages.

The method returns the results to the presentation tier in the form of a SearchResults class:

```
// Class that stores the results of a product catalog search
class SearchResults
{
  public $mProducts; // list of products
  public $mSearchedWords; // words used for searching
  public $mIgnoredWords; // words that were ignored
}
```

To see what words are shorter than a given size, the search string is split into separate words using the strtok function. When calling this function for the first time, you need to pass the whole string to be split, and a string containing the splitting characters, and the strtok function will return the first word in the string. On subsequent calls, you just need to supply the splitting characters:

```
/* on the first call to strtok you supply the whole search string
and the list of delimiters. It returns the first word of the string */
$word = strtok($searchString, $delimiters);
$accepted_words = array();
$ignored_words = array();
// parse the search string word by word until there are no more words
while ($word)
{
  // short words are added to the ignored_words lists
  if (strlen($word) < FT_MIN_WORD_LEN)
    $ignored_words[] = $word;
  else
    $accepted_words[] = $word;
  // get the next word of the search string
  $word = strtok($delimiters);
}
```

The words that will be used for full-text searching are saved in a new array named $accepted_words, whereas the others are saved in an array named $ignored_words. The list of accepted words is sent to the data tier for performing the full-text search:

```
// if there are any accepted words...
if (count($accepted_words))
{
  // get the search results by calling the data tier Search method
  $search_results->mProducts = $this->mDoCatalog->Search
  ($accepted_words, $allWords, $pageNo, $rTotalPages);
}
```

You could send the complete list of words to the data tier, but this would have made no difference—the words that are saved in $ignored_words would have been ignored by MySQL anyway.

The $ignored_words and $accepted_words lists are transformed into strings using the implode function; these strings together with the search results products are saved to a SearchResults object, which is returned to the calling method of the presentation tier:

```
// save the list of accepted words and ignored words
if ($accepted_words != null)
  $search_results->mSearchedWords = implode(", ", $accepted_words);
if ($ignored_words != null)
  $search_results->mIgnoredWords = implode(", ", $ignored_words);
// return results
return $search_results;
}
```

Implementing the Presentation Tier

Yep, it's time to see some colors in front of your eyes!

The Search Catalog feature has two separate interface elements that you need to implement. The first one is the place where the visitor enters the search string. As you have already seen, it looks like Figure 5-8.

Figure 5-8. *The search box*

This part of the user interface will be implemented as a separate componentized template named search_box, whose role is to provide the means to enter the search string for the visitor.

The other part of the user interface consists of a componentized template named search_results, which displays the products matching the search criteria (see Figure 5-9).

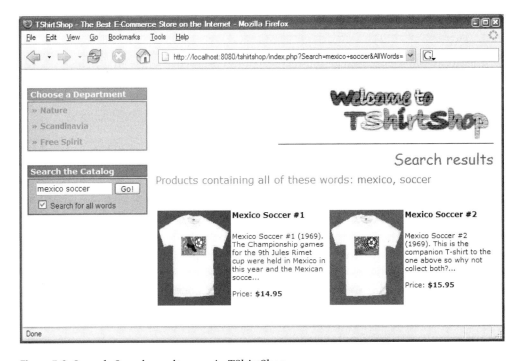

Figure 5-9. *Sample Search results page in TShirtShop*

You'll create the two componentized templates in two separate exercises.

Exercise: Creating the search_box Componentized Template

Follow these steps to create the search_box componentized template:

1. Create a new template file named search_box.tpl in the templates folder and add the following code to it:

```
{* search_box.tpl *}
{load_search_box assign="search_box"}
<br />
<table border="0" cellpadding="0" cellspacing="1" width="200">
 <tr>
  <td class="SearchBoxHead"> Search the Catalog </td>
 </tr>
 <tr>
  <td class="SearchBoxContent">
   <form action="index.php">
    <input class="SearchBox" maxlength="100" id="Search" name="Search"
           value="{$search_box->mSearchString}" size="18"/>
    <input class="SearchBox" type="submit" value="Go!"/><br />
    <input type="checkbox" id="AllWords"  name="AllWords"
    {if $search_box->mAllWords == "on" } checked="checked" {/if}/>
      Search for all words
   </form>
  </td>
 </tr>
</table>
{* end search_box.tpl *}
```

2. Create a new smarty function plugin file named function.load_search_box.php in the smarty_plugins folder with the following code in it:

```
<?php
// plugin functions inside plugin files must be named: smarty_type_name
function smarty_function_load_search_box($params, $smarty)
{
  $search_box = new SearchBox();
  // assign template variable
  $smarty->assign($params['assign'], $search_box);
}
// class that manages the search box
class SearchBox
{
  /* public variables for the smarty template */
  public $mSearchString = "";
  public $mAllWords = "off";
  /* constructor */
  function __construct()
  {
```

```
    $this->mBoCatalog = new BoCatalog();
    if (isset($_GET['Search']))
      $this->mSearchString = $_GET['Search'];
    if (isset($_GET['AllWords']))
      $this->mAllWords = $_GET['AllWords'];
  }
} //end class
?>
```

3. Add the following styles needed in the preceding template file to the `tshirtshop.css` file:

```
.SearchBoxHead
{
  border-right: #0468a4 2px solid;
  border-top: #0468a4 2px solid;
  border-bottom: #0468a4 2px solid;
  border-left: #0468a4 2px solid;
  background-color: #0583b5;
  font-family: Verdana, Arial;
  font-weight: bold;
  font-size: 10pt;
  color: #f5f5dc;
  padding-left: 3px
}
.SearchBoxContent
{
  border-right: #0468a4 2px solid;
  border-top: #0468a4 2px solid;
  border-left: #0468a4 2px solid;
  border-bottom: #0468a4 2px solid;
  background-color: #8bc8dd;
  font-family: Arial, Verdana;
  font-size: 9pt;
  color: darkblue;
  padding-top: 5px;
  padding-left: 12px;
  padding-bottom: 5px
}
.SearchBox
{
  font-family: Verdana, Helvetica, sans-serif;
  font-size: 9pt;
  margin-bottom: 5px
}
```

4. Modify the `index.tpl` file to load the newly created template file:

...

```
{include file="departments_list.tpl"}
{include file="$categoriesCell"}
{include file="search_box.tpl"}
```

...

5. Load your project in a browser and you'll see the search box resting nicely in its place (see Figure 5-10).

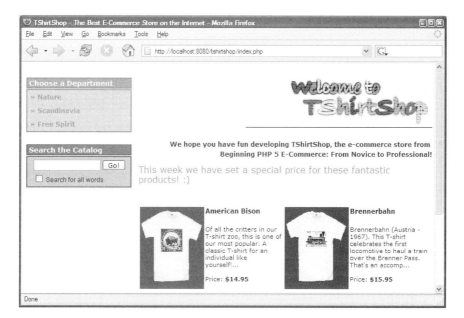

Figure 5-10. *The Search Box in action*

How It Works: The search_box Componentized Template

By now you're used to the way we use function plugins in conjunction with Smarty templates. In this case, we use the plugin to maintain the state of the search box after performing a search. When the page is reloaded after clicking the Go! button, we want to keep the entered string in the text box and also maintain the state of the AllWords check box.

The `load_search_box` function plugin simply saves the values of the Search and AllWords query string parameters, while checking to make sure these parameters actually exist in the query string. These values are then used in the `search_box.tpl` Smarty template to recreate the previous controls' state.

Note that we could have implemented this functionality by reading the values of the Search and AllWords query string parameters using $smarty.get.Search and $smarty.get.AllWords instead of a plugin. However, having a plugin gives you more control over the process, and also avoids generating warnings in case the mentioned parameters don't exist in the query string.

Exercise: Creating the search_results Componentized Template

In this exercise, you'll create the componentized template that displays the search results. To make your life easier, you can reuse the product_list componentized template to display the actual list of products. This is the componentized template that we have used so far to list products for the main page, for departments, and for categories. Of course, if you want to have the search results displayed in another format, you must create another user control.

You'll need to modify the templates-logic file of the products list (products_list.php) to recognize when it's being called to display search results, so it calls the correct method of the business tier to get the list of products.

Let's create the search_result template and update the templates-logic of the products_list componentized template, in the following exercise:

1. Create a new template file in the templates directory named search_results.tpl, and add the following to it:

```
{* search_results.tpl *}
<p align="right">
  <span class="DepartmentTitle">Search results</span>
</p>
<p align="left">
  {include file="products_list.tpl"}
</p>
```

2. Modify the smarty_plugins/function.load_products_list.php file by adding the following lines at the end of the constructor method of the ProductList class (__construct):

```
// get Search from query string
if (isset($_GET['Search']))
  $this->mSearchString=$_GET['Search'];
// get AllWords from query string
if (isset($_GET['AllWords']))
  $this->mAllWords=$_GET['AllWords'];
```

3. Add the $mSearchResultsTitle, $mSearch, and $mAllWords members to the ProductsList class:

```
class ProductsList
{
  /* public variables to be read from smarty template */
  public $mProducts;
  public $mPageNo;
  public $mrTotalPages;
  public $mNextLink;
  public $mPreviousLink;
  public $mSearchResultsTitle;
  public $mSearch = "";
  public $mAllWords = "off";
```

4. Modify the init method in ProductsList like this:

```
/* init */
function init()
{
  // if searching the catalog, get the list of products by calling
  // the Search busines tier method
  if (isset($this->mSearchString))
  {
    // get a SearchResults object
    $search_results = $this->mBoCatalog->Search(
                          $this->mSearchString, $this->mAllWords,
                          $this->mPageNo, $this->mrTotalPages);
    // get the list of products from the SearchResults object
    $this->mProducts = & $search_results->mProducts;
    // build the title for the list of products
    if (!empty($search_results->mSearchedWords))
        $this->mSearchResultsTitle =
          "Products containing <font color=\"red\">"
          . ($this->mAllWords == "on" ? "all" : "any") . "</font>"
          . " of these words: <font color=\"red\">"
          . $search_results->mSearchedWords . "</font><br>";
    if (!empty($search_results->mIgnoredWords))
        $this->mSearchResultsTitle .=
          "Ignored words: <font color=\"red\">"
          . $search_results->mIgnoredWords . "</font><br/>";
    if (empty($search_results->mProducts))
        $this->mSearchResultsTitle .=
          "Your search generated no results.<br/>";
    $this->mSearchResultsTitle .= "<br/>";
  }
  // if browsing a category, get the list of products by calling
  // the GetProductsInCategory business tier method
  elseif (isset($this->mCategoryId))
    $this->mProducts = $this->mBoCatalog->GetProductsInCategory($this
      ->mCategoryId, $this->mPageNo, $this->mrTotalPages);
  ...
```

5. Add the following line in products_list.tpl, just below the load_products_list line:

```
{* products_list.tpl *}
{load_products_list assign="products_list"}
<span class="ListDescription">{$products_list->mSearchResultsTitle}
</span>
```

6. Modify the index.php file to load the search_results componentized template when a search is performed, by adding these lines:

```
...
if (isset($_GET['DepartmentID']))
{
  $pageContentsCell = "department.tpl";
  $categoriesCell = "categories_list.tpl";
}
if (isset($_GET['Search']))
  $pageContentsCell="search_results.tpl";
if (isset($_GET['ProductID']))
  $pageContentsCell = "product.tpl";
$page->assign("pageContentsCell", $pageContentsCell);
$page->assign("categoriesCell", $categoriesCell);
...
```

7. Load your project in your favorite browser and type **mexico** to get an output similar to Figure 5-11.

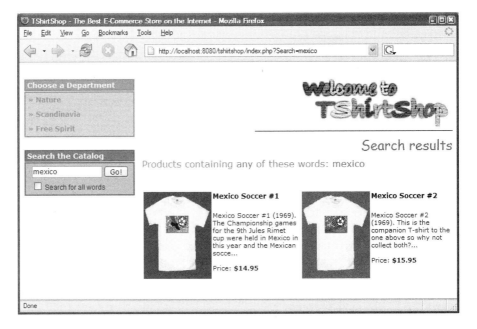

Figure 5-11. *Sample TShirtShop search results page*

How It Works: The Searchable Product Catalog

Congratulations, you have a searchable product catalog! There was quite a bit to write, but the code wasn't very complicated, was it?

Because you've used much of the already existing code and added bits to the already working architecture, there weren't any surprises. The list of products is still displayed by the `products_list` template you built earlier, which is now updated to recognize the Search element in the query string, in which case it uses the `Search` method of the business tier to get the list of products for the visitor.

The `Search` method of the business tier returns a `SearchResults` object that contains, apart from the list of returned products, the list of words that were used for searching, and the list of words that were ignored (words shorter than a predefined number of characters). These details are shown to the visitor.

Summary

In this chapter, you implemented the search functionality of TShirtShop by using the full-text searching functionality of MySQL. The search mechanism integrated very well with the current web site structure, and the paging functionality built in Chapter 4. The most interesting new detail you learned in this chapter was about performing full-text searches with MySQL. This was also the first instance where the business tier had some functionality of its own instead of simply passing data back and forth between the data tier and the presentation tier.

In Chapter 6, you'll learn how to sell your products using PayPal.

■■■

CHAPTER 6

Receiving Payments Using PayPal

Let's collect some money! Your e-commerce web site needs a way to receive payments from customers. The preferred solution for established companies is to open a merchant account, but many small businesses choose to start with a solution that's simpler to implement, where they don't have to process credit card or payment information themselves.

A number of companies and web sites can help individuals or small businesses that don't have the resources to process credit cards and wire transactions. These companies can be used to intermediate the payment between online businesses and their customers. Many of these payment-processing companies are relatively new and the handling of any individual's financial details is very sensitive. Additionally, a quick search on the Internet will produce reports from both satisfied and unsatisfied customers for almost all of these companies. For these reasons, we are not recommending any third-party company.

Instead, this chapter lists some of the companies currently providing these services, and then demonstrates some of the functionality they provide with PayPal. You'll learn how to integrate PayPal with TShirtShop in the first two stages of development. In this chapter, you will

- Learn how to create a new PayPal account

- Learn how to integrate PayPal in stage 1 of development, where you'll need a shopping cart and custom checkout mechanism

- Learn how to integrate PayPal in stage 2 of development, where you'll have your own shopping cart, so you'll need to guide the visitor directly to a payment page

- Learn how to configure PayPal to automatically calculate shipping costs

---

Note This chapter is not a PayPal manual, but a quick guide to using PayPal. For any complex queries about the services provided, please contact PayPal (http://www.paypal.com), or the Internet Payment Service Provider you decide to use.

Considering Internet Payment Service Providers

Take a look at this list of Internet Payment Service Provider web sites. This is a diverse group, each having its advantages. Some of the providers transfer money person to person and payments need to be verified manually; others have sophisticated integration with your web site. Some work anywhere on the globe, while others work only for a single country.

The following list is not complete—you can find more detailed lists of payment systems on a number of web sites, such as `http://www.online-payment-processing.com`, or `http://www.computerbits.com/archive/2003/0800/credicards.html`.

- *2Checkout*: `http://www.2checkout.com`

- *AnyPay*: `http://www.anypay.com`

- *CCNow*: `http://www.ccnow.com`

- *Electronic Transfer*: `http://www.electronictransfer.com`

- *Moneybookers*: `http://www.moneybookers.com`

- *MultiCards*: `http://www.multicards.com`

- *Pay By Web*: `http://www.paybyweb.com`

- *Paymate*: `http://www.paymate.com.au`

- *PayPal*: `http://www.paypal.com`

- *PaySystems:* `http://www.paysystems.com`

- *ProPay*: `http://www.propay.com`

- *QuickPayPro*: `http://www.quickpaypro.com`

- *WorldPay*: `http://worldpay.com`

For the demonstration in this chapter, we chose to use PayPal. Apart from being popular, PayPal offers services that fit very well into our web site for the first two stages of development. PayPal is available in a number of countries—the most up-to-date list can be found at `http://www.paypal.com`.

For the first stage of development (the current stage)—where you only have a searchable product catalog—and with only a few lines of HTML code, PayPal enables you to add a shopping cart with checkout functionality. For the second stage of development, in which you will implement your own shopping cart, PayPal has a feature called Single Item Purchases that can be used to send the visitor directly to a payment page without the intermediate shopping cart. You'll use this feature of PayPal in Chapter 9.

For a summary of the features provided by PayPal, point your browser to `http://www.paypal.com` and click the `Merchant Tools` link. That page contains a few other useful links that will show you the main features available.

Getting Started with PayPal

Probably the best description of this service is the one found on its web site: "PayPal is an account-based system that lets anyone with an email address securely send and receive online payments using their credit card or bank account."

PayPal is one of the companies that allow a small business like the TShirtShop electronic store to receive payments from its customers. The visitor, instead of paying the client directly, pays PayPal using a credit card or bank account. The client then uses its PayPal account to get the money received from the customers. At the time of writing, there is no cost involved in creating a new PayPal account and the service is free for the buyer. The fees involved when receiving money are shown at `http://www.paypal.com/cgi-bin/webscr?cmd=_display-fees-outside`.

Visit the PayPal web site to get updated and complete information, and, of course, visit its competitors before making a decision for your own e-commerce site. Be sure to check which of the services are available in your country, and what kind of credit cards and payment methods each company accepts.

If you want to use PayPal beyond the exercises with TShirtShop, you'll want to learn more about its service. On the main PayPal web page, click the `Help` link, which opens up the Help pages. These pages are well structured and provide a search feature. You might also want to check the PayPal Developer Network site at `https://www.paypal.com/pdn`. Another useful web site for PayPal developers is `http://www.paypaldev.org`, which according to the site is an "independent forum for PayPal developers." This web site provides a number of useful links, including links to the five PayPal manuals in PDF format (Single Item Purchases, Shopping Cart, Instant Payment Notification, Donations, Subscriptions).

In the following exercises, you'll create a new PayPal account, and then integrate it with TShirtShop.

■**Tip** The steps to create a PayPal account are also described in more detail in the PayPal manuals mentioned earlier.

Exercise: Creating the PayPal Account

To create your PayPal account, follow these steps:

1. Browse to `http://www.paypal.com` using your favorite web browser.

2. Click the `Sign Up` link.

3. PayPal supports two account types: Personal and Business. To receive credit card payments, you need to open a Business account. Choose your country from the combo box, and click Continue.

4. Complete all of the requested information and you will receive an email asking you to revisit the PayPal site to confirm the details you have entered.

How It Works: The PayPal Account

After the PayPal account is set up, the email address you provided will be your PayPal ID.

A lot of functionality is available within the PayPal service—because the site is easy to use and many of the functions are self-explanatory, we won't describe everything here. Remember that these sites are there for your business, so they're more than happy to assist with any of your queries.

Now let's see how you can actually use the new account for the web site.

Integrating the PayPal Shopping Cart and Checkout

In the first stage of development (the current stage), you need to integrate the shopping cart and checkout functionality from PayPal. In the second stage of development, after you create your own shopping cart, you'll only need to rely on PayPal's checkout mechanism.

To accept payments, you need to add two important elements to the user interface (UI) part of the site: Add to Cart buttons for each product and a View Cart button somewhere on the page. PayPal makes adding these buttons a piece of cake.

The functionality of those buttons is performed by secure links to the PayPal web site. For example, the following form represents the Add to Cart button for a product named "American Bison" that costs $14.00:

```
<form target="paypal" action="https://www.paypal.com/cgi-bin/webscr"
    method="post">
<input type="hidden" name="cmd" value="_cart">
<input type="hidden" name="business" value="your_email_address">
<input type="hidden" name="item_name" value="American Bison">
<input type="hidden" name="amount" value="14.00">
<input type="image" src="images/add_to_cart.gif" name="submit">
<input type="hidden" name="add" value="1">
</form>
```

■**Note** The fields are predefined and their names are self-explanatory. The most important is business, which must be the email address you used when you registered the PayPal account (the email address that will receive the money). Consult PayPal's Shopping Cart Manual for more details. You can download it at https://www.paypal.com/en_US/pdf/shopping_cart.pdf.

You need to make sure this HTML code gets added to each product, so you'll have Add to Cart buttons for each product. To do this, you must modify the products_list.tpl file. Next, you'll add the View Cart button somewhere on index.tpl, so it will be accessible at any time for the visitor.

Tip Although we won't use them for our site, it's good to know that PayPal provides button generators based on certain data you provide (product name, product price), giving you an HTML block similar to the one shown previously. Click the Developers link at the bottom of the first page and then click PayPal Solutions in the menu on the left to find the button generators.

After adding the Add to Cart and View Cart buttons, the web site will look like Figure 6-1.

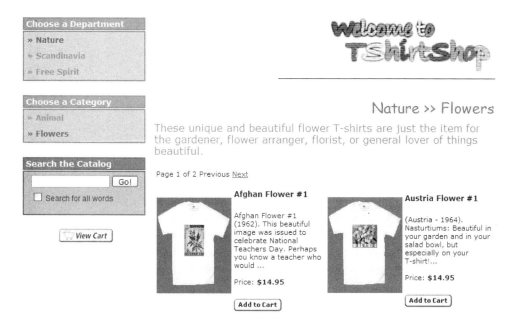

Figure 6-1. *TShirtShop with Add to Cart and View Cart buttons*

You'll implement the PayPal integration in the next exercise.

Exercise: Integrating the PayPal Shopping Cart and Custom Checkout

To add the PayPal shopping cart to TShirtShop, follow these steps:

1. Open index.tpl and add the OpenPayPalWindow JavaScript function inside the <head> element, as shown in the following code listing. This function is used to open the PayPal shopping cart window when the visitor clicks on one of the Add to Cart buttons.

```
<head>
  <title>{#sitetitle#}</title>
  <link href="tshirtshop.css" type="text/css" rel="stylesheet"/>
  {literal}
  <script language="JavaScript" type="text/javascript">
  <!--
```

```
    var PayPalWindow = null;
    function OpenPayPalWindow(url)
    {
      if ((!PayPalWindow) || PayPalWindow.closed)
        // If the PayPal window doesn't exist, we open it
        PayPalWindow = window.open(url,"cart","height=300, width=500");
      else
      {
        // If the PayPal window exists, we make it show
        PayPalWindow.location.href = url;
        PayPalWindow.focus();
      }
    }
    // -->
    </script>
    {/literal}
  </head>
```

■**Note** Any JavaScript code you place in a Smarty template should be enclosed between {literal} and {/literal} elements because the JavaScript code uses { and } characters, which are the default delimiters for Smarty. This way, Smarty will not parse your JavaScript code.

---

2. Now, add the View Cart button on the main page, just below the search box. Open index.tpl and modify it like this:

```
<td valign="top" height="100%">
  <br />
  {include file="departments_list.tpl"}
  {include file="$categoriesCell"}
  {include file="search_box.tpl"}
  <br />
        
         
  <a href=
  "JavaScript: OpenPayPalWindow('https://www.paypal.com/cgi-bin/webscr?
        cmd=_cart
        &amp;business=youremail@yourserver.com
        &amp;display=1
        &amp;return=www.yourwebsite.com
        &amp;cancel_return=www.yourwebsite.com')">
```

```
   <img src="images/view_cart.gif" border="0" alt="view cart"/>
  </a>
</td>
```

■**Note** You must write the `OpenPayPalWindow` call on a single line in the HTML source. We split it on multiple lines in the code snippet to make it easier to read.

---

3. Add the PayPal Add to Cart button in `products_list.tpl`, just below the product price:

```
<br /><br />
<a href=
  "JavaScript: OpenPayPalWindow('https://www.paypal.com/cgi-bin/webscr?
    cmd=_cart
    &amp;business=youremail@yourserver.com
    &amp;item_name=' + escape('{$products_list->mProducts[k].name}') +
    '&amp;amount={$products_list->mProducts[k].price}
    &amp;add=1
    &amp;return=www.yourwebsite.com
    &amp;cancel_return=www.yourwebsite.com')">
 <img src="images/add_to_cart.gif" border="0" alt="add to cart"/>
</a>
```

■**Note** You must write the `OpenPayPalWindow` call on a single line in the HTML source. We split it on multiple lines in the code snippet to make it easier to read.

---

4. Make sure you replace `youremail@yourserver.com` with the email address you submitted when you created your PayPal account for both Add to Cart and View Cart buttons! Also, replace `www.yourwebsite.com` with the address of your e-commerce store Alternatively, you can remove the `return` and `cancel_return` variables if you don't want PayPal to redirect to your web site after the customer completes or cancels a payment.

■**Caution** You need to use the correct email address if you want the money to get into your account!

---

5. Load the `index.php` page in a browser, and click one of the Add to Cart buttons. You should get the PayPal shopping cart, which looks like Figure 6-2.

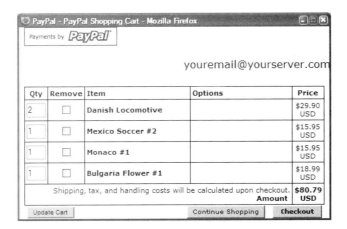

Figure 6-2. *Integrating the PayPal shopping cart*

Experiment with the PayPal shopping cart to see that it works as advertised.

How It Works: PayPal Integration

Yes, it was just that simple. Now, all visitors are potential customers! They can click the Checkout button of the PayPal shopping cart, and then buy the products!

For building the PayPal call, we use the `escape` JavaScript command to ensure the product's name is correctly formed in case it contains nonportable characters (such as #). See more details about the escape method at `http://www.devguru.com/Technologies/ecmascript/quickref/escape.html` or in your favorite JavaScript reference.

■**Note** You can add a `currency_code` field to the PayPal Add to Cart link to specify the currency in which the product's price will appear. If you omit this field, it defaults to the currency of your primary balance. A shopping cart can't contain products with different currencies. At the time of this writing, accepted values for the `currency_code` field are USD (US Dollar), EUR (Euro), GBP (Pound Sterling), CAD (Canadian Dollar) and JPY (Yen). Check PayPal's shopping cart manual for updated information.

After a customer makes a payment on the web site, an email notification is sent to the email address registered on PayPal, and also to the customer. Your PayPal account will reflect the payment, and you can view the transaction information in your account history or as a part of the history transaction log.

After PayPal confirms the payment, you can ship the products to your customer.

Caution On each payment, you need to carefully check that the product prices correspond to the correct amounts, because it's very easy for anyone to add a fake product to the shopping cart, or an existing product with a modified price. This can be done by fabricating one of those PayPal `Add to Cart` links and navigating to it. You can read a detailed article about this problem at `http://www.alphabetware.com/pptamper.asp`.

We touched on a few of the details of the PayPal shopping cart, but for a complete description of its functionality, you should read the PayPal Shopping Cart manual, which is available for download at `https://www.paypal.com/en_US/pdf/shopping_cart.pdf`.

If you decide to use PayPal for your own web site, make sure you learn about all of its features. For example, you can teach PayPal to automatically calculate shipping costs and tax for each order.

Using the PayPal Single Item Purchases Feature

Single Item Purchases is a PayPal feature that allows you to send the visitor directly to a payment page instead of the PayPal shopping cart. The PayPal shopping cart will become useless in Chapter 8, where you'll create your own shopping cart.

In Chapter 9, you'll implement the "Place Order" button in the shopping cart, which saves the order into the database and forwards to a PayPal payment page. To call the PayPal payment page (bypassing the PayPal shopping cart), you redirect to a link like the following:

```
https://www.paypal.com/xclick/business=youremail@yourserver.com&item_name=Order#1
23&item_number=123&amount=$123
```

The latest version of the PayPal Single Item Purchases manual can be found at `https://www.paypal.com/en_US/pdf/single_item.pdf`, which includes all the options available for this feature.

Tip You will create your own complete order-processing system in the third phase of development (starting with Chapter 12), where you'll process credit card transactions.

When you implement the PayPal Single Item Purchases in Chapter 9 (just after creating the Place Order button), you'll need to add the following code at the beginning of the init() method from the ShoppingCart class, in smarty_plugins/function.load_shopping_cart.php:

```
// calculate the total amount for the shopping cart
$this->mTotalAmount = $this->mShoppingCart->GetTotalAmount();
// if the Place Order button was clicked...
if(isset($_POST['place_order']))
{
  // create the order and get the order ID
  $order_id = $this->mShoppingCart->CreateOrder();
  // this will contain the PayPal link
  $redirect =
    "https://www.paypal.com/xclick/business=youremail@server.com" .
    "&item_name=TShirtShop Order " . $order_id .
    "&item_number=" . $order_id .
    "&amount=" . $this->mTotalAmount .
    "&return=http://www.YourWebSite.com" .
    "&cancel_return=http://www.YourWebSite.com";
  // redirection to the payment page
  header("Location: " . $redirect);
  exit;
}
```

Of course, don't forget to replace youremail@server.com with your registered PayPal email address, and http://www.YourWebSite.com with the address of your e-commerce store. The return and cancel_return parameters specify the web pages to return to after the payment is made or canceled. Figure 6-3 shows the PayPal Single Item Purchase screen.

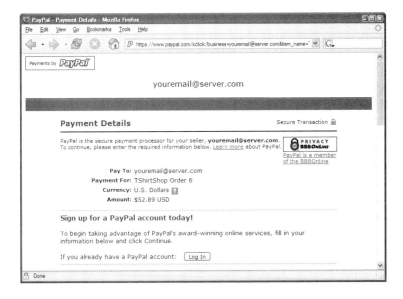

Figure 6-3. *The PayPal Single Item Purchase screen*

Summary

In this chapter, you saw how to integrate PayPal into an e-commerce site—a simple payment solution that many small businesses choose so they don't have to process credit card or payment information themselves.

First, we listed some of the alternatives to PayPal, before guiding you through the creation of a new PayPal account. We then covered how to integrate PayPal in stages 1 and 2 of development, first discussing a shopping cart, a custom checkout mechanism, and then how to direct the visitor directly to the payment page.

In the next chapter, we will move on to look at a catalog administration page for TShirtShop.

CHAPTER 7

■■■

Catalog Administration

In the previous chapters, you worked with catalog information that already existed in the database. You have probably inserted some records yourself, or maybe you downloaded the department, category, and product information from the book's accompanying source code. Obviously, for a real web site both ways are unacceptable, so you need to write some code to allow easy management of the web store data. That said, the final detail to take care of before launching a web site is to create its administrative interface. Although visitors will never see this part, it's key to delivering a quality web site to your client.

In this chapter, you'll implement a catalog administration page. With this feature, you complete the first stage of your web site's development! Because this page can be implemented in many ways, a serious discussion with the client is required to get the specific list of required features. In our case, the catalog administration page should allow your client to do the following:

- Add and remove departments

- Modify existing departments' information (name, description)

- View the list of categories that belong to a department

- Manage department categories

- Edit existing categories' information (name, description)

- View the list of products in a specific category

- Edit product details

- Assign an existing product to an additional category (a product can belong to multiple categories), or move it to another category

- View the categories a department is associated with

- Remove a product from a category

- Delete a product from the catalog

The administration page also must require a username and password, so only the site administrators can perform administrative tasks.

Previewing the Catalog Administration Page

Although the long list of objectives might look intimidating at first, it is easy to implement. We have already covered most of the theory in the previous chapters, but you'll still learn quite a bit in this chapter.

The first step toward creating the catalog administration page is to create a login mechanism, which will be implemented as a simple login page that you can see in Figure 7-1.

Figure 7-1. *The TShirtShop login page*

Next, you build the site administration part of the site by creating its main page (catalog_admin.php), its associated Smarty template (catalog_admin.tpl), and a number of componentized templates that it uses (admin_departments, admin_categories, admin_products, and admin_product_details).

After logging in, the administrator is presented with the list of departments (generated by the admin_departments Smarty template, which is loaded from the main admin page, catalog_admin.php), as shown in Figure 7-2.

The functionality you'll implement for departments is much the same as you'll see for categories and products. More specifically, the administrator can

- Edit the department's name or description by clicking the Edit button.

- Edit the categories for a specific department by clicking the Edit Categories button.

- Completely remove a department from the database by clicking the Delete button (this works only if the department has no related categories).

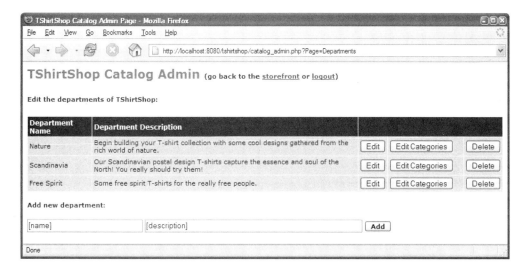

Figure 7-2. *The TShirtShop departments admin page*

When clicking the Edit button, the corresponding row from the table enters edit mode and its fields become editable, as shown in Figure 7-3. Also, as you can see, instead of the Edit button, you get Update and Cancel buttons. Clicking Update updates the database with the changes, while clicking Cancel simply quits edit mode.

Figure 7-3. *Editing department information*

The administrator can add new departments by entering the new department's name and description in the text boxes below the table, and clicking the Add button.

When the administrator clicks the Edit Categories button, the `catalog_admin.php` page is reloaded, but with an additional parameter in the query string: `DepartmentID`. This parameter tells `catalog_admin.php` to load the `admin_categories` Smarty template, which lets the administrator edit the categories that belong to the selected department (see Figure 7-4).

Figure 7-4. *The TShirtShop categories admin page*

This page works similar to the one for editing departments. You also get a link (`back to departments…`) that redirects back to the department's administration page.

The navigation logic between the department, category, and product administration pages is done using query string parameters. As you can see in Figure 7-4, when a department is selected, its ID is appended to the query string.

You already implemented this kind of functionality in the `index.php` page. There you decided which componentized template to load (at runtime) by analyzing the query string parameters.

We'll discuss more about `catalog_admin.php` and its four componentized templates later, while you're building them. For now, let's start by dealing with the security mechanism.

Setting Up the Catalog Administration Page

The catalog administration part of the site will consist of the `catalog_admin.php` page and a number of other PHP files and Smarty templates. You'll build each of these components one at a time. For each component, you'll first implement the presentation layer, then write the business tier code, and finally write the data tier methods.

Authenticating Administrators

Because you want only certain users to access the catalog administration page, you need to implement some sort of security mechanism that controls access to the sensitive pages in the site.

Implementing security requires dealing with two important concepts: **authentication** and **authorization**. Authentication is the process in which users are uniquely identified (most often by supplying a username and password), while authorization refers to which resources the authenticated user can access.

Users who want to access the catalog administration page should first *authenticate* themselves. After you know who they are, you decide whether they are authorized to access the administration page.

In TShirtShop, you'll use an authentication method called **Forms authentication**, which allows you to control the login process through an HTML form. After the client is authenticated, PHP automatically generates a cookie on the client, which is used to authenticate all subsequent requests. If the cookie is not found, the client is shown the login HTML form.

■**Note** We assume the administrator accesses the administrative pages from a client that has cookies enabled.

The username and password combinations can be physically stored in various ways. For example, in Chapter 11, you'll see how to store hashed (encrypted) customer passwords in the database.

■**Tip** Hashing is a common method for storing passwords. The hash value of a password is calculated by applying a mathematical function (hash algorithm) to it. When the user tries to authenticate, the password is hashed, and the resulting hash value is compared to the hash value of the original (correct) password. If the two values are identical, then the entered password is correct. The essential property about the hash algorithm is that theoretically you cannot obtain the original password from its hash value (the algorithm is one-way). In practice, scientists have recently found vulnerabilities with the popular MD5, SHA-0, and SHA-1 hashing algorithms (see `http://www.broadbandreports.com/shownews/52284`).

A simpler method is to store the username and password combination in your PHP file. This method isn't as flexible as using the database, but it's fast and easy to implement.

When storing the username/password combination in your script file, you can choose to store the password either in clear text, or hashed with a hashing algorithm such as MD5 or SHA1.

In the following exercise, you'll simply store the password in clear text, but it's good to know you have other options as well. You'll learn more about hashing in Chapter 11.

Exercise: Implementing the Skeleton of the Admin page

Follow these steps to create the skeleton of the catalog admin page and the security mechanism:

1. Modify the templates/first_page_contents.tpl file to add a link to the catalog admin page:

```
Beginning PHP 5 E-Commerce: From Novice to Professional!
<br /><br />
Access the <a href="catalog_admin.php"> catalog admin page </a>.
</span>
</p>
```

2. Add the following styles to tshirtshop.css:

```css
.TableHeader
{
  font-family: Verdana;
  font-weight: bold;
  font-size: 12px;
  color: #ffffff;
  background: #00008b
}
.TableRow
{
  font-family: Verdana;
  font-size: 11px;
  background: #dcdcdc
}
.Title
{
  font-family: Verdana;
  font-weight: bold;
  font-size: 16pt;
  color: #228aaa;
  padding-right: 3px;
  text-align: left;
}
.AdminPageText
{
  color: Navy;
  font-family: Verdana, Helvetica, sans-serif;
  text-decoration: none;
  font-size: 11px;
  font-weight: bold;
  line-height: 12px;
}
.AdminErrorText
{
  font-weight: bold;
  font-size: 12px;
  color: red;
```

```
   font-style: italic;
   font-family: Verdana, Helvetica, sans-serif;
}
.AdminButtonText
{
   color: Black;
   font-family: Verdana, Helvetica, sans-serif;
   font-weight: bold;
   font-size: 11px;
}
```

3. Modify include/app_top.php by adding the following two lines at its beginning. Calling ob_start() (http://www.php.net/ob_start) turns on output buffering, which improves performance and ensures that page redirections with the header function (see catalog_admin.php at the next step) don't generate errors.

```php
<?php
// turn on output buffering
ob_start();
// turn on session
session_start();
```

4. In your site root, create a new file named catalog_admin.php and write the following code in it:

```php
<?php
// Reference config files and business tier
require_once 'include/app_top.php';
require_once SITE_ROOT . '/business_objects/bo_catalog.php';
// If admin is not logged, redirect to the login page
if (!(isset($_SESSION['AdminLogged'])) || $_SESSION['AdminLogged'] !=true)
{
  header('Location: admin_login.php?ReturnPage=catalog_admin.php');
  exit;
}
// If logging out ...
if (isset($_GET['Page']) && $_GET['Page'] == "Logout")
{
  unset($_SESSION['AdminLogged']);
  header("Location: index.php");
  exit;
}
// Load the page
$page = new Page();
$pageContent = "blank.tpl";
$page->assign("pageContent", $pageContent);
$page->display('catalog_admin.tpl');
// Load app_bottom which closes the database connection
require_once 'include/app_bottom.php';
?>
```

5. Create the `templates/catalog_admin.tpl` template file, which is loaded from `catalog_admin.php`, and add the following code in it:

```
{* catalog_admin.tpl *}
<!DOCTYPE html
PUBLIC "-//W3C//DTD XHTML 1.0 Transitional//EN"
"http://www.w3.org/TR/xhtml1/DTD/xhtml1-transitional.dtd">
<html>
 <head>
  <title>TShirtShop Catalog Admin Page</title>
  <link href="tshirtshop.css" type="text/css" rel="stylesheet"/>
 </head>
 <body>
  <table cellpadding="0" cellspacing="0" border="0" width="100%">
    <tr>
      <td>
        <span class="Title">TShirtShop Catalog Admin</span>
        <span class="AdminPageText">
          (go back to the <a href="index.php">storefront</a> or
          <a href="catalog_admin.php?Page=Logout">logout</a>)
        </span>
      </td>
    </tr>
  </table>
  <br />
  {include file="$pageContent"}
 </body>
</html>
```

6. Add the administrator login information at the end of `config.inc.php`:

```
// administrator login information
define("ADMIN_USERNAME", "admin");
define("ADMIN_PASSWORD", "admin");
```

■**Note** As stated earlier, in Chapter 11 you'll learn about hashing and how to work with hashed passwords stored in the database. If you want to use hashing now, you need to store the hash value of the password in the `config` file instead of storing the password in clear text ("admin" in this case). At login time, you compare the hash value of the string entered by the user to the hash value you saved in the `config` file. You can calculate the hash value of a string by applying the `sha1` function to it (the `sha1` function calculates the hash value using the `SHA1` algorithm). Don't worry if this sounds too advanced at this moment, Chapter 11 will show you'll the process in more detail.

---

7. Now create the admin_login.php script in the root directory of your site to supervise the login moment:

```php
<?php
// Load Smarty library and config files
require_once 'include/app_top.php';
// Load the page
$page = new Page();
$admin_login = new AdminLogin();
$page->assign_by_ref("admin_login", $admin_login);
$page->display('admin_login.tpl');
// app_bottom closes database connection and flushes output buffering
require_once 'include/app_bottom.php';

// class that deals with authenticating administrators
class AdminLogin
{
  // public variables available in smarty template
  public $mUsername;
  public $mLoginMessage = "";
  public $mReturnPage;
  // class constructor
  function __construct()
  {
    // page the user is forwarded to in case the password is correct
    if (isset($_GET['ReturnPage']))
      $this->mReturnPage = $_GET['ReturnPage'];
    // If admin is already logged, redirect to the requested page
    if (isset($_SESSION['AdminLogged'])
        && $_SESSION['AdminLogged'] ==  true)
    {
      header('Location: ' . $this->mReturnPage);
      exit;
    }
    // verify if the correct username and password have been supplied
    if(isset($_POST['Submit']))
    {
      if($_POST['username'] == ADMIN_USERNAME
         && $_POST['password'] == ADMIN_PASSWORD)
      {
        $_SESSION['AdminLogged'] = true;
        header("Location: " . $this->mReturnPage);
        exit;
      }
      else
        $this->mLoginMessage = "<br />Login failed. Please try again:";
    }
  }
}
?>
```

8. Create a new template file named `admin_login.tpl` in the `templates` folder and add the following code to it:

```
{* admin_login.tpl *}
<!DOCTYPE html
PUBLIC "-//W3C//DTD XHTML 1.0 Transitional//EN"
"http://www.w3.org/TR/xhtml1/DTD/xhtml1-transitional.dtd">
<html>
 <head>
  <title>TShirtShop Login</title>
  <link href="tshirtshop.css" type="text/css" rel="stylesheet" />
 </head>
 <body>
  <br />
  <span class="Title">
   TShirtShop Login
  </span><br /><br />
  <span class="AdminPageText">
   Enter login information or go back to
   <a href="index.php">storefront</a>
  </span><br />
  <span class="AdminErrorText">
   {$admin_login->mLoginMessage}
  </span>
  <br />
  <form method="post"
        action="admin_login.php?ReturnPage={$admin_login->mReturnPage}">
   <table cellpadding="3" cellspacing="1" border="0">
    <tr>
     <td>Username:</td>
     <td>
      <input class="Button" type="text" name="username"
             value="{$admin_login->mUsername}"/>
     </td>
    </tr>
    <tr>
     <td>Password:</td>
     <td>
      <input class="button" type="password" value="" name="password"/>
     </td>
    </tr>
    <tr>
     <td colspan="2">
      <br />
```

```
        <input class="button" type="submit" value="Login" name="Submit"/>
      </td>
    </tr>
   </table>
  </form>
 </body>
</html>
```

9. Load `index.php` in your favorite browser page and you'll see the `catalog admin page` link in the welcome message. Click it and an HTML login form will be displayed as shown in Figure 7-5.

Figure 7-5. *The login page*

After you supplied the correct login info (`admin`/`admin`) you'll be redirected to the admin page. The admin page contains a link to the TShirtShop main page, and a logout link that unauthenticates the administrator (see Figure 7-6).

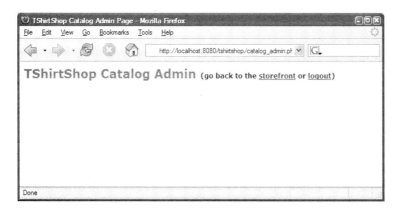

Figure 7-6. `catalog_admin.php` *in action*

How It Works: The catalog_admin Page

You created two PHP scripts in this exercise: catalog_admin.php and admin_login.php. catalog_admin.php is the page that you'll continue to develop in the rest of the chapter to allow the user to administer catalog data. admin_login.php contains the admin authentication and authorization functionality.

All the fun begins in catalog_admin.php, which checks to see whether the visitor has been authenticated as administrator (by checking if the AdminLogged session variable is true). In case the visitor is not logged in as administrator, he or she is forwarded to the login page, admin_login.php:

```
// If admin is not logged, redirect to the login page
if (!(isset($_SESSION['AdminLogged'])) || $_SESSION['AdminLogged'] !=true)
{
  header('Location: admin_login.php?ReturnPage=catalog_admin.php');
  exit;
}
```

The login mechanism in the AdminLogin class stores the current authentication state in the visitor's session under a variable named AdminLogged. If its value is true, that means the user has already been authenticated as administrator, and is forwarded to the originally requested page:

```
    // If admin is already logged, redirect to the requested page
    if (isset($_SESSION['AdminLogged'])
        && $_SESSION['AdminLogged'] ==  true)
    {
      header('Location: ' . $this->mReturnPage);
      exit;
    }
```

Otherwise, the script tests whether the supplied username and password match the values stored in config.inc.php as ADMIN_USERNAME and ADMIN_PASSWORD:

```
    // verify if the correct username and password have been supplied
    if(isset($_POST['Submit']))
    {
      if($_POST['username'] == ADMIN_USERNAME
        && $_POST['password'] == ADMIN_PASSWORD)
      {
        $_SESSION['AdminLogged'] = true;
        header("Location: " . $this->mReturnPage);
        exit;
      }
      else $this->mLoginMessage = "Login Error";
    }
```

The logout link in `catalog_admin.php` simply unsets the `AdminLogged` session variable and redirects the administrator to `index.php`. This way, on the next attempt to access the admin page, the administrator will be redirected to the login page.

```
// If logging out ...
if (isset($_GET['Page']) && $_GET['Page'] == "Logout")
{
  unset($_SESSION['AdminLogged']);
  header("Location: index.php");
  exit;
}
```

Administering Departments

The department administration section allows the client to add, remove, or change department information. To implement this functionality, you'll need to write the necessary code for the presentation, business, and data layers.

One fundamental truth regarding *n*-Tiered applications (which also applies to this particular case) is that the business and data tiers are ultimately created to support the presentation tier. Drawing on paper and establishing exactly how you want the site to look (in other words, what functionality needs to be supported by the user interface) is a good indication of what the database and business tier will contain.

With the proper design work, you can know exactly what to place in each tier, so the order of writing the code doesn't matter. When the design is clearly established, a team of programmers can work at the same time and implement the three tiers concurrently, which is one of the benefits of having a tiered architecture.

However, this rarely happens in practice, except for the largest projects that really need very careful design and planning. In our case, usually the best way is to start with the lower levels (the database and data object), to have the basics established before creating the UI (user interface). For this to happen, first you need to analyze what functionality you'll need for the UI, otherwise you won't know what to write in the data and business tiers.

In this chapter, we will always start with the presentation tier. You can do this because now you have a good overview of the architecture, and know beforehand how you'll implement the other two tiers. This knowledge is necessary because in the presentation tier, you call methods from the business tier (which you haven't created yet), and in the business tier, you call the data tier (which, again, you haven't yet created). If you don't have a clear idea of how to implement the other tiers, starting with the presentation tier can be trickier in the long run.

Because you already have a working architecture, it will be simple to write components as needed for each tier. Of course, if you had to implement something new or more complicated, we would have spent some time analyzing the full implications, but here you won't do anything more complicated than the code in the previous chapters. You'll apply the same technique for all componentized templates you'll build in this chapter.

Implementing the Presentation Tier

Let's take another look at what the admin_departments componentized template looks like in action (see Figure 7-7).

Edit the departments of TShirtShop:

Department Name	Department Description			
Nature	Begin building your T-shirt collection with some cool designs gathered from the rich world of nature.	Edit	Edit Categories	Delete
Scandinavia	Our Scandinavian postal design T-shirts capture the essence and soul of the North! You really should try them!	Edit	Edit Categories	Delete
Free Spirit	Some free spirit T-shirts for the really free people.	Edit	Edit Categories	Delete

Add new department:

[name]	[description]	Add

Figure 7-7. *The* admin_departments *componentized template in action*

This componentized template will generate a list populated with the departments' information, and it also has a label, two text boxes, and a button used to add new departments to the list.

When you click on a department's Edit button, the name and the description of that department becomes editable and the Update and Cancel buttons appear in place of the Edit button, as shown in Figure 7-8.

Edit the departments of TShirtShop:

Department Name	Department Description			
Nature	Begin building your T-shirt collection with some cool designs gathered from the rich world of nature.	Update Cancel	Edit Categories	Delete
Scandinavia	Our Scandinavian postal design T-shirts capture the essence and soul of the North! You really should try them!	Edit	Edit Categories	Delete
Free Spirit	Some free spirit T-shirts for the really free people.	Edit	Edit Categories	Delete

Add new department:

[name]	[description]	Add

Figure 7-8. *The* admin_departments *componentized template in edit mode*

Exercise: Implementing admin_departments Componentized Template

Follow these steps to make your departments live:

1. Create a new template file named admin_departments.tpl in the templates folder file and add the following code to it:

```
{load_admin_departments assign="admin_departments"}
<span class="AdminPageText">Edit the departments of TShirtShop:</span>
<br/><br/>
<span class="AdminErrorText">{$admin_departments->mErrorMessage}</span>
{if $admin_departments->mDepartmentsCount eq 0}
```

```
<b>There are no departments in your database</b>
{else}
<form action="catalog_admin.php?Page=Departments" method="post">
<table cellpadding="3" cellspacing="1" border="0" width="100%">
 <tr class="TableHeader">
  <td>Department Name</td>
  <td>Department Description</td>
  <td colspan="3"> </td>
 </tr>
 {section name=cDepartments loop=$admin_departments->mDepartments}
  {if $admin_departments->mEditItem ==
       $admin_departments->mDepartments[cDepartments].department_id}
 <tr class="TableRow">
  <td>
   <input type="text" name="dep_name"
     value="{$admin_departments->mDepartments[cDepartments].name}" />
  </td>
  <td>
   <textarea name="dep_description" rows="3" cols="50">
{$admin_departments->mDepartments[cDepartments].description}
   </textarea>
  </td>
  <td width="30">
   <input type="submit" name="submit_update_dep_{$admin_departments->
mDepartments[cDepartments].department_id}" value="Update"/><br />
   <input type="submit" name="submit_cancel_dep_{$admin_departments->
mDepartments[cDepartments].department_id}" value="Cancel" />
  </td>
  <td width="130">
   <input type="submit" name="submit_edit_categ_{$admin_departments->
mDepartments[cDepartments].department_id}"
     value="Edit Categories"/></td>
  <td width="50"><input type="submit"
    name="submit_delete_dep_{$admin_departments->
mDepartments[cDepartments].department_id}" value="Delete"/></td>
 </tr>
 {else}
  <tr class="TableRow">
   <td>{$admin_departments->mDepartments[cDepartments].name}</td>
   <td>{$admin_departments->mDepartments[cDepartments].description}</td>
   <td width="30">
    <input type="submit" name="submit_edit_dep_{$admin_departments->
mDepartments[cDepartments].department_id}" value="Edit"/>
   </td>
   <td width="130">
    <input type="submit" name="submit_edit_categ_{$admin_departments->
mDepartments[cDepartments].department_id}" value="Edit Categories"/>
   </td>
```

```
    <td width="50">
      <input type="submit" name="submit_delete_dep_{$admin_departments->
mDepartments[cDepartments].department_id}" value="Delete"/>
    </td>
   </tr>
   {/if}
  {/section}
 </table>
 </form>
{/if}

<form action="catalog_admin.php?Page=Departments" method="post">
 <span class="AdminPageText">Add new department:</span><br /><br />
 <input  type="text" size="30" name="dep_name"
    value="[name]"/>
 <input type="text" size="60" name="dep_description"
        value="[description]"/>
 <input type="submit" name="submit_add_dep_0"
        class="AdminButtonText" value="Add"/>
 </form>
```

2. Create a new plugin file named function.load_admin_departments.php in the
   smarty_plugins folder and add the following to it:

```php
<?php
/* smarty plugin function that gets called when the
   load_admin_departments function plugin is loaded from a template */
function smarty_function_load_admin_departments($params, $smarty)
{
  $admin_departments = new AdminDepartments();
  $admin_departments->init();
  // assign template variable
  $smarty->assign($params['assign'], $admin_departments);
}

// class that supports departments admin functionality
class AdminDepartments
{
  // public variables available in smarty template
  public $mDepartmentsCount;
  public $mDepartments;
  public $mErrorMessage = "";
  public $mEditItem;
  // private members
  private $mCatalog;
  public $mAction = "";
  public $mActionedDepId;
  // class constructor
```

```
function __construct()
{
  $this->mCatalog = new BoCatalog();
  // parse the list with posted variables
  foreach ($_POST as $key => $value)
   // if a submit button was clicked...
   if (substr($key,0,6) == "submit")
   {
     // get the position of the last '_' underscore
     // from submit button name
     // e.g. strtpos("submit_edit_dep_1", "_") is 16
     $last_underscore = strrpos($key, "_");
     // get the scope of submit button
     // (e.g 'edit_dep' from 'submit_edit_dep_1')
     $this->mAction = substr($key, strlen("submit_"),
                             $last_underscore-strlen("submit_"));
     // get the department id targeted by submit button
     // (the number at the end of submit button name )
     // e.g '1' from 'submit_edit_dep_1'
     $this->mActionedDepId = substr($key,$last_underscore+1);
     break;
   }
}
// init
function init()
{
  // if adding a new department ...
  if ($this->mAction == "add_dep")
  {
    $department_name = $_POST['dep_name'];
    $department_description = $_POST['dep_description'];
    if ($department_name == null)
      $this->mErrorMessage = "Department name required";
    if ($this->mErrorMessage == null)
      $this->mCatalog->AddDepartment($department_name,
                                     $department_description);
  }
  // if editing an existing department ...
  if ($this->mAction == 'edit_dep')
    $this->mEditItem = $this->mActionedDepId;
  // if updating a department ...
  if ($this->mAction == 'update_dep')
  {
    $department_name = $_POST['dep_name'];
    $department_description = $_POST['dep_description'];
    if ($department_name == null)
      $this->mErrorMessage = "Department name required";
```

```
        if ($this->mErrorMessage == null)
          $this->mCatalog->UpdateDepartment($this->mActionedDepId,
                          $department_name, $department_description);
      }
      // if deleting a department ...
      if ($this->mAction == "delete_dep")
      {
        $status=$this->mCatalog->DeleteDepartment($this->mActionedDepId);
        if ($status < 0) $this->mErrorMessage = "Department not empty";
      }
      // if editing department's categories ...
      if ($this->mAction == "edit_categ")
      {
        header("Location:catalog_admin.php?Page=Categories&" .
         "DepartmentID=$this->mActionedDepId");
        exit;
      }
      // load the list of departments
      $this->mDepartments = $this->mCatalog->GetDepartmentsWithDescriptions();
      $this->mDepartmentsCount = count($this->mDepartments);
    }
} //end class
?>
```

3. Modify the `catalog_admin.php` file to load the newly created `admin_departments` componentized template:

```
// Load the page
$page = new Page();
$pageContent = "blank.tpl";
// If Page is not explicitly set, assume the Departments page
if(isset($_GET['Page']))
  $admin_page = $_GET['Page'];
else
  $admin_page = "Departments";
// Choose what admin page to load ...
if ($admin_page == "Departments")
  $pageContent = "admin_departments.tpl";
$page->assign("pageContent", $pageContent);
$page->display('catalog_admin.tpl');
```

How It Works: The admin_departments Componentized Template

You wrote a lot of code in this exercise, and you still can't test anything. This is the tough part about creating the UI first. Still, the code is not that complicated if you look at it. Let's see how the `admin_departments.tpl` template is done.

Here's a scheme of the {section} construct used to build the rows of the table:

```
{section name=cDepartments loop=$admin_departments->mDepartments}
  {if $admin_departments->mEditItem ==
      $admin_departments->mDepartments[cDepartments].department_id}
>> here goes a form where the administrator can edit the department name    <<
>> and description with Update/Cancel, Edit Categories, and Delete buttons. <<
  {else}
>> here goes a form that displays the department name and description, and   <<
>> also Edit, Edit Categories, and Delete buttons.                          <<
  {/if}
{/section}
```

By default, the department name and description are not editable, but when you click the Edit button of one department, $admin_departments->mEditItem is set to the department_id value of the clicked department, and the smarty presentation logic generates editable text boxes instead of labels. This will allow the administrator to edit the selected department's details (in edit mode, Update/Cancel buttons appear instead of the Edit button, as you saw in the earlier figures).

The Smarty plugin function loaded from the admin_departments template (in function.load_admin_departments.php) is executed whenever the user clicks any of these buttons, and reacts to the visitor's action. The function recognizes what button was clicked and knows what to do after parsing the list of posted variables and reading the clicked button's name. In the departments admin page (see the admin_departments.tpl template file), buttons have names such as submit_edit_dep_1.

All button names start with submit and end with the ID of the department. In the middle of the name is the code for the button type, which specifies what operation to do with the mentioned department. A button named submit_edit_dep_1 tells the plugin function to enter edit mode for the department with a department_id value of 1.

Note that with the Add department button, the department's ID specified in the button name becomes irrelevant, because its value is automatically generated by the database (department_id is an AUTO_INCREMENT column).

In our case, the button type can be

- add_dep for the Add department buttons

- edit_dep for the Edit department buttons

- update_dep for the Update buttons

- delete_dep for the Delete buttons

- edit_categ for the Edit Categories buttons

Depending on the type of the clicked button, one of the corresponding business tier methods is called. Let's consider these methods next.

Implementing the Business Tier

You called four middle-tier methods from the AdminDepartments class. Now it's time to add their business tier counterparts:

- GetDepartmentsWithDescriptions returns the list of departments to be displayed in the departments admin page.

- UpdateDepartment changes a department's details. Its parameters are the department's department_id value, its new name, and its new description.

- DeleteDepartment deletes the department specified by the department_id parameter.

- AddDepartment needs the name and description for the new department, because the department_id value is automatically generated by the database (the department_id column in the department table is an AUTO-INCREMENT column).

Apart from these methods, you also used the GetDepartmentDetails and GetCategory-Details methods that already exist in the BoCatalog class.

Exercise: Adding the Methods

Now it's time to implement the new methods. Add this code to the BoCatalog class in business_objects/bo_catalog.php:

```
// retrieves all departments with their descriptions
public function GetDepartmentsWithDescriptions()
{
  $result = $this->mDoCatalog->GetDepartmentsWithDescriptions();
  return $result;
}

// updates department details
public function UpdateDepartment($departmentId, $departmentName,
                                           $departmentDescription)
{
  $this->mDoCatalog->UpdateDepartment($departmentId, $departmentName,
                                           $departmentDescription);
}

// deletes a department
public function DeleteDepartment($departmentId)
{
  return $this->mDoCatalog->DeleteDepartment($departmentId);
}

// adds a department
public function AddDepartment($departmentName, $departmentDescription)
{
  $this->mDoCatalog->AddDepartment($departmentName, $departmentDescription);
}
```

Implementing the Data Tier

You'll add four methods in the data tier that correspond to the four business tier methods you wrote earlier. You'll also add a method to the DbManager class (DbEscapeSimple) to support functionality required by the other methods. Let's see what this is all about.

DbEscapeSimple

The DbEscapeSimple method calls the database-specific escapeSimple method. This method escapes a string according to the current DBMS's (Database Management System—MySQL in our case) standards, which is necessary in case you do database operations with strings that can contain characters such as " or ".

However, escapeSimple is called only if the user input strings aren't automatically escaped by PHP (this is tested using the get_magic_quotes_gpc() PHP function).

Add the following method to the DbManager class in include/database.php:

```
// wrapper class for the escapeSimple() method
public function DbEscapeSimple($string)
{
  if (get_magic_quotes_gpc())
    return $string;
  else
    return $this->db->escapeSimple($string);
}
```

GetDepartmentsWithDescriptions

GetDepartmentsWithDescriptions is the simplest method you'll implement here. It returns the complete list of departments with their identities, names, and descriptions. This is similar to the GetDepartments method called to fill the departments list from the storefront, but this one also returns the descriptions.

Add the GetDepartmentsWithDescriptions method to the DoCatalog class (located in data_objects/do_catalog.php):

```
// retrieves all departments with their descriptions
public function GetDepartmentsWithDescriptions()
{
  $query_string = "SELECT department_id, name, description FROM department";
  $result = $this->dbManager->DbGetAll($query_string);
  return $result;
}
```

UpdateDepartment

The UpdateDepartment method updates the name and description of an existing department using the UPDATE SQL statement. Add the UpdateDepartment method to the DoCatalog class:

```
// updates a department
public function UpdateDepartment($departmentId, $departmentName,
                                $departmentDescription)
```

```
{
  $query_string =
    "UPDATE department
    SET name = '" . $this->dbManager->DbEscapeSimple($departmentName) .
    "', description = '" .
    $this->dbManager->DbEscapeSimple($departmentDescription) .
    "' WHERE department_id = $departmentId";
  $result = $this->dbManager->DbQuery($query_string);
}
```

DeleteDepartment

DeleteDepartment deletes an existing department from the database, but only if no categories are related to it. Add the DeleteDepartment method to the DoCatalog class:

```
// deletes a department if it has no related categories
public function DeleteDepartment($departmentId)
{
  $query_string =
    "SELECT COUNT(*)
    FROM category WHERE department_id = $departmentId";
  $counter = $this->dbManager->DbGetOne($query_string);
  if ($counter == 0)
  {
    $query_string =
      "DELETE FROM department WHERE department_id = $departmentId";
    $result = $this->dbManager->DbQuery($query_string);
    return 1;
  }
  return -1;
}
```

AddDepartment

AddDepartment inserts a new department into the database:

```
// add a department
public function AddDepartment($departmentName, $departmentDescription)
{
  $query_string =
    "INSERT INTO department (name, description)
    VALUES ('" . $this->dbManager->DbEscapeSimple($departmentName) .
    "', '" . $this->dbManager->DbEscapeSimple($departmentDescription)
    . "')";
  $result = $this->dbManager->DbQuery($query_string);
}
```

Finally, load the catalog_admin.php page in your browser and admire your results (see Figure 7.9). Check all the buttons carefully.

TShirtShop Catalog Admin (go back to the storefront or logout)

Edit the departments of TShirtShop:

Department Name	Department Description			
Nature	Begin building your T-shirt collection with some cool designs gathered from the rich world of nature.	Edit	Edit Categories	Delete
Scandinavia	Our Scandinavian postal design T-shirts capture the essence and soul of the North! You really should try them!	Edit	Edit Categories	Delete
Free Spirit	Some free spirit T-shirts for the really free people.	Edit	Edit Categories	Delete

Add new department:

[name]	[description]	Add

Figure 7-9. *The* admin_departments *componentized template in action*

Administering Categories and Products

Because the pages that administer categories and products are based on the same steps and concepts as the departments admin page, it is more efficient now to just use the files from the code download. Follow these steps to update your web site to handle administering categories and products:

1. From the Downloads section for this chapter on the Apress web site (http://www.apress.com), copy the following template files to your project's templates folder: admin_categories.tpl and admin_products.tpl.

2. From the code download to the smarty_plugins folder of your project, copy the function.load_admin_categories.php and function.load_admin_products.php plugin files to the corresponding place in your site directories.

3. Either copy the bo_catalog.php file, or add the following methods from the BoCatalog class in the code download of this chapter to your BoCatalog class: GetCategories-InDepartmentWithDescriptions, AddCategory, DeleteCategory, UpdateCategory, GetProductsInCategoryAdmin, CreateProductToCategory, UpdateProduct, and GetProductDetails.

4. Either copy the do_catalog.php file, or add the following methods from the DoCatalog class in the code download to your DoCatalog class: GetCategoriesInDepartmentWith-Descriptions, AddCategory, DeleteCategory, UpdateCategory, GetProductsInCategory-Admin, CreateProductToCategory, UpdateProduct, and GetProductDetails.

5. Modify the catalog_admin.php page to load the newly added componentized templates:

```
// Choose what admin page to load ...
if ($admin_page == "Departments")
  $pageContent = "admin_departments.tpl";
if ($admin_page == "Categories")
  $pageContent = "admin_categories.tpl";
if ($admin_page == "Products")
```

```
    $pageContent = "admin_products.tpl";
$page->assign("pageContent", $pageContent);
$page->display('catalog_admin.tpl');
```

6. Load catalog_admin.php in your browser, choose a department, and click its Edit Categories button. The admin_categories componentized template loads and a page like the one in Figure 7-10 appears.

TShirtShop Catalog Admin (go back to the storefront or logout)

Editing categories for department: Nature (back to departments...)

Category Name	Category Description			
Animal	Our ever-growing selection of beautiful animal T-shirts represents critters from everywhere, both wild and domestic.	Edit	Edit Products	Delete
Flowers	These unique and beautiful flower T-shirts are just the item for the gardener, flower arranger, florist, or general lover of things beautiful.	Edit	Edit Products	Delete

Add new category:

[name]	[description]	Add

Figure 7-10. *The* admin_categories *componentized template*

Choose a category and click on its Edit Products button to see the admin_products componentized template as shown in Figure 7-11.

TShirtShop Catalog Admin (go back to the storefront or logout)

Editing products for category: Animal (back to categories...)

ID	Name	Description	Price	Image1	Image2	Dept. Prom.	Cat. Prom.		
1	Sambar	Sambar (North Borneo - 1892). This handsome Malayan Sambar was a pain in the neck to get to pose like this, and all so you could have this beautiful retro T-shirt!	14.95	BorneoDeer.gif	BorneoDeer.stamp.jpg	☐	☐	Edit	Select
2	American Bison	Of all the critters in our T-shirt zoo, this is one of our most popular. A classic T-shirt for an individual like yourself!	14.95	Buffalo.gif	Buffalo.stamp.jpg	☑	☑	Edit	Select
3	Cameroun Monkey	Mustache Monkey (Cameroun - 1962). This fellow is more than equipped to hang out with that tail of his, just like you'll be fit for hanging out with this great T-shirt!	12.99	CameroonMonkey.gif	CamerounMonkey.stamp.jpg	☐	☐	Edit	Select

Figure 7-11. *The* admin_products *componentized template*

How It Works: Administering Categories and Products

This time, we chose to quickly show you how to add the new functionality by using the code download. We did this because the code for administering categories and products follows the same patterns as the code for administering departments.

Have a close look at the new code that you added to make sure you understand exactly how it works before moving on to administering product details.

Administering Product Details

The products list you built earlier is wonderful, but it lacks a few important features. The final componentized template you're implementing, `admin_product_details`, enables you to

- View the product's picture.

- Remove the product from a category.

- Remove the product from the database completely.

- Assign the current product to an additional category.

- Move the current product to another category.

When it comes to product removal, things aren't so straightforward. You can either unassign the product from a category by removing the record from the `product_category` table, or you can effectively remove the product from the `product` table. Because products are accessed in the catalog by selecting a category, you must make sure there are no orphaned products (products that don't belong to any category), because they couldn't be accessed using the current administration interface.

So, if you added a Delete button for a product, what would it actually do? Delete the product from the database? This would work, but it's a bit awkward if you have a product assigned to multiple categories and you only want to remove it from a single category. On the other hand, if the Delete button removes the product from the current category, you can create orphaned products because they exist in the `product` table, but they don't belong to any category so they can't be accessed. You could fix that by allowing the site administrator to see the complete list of products without locating them by department and category.

The simple solution implemented in this chapter is like that. There will be two delete buttons: a "Remove from category" button, which allows removing the product from a single category, and a "Remove from catalog" button, which completely removes the product from the catalog by deleting its entries in the `product` and `product_category` tables. In case the product belongs to more categories, only the "Remove from category" button will be active. In case the product belongs to a single category, only the "Remove from catalog" button will be available, because removing it only from its category would generate an orphan product in the `product` table (a product that doesn't belongs to any category, thus inaccessible through the current interface).

With this componentized template, apart from permitting the administrator to remove products, you'll also see how to assign the currently selected product to an additional category, or to move the product to another category.

Implementing the Presentation Tier

Figure 7-12 shows how the product details admin page will look for the Norway Post product.

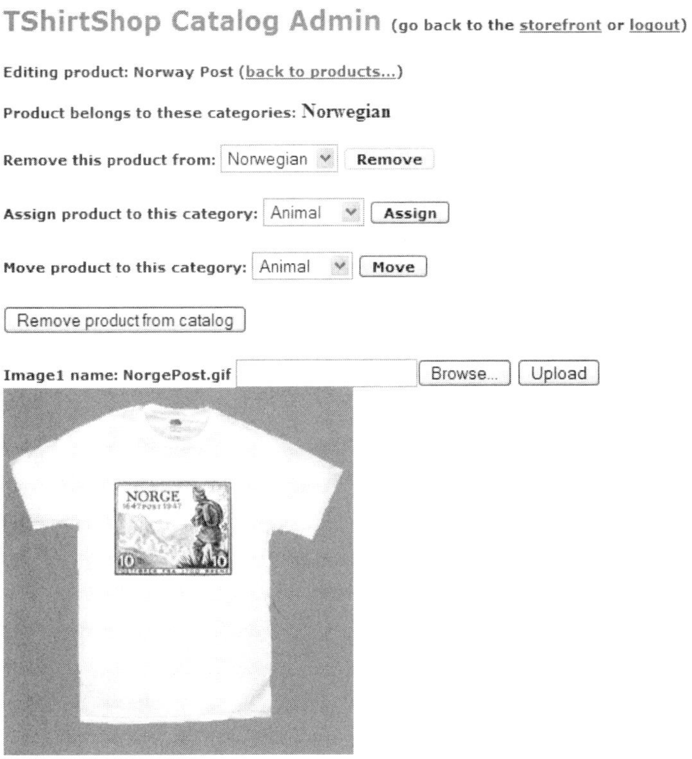

Figure 7-12. *Administering product details*

You'll implement the admin_product_details Smarty componentized template in the following exercise.

Exercise: Implementing admin_product_details

To implement admin_product_details, follow these steps:

1. Create the templates/admin_product_details.tpl file and add the following in it:

```
{load_admin_product_details assign="admin_product_details"}
<form enctype="multipart/form-data"
action="catalog_admin.php?Page=ProductDetails
&amp;DepartmentID={$admin_product_details->mDepartmentId}
&amp;CategoryID={$admin_product_details->mCategoryId}
&amp;ProductID={$admin_product_details->mProductId}" method="post">

<span class="AdminPageText">Editing product:
{$admin_product_details->mProductName}
(<a href="catalog_admin.php?Page=Products
```

```
&amp;DepartmentID={$admin_product_details->mDepartmentId}
&amp;CategoryID={$admin_product_details->mCategoryId}">back to
products...</a>)
</span>
<p>
 <span class="AdminPageText">Product belongs to these categories:</span>
 <span><b>{$admin_product_details->mProductCategoriesString}</b></span>
</p>
<span class="AdminPageText">Remove this product from:</span>
<select name="TargetCategoryIdRemove">
 {html_options options=$admin_product_details->mRemoveFromCategories}
</select>
<input type="submit" name="RemoveFromCategory" class="AdminButtonText"
value="Remove"
{if $admin_product_details->mRemoveFromCategoryButtonDisabled}
disabled="disabled" {/if}/>
<br/><br/>
<span class="AdminPageText">Assign product to this category:</span>
<select name="TargetCategoryIdAssign">
 {html_options options=$admin_product_details->mAssignOrMoveTo}
</select>
<input type="submit" name="Assign" class="AdminButtonText" value="Assign"/>
<br/><br/>
<span class="AdminPageText">Move product to this category:</span>
<select name="TargetCategoryIdMove">
 {html_options options=$admin_product_details->mAssignOrMoveTo}
</select>
<input type="submit" name="Move" class="AdminButtonText" value="Move"/>
<br/><br/>
<input type="submit" name="RemoveFromCatalog"
       value="Remove product from catalog"
 {if !$admin_product_details->mRemoveFromCategoryButtonDisabled}
disabled="disabled" {/if} />
<br/><br/>

<span class="AdminPageText">
 Image1 name: {$admin_product_details->mProductImage1}
 <input name="Image1Upload" type="file" value="Upload"/>
 <input type="submit" name="Upload" value="Upload"/> <br/>
 <img src="product_images/{$admin_product_details->mProductImage1}"
border="0" alt="image here"/>
 <br/>
 Image2 name: {$admin_product_details->mProductImage2}
 <input name="Image2Upload" type="file" value="Upload"/>
 <input type="submit" name="Upload" value="Upload"/> <br/>
 <img src="product_images/{$admin_product_details->mProductImage2}"
border="0" alt="image here"/>
</span>
</form>
```

2. Create the smarty_plugins/function.load_admin_product_details.php file and add
the following in it:

```php
<?php
/* smarty plugin function that gets called when the
load_admin_product_details function plugin is loaded from a template */
function smarty_function_load_admin_product_details($params, $smarty)
{
  $admin_product = new AdminProduct();
  $admin_product->init();
  // assign template variable
  $smarty->assign($params['assign'], $admin_product);
}

// class that deals with product administration
class AdminProduct
{
  //public attributes
  public $mProductName;
  public $mProductImage1;
  public $mProductImage2;
  public $mProductCategoriesString;
  public $mRemoveFromCategories;
  public $mProductId;
  public $mCategoryId;
  public $mDepartmentId;
  public $mRemoveFromCategoryButtonDisabled = false;
  //private attributes
  private $mCatalog;
  private $mTargetCategoryId;
  // class constructor
  function __construct()
  {
    // business tier class
    $this->mCatalog = new BoCatalog();
    // need to have DepartmentID in the query string
    if (!isset($_GET['DepartmentID']))
      trigger_error("DepartmentID not set");
    else
      $this->mDepartmentId = (int)$_GET['DepartmentID'];
    // need to have CategoryID in the query string
    if (!isset($_GET['CategoryID']))
      trigger_error("CategoryID not set");
    else
      $this->mCategoryId = (int)$_GET['CategoryID'];
    // need to have ProductID in the query string
    if (!isset($_GET['ProductID']))
      trigger_error("ProductID not set");
```

```php
    else
      $this->mProductId = (int)$_GET['ProductID'];
}
// init
public function init()
{
  // if uploading a product picture ...
  if (isset($_POST['Upload']))
  {
    // check whether we have write permission on the product_images folder
    if (!is_writeable(SITE_ROOT . '/product_images/'))
    {
      echo "Can't write to the product_images folder";
      exit;
    }
    // if the error code is 0, the first file was uploaded ok
    if ($_FILES['Image1Upload']['error'] == 0)
    {
      // use the move_uploaded_file PHP function to move the file
      // from its temporary location to the product_images folder
      move_uploaded_file($_FILES['Image1Upload']['tmp_name'],
        SITE_ROOT . '/product_images/' . $_FILES['Image1Upload']['name']);
      // update the product's information in the database
      $this->mCatalog->SetPicture1($this->mProductId,
        $_FILES['Image1Upload']['name']);
    }
    // if the error code is 0, the second file was uploaded ok
    if ($_FILES['Image2Upload']['error'] == 0)
    {
      // move the uploaded file to the product_images folder
      move_uploaded_file($_FILES['Image2Upload']['tmp_name'],
        SITE_ROOT . '/product_images/' . $_FILES['Image2Upload']['name']);
      // update the product's information in the database
      $this->mCatalog->SetPicture2($this->mProductId,
        $_FILES['Image2Upload']['name']);
    }
  }
  // if removing the product from a category...
  if (isset($_POST['RemoveFromCategory']))
  {
    $target_category_id = $_POST['TargetCategoryIdRemove'];
    $still_exists = $this->mCatalog->RemoveProductFromCategory(
                         $this->mProductId, $target_category_id);
    if ($still_exists == 0)
    {
      header(
        "Location:catalog_admin.php?Page=Products&DepartmentID=" .
```

```php
        "$this->mDepartmentId&CategoryID=$this->mCategoryId");
      exit;
    }
  }
  // if removing the product from catalog...
  if (isset($_POST['RemoveFromCatalog']))
  {
    $this->mCatalog->DeleteProduct($this->mProductId);
    header(
      "Location:catalog_admin.php?Page=Products&DepartmentID=" .
      "$this->mDepartmentId&CategoryID=$this->mCategoryId");
    exit;
  }
  // if assigning the product to another category ...
  if (isset($_POST['Assign']))
  {
    $target_category_id = $_POST['TargetCategoryIdAssign'];
    $this->mCatalog->AssignProductToCategory($this->mProductId,
      $target_category_id);
  }
  // if moving the product to another category ...
  if (isset($_POST['Move']))
  {
    $target_category_id = $_POST['TargetCategoryIdMove'];
    $this->mCatalog->MoveProductToCategory($this->mProductId,
                    $this->mCategoryId,$target_category_id);
    header(
      "Location:catalog_admin.php?Page=ProductDetails".
      "&DepartmentID=$this->mDepartmentId&CategoryID=$target_category_id".
      "&ProductID=$this->mProductId");
    exit;
  }
  // get product details and show them to user
  $product_details =
    $this->mCatalog->GetProductDetails($this->mProductId);
  $this->mProductName = $product_details['name'];
  $this->mProductImage1 = $product_details['image_file_1'];
  $this->mProductImage2 = $product_details['image_file_2'];
  $product_categories =
    $this->mCatalog->GetCategoriesForProduct($this->mProductId);
  if (count($product_categories) == 1)
    $this->mRemoveFromCategoryButtonDisabled = true;
  // show the categories the product belongs to
  for ($i = 0; $i < count($product_categories); $i++)
    $temp1[$product_categories[$i]['category_id']] =
      $product_categories[$i]['name'];
  $this->mRemoveFromCategories = $temp1;
```

```
      $this->mProductCategoriesString = implode(",", $temp1);
      $all_categories = $this->mCatalog->GetCategories();
      for ($i = 0; $i < count($all_categories); $i++)
        $temp2[$all_categories[$i]['category_id']] =
$all_categories[$i]['name'];
      $this->mAssignOrMoveTo = array_diff($temp2, $temp1);
    }
  } //end class
  ?>
```

3. Modify the catalog_admin.php page to load the admin_product_details componentized template:

```
if ($admin_page == "Departments")
  $pageContent = "admin_departments.tpl";
if ($admin_page == "Categories")
  $pageContent = "admin_categories.tpl";
if ($admin_page == "Products")
  $pageContent = "admin_products.tpl";
if ($admin_page == "ProductDetails")
  $pageContent = "admin_product_details.tpl";
```

How It Works: admin_product_details

Even though you can't execute the page yet, it's worth taking a look at the new elements the
new template contains.

The admin_product_details.tpl template contains a single form with the enctype=
"multipart/form-data" attribute. This attribute is needed for uploading product pictures,
and works in conjunction with the HTML code that enables file uploading:

```
...
  <input name="Image1Upload" type="file" value="Upload" />
  <input type="submit" name="Upload" value="Upload" /> <br />
...
```

At the end of the admin_product_details.tpl template file, you'll find a similar piece of
code used for uploading the second image of the product:

```
...
<input name="Image2Upload" type="file" value="Upload" />
<input type="submit" name="Upload" value="Upload"> <br />
...
```

The reaction to clicking these Upload buttons is implemented in the init() method from
the AdminProduct class (in smarty_plugins/function.load_admin_product_details.php):

```
// if uploading a product picture ...
if (isset($_POST['Upload']))
{
  // check whether we have write permission on the product_images folder
```

```
    if (!is_writeable(SITE_ROOT . '/product_images/'))
    {
      echo "Can't write to the product_images folder";
      exit;
    }
    // if the error code is 0, the first file was uploaded ok
    if ($_FILES['Image1Upload']['error'] == 0)
    {
      // use the move_uploaded_file PHP function to move the file
      // from its temporary location to the product_images folder
      move_uploaded_file($_FILES['Image1Upload']['tmp_name'],
        SITE_ROOT . '/product_images/' . $_FILES['Image1Upload']['name']);
      // update the product's information in the database
      $this->mCatalog->SetPicture1($this->mProductId,
        $_FILES['Image1Upload']['name']);
    }
    // if the error code is 0, the second file was uploaded ok
    if ($_FILES['Image2Upload']['error'] == 0)
    {
      // move the uploaded file to the product_images folder
      move_uploaded_file($_FILES['Image2Upload']['tmp_name'],
        SITE_ROOT . '/product_images/' . $_FILES['Image2Upload']['name']);
      // update the product's information in the database
      $this->mCatalog->SetPicture2($this->mProductId,
        $_FILES['Image2Upload']['name']);
    }
  }
```

The `$_FILES` superglobal variable is a two-dimensional array that stores information about your uploaded file (or files). If the `$_FILES['Image1Upload']['error']` variable is set to 0, then the main image of the product has uploaded successfully and must be handled. The `$_FILES['Image1Upload']['tmp_name']` variable stores the temporary file name of the uploaded file on the server, and the `$_FILES['Image1Upload']['name']` variable stores the name of the file as specified when uploaded to the server.

Note A complete description of the `$_FILES` superglobal is available at `http://www.php.net/manual/en/features.file-upload.php`.

The `move_uploaded_file` PHP function is used to move the file from the temporary location to the `product_images` folder:

```
    // use the move_uploaded_file PHP function to move the file
    // from its temporary location to the product_images folder
    move_uploaded_file($_FILES['Image1Upload']['tmp_name'],
      SITE_ROOT . '/product_images/' . $_FILES['Image1Upload']['name']);
```

After uploading a product picture, the file name must be stored in the database (otherwise, the file upload has no effect):

```
$this->mCatalog->SetPicture1($this->mProductId,
  $_FILES['Image1Upload']['name']);
```

As you can see, it's pretty simple to handle file uploads with PHP.

Implementing the Business Tier

To implement the business tier, you'll need to add the following methods to the BoCatalog class:

- DeleteProduct completely removes a product from the catalog.

- RemoveProductFromCategory is called when the "Remove from category" button is clicked to unassign the product from a category.

- GetCategories returns all the categories from our catalog.

- GetCategoriesForProduct is used to get the list of categories that are related to the specified product.

- AssignProductToCategory assigns a product to a category.

- MoveProductToCategory moves a product from one category to another.

- SetPicture1 changes the image file name in the database for a certain product.

- SetPicture2 changes the second image file name for a certain product.

Because their functionality is better expressed by the data tier methods they call, we'll discuss more about them when implementing the data tier. Add the following code to the BoCatalog class:

```
// removes a product from the product catalog
public function DeleteProduct($productId)
{
  $this->mDoCatalog->DeleteProduct($productId);
}

// unassigns a product from a category
public function RemoveProductFromCategory($productId, $categoryId)
{
  return $this->mDoCatalog->RemoveProductFromCategory($productId,
                                                      $categoryId);
}

// retrieves the complete list of categories
public function GetCategories()
{
  return $this->mDoCatalog->GetCategories();
}
```

```
// retrieves the list of categories a product belongs to
public function GetCategoriesForProduct($productId)
{
  return $this->mDoCatalog->GetCategoriesForProduct($productId);
}

// assigns a product to a category
public function AssignProductToCategory($productId, $categoryId)
{
  $this->mDoCatalog->AssignProductToCategory($productId, $categoryId);
}

// moves a product from one category to another
public function MoveProductToCategory($productId,
                                      $sourceCategoryId,
                                      $targetCategoryId)
{
  return $this->mDoCatalog->MoveProductToCategory($productId,
                                                  $sourceCategoryId,
                                                  $targetCategoryId);
}

// changes the name of the first product image file in the database
public function SetPicture1($productId,$pictureName)
{
  $this->mDoCatalog->SetPicture1($productId,$pictureName);
}

// changes the name of the second product image file in the database
public function SetPicture2($productId,$pictureName)
{
  $this->mDoCatalog->SetPicture2($productId,$pictureName);
}
```

Implementing the Data Tier

In the data tier, you add the corresponding methods in the DoCatalog class for the business tier methods you have just seen.

DeleteProduct

The DeleteProduct method completely removes a product from the catalog by deleting its entries in the product_category and product tables.

```
public function DeleteProduct($productId)
{
  $query_string = "DELETE FROM product_category WHERE product_id = $productId";
  $this->dbManager->DbQuery($query_string);
  $query_string = "DELETE FROM product WHERE product_id = $productId";
  $this->dbManager->DbQuery($query_string);
}
```

RemoveProductFromCategory

The RemoveProductFromCategory method verifies how many categories the product exists in. If the product exists in more than one category, then it just removes the product from the specified category (ID received as a parameter). If the product is associated with a single category, it is removed completely from the database.

```
public function RemoveProductFromCategory($productId, $categoryId)
{
  $query_string = "SELECT COUNT(*) FROM product_category
                   WHERE product_id=$productId";
  $counter = $this->dbManager->DbGetOne($query_string);
  if ($counter == 1)
  {
    $this->DeleteProduct($productId);
    return 0;
  }
  else
  {
    $query_string =
      "DELETE FROM product_category
       WHERE category_id = $categoryId AND product_id = $productId";
    $this->dbManager->DbQuery($query_string);
    return 1;
  }
}
```

GetCategories

GetCategories simply returns all the categories from your catalog:

```
public function GetCategories()
{
  $query_string = "SELECT category_id, name, description FROM category";
  $result=$this->dbManager->DbGetAll($query_string);
  return $result;
}
```

GetCategoriesForProduct

The GetCategoriesForProduct method returns a list of the categories that belong to the specified product. Only their IDs and names are returned because this is the only information we're interested in.

```
public function GetCategoriesForProduct($productId)
{
  $query_string =
   "SELECT category.category_id, category.department_id, category.name
    FROM category JOIN product_category
    ON category.category_id = product_category.category_id
    WHERE product_category.product_id = $productId";
  $result = $this->dbManager->DbGetAll($query_string);
  return $result;
}
```

AssignProductToCategory

The AssignProductToCategory method associates a product with a category by adding a (product_id, category_id) value pair into the product_category table:

```
public function AssignProductToCategory($productId, $categoryId)
{
  $query_string =
    "INSERT INTO product_category (product_id, category_id)
     VALUES ($productId, $categoryId)";
  $this->dbManager->DbQuery($query_string);
}
```

MoveProductToCategory

The MoveProductToCategory method removes a product from a category and places it in another one:

```
public function MoveProductToCategory($productId, $sourceCategoryId,
                                      $targetCategoryId)
{
  $query_string = "UPDATE product_category
                   SET category_id=$targetCategoryId
                   WHERE product_id = $productId AND
                         category_id = $sourceCategoryId";
  $this->dbManager->DbQuery($query_string);
}
```

SetPicture1 and SetPicture2

We need these methods to change the image name of a product when uploading a new picture:

```
public function SetPicture1($productId, $pictureName)
{
  $query_string = "UPDATE product
                   SET image_file_1 = '$pictureName'
                   WHERE product_id = $productId";
  $this->dbManager->DbQuery($query_string);
}

public function SetPicture2($productId, $pictureName)
{
  $query_string = "UPDATE product
                   SET image_file_2 = '$pictureName'
                   WHERE product_id = $productId";
  $this->dbManager->DbQuery($query_string);
}
```

Summary

You've done quite a lot of coding in this chapter. You implemented a number of componentized templates, along with their middle-tier methods and methods for the data tier. You learned how to implement a simple authentication scheme so only administrators are allowed to access the catalog administration page. At the conclusion of the chapter, you learned how to upload files from the client to the server using PHP.

In the next chapter, you enter the second stage of development by implementing a custom shopping basket into your web site.

PART 2

■■■

Phase II
of Development

■ ■ ■

CHAPTER 8

The Shopping Basket

Welcome to the second stage of development! At this stage, you start improving and adding new features to the already existing, fully functional e-commerce site.

So, what can you improve about it? Well, the answer to this question isn't hard to find if you take a quick look at the popular e-commerce sites on the web. They personalize the experience for the user, provide product recommendations, remember customers' preferences, and boast many other features that make the site easy to remember and hard to leave without first buying something.

Because in the first stage of development you extensively relied on a third party-payment processor (PayPal), which supplied an integrated shopping basket, you didn't record any shopping cart or order info in the database. Right now, your site isn't capable of displaying a list of "most wanted" products, or any other information about the products that have been sold through the web site because, at this stage, you aren't tracking the products sold. This makes it impossible to implement any of these improvements.

Obviously, saving order information in the database is your first priority. In fact, most of the features you'll want to implement next rely on having a record of the products sold. To achieve this functionality, in this chapter you'll implement a custom shopping basket and a custom checkout.

In this chapter, you will implement the custom shopping basket, which will store data in the local tshirtshop database. This will provide you with more flexibility than the PayPal shopping basket over which you have no control and which cannot be easily saved into your database for further processing and analysis. With the custom shopping basket, when the visitor clicks the Add to Cart button for a product, the product is added to the visitor's shopping cart. When the visitor clicks the View Cart button, a page like the one shown in Figure 8-1 appears.

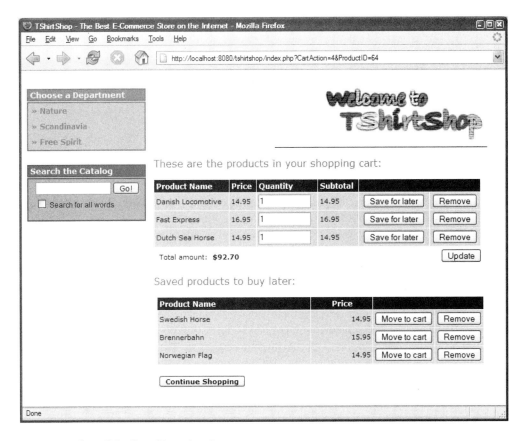

Figure 8-1. *The TShirtShop Shopping Cart*

In all the other pages except the shopping cart page, the visitor will be able to see a shopping cart summary in the left part of the screen as shown in Figure 8-2.

At the end of this chapter, you'll have a functional shopping basket, but the visitor will not yet be able to order the products contained in it. You'll add this functionality in the next chapter, when you implement a custom checkout—the Proceed to Checkout button. When the visitor clicks this button, the products in the shopping basket are saved as a separate order in the database, and the visitor is redirected to a page to pay. If you integrated the PayPal shopping cart for the first development stage, starting with the next chapter, PayPal will only be used to handle payments, and you won't rely on its shopping cart anymore.

Specifically, in this chapter you'll learn how to

- Design a shopping cart

- Add a new database table to store shopping cart records

- Create the data tier methods that work with the new table

- Implement the business layer methods

- Implement the Add to Cart and View Cart buttons (or make them work with the new shopping cart if you already implemented them in the PayPal chapter)

- Implement the presentation layer part of the custom shopping cart

Figure 8-2. *Displaying the shopping cart summary*

Designing the Shopping Cart

Before starting to write the code for the shopping cart, let's take a closer look at what you're going to do.

First, note that you won't have any user personalization features at this stage of the site. It doesn't matter who buys your products at this point, you just want to know what products were sold and when. When you add user customization features in the later chapters, your task will be fairly simple: when the visitor authenticates, the visitor's temporary (anonymous) shopping cart will be associated with the visitor's account. Because you work with temporary shopping carts, even after implementing the customer account system, the visitor isn't required to supply additional information (log in) earlier than necessary.

Probably the best way to store shopping cart information is to generate a unique cart ID for each shopping cart and save it on the visitor's computer as a cookie. When the visitor clicks the Add to Cart button, the server first verifies whether the cookie exists on the client computer. If it does, the specified product is added to the existing cart. Otherwise, the server generates another cart ID, saves it to the client's cookie, and then adds the product to the newly generated shopping cart.

In the previous chapter, you created the componentized templates by starting with the presentation layer components. However, this strategy doesn't work here because now you need to do a bit more design work beforehand, so we'll take the more common approach, and start with the database tier.

Storing Shopping Cart Information

You will store all the information from the shopping carts in a single table named shopping_cart. Execute the following SQL commands to add the shopping_cart table to the tshirtshop database, and then we'll comment upon it (of course, you can always use the script from the Downloads section of the Apress web site at http://www.apress.com).

```
USE tshirtshop;
# Table structure for table 'shopping_cart'
DROP TABLE IF EXISTS shopping_cart;
CREATE TABLE shopping_cart (
  cart_id char(32) NOT NULL default '',
  product_id int(11) NOT NULL default '0',
  quantity int(11) NOT NULL default '0',
  when_to_buy set('now','later') NOT NULL default 'now',
  date_product_added datetime NOT NULL default '0000-00-00 00:00:00',
  PRIMARY KEY  (cart_id, product_id)
);
```

Let's look at each field in shopping_cart:

- cart_id stores a unique ID that you'll generate for each shopping cart. This is not an integer field like other ID columns you've created so far. It is a char field and will be filled with an MD5 hash of a unique ID, which will result in a 32-character length string.

- product_id references the ID of an existing product.

- quantity stores the product's shopping cart quantity.

- when_to_buy helps you implement the "save to buy later" functionality. The when_to_buy field is a set type, defined to accept two values: now and later. When the customer proceeds to check out, only the products that have this value set to "now" are added to the order, while the "save for later" products remain in the shopping cart. This useful feature allows the visitor to keep more products in the shopping cart than he or she can afford at the moment, and order only a selection of the products in the shopping cart.

- date_product_added will be populated with the current date when a new product is added to the cart, and is useful when deleting old shopping carts from the database.

■**Note** The shopping_cart table has a composite primary key formed of both cart_id and product_id fields. This make sense, because a particular product can exist only once in a particular shopping cart, so a (cart_id, product_id) pair shouldn't appear more than once in the table.

Implementing the Data Tier

In this section, you'll create the usual methods that query the database for shopping cart operation. Before writing the methods, you need to take care of a couple of issues:

1. First, add the following two lines at the end of your config.inc.php file. These constants are used to differentiate between current shopping cart items, and items that are saved for later:

```
// shopping cart item types
define("GET_CART_PRODUCTS",1);
define("GET_CART_SAVED_PRODUCTS",2);
```

2. Create a new file in the data_objects folder named do_shopping_cart.php, which will contain all the shopping cart-related data logic. Insert the following code into this file:

```php
<?php
// data tier class for shopping cart operations
class DoShoppingCart
{
  // constructor
  function __construct()
  {
    // get the global DbManager instance (created in app_top.php)
    $this->dbManager = $GLOBALS['gDbManager'];
  }
}
?>
```

Implementing the Methods

Before going further with the code, let's review the methods you'll add to the DoShoppingCart class:

- AddProduct adds a product to the shopping cart.

- Update modifies shopping cart products' quantities.

- RemoveProduct deletes a record from the visitor's shopping cart.

- GetProducts gets the list of products in the specified shopping cart, and is called when you want to show the user his shopping cart.

- GetTotalAmount returns the total costs of the products in the specified product cart.

- SaveProductToBuyLater saves a product to a shopping cart for later purchase.

- MoveProductToCart moves a product from the "save for later" list back to the "main" shopping cart.

Now let's create each method one at a time.

AddProduct

The AddProduct method is called when the visitor clicks on the Add to Cart button for one of the products. If the selected product already exists in the shopping cart, its quantity should be increased by one; if the product doesn't exist, one unit is added to the shopping cart (a new shopping_cart record is created).

Not surprisingly, AddProduct receives two parameters, namely $productId and, of course, $cartId.

The method first determines whether the product mentioned by $productId exists in the cart referred to by the $mCartId class member. It does this by testing whether a ($cartId, $productId) pair is in the shopping_cart table. If the product is in the cart, AddProduct updates the current product quantity in the shopping cart by adding one unit. Otherwise, AddProduct creates a new record for the product in shopping_cart with a default quantity of 1, but not before checking whether the mentioned $productId is valid.

Add the AddProduct method to the DoShoppingCart class:

```
// adds a product to the shopping cart
public function AddProduct($productId, $cartId)
{
  // first we check if $productId exists in shopping cart
  $query_string = "SELECT quantity
              FROM shopping_cart
              WHERE product_id = $productId AND cart_id = '$cartId'";
  // if the product doesn't exist in the shopping cart...
  if ($this->dbManager->DbGetOne($query_string) == null)
  {
    // add the product to the shopping cart
    $query_string = "INSERT INTO shopping_cart
                  (cart_id, product_id, quantity, date_product_added)
                  VALUES ('$cartId', $productId , 1, now())";
  }
  // if the product already exists in the shopping cart...
  else
  {
    // increase product quantity by one and set the 'when_to_buy'
    // column to 'now' (in case the product was being saved for later)
      $query_string = "UPDATE shopping_cart
                    SET quantity = quantity + 1,
                        when_to_buy='now'
                    WHERE product_id = $productId
                      AND cart_id = '$cartId'";
  }
  $this->dbManager->DbQuery($query_string);
}
```

The now() MySQL function retrieves the current date and manually populates the date_product_added field.

Update

The Update method is used when you want to update the quantity of one or more existing shopping cart items. This method is called when the visitor clicks the Update button.

Update receives as parameters two array values: $product_id and $quantity.

If $quantity[i] is zero or less, Update removes the mentioned product from the shopping cart. Otherwise, it updates the quantity of the product in the shopping cart and also updates date_product_added to accurately reflect the time the record was last modified.

Updating the date_product_added field is particularly useful for the administration page, when you'll want to remove shopping carts that haven't been updated in a long time.

Add the Update method to the DoShoppingCart class:

```
// updates the shopping cart
public function Update($productId, $quantity,$cartId)
{
  // here we update the shopping cart quantities
  for($i=0; $i<count($productId); $i++)
  {
    if (is_numeric($quantity[$i]))
      // if quantity is positive, update the quantity
      if($quantity[$i] > 0)
        $query_string =
          "UPDATE shopping_cart
           SET quantity = $quantity[$i], date_product_added = now()
           WHERE cart_id = '$cartId' AND product_id = $productId[$i]";
      // if the new quantity is negative or zero, remove the product
      else
        $query_string =
          "DELETE FROM shopping_cart
           WHERE cart_id = '$cartId' AND product_id = $productId[$i]";
    $this->dbManager->DbQuery($query_string);
  }
}
```

RemoveProduct

The RemoveProduct method removes a product from the shopping cart when a visitor clicks the Remove button for one of the products in the shopping cart.

```
// removes product from the shopping cart
public function RemoveProduct($productId, $cartId)
{
  $query_string = "DELETE FROM shopping_cart
                   WHERE product_id = $productId
                   AND cart_id = '$cartId'";
  $this->dbManager->DbQuery($query_string);
}
```

GetProducts

The GetProducts method returns the products in the shopping cart mentioned by the $cartId parameter. It also receives $cartProductsType as a parameter, which determines whether you're looking for the current shopping cart products or for the products saved for later.

If the $cartProductsType is equal to the GET_CART_PRODUCTS constant, GetProducts will return the shopping cart products. If the $cartProductsType is equal to the GET_CART_SAVED_PRODUCTS constant, GetProducts will return the "save for later" products. If $cartProductsType is neither GET_CART_PRODUCTS or GET_CART_SAVED_PRODUCTS, the method will raise an error. Because the shopping_cart table only stores the product_id for each product it stores, you need to join the shopping_cart and product tables to get the information you need.

```
// gets shopping cart products
public function GetProducts($cartProductsType, $cartId)
{
  // if retrieving "active" shopping cart products...
  if ($cartProductsType == GET_CART_PRODUCTS)
  {
   $query_string =
      "SELECT product.product_id, product.name,
              product.price, shopping_cart.quantity,
              product.price * shopping_cart.quantity AS subtotal
       FROM shopping_cart INNER JOIN product
         ON shopping_cart.product_id = product.product_id
       WHERE shopping_cart.cart_id = '$cartId'
         AND when_to_buy='now'";
  }
  // if retrieving products saved for later...
  elseif ($cartProductsType == GET_CART_SAVED_PRODUCTS)
  {
   $query_string =
      "SELECT product.product_id, product.name, product.price
       FROM shopping_cart INNER JOIN product
         ON shopping_cart.product_id = product.product_id
       WHERE shopping_cart.cart_id = '$cartId'
         AND when_to_buy='later'";
  }
  else
    trigger_error("$cartProductsType value unknown", E_USER_ERROR);
  return $this->dbManager->DbGetAll($query_string);
}
```

■**Note**   The subtotal column that GetProducts() returns is called a *calculated column*. It doesn't exist in any of the joined tables, but is generated using a formula, which, in this case, is the price of the product multiplied by its quantity. When sending back the results, subtotal is regarded as a separate column.

GetTotalAmount

The GetTotalAmount method returns the total value of the products in the shopping cart. This is called when displaying the total amount for the shopping cart.

```
// gets total amount of the shopping cart products
public function GetTotalAmount($cartId)
{
  $query_string =
      "SELECT SUM(product.price * shopping_cart.quantity) AS total_amount
       FROM shopping_cart INNER JOIN product
         ON shopping_cart.product_id = product.product_id
       WHERE shopping_cart.cart_id = '$cartId'";
  $result = $this->dbManager->DbGetOne($query_string);
  return $result;
}
```

If the cart is empty, total_amount will be 0.

SaveProductToBuyLater

The SaveProductToBuyLater method saves a shopping cart product to the "save for later" list so the visitor can buy it later (the product isn't sent to checkout when placing the order). This is done by setting the value of the when_to_buy field to 'later'.

```
// moves a shopping cart product to the "save for later" list
public function SaveProductToBuyLater($productId, $cartId)
{
  $query_string = "UPDATE shopping_cart
                   SET when_to_buy = 'later', quantity = 1
                   WHERE product_id = $productId
                     AND cart_id = '$cartId'";
  $result = $this->dbManager->DbQuery($query_string);
}
```

MoveProductToCart

The MoveProductToCart method sets a product's when_to_buy state to 'now', so the visitor can buy the product when placing the order.

```
// moves a product from the "save for later" list to the shopping cart
public function MoveProductToCart($productId, $cartId)
{
  $query_string = "UPDATE shopping_cart
                   SET when_to_buy='now'
                   WHERE product_id = $productId
                     AND cart_id = '$cartId'";
  $result = $this->dbManager->DbQuery($query_string);
}
```

Implementing the Business Tier

To implement the business tier, you'll need to create the usual methods that call the data object layer methods you've just written, and you'll add some new ones that manage business logic.

Exercise: Implementing the Shopping Cart Business Logic

Follow the steps to create the bo_shopping_cart.php business logic file:

1. First, include a reference to bo_shopping_cart.php in index.php:

```
// Load Business Tier
require_once SITE_ROOT . '/business_objects/bo_catalog.php';
require_once SITE_ROOT . '/business_objects/bo_shopping_cart.php';
```

2. Create a new file called bo_shopping_cart.php in the business_objects folder. Add the following code to the file, and then we'll comment upon it in the "How It Works" section:

```php
<?php
// reference data tier class for shopping cart management
require_once SITE_ROOT . '/data_objects/do_shopping_cart.php';

// business tier class for the shopping cart
class BoShoppingCart
{
  // instance of the data tier shopping cart class
  private $mDoShoppingCart;
  // stores the visitor's Cart ID
  private static $mCartId;
  // constructor
  public function __construct()
  {
    // initialize data tier object
    $this->mDoShoppingCart = new DoShoppingCart();
    // ensure we have a cart id for the current visitor in the session
    $this->SetCartId();
  }

  // called at the beginning of index.php to ensure we have the
  // visitor's cart ID in the visitor's session
  public static function SetCartId()
  {
    // if the cart ID hasn't already been set...
    if (self::$mCartId == "")
    {
      // if the visitor's cart ID is in the session, get it from there
      if (isset($_SESSION['cartId']))
```

```
    {
      self::$mCartId = $_SESSION['cartId'];
    }
    // if not, check if the cart ID was saved as a cookie
    elseif (isset($_COOKIE['cartId']))
    {
      // save the cart ID from the cookie
      self::$mCartId = $_COOKIE['cartId'];
      $_SESSION['cartId'] = self::$mCartId;
    }
    else
    {
      // generate cart id and save it to the $mCartId class member,
      // the session and a cookie (on subsequent requests mCartId
      // will be populated from the session)
      self::$mCartId = md5(uniqid(rand(), true));
      // store cart id in session
      $_SESSION['cartId'] = self::$mCartId;
      // cookie will be valid for 7 days
      setcookie('cartId', self::$mCartId, time() + 432000);
    }
  }
}

// returns the current visitor's card id
public function GetCartId()
{
  return self::$mCartId;
}

// adds product to the shopping cart
public function AddProduct($productId)
{
  $this->mDoShoppingCart->AddProduct($productId, $this->GetCartId());
}

// updated the shopping cart with new product quantities
// ($productId and $quantity are arrays that contain product ids
//   and their respective quantities)
public function Update($productId, $quantity)
{
  $this->mDoShoppingCart->Update($productId, $quantity,
                                 $this->GetCartId());
}

// removes product from shopping cart
public function RemoveProduct($productId)
```

```php
    {
      $this->mDoShoppingCart->RemoveProduct($productId,
                                      $this->GetCartId());
    }

    // save product to the "save for later" list
    public function SaveProductToBuyLater($productId)
    {
      $this->mDoShoppingCart->SaveProductToBuyLater($productId,
                                        $this->GetCartId());
    }

    // get product from the "save for later" list back to the cart
    public function MoveProductToCart($productId)
    {
      $this->mDoShoppingCart->MoveProductToCart($productId,
                                      $this->GetCartId());
    }

    // get shopping cart products
    public function GetCartProducts($cartProductsType)
    {
      return $this->mDoShoppingCart->GetProducts($cartProductsType,
                                          $this->GetCartId ());
    }

    // gets total amount of shopping cart products
    // (not including the ones that are being saved for later)
    public function GetTotalAmount()
    {
      return $this->mDoShoppingCart->GetTotalAmount($this->GetCartId());
    }
  }
?>
```

How It Works: The Business Tier Part of the Shopping Cart

When a visitor enters your site, you'll have to generate a shopping cart ID for the visitor if he doesn't have one. You take care of this in the BoShoppingCart class constructor, which uses the SetCartId method to ensure the visitor's cart ID is saved in the mCartID member of the BoShoppingCart class. The shopping cart ID is cached in the visitor's session and in a persistent cookie.

This cart ID will be stored in a cookie that is set to expire in seven days (a persistent cookie), which is a reasonable time for the visitors to buy the products in their carts. The expiration time is extended every time the visitors revisit TShirtShop.

You also store the cart ID in the session. The session relies on the session ID, which is a unique ID assigned to every visitor that accesses your web site. The session ID can be propagated in two ways: through cookies or by using a URL parameter. Using cookies to store session IDs is optimal and it's assumed that client browsers accept the cookies.

Now let's look at the SetCartId method that manages the cart ID:

```
// called at the beginning of index.php to ensure we have the
// visitor's cart ID in the visitor's session
public static function SetCartId()
{
  // if the cart ID hasn't already been set...
  if (self::$mCartId == "")
  {
    // if the visitor's cart ID is in the session, get it from there
    if (isset($_SESSION['cartId']))
    {
      self::$mCartId = $_SESSION['cartId'];
    }
    // if not, check if the cart ID was saved as a cookie
    elseif (isset($_COOKIE['cartId']))
    {
      // save the cart ID from the cookie
      self::$mCartId = $_COOKIE['cartId'];
      $_SESSION['cartId'] = self::$mCartId;
    }
    else
    {
      // generate cart id and save it to the $mCartId class member,
      // the session, and a cookie (on subsequent requests, mCartId
      // will be populated from the session)
      self::$mCartId = md5(uniqid(rand(), true));
      // store cart id in session
      $_SESSION['cartId'] = self::$mCartId;
      // cookie will be valid for 7 days
      setcookie('cartId', self::$mCartId, time() + 432000);
    }
  }
}
```

The goal of this method is to have the cart ID saved to the mCartId member of the BoShoppingCart class, which is returned by the GetCartId method. mCartId is a static member, which means it has a single "global" value that applies to any instance of BoShoppingCart created during a single user request.

Three functions are used to obtain the cart ID: md5, uniqid, and rand. The call to md5(uniqid(rand(),true)) generates a unique, difficult to predict, 32-byte value. The md5 function returns the cart ID, which is an MD5 hash (calculated using the RSA Data Security,

Inc. MD5 Message-Digest Algorithm) of the unique ID generated by the uniqid function. The resulting hash is a 32-character hexadecimal number.

The uniqid function returns a unique identifier based on the current time in microseconds; its first parameter is the prefix to be appended to its generated value, in this case, the rand() function that returns a pseudo-random value between 0 and RAND_MAX, which is platform dependent. If the second parameter of uniqid is true, uniqid adds an additional "combined LCG" (combined Linear Congruential Generator) entropy at the end of the return value, which should make the results even more unique.

In short, uniquid(rand(), true) generates a very unique value, which is passed through md5 to ensure it has an even more unpredictable value, with a standard length of 32 bytes.

Implementing the Presentation Tier

The rest of this chapter deals with building the user interface (UI) part of the shopping cart. After updating the storefront, you'll have Add to Cart buttons for each product and a View Cart link in the cart summary box in the left part of the page. If the visitor's cart is empty, the link isn't displayed anymore, as you can see in Figure 8-3.

Figure 8-3. *The "View Cart" link doesn't show up if the cart is empty.*

If you added PayPal integration as presented in Chapter 6, you'll already have these buttons on your site, and you'll update their functionality here.

When clicking on View Cart, the shopping cart componentized template (which you'll build later) is loaded in index.tpl. You can see this componentized component in action in Figure 8-4.

Figure 8-4. *The TShirtShop shopping cart*

The mechanism for loading the shopping cart componentized component is the same one you already used in index.php to load other components. When the Add to Cart button is clicked, index.php is reloaded with an additional parameter (CartAction) in the query string:

http://localhost/tshirtshop/index.php?CartAction=1&ProductID=10

When clicking on View Cart, the CartAction parameter added to the query string doesn't take any value.

The shopping cart will have five cart actions, which are described using the following self-explanatory constants in the configuration file (include/config.inc.php): ADD_PRODUCT, REMOVE_PRODUCT, UPDATE_PRODUCTS_QUANTITIES, SAVE_PRODUCT_FOR_LATER, and MOVE_PRODUCT_TO_CART.

Before moving on, let's recap the main steps you'll take to implement the whole UI of the shopping cart:

- Modify the Add to Cart buttons to use the custom shopping cart.

- Add a "shopping cart summary" box to index.tpl instead of the View Cart button.

- Modify index.php to recognize the CartAction query string parameter.

- Implement the shopping_cart componentized template.

Updating the Add to Cart Buttons

You need to change the code of products_list.tpl so that each displayed product includes an Add to Cart button with a link like the ones shown earlier (a link to index.php with an additional CartAction parameter in the query string).

1. Add the following code at the end of include/config.inc.php:

```
// cart actions
define("ADD_PRODUCT",1);
define("REMOVE_PRODUCT",2);
define("UPDATE_PRODUCTS_QUANTITIES",3);
define("SAVE_PRODUCT_FOR_LATER",4);
define("MOVE_PRODUCT_TO_CART",5);
```

2. If you implemented the PayPal shopping cart, you need to change the Add to Cart buttons to link to the TShirtShop web site instead of PayPal. Open products_list.tpl and product.tpl, and delete the following call to the OpenPayPalWindow() function:

```
<a href="JavaScript: OpenPayPalWindow('...')">
  <IMG src="Images/AddToCart.gif" border="0">
</a>
```

3. Whether you used PayPal or not, the resulting code should be the same. Update the template code of your products_list.tpl as shown in the following code snippet. The new code is highlighted:

```
<td valign="top" width="200">
  <span class="ProductName">
    <a href="{$products_list->mProducts[k].onclick}"
       class="ProductName">
      {$products_list->mProducts[k].name}
    </a>
  </span>
  <br><br>
  <span class="ProductDescription">
    {$products_list->mProducts[k].description}
    <br><br>
    Price:
  </span>
  <span class="ProductPrice">
    ${$products_list->mProducts[k].price}
  </span>
  <br><br>
  <a href=
  "{$products_list->mProducts[k].onclick_add|escape:"html"}">
  <img src="images/add_to_cart.gif" border="0"
       alt="add to cart"/>
  </a>
</td>
```

4. Let's also create Add to Cart links in product.tpl. First, open smarty_plugins/function.load_product.php, and add the following line at the end of the init() method of the Product class. This will create the link for the Add to Cart button:

```
$this->mAddToCartLink = "index.php?CartAction=" . ADD_PRODUCT .
                        "&ProductID=" . $this->mProductId;
```

5. Add the following code to product.tpl in place of your old Add to Cart button:

```
<a href="{$product->mAddToCartLink|escape:"html"}">
  <img src="images/add_to_cart.gif" border="0" alt="add to cart"/>
</a>
```

6. Modify the init() method in smarty_plugins/function.load_products_list.php as follows to add the CartAction parameter:

```
...
    // if browsing the first page, get the list of products by calling
    // the GetProductsOnCatalogPromotion business tier method
    else
      $this->mProducts =
        $this->mBoCatalog->GetProductsOnCatalogPromotion($this->mPageNo,
                                           $this->mrTotalPages);
    // build the "add to cart" links
    $base = "index.php?CartAction=" . ADD_PRODUCT . "&ProductID=";
    for ($i=0;$i<count($this->mProducts);$i++)
      $this->mProducts[$i]['onclick_add'] =
            $base . $this->mProducts[$i]['product_id'];
    // if there are subpages of products, display navigation controls
    if ($this->mrTotalPages > 1)
    {
      // read the query string
      $query_string = $_SERVER['QUERY_STRING'];
      // find  if we have PageNo in the query string
...
```

7. With this piece of code, you create Add to Cart buttons that link to index.php with an additional CartAction parameter to the original query string. After making this change, execute the page to make sure the buttons work. Now browse to your favorite department and click the Add to Cart button of one of the products. You'll see that index.php is reloaded with the additional CartAction parameter appended at the beginning of the query string:

```
http://localhost/tshirtshop/index.php?CartAction=1&ProductID=10
```

The value of the CartAction parameter represents the value of one of the constants you just added to config.inc.php.

Displaying the Cart Summary in the Main Page

Instead of the View Cart PayPal buttons, we want to have a cart summary component, with a "view cart" link, as shown in the screenshots at the beginning of this chapter.

When that View Cart link is clicked, instead of forwarding to PayPal, now we add the CartAction parameter to the query string. If you had a PayPal shopping cart, locate the following code in index.tpl, and delete it (feel free to also remove the OpenPayPalWindow function completely):

```
<a href="JavaScript: OpenPayPalWindow(…)">
  <IMG src="images/view_cart.gif" border="0">
</a>
```

Now follow the steps to implement the cart_summary componentized template, by following the steps:

1. Open index.php and update it as highlighted in the following code snippet. This way
   index.php will recognize the CartAction query string parameter.

```
if (isset($_GET['Search']))
  $pageContentsCell="search_results.tpl";
if (isset($_GET['ProductID']))
  $pageContentsCell = "product.tpl";
if (isset($_GET['CartAction']))
{
  $pageContentsCell = "shopping_cart.tpl";
  $cartSummaryCell = "blank.tpl";
}
else
  $cartSummaryCell="cart_summary.tpl";
$page->assign("cartSummaryCell",$cartSummaryCell);
$page->assign("pageContentsCell", $pageContentsCell);
```

2. Edit index.tpl by adding a reference to the cart summary component:

```
{include file="departments_list.tpl"}
{include file="$categoriesCell"}
{include file="search_box.tpl"}
{include file="$cartSummaryCell"}
```

3. Add the following style to tshirtshop.css:

```
.CartSummary
{
  border-right: #0468a4 2px solid;
  border-top: #0468a4 2px solid;
  border-left: #0468a4 2px solid;
  border-bottom: #0468a4 2px solid;
  background-color: #38bc8dd;
  font-family: Arial, Verdana;
  font-size: 9pt;
  color: darkblue;
  padding-top: 3px;
  padding-left: 2px;
  padding-bottom: 5px
}
```

4. Create a new file in the templates folder named cart_summary.tpl, and write the following code to it:

```
{load_cart_summary assign="cart_summary"}
<br />
{* start cart summary *}
```

```
<table border="0" cellpadding="0" cellspacing="1" width="200">
 <tr>
  <td class="CartSummary">
   {if $cart_summary->mEmptyCart}
     Your shopping cart is empty!
   {else}
    <b>Cart summary </b>
     (<a class href="index.php?CartAction">view details</a>)
    <br/>
    {section name=cSum loop=$cart_summary->mItems}
     {$cart_summary->mItems[cSum].quantity} x
     {$cart_summary->mItems[cSum].name}
     <br/>
    {/section}
    <img src="images/1n.gif" border="0" width="99%" height="1"
alt="line here"/>
    <span class="ProductPrice">
    ${$cart_summary->mTotalAmount}
   {/if}
  </td>
 </tr>
</table>
```

5. Write the function plugin file smarty_plugins/function.load_cart_summary.php:

```php
<?php
// plugin functions inside plugin files must be named: smarty_type_name
function smarty_function_load_cart_summary($params, $smarty)
{
  $cart_summary = new CartSummary();
  // assign template variable
  $smarty->assign($params['assign'], $cart_summary);
}
// class that deals with managing the shopping cart summary
class CartSummary
{
  public $mTotalAmount;
  public $mItems;
  function __construct()
  {
    // creating the middle tier object
    $shopping_cart = new BoShoppingCart();
    // calculate the total amount for the shopping cart
    $this->mTotalAmount = $shopping_cart->GetTotalAmount();
    // get shopping cart products
    $this->mItems =
        $shopping_cart->GetCartProducts(GET_CART_PRODUCTS);
    if (empty($this->mItems))
```

```
        $this->mEmptyCart = true;
      else
        $this->mEmptyCart = false;
    }
  }
?>
```

Creating the Shopping Cart

Right now, clicking on the Add to Cart or View Cart buttons generates an error because you haven't written the shopping_cart componentized template yet (this displays the visitor's shopping cart.) To create the new componentized template, you first create a new template named shopping_cart.tpl in the templates folder. Next, you create the function.load_shopping_cart.php file that will keep your function plugin behind the shopping_cart.tpl template.

Exercise: Creating the shopping_cart **Template**

Follow the detailed steps to create the template:

1. Update index.php to save the PageLink session item:

    ```
    /* if not visiting a product page or the shopping cart, save the link
       to the current page in the PageLink session variable; it will be used
       to create the Continue Shopping link in the product details page and
       the links to product details pages */
    if (!isset($_GET['ProductID']) && !isset($_GET['CartAction']))
      $_SESSION['PageLink'] = "http://" . $_SERVER['SERVER_NAME'] .
            ":" . $_SERVER['SERVER_PORT'] . $_SERVER['REQUEST_URI'];
    ```

2. Create a new file named smarty_plugins/function.load_shopping_cart.php and add the following code to it:

    ```php
    <?php
    // plugin functions inside plugin files must be named: smarty_type_name
    function smarty_function_load_shopping_cart($params, $smarty)
    {
      $shopping_cart = new ShoppingCart();
      $shopping_cart->init();
      // assign template variable
      $smarty->assign($params['assign'], $shopping_cart);
    }
    // class that deals with managing the shopping cart
    class ShoppingCart
    {
      /* public variables available in smarty template */
      public $mShoppingCartProducts;
      public $mSavedShoppingCartProducts;
      public $mTotalAmount;
      public $mIsCartNowEmpty = 0; // is the shopping cart empty?
    ```

```
  public $mIsCartLaterEmpty = 0; // is the 'saved for later' list empty?
  public $mShoppingCartReferrer = "index.php";
  /* private attributes */
  private $mShoppingCart;
  private $mProductId;
  private $mShoppingCartAction;
  //class constructor
  function __construct()
  {
    //setting the "Continue shopping" button target
    if (isset($_SESSION['PageLink']))
      $this->mShoppingCartReferrer = $_SESSION['PageLink'];
    // creating the middle tier object
    $this->mShoppingCart = new BoShoppingCart();
    if (isset($_GET['CartAction']))
      $this->mShoppingCartAction = $_GET['CartAction'];
    else
      trigger_error("CartAction not set", E_USER_ERROR);
    // these cart operations require a valid product id
    if ($this->mShoppingCartAction == ADD_PRODUCT ||
        $this->mShoppingCartAction == REMOVE_PRODUCT ||
        $this->mShoppingCartAction == SAVE_PRODUCT_FOR_LATER ||
        $this->mShoppingCartAction == MOVE_PRODUCT_TO_CART)
      if (isset($_GET['ProductID']))
        $this->mProductId = $_GET['ProductID'];
      else
        trigger_error("ProductID must be set for this type of request",
E_USER_ERROR);
  }
  //init
  function init()
  {
    switch ($this->mShoppingCartAction)
    {
      case ADD_PRODUCT:
        $this->mShoppingCart->AddProduct($this->mProductId);
        header("Location: $this->mShoppingCartReferrer");
        break;
    case REMOVE_PRODUCT:
        $this->mShoppingCart->RemoveProduct($this->mProductId);
        break;
      case UPDATE_PRODUCTS_QUANTITIES:
        $this->mShoppingCart->Update($_POST['productID'],
                                      $_POST['quantity']);
        break;
      case SAVE_PRODUCT_FOR_LATER:
        $this->mShoppingCart->SaveProductToBuyLater($this->mProductId);
```

```
        break;
      case MOVE_PRODUCT_TO_CART:
        $this->mShoppingCart->MoveProductToCart($this->mProductId);
        break;
      default:
        // do nothing
        break;
    }
    // calculate the total amount for the shopping cart
    $this->mTotalAmount = $this->mShoppingCart->GetTotalAmount();
    // get shopping cart products
    $this->mShoppingCartProducts =
        $this->mShoppingCart->GetCartProducts(GET_CART_PRODUCTS);
    // gets the 'saved for later' products
    $this->mSavedShoppingCartProducts =
        $this->mShoppingCart->GetCartProducts(GET_CART_SAVED_PRODUCTS);
    // check whether we have an empty shopping cart
    if (count($this->mShoppingCartProducts) == 0)
      $this->mIsCartNowEmpty = 1;
    // check whether we have an empty 'saved for later' list
    if (count($this->mSavedShoppingCartProducts) == 0)
      $this->mIsCartLaterEmpty = 1;
  }
} //end class
?>
```

3. Create a new file named shopping_cart.tpl in the templates folder and add the following code to it:

```
{load_shopping_cart assign="shopping_cart"}
{if ($shopping_cart->mIsCartNowEmpty == 1)}
 <p>
  <span class="ListDescription">Your shopping cart is empty!</span>
 </p>
{else}
 <p>
  <span class="ListDescription">
  These are the products in your shopping cart:
  </span>
 </p>
 <form action="index.php?CartAction=
      {$smarty.const.UPDATE_PRODUCTS_QUANTITIES}" method="post">
 <table cellpadding="3" cellspacing="1" border="0" width="98%">
  <tr class="TableHeader">
   <td>Product Name</td>
   <td>Price</td>
   <td>Quantity</td>
   <td>Subtotal</td>
```

```
    <td colspan="2"> </td>
   </tr>
   {section name=cCart
           loop=$shopping_cart->mShoppingCartProducts}
    <input name="productID[]" type="hidden" value=
"{$shopping_cart->mShoppingCartProducts[cCart].product_id}"/>
    <tr class="TableRow">
    <td>
     {$shopping_cart->mShoppingCartProducts[cCart].name}
    </td>
    <td>
     {$shopping_cart->mShoppingCartProducts[cCart].price}
    </td>
    <td>
     <input type="text" size="10" name="quantity[]" value=
"{$shopping_cart->mShoppingCartProducts[cCart].quantity}"/>
    </td>
    <td>
     {$shopping_cart->mShoppingCartProducts[cCart].subtotal}
    </td>
    <td align="center">
     <input type="button" name="saveForLater" value="Save for later"
onclick="window.location='index.php?CartAction=
{$smarty.const.SAVE_PRODUCT_FOR_LATER}&amp;ProductID=
{$shopping_cart->mShoppingCartProducts[cCart].product_id}';"/>
    </td>
    <td align="center">
     <input type="button" name="remove" value="Remove"
onclick="window.location='index.php?CartAction=
{$smarty.const.REMOVE_PRODUCT}&amp;ProductID=
{$shopping_cart->mShoppingCartProducts[cCart].product_id}';"/>
    </td>
   </tr>
   {/section}
  </table>
  <table width="98%" cellpadding="3" cellspacing="1"
        border="0" align="center">
   <tr>
    <td>
     <span class="ProductDescription">Total amount:</span> 
     <span class="ProductPrice">${$shopping_cart->mTotalAmount}</span>
    </td>
    <td align="right">
     <input type="submit" name="update" value="Update"/>
    </td>
   </tr>
  </table>
```

```
  </form>
{/if}
{if ($shopping_cart->mIsCartLaterEmpty == 0)}
 <p>
  <span class="ListDescription">Saved products to buy later:</span>
 </p>
 <table width="98%" cellpadding="3" cellspacing="1"
        border="0" align="center">
  <tr class="TableHeader">
   <td>Product Name</td>
   <td align="center">Price</td>
   <td colspan="2"> </td>
  </tr>
  {section name=cLCart loop=$shopping_cart->mSavedShoppingCartProducts}
  <tr class="TableRow">
   <td>
    {$shopping_cart->mSavedShoppingCartProducts[cLCart].name}
   </td>
   <td align="right">
    {$shopping_cart->mSavedShoppingCartProducts[cLCart].price}
   </td>
   <td align="center" width="85">
    <input type="button" name="moveToCart" value="Move to cart"
onclick="window.location='index.php?CartAction=
{$smarty.const.MOVE_PRODUCT_TO_CART}&amp;ProductID=
{$shopping_cart->mSavedShoppingCartProducts[cLCart].product_id}';"/>
   </td>
   <td align="center" width="65">
    <input type="button" name="remove" value="Remove"
onclick="window.location='index.php?CartAction=
{$smarty.const.REMOVE_PRODUCT}&amp;ProductID=
{$shopping_cart->mSavedShoppingCartProducts[cLCart].product_id}';"/>
   </td>
  </tr>
  {/section}
 </table>
{/if}
 <p> 
 <input type="button" name="continueShopping"
value="Continue Shopping" class="AdminButtonText"
onclick="window.location='{$shopping_cart->mShoppingCartReferrer}';"/>
 </p>
```

■**Note**   You will need to write the `window.location` JavaScript calls on single lines, not split like shown in the previous code listing.

You just finished the code for this chapter, so now it's time to try it out and make sure everything works as expected. Test it by adding products to the shopping cart, changing the quantity, and removing items.

How It Works: The Shopping Cart

The actions that the shopping cart can execute are defined by the following constants defined in `config.inc.php`: ADD_PRODUCT, REMOVE_PRODUCT, UPDATE_PRODUCTS_QUANTITIES, SAVE_PRODUCT_FOR_LATER, and MOVE_PRODUCT_TO_CART. Note that we didn't define any variable for viewing the shopping cart, so if `CartAction` does not take any value or its value is not equal to one of the action variables, it will simply display the shopping cart content.

Every shopping cart action, except viewing and updating the shopping cart, relies on the `ProductID` query string parameter (an error is raised if it isn't set). If the proper conditions are met, the business tier method that corresponds to the visitor's action is called.

Administering the Shopping Cart

Now that you've finished writing the shopping cart, there are two more things you need to take into account, both related to administration issues:

- How to delete a product that exists in shopping carts from the product catalog.

- How to remove old shopping cart elements by building a simple shopping cart administration page. This is important, because without this feature, the shopping_cart table keeps growing.

Deleting Products that Exist in Shopping Carts

The catalog administration pages enable you to completely delete products from the catalog. Before removing a product, you should also remove its appearances in visitors' shopping carts.

Update the `DeleteProduct` method in the `DoCatalog` class (in `do_catalog.php`) as follows:

```
public function DeleteProduct($productId)
{
  $query_string = "DELETE FROM product_category WHERE product_id = $productId";
  $this->dbManager->DbQuery($query_string);
  $query_string = "DELETE FROM shopping_cart WHERE product_id = $productId";
  $this->dbManager->DbQuery($query_string);
  $query_string = "DELETE FROM product WHERE product_id = $productId";
  $this->dbManager->DbQuery($query_string);
}
```

Building the Shopping Cart Admin Page

The second problem with the shopping cart is that at this moment no mechanism exists to delete the old records from the shopping_cart table. On a high activity web site, the shopping_cart table can grow very large.

With the current version of the code, shopping cart IDs are stored at the client browser for seven days. As a result, you can assume that any shopping carts that haven't been updated in the last ten days are invalid, and can be safely removed.

In the following exercise, you'll quickly implement a simple shopping cart administration page, where the administrator can see how many old shopping cart entries exist, and can delete them if necessary.

The most interesting aspect you need to understand is the SQL logic that deletes all shopping carts that haven't been updated in a certain amount of time. This isn't as simple as it sounds—at first sight, you might think all you have to do is delete all the records in shopping_cart whose date_product_added is older than a specified date. However, this strategy doesn't work with shopping carts that are modified over time (say, the visitor has been adding items to the cart each week in the past three months). If the last change to the shopping cart is recent, none of its elements should be deleted, even if some are very old. In other words, you should either remove all elements in a shopping cart, or none of them. The age of a shopping cart is given by the age of its most recently modified or added product.

This being said, implement the new functionality by following these steps:

1. Add the following data tier method to the DoShoppingCart method in do_shopping_cart.php:

```
// deletes old shopping carts
public function DeleteOldShoppingCarts($days)
{
  // query that gets the card_ids for old carts
  $query_string =
    "SELECT cart_id, date_product_added
     FROM shopping_cart
     GROUP BY cart_id
     HAVING DATE_SUB(CURDATE(), INTERVAL $days DAY)
            >= MAX(date_product_added)";
  $result = $this->dbManager->DbGetAll($query_string);
  // removes all items from the old carts
  for ($i=0; $i<count($result); $i++)
  {
    $query_string="DELETE FROM shopping_cart
                   WHERE cart_id='{$result[$i]['cart_id']}'";
    $this->dbManager->DbQuery($query_string);
  }
  return count($result);

}
```

2. Add the following business tier method to bo_shopping_cart.php:

```
// deletes old shopping carts
public function DeleteOldShoppingCarts($days)
{
  return $this->mDoShoppingCart->DeleteOldShoppingCarts($days,
                                    $this->GetCartId());
}
```

3. Create a new file named cart_admin.php in your project's root (the tshirtshop folder) with the following contents:

```php
<?php
// Reference config files and business tier
require_once 'include/app_top.php';
require_once SITE_ROOT . '/business_objects/bo_shopping_cart.php';
// If admin is already logged, redirect to the requested page
if (!isset($_SESSION['AdminLogged']) || !$_SESSION['AdminLogged'])
{
  header('Location: admin_login.php?ReturnPage=cart_admin.php');
  exit;
}
// If logging out ...
if (isset($_GET['Page']) && $_GET['Page'] == "Logout")
{
  unset($_SESSION['AdminLogged']);
  header("Location: index.php");
  exit;
}
$message = "";
$selected = 1;
if (isset($_GET['days']))
{
  $shopping_cart = new BoShoppingCart();
  $affected = $shopping_cart->DeleteOldShoppingCarts((int)$_GET['days']);
   $message = "You deleted " . $affected .
              " carts older than {$_GET['days']} days.";
  $selected=(int)$_GET['days'];
}
// Load the page
$page = new Page();
$page->assign('days_ids', array(1,3,5,10,15,30));
$page->assign('message', $message);
$page->assign('selected', $selected);
$page->display('cart_admin.tpl');
// Load app_bottom which closes the database connection
require_once 'include/app_bottom.php';
?>
```

4. Create cart_admin.tpl in the templates folder:

```
{* cart_admin.tpl *}
<!DOCTYPE html
PUBLIC "-//W3C//DTD XHTML 1.0 Transitional//EN"
"http://www.w3.org/TR/xhtml1/DTD/xhtml1-transitional.dtd">
<html>
 <head>
```

```
    <title>TShirtShop Shopping Cart Admin Page</title>
    <link href="tshirtshop.css" type="text/css" rel="stylesheet"/>
   </head>
   <body>
    <span class="Title">TShirtShop Shopping Cart Admin</span>
    <span class="AdminPageText">
     (go back to the <a href="index.php">storefront</a> or
     <a href="catalog_admin.php?Page=Logout">logout</a>)
    </span>
    <br/><br/>
    <span class="AdminPageText">
     {$message}<br/><br/>
     Delete carts older than
     <form action="cart_admin.php" method="get">
      <select name="days">
      {html_options values=$days_ids selected=$selected output=$days_ids}
      </select>
      days
      <input type="submit" value="Delete"/>
     </form>
    </span>
   </body>
  </html>
```

5. Add a link to the cart admin page in templates/first_page_contents.tpl:

```
    Access the <a href="catalog_admin.php"> catalog admin page </a> or
    <a href="cart_admin.php">cart admin page</a>.
```

Summary

In this chapter, you learned how to store the shopping cart information in the database, and you learned a few things in the process as well. Probably the most interesting was the way you can store the shopping cart ID as a cookie on the client, since you haven't done anything similar so far in this book.

After working through the process of creating the shopping cart, starting with the database and ending with the presentation tier, we also touched on the new administrative challenges.

You'll complete the functionality offered by the custom shopping cart in the next chapter with a custom checkout system. You'll add a Place Order button to the shopping cart, which will allow you to save the shopping cart information as a separate order in the database.

■ ■ ■

CHAPTER 9

Dealing with Customer Orders

The good news is that your shopping cart looks good and is fully functional. The bad news is that it doesn't allow the visitor to actually place an order, making it totally useless in the context of a production system. We'll deal with that problem in this chapter, in two separate stages. In the first part of the chapter, you'll implement the client-side part of the order-placing mechanism. More precisely, you'll add a Place Order button to the shopping cart control, which will allow the visitor to order the products in the shopping cart.

In the second part of the chapter, you'll implement a simple orders administration page where the site administrator can view and handle pending orders.

The code for each part of the site will be presented in the usual way, starting with the database tier, continuing with the business tier, and finishing with the user interface (UI).

Implementing an Order Placing System

The whole order placing system is related to the **Place Order** button mentioned earlier. Figure 9-1 shows how this button will look after you update the shopping_cart componentized template in this chapter.

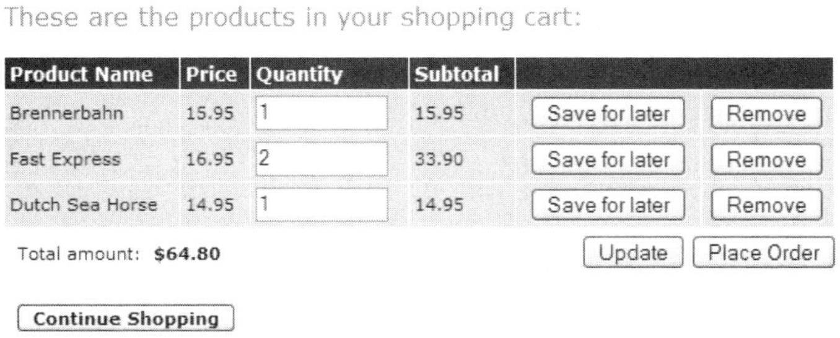

These are the products in your shopping cart:

Product Name	Price	Quantity	Subtotal		
Brennerbahn	15.95	1	15.95	Save for later	Remove
Fast Express	16.95	2	33.90	Save for later	Remove
Dutch Sea Horse	14.95	1	14.95	Save for later	Remove

Total amount: **$64.80**   Update   Place Order

Continue Shopping

Figure 9-1. *The shopping cart with a Place Order button*

The button looks quite boring for something that we can honestly say is the center of this chapter's universe. Still, a lot of logic is hidden behind it, so let's talk about what should happen when the customer clicks that button. Remember that at this stage we don't care who places the order, but we do want to store information in the database about the products that were ordered.

Basically, two things need to happen when the customer clicks the Place Order button:

- First, the order must be stored somewhere in the database. This means that you must save the shopping cart's products to an order named TShirtShop Order *nnn* and clear the shopping cart.

- Secondly, the customer is redirected to a PayPal payment page where the customer pays the necessary amount for the order.

■**Note** For the second development stage, we still don't process payments ourselves, but use a third-party payment processor instead. Now we no longer need the PayPal shopping cart because we implemented our own in the previous chapter. Instead, we'll use the Single Item Purchases option of PayPal, which redirects the visitor directly to a payment page.

A problem that arises when using a third-party payment processor is that the customer can change his mind and cancel the order while at the checkout page. This can result in orders that are saved to the database (the order is saved before the page is redirected to the payment page), but for which payment wasn't completed. Obviously, we need a payment confirmation system, along with a database structure that is able to store status information about each order.

The confirmation system that you'll implement is simple. Every payment processor, including PayPal, can be instructed to send a confirmation message after a payment has been processed. We'll allow the site administrator to manually check, in the administration page, which orders have been paid for. These orders are known as verified orders. You'll see later in this chapter how to manage them in the orders management part of the site.

■**Note** PayPal and its competitors offer automated systems that inform your web site when a payment has been completed or canceled. However, this book doesn't visit the intimate details of any of these payment systems—you'll need to do your homework and study the documentation of your company of choice. The PayPal Instant Payment Notification manual can be downloaded at https://www.paypal.com/en_US/pdf/ipn.pdf.

Now that you have an idea of what to do with that Place Order button, the next major concerns are what order information to store in the database and how to store it. As you saw in previous chapters, deciding how to store information helps you get a better idea of how the whole system works.

Storing Orders in the Database

Two kinds of order information need to be stored:

- General details about the order, such as the date the order was created; whether and when the products have been shipped; whether the order is verified, completed, or canceled; and a few other details

- The products that belong to that order and their quantities

In the orders administration page that you'll create later in this chapter, you'll be able to see and modify the general order information.

Creating the New Data Tables

Due to the nature of the information that will be stored, you need two data tables: `orders` and `order_detail`. The `orders` table stores information regarding the `order` as a whole, while `order_detail` contains the products that belong to each order.

Tip So far we have been consistent about naming our tables in singular form (`shopping_cart`, `department`, and so on). However, here we make an exception for the `orders` table because `ORDER` is also an SQL keyword. For the purposes of this book, we prefer to break the naming convention to avoid any confusion while writing the SQL code, and generally speaking, it isn't good practice to use SQL keywords as object names.

These tables have a one-to-many relationship, enforced through a foreign-key constraint on their `order_id` fields. One-to-many is the usual relationship implemented between an `orders` table and an `order_detail` table. The `order_detail` table contains many records that belong to one order. You might want to revisit Chapter 4 where the table relationships are explained in more detail.

You'll implement the tables in the following exercise.

Exercise: Adding the orders and the order_detail Tables to the Database

Follow these steps to add the new data tables to the tshirtshop database:

1. Use phpMyAdmin (or your preferred database interface) to create a new data table named orders with 11 fields, as shown in Figure 9-2.

Server: localhost ▸ Database: tshirtshop ▸ Table: orders

Field	Type⑦	Length/Values*	Attributes	Null	Default**	Extra					
order_id	INT ∨		UNSIGNED ∨	not null ∨		auto_increment ∨	⊙	○	○	○	☐
total_amount	DECIMAL ∨	10.2	∨	not null ∨	0	∨	○	○	○	⊙	☐
date_created	DATETIME ∨		∨	not null ∨		∨	○	○	○	⊙	☐
date_shipped	DATETIME ∨		∨	null ∨		∨	○	○	○	⊙	☐
verified	TINYINT ∨	1	∨	not null ∨	0	∨	○	○	○	⊙	☐
completed	TINYINT ∨	1	∨	not null ∨	0	∨	○	○	○	⊙	☐
canceled	TINYINT ∨	1	∨	not null ∨	0	∨	○	○	○	⊙	☐
comments	VARCHAR ∨	255	∨	null ∨		∨	○	○	○	⊙	☐
customer_name	VARCHAR ∨	50	∨	null ∨		∨	○	○	○	⊙	☐
shipping_addres	VARCHAR ∨	255	∨	null ∨		∨	○	○	○	⊙	☐
customer_email	VARCHAR ∨	50	∨	null ∨		∨	○	○	○	⊙	☐

Table comments: Table type:
                              INNO DB ∨

Figure 9-2. *Designing the* orders *table*

■**Caution** Don't forget to set order_id as both a primary key and an auto_increment column! Also, you must select INNO DB for the table type if you want to take advantage of referential integrity (we'll enforce the relationship between orders and order_detail using a foreign key).

If you prefer not to use a visual tool, you can either use the code from the Downloads section of the Apress web site (http://www.apress.com) or execute the following query in your tshirtshop database:

```
CREATE TABLE orders (
order_id INT UNSIGNED NOT NULL auto_increment,
total_amount DECIMAL(10,2) NOT NULL,
date_created DATETIME NOT NULL,
date_shipped DATETIME NULL,
verified TINYINT(1) DEFAULT '0' NOT NULL,
completed TINYINT(1) DEFAULT '0' NOT NULL,
canceled TINYINT(1) DEFAULT '0' NOT NULL,
comments VARCHAR(255),
customer_name VARCHAR(50),
shipping_address VARCHAR(255),
customer_email VARCHAR(50),
PRIMARY KEY (order_id)
) TYPE = InnoDB;
```

2. Next, add the `order_detail` table as shown in Figure 9-3.

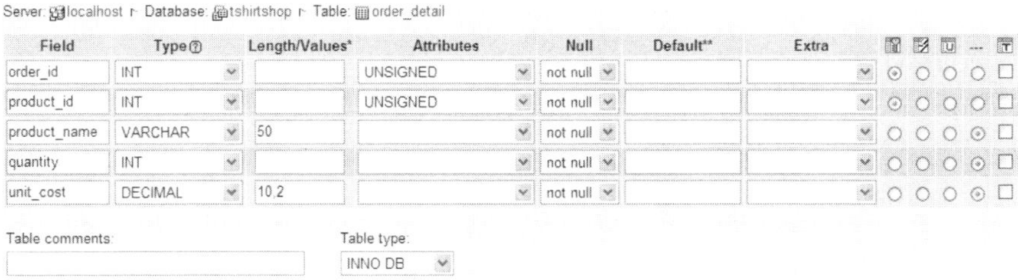

Server: ⃞localhost ⊦ Database: ⃞tshirtshop ⊦ Table: ⃞order_detail

Field	Type⑦	Length/Values*	Attributes	Null	Default**	Extra					
order_id	INT ⌄		UNSIGNED ⌄	not null ⌄		⌄	⊙	○	○	○	☐
product_id	INT ⌄		UNSIGNED ⌄	not null ⌄		⌄	⊙	○	○	○	☐
product_name	VARCHAR ⌄	50	⌄	not null ⌄		⌄	○	○	○	⊙	☐
quantity	INT ⌄		⌄	not null ⌄		⌄	○	○	○	⊙	☐
unit_cost	DECIMAL ⌄	10.2	⌄	not null ⌄		⌄	○	○	○	⊙	☐

Table comments: Table type:

                                    INNO DB ⌄

Figure 9-3. Designing the `order_detail` *table*

■**Caution** Don't forget to set the composite primary key formed of `order_id` and `product_id`.

The SQL query that creates this table is

```
CREATE TABLE order_detail (
order_id INT UNSIGNED NOT NULL,
product_id INT UNSIGNED NOT NULL,
product_name VARCHAR(50) NOT NULL,
quantity INT NOT NULL,
unit_cost DECIMAL(10, 2) NOT NULL,
PRIMARY KEY (order_id, product_id)
) TYPE = InnoDB;
```

3. Enforce the relationship between the `orders` and `order_detail` tables by creating a foreign key that links the `order_id` field in `order_detail` to the `order_id` field in `orders`. If you prefer using phpMyAdmin, open `order_detail`'s table properties page, click the `Relation view` link, enforce the relationship as shown in Figure 9-4, and click the Go button.

Server: ⃞localhost ⊦ Database: ⃞tshirtshop ⊦ Table: ⃞order_detail

| ⃞Structure | ⃞Browse | ⃞SQL | ⃞Search | ⃞Insert | ⃞Export | ⃞Operations | ⃞Empty | ⃞Drop |

	Links to				
		InnoDB			
order_id	orders->order_id ⌄	ON DELETE	-- ⌄	ON UPDATE	-- ⌄
product_id	-- ⌄	ON DELETE	-- ⌄	ON UPDATE	-- ⌄
product_name	-- ⌄	ON DELETE	-- ⌄	ON UPDATE	-- ⌄
quantity	-- ⌄	ON DELETE	-- ⌄	ON UPDATE	-- ⌄
unit_cost	-- ⌄	ON DELETE	-- ⌄	ON UPDATE	-- ⌄
		Go			

Figure 9-4. Using phpMyAdmin to create a `FOREIGN KEY` *constraint*

Alternatively, you can build the FOREIGN KEY constraint with the following SQL query:

```
ALTER TABLE order_detail
ADD CONSTRAINT fk_order_id
    FOREIGN KEY (order_id)
    REFERENCES orders(order_id)
```

How It Works: The Data Tables and the Relationship

Now that you've created the tables, let's take a closer look at their structure and relationships.

The orders Table

The orders table contains two categories of information: data about the order itself (the first eight fields) and data about the customer that made the order (last three fields).

An alternative would be to store the customer information in a separate table named customer and store only the customer_id value in the orders table. However, storing customer data is not one of the goals of this development stage. At this stage, we prefer to keep things simple because it doesn't matter who made the order, just what products have been sold. You'll deal with creating a separate customer table in Chapter 11.

Third-party payment processors like PayPal store and manage the complete customer information, so it doesn't need to be stored in your database as well. We have added the customer_name, shipping_address, and customer_email fields as optional fields that can be filled by the administrator if it's easier to have this information at hand for certain (or all) orders.

The field names are self-explanatory. order_id is the primary key of the table. total_amount stores the total value of the order. date_created, and date_shipped specify when the order was created and shipped (the latter supports NULLs in case the order hasn't been shipped yet).

The three bit fields (verified, completed and canceled) show the status of the order. These fields store 0 for "No" and 1 for "Yes". Note that instead of having more bit fields, we could have a single status field, which would contain the order status coded as an integer value, for example 1 for "processing," 2 for "completed," 3 for "canceled," and so on. In Chapters 12 and 13, you'll learn how to implement a professional order pipeline, but an easy order tracking system is enough for your web site in this stage of development.

At the moment an order is created, all three bit fields are set to 0. The verified field is set to 1 after PayPal confirms the payment. The site administrator marks an order as "verified" upon receipt of the payment confirmation email. After the payment is confirmed (and the order is verified), the products are shipped, the date_shipped field is populated, and the completed bit is set to 1. The administrator marks an order as completed when the order has been assembled, addressed, and mailed to the purchaser.

The administrator might want to mark an order as canceled (by setting the canceled bit to 1) if it hasn't been verified in a certain amount of time, or for other various reasons. The comments field is used to record whatever special information might show up about the order.

■Note PayPal can automatically tell your web site when a payment is completed through the Instant Payment Notification feature. Using this feature can make things easier for the site administrator because he or she wouldn't need to manually check orders for which payment was received; however we won't use this feature in TShirtShop because it's too specific to PayPal. Consult the documentation of the payment provider you choose to check what specific features they have prepared for you to play with.

The order_detail Table

Let's see what information the order_detail table contains. Take a look at Figure 9-5 to see some typical order_detail records.

order_id	product_id	product_name	quantity	unit_cost
7	35	Brennerbahn	1	15.95
7	76	Fast Express	2	16.95
7	83	Dutch Sea Horse	1	14.95
8	12	Norway Post	1	15.95
8	14	Swedish Horse	1	14.95
8	23	Danish Locomotive	1	14.95

Figure 9-5. *Sample data in the* order_detail *table*

Each record in order_detail represents an ordered product that belongs to the order specified by order_id. The primary key is formed by both order_id and product_id because a particular product can be ordered only once in one order. A quantity field contains the number of ordered items, so it wouldn't make any sense to have one product_id recorded more than once for one order.

You might be wondering why the product_id *and* the price and product name are recorded in the order_detail table, especially since if you have the product id, you can get all of the product's details from the product table without having any duplicated information.

We chose to duplicate the product data (the product's name and price) in the order_detail table to guard against product information changes; products can be removed from the database, and their name and price can change, but this shouldn't affect the orders' data.

We store the product_id because, apart from being the only programmatic way to link back to the original product info (if the product still exists), product_id used to create the primary key of order_detail. product_id comes in very handy here, because having it in the composite primary key in order_detail saves you from needing to add another primary key field, and also ensures that you won't have the same product more than once in a single order.

The Foreign Key

This is the first chapter where you get to play with foreign keys. We had a short discussion about them in Chapter 4, which you might want to review.

Note Foreign keys are only supported by INNO DB tables.

Foreign keys are all about enforcing referential integrity. Enforcing the relationship between orders and order_detail ensures that every record in order_detail is related to an existing record in orders (so each order detail belongs to a valid order). The database won't allow you to add order_detail records with invalid order_id values, and won't allow you to remove records from the orders table if order_detail records belong to those records (in which case, removing records from the orders table would generate orphaned order_detail records).

Tip After adding some orders to your database, later in this chapter, try to manually remove a record from the orders table and you'll see that the database won't allow it, because the record will have related records in the order_details table.

Let's reexamine the SQL query that added the foreign key:

```
ALTER TABLE order_detail
ADD CONSTRAINT fk_order_id
    FOREIGN KEY (order_id)
    REFERENCES orders(order_id)
```

The ADD CONSTRAINT fk_order_id part specifies that you're adding a new constraint named FK_ORDER_ID. The FOREIGN KEY (order_id) part specifies that you're adding a FOREIGN KEY type of constraint, on the order_id field, which references the order_id field in orders (REFERENCES orders(order_id)).

Perhaps you noticed the ON DELETE and ON UPDATE fields on the phpMyAdmin form for implementing relationships. These are options you can set when implementing new relationships:

- ON UPDATE: This option tells MySQL how to behave when updating data that is related to data in another table. The ON UPDATE CASCADE option can be used for maintaining data integrity in such cases. With ON UPDATE CASCADE, if the order_id field of an existing order is changed, SQL Server also changes the order_id fields of all order_detail records that relate to that order—this way, even after you change the order's ID, its related records still belong to it. You can leave this option unchecked because you won't need to change order IDs.

- ON DELETE: Selecting ON DELETE CASCADE is a radical solution for keeping data integrity. If this is selected and you delete a record from the orders table, all its related order_detail entries are automatically deleted by MySQL. You should be very careful with this sensitive option. You won't use it in the TShirtShop project.

Implementing the Data Tier

At this stage, you need to add two additional data tier methods in the DoShoppingCart class. The most important is CreateOrder, which takes the products from the shopping cart and creates an order with them. The other procedure is EmptyShoppingCart, which empties the visitor's cart after the order has been placed.

Start with EmptyShoppingCart because this is called from CreateOrder.

EmptyShoppingCart

This isn't the most interesting data tier method you'll ever write, but nevertheless it's important for the TShirtShop store. The customer expects the shopping cart to be empty after buying the products. Add the EmptyShoppingCart method to the DoShoppingCart class:

```
// empties visitor's shopping cart
public function EmptyShoppingCart($cartId)
{
  $query_string = "DELETE FROM shopping_cart
                    WHERE cart_id='$cartId'";
  $this->dbManager->DbQuery($query_string);
}
```

CreateOrder

The heart of the order-placing mechanism is the CreateOrder method. This method gets called when the customer decides to buy the products in the shopping cart and clicks the **Place Order** button.

The role of CreateOrder is to create a new order based on the products in the customer's shopping cart. This implies adding a new record to the orders table and a number of records (one record for each product) in the order_detail table.

Add the following CreateOrder method to the DoShoppingCart class and then we'll talk a bit more about it:

```
// create a new order
public function CreateOrder($cartId)
{
  // Insert a new record into orders
  $query_string = "INSERT INTO orders (date_created) VALUES (NOW())";
  $this->dbManager->DbQuery($query_string);
  // Obtain the new Order ID
  $query_string="SELECT LAST_INSERT_ID()";
  $order_id = $this->dbManager->DbGetOne($query_string);
  //prepare order details to be inserted in order_detail table
  $query_string =
    "SELECT product.product_id, product.name,
            shopping_cart.quantity, product.price
      FROM product JOIN shopping_cart
        ON product.product_id = shopping_cart.product_id
      WHERE shopping_cart.cart_id = '$cartId'";
```

```
$cart_items = $this->dbManager->DbGetAll($query_string);
// save shopping cart items as order details
$sum = 0;
for ($i=0; $i<count($cart_items); $i++)
{
  // add a shopping cart item to order_detail
  $query_string =
    "INSERT INTO order_detail
            (order_id, product_id, product_name, quantity, unit_cost)
      VALUES ($order_id,
            {$cart_items[$i]['product_id']},
            '{$cart_items[$i]['name']}',
            {$cart_items[$i]['quantity']},
            {$cart_items[$i]['price']})";
  $this->dbManager->DbQuery($query_string);
  // add item's price to the total amount
  $sum += $cart_items[$i]['quantity']
          * $cart_items[$i]['price'];
}
// save the order's total amount
$query_string =
  "UPDATE orders SET total_amount = $sum WHERE order_id = $order_id";
$this->dbManager->DbQuery($query_string);
// Clear the shopping cart
$this->EmptyShoppingCart($cartId);
//return the Order ID
return $order_id;
}
```

The first step in this method involves creating the new record in the orders table. You need to do this at the beginning to find out what order_id was generated for the new order. Remember that the order_id field is an autoincrement column and is automatically generated by the database, so you need to retrieve its value after inserting a record into orders:

```
// Insert a new record into orders
$query_string = "INSERT INTO orders (date_created) VALUES (NOW())";
$this->dbManager->DbQuery($query_string);
// Obtain the new Order ID
$query_string="SELECT LAST_INSERT_ID()";
$order_id = $this->dbManager->DbGetOne($query_string);
```

This is the basic mechanism of extracting the newly generated ID. After the INSERT statement, you save the value of LAST_INSERT_ID() to a variable. You must do this immediately after inserting the new row, because the value of LAST_INSERT_ID() is reset after the next successful insert operation.

Using the order_id variable, you add the order_detail records by gathering information from the product and shopping_cart tables. You get the list of the products and their quantities from shopping_cart, get their names and prices from product, and save these records one by one to the order_detail table.

```
for ($i=0; $i<count($cart_items); $i++)
{
  // add a shopping cart item to order_detail
  $query_string =
    "INSERT INTO order_detail
            (order_id, product_id, product_name, quantity, unit_cost)
     VALUES ($order_id,
              {$cart_items[$i]['product_id']},
              '{$cart_items[$i]['name']}',
              {$cart_items[$i]['quantity']},
              {$cart_items[$i]['price']})";
  $this->dbManager->DbQuery($query_string);
  // add item's price to the total amount
  $sum += $cart_items[$i]['quantity']
          * $cart_items[$i]['price'];
}
```

Tip When joining product and shopping_cart, you get the product_id from product, but you could also get it from shopping_cart; the result would be the same because the table join is made on the product_id column.

While saving the products, the method also calculates the total amount of the order by adding each product's price multiplied by its quantity. This value is then saved as the order's total_amount:

```
// save the order's total amount
$query_string =
  "UPDATE ORDERS SET total_amount=$sum WHERE order_id = $order_id";
$this->dbManager->DbQuery($query_string);
```

In the end, the method empties the visitor's shopping cart, and returns the order's ID:

```
// Clear the shopping cart
$this->EmptyShoppingCart($cartId);
//return the Order ID
return $order_id;
```

Implementing the Business Tier

In this step, you only need a single method, CreateOrder, which you'll add to the BoShopping-Cart class:

```
// create a new order from the shopping cart
public function CreateOrder()
{
  return $this->mDoShoppingCart->CreateOrder($this->GetCartId());
}
```

The method calls the CreateOrder data tier method, returning the order_id of the newly created order.

Implementing the Presentation Tier

You've finally arrived at the part of the process where you'll put the code you've written into action. The UI consists of the star player, the Place Order button along with all the logic behind it, which allows the visitor to become a customer.

This button is the only addition on the visitor side for the custom checkout. Let's first place the button on the shopping_cart template file, and then implement its functionality.

To get the desired functionality, you just follow a few simple steps. The first one involves adding the Place Order button to the shopping cart.

Adding the Place Order Button

Modify shopping_cart.tpl by adding a new column just after the Update button, as high-lighted in the following code snippet:

```
<tr>
  <td>
   <span class="ProductDescription">Total amount:</span> 
   <span class="ProductPrice">${$shopping_cart->mTotalAmount}</span>
  </td>
  <td align="right">
   <input type="submit" name="update" value="Update"/>
   <input type="submit" name="place_order" value="Place Order"/>
  </td>
</tr>
```

Cool, now you have a Place Order button in the shopping cart.

Implementing the Order Placement Functionality

Now it's time to implement the Place Order button's functionality. Because this functionality depends on the company that processes your payments, you might need to adapt it to the behavior of your payment processing company. If you use PayPal, the code that redirects the visitor to a payment was already presented in "Using the PayPal Single Item Purchases Feature" section of Chapter 6.

Add the following code at the beginning of the init() method of the ShoppingCart class in smarty_plugins/function.load_shopping_cart.php:

```
// calculate the total amount for the shopping cart
$this->mTotalAmount = $this->mShoppingCart->GetTotalAmount();
// if the Place Order button was clicked...
if(isset($_POST['place_order']))
{
  // create the order and get the order ID
  $order_id = $this->mShoppingCart->CreateOrder();
  // this will contain the PayPal link
  $redirect =
    "https://www.paypal.com/xclick/business=youremail@server.com" .
    "&item_name=TShirtShop Order " . $order_id .
    "&item_number=" . $order_id .
    "&amount=" . $this->mTotalAmount .
    "&return=http://www.YourWebSite.com" .
    "&cancel_return=http://www.YourWebSite.com";
  // redirection to the payment page
  header("Location: " . $redirect);
  exit;
}
```

Of course, if you use another company to process your payments, you'll need to modify the code accordingly.

When a visitor clicks the Place Order button, two important actions happen. First, the order is created in the database by calling the CreateOrder method of the BoShoppingCart class. This function calls its corresponding function from DoShoppingCart class to create a new order with the products in the shopping cart, and returns the ID of the new order:

```
// create the order and get the order ID
$order_id = $this->mShoppingCart->CreateOrder();
```

Second, the visitor is redirected to the payment page, which requests payment for an item named "TShirtShop Order *XXX*" with a value that amounts to the total value of the order.

Administering Orders

So your visitor just made an order. Now what?

After giving visitors the option to pay for your products, you need to make sure they actually get what they paid for. TShirtShop needs a carefully designed administration page, where the administrator can quickly see the status of pending orders.

▪**Note** This chapter doesn't intend to help you create a perfect order administration system, but rather something that is simple and functional enough to get you on the right track.

The orders administration part of the site will consist of the orders_admin.php page and two componentized templates named orders_list_admin and order_details_admin.

The orders_admin.php page always loads the orders_list_admin componentized template that offers the capability to filter the orders. When first loaded, it offers you various ways of selecting orders as shown in Figure 9-6.

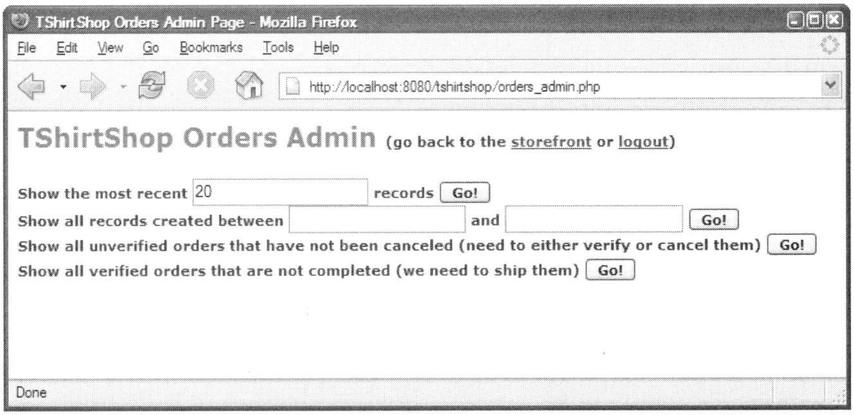

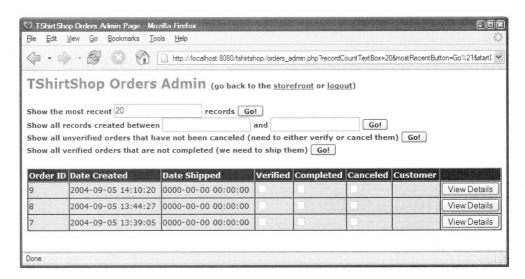

Figure 9-6. *The Orders Admin page*

After clicking one of the Go! buttons, the matching orders appear in a table (see Figure 9-7).

Figure 9-7. *Selecting the most recent orders in the Orders Admin page*

When you click the View Details button for an order, you are sent to a page where you can view and update order information, as shown in Figure 9-8.

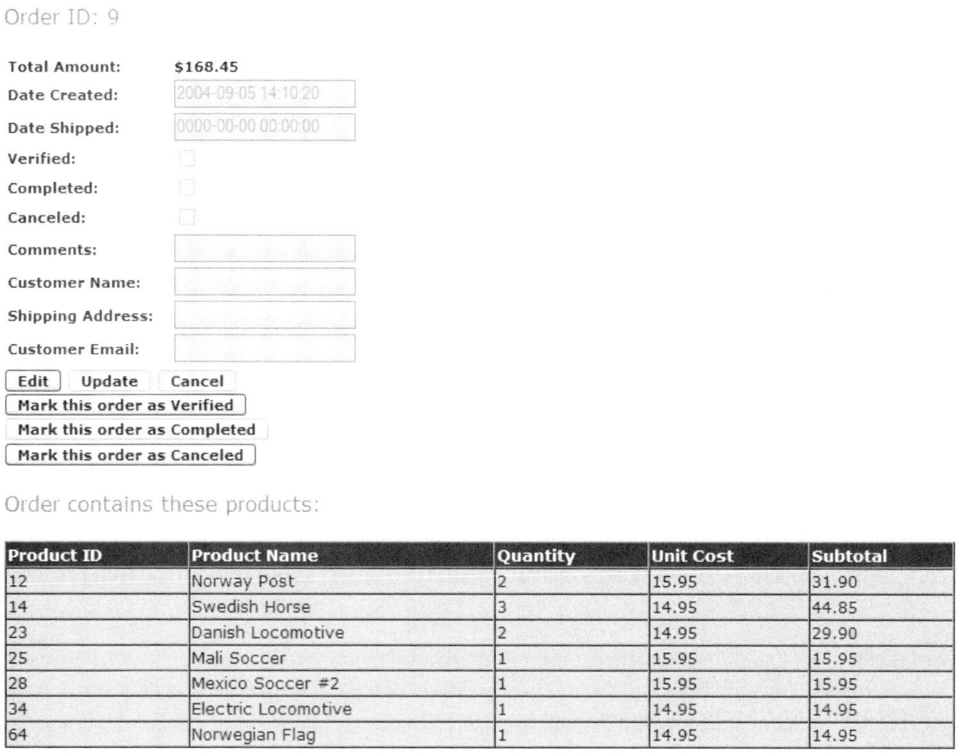

Order ID: 9

Total Amount:	$168.45
Date Created:	2004-09-05 14:10:20
Date Shipped:	0000-00-00 00:00:00
Verified:	☐
Completed:	☐
Canceled:	☐
Comments:	
Customer Name:	
Shipping Address:	
Customer Email:	

Edit   Update   Cancel
Mark this order as Verified
Mark this order as Completed
Mark this order as Canceled

Order contains these products:

Product ID	Product Name	Quantity	Unit Cost	Subtotal
12	Norway Post	2	15.95	31.90
14	Swedish Horse	3	14.95	44.85
23	Danish Locomotive	2	14.95	29.90
25	Mali Soccer	1	15.95	15.95
28	Mexico Soccer #2	1	15.95	15.95
34	Electric Locomotive	1	14.95	14.95
64	Norwegian Flag	1	14.95	14.95

Figure 9-8. *Administering order details*

The orders_admin.php Page

This page first checks whether you are authenticated as admin and then loads the orders_list_admin and order_details_admin componentized templates. You'll create the orders_admin.php page in the following exercise.

Exercise: Creating the orders_admin.php **Page**

To create the orders_admin.php page, follow these steps:

1. Start with the template file. Add a new file named orders_admin.tpl in the templates directory, and write the following code in it:

```
<!DOCTYPE html
PUBLIC "-//W3C//DTD XHTML 1.0 Transitional//EN"
"http://www.w3.org/TR/xhtml1/DTD/xhtml1-transitional.dtd">
<html>
 <head>
  <title>TShirtShop Orders Admin Page</title>
  <link href="tshirtshop.css" type="text/css" rel="stylesheet"/>
 </head>
```

```
<body>
 <table cellpadding="0" cellspacing="0" border="0" width="100%">
   <tr>
     <td>
       <span class="Title">TShirtShop Orders Admin</span>
       <span class="AdminPageText">
         (go back to the <a href="index.php">storefront</a> or
         <a href="orders_admin.php?logout">logout</a>)
       </span>
     </td>
   </tr>
 </table>
 <br/>
 {include file="orders_list_admin.tpl"}
 {include file="$orderDetailsCell"}
 </body>
</html>
```

2. Create a new file named orders_admin.php in the project's root folder (the tshirtshop folder):

```php
<?php
// load config files
require_once 'include/app_top.php';
// load business objects
require_once 'business_objects/bo_order_manager.php';
// if admin is not logged in, redirect to admin_login.php page
if (!isset($_SESSION['AdminLogged']) || $_SESSION['AdminLogged'] != true)
{
  header('Location: admin_login.php?ReturnPage=orders_admin.php');
  exit;
}
// if logging out ...
if (isset($_GET['logout']))
{
  unset($_SESSION['AdminLogged']);
  header("Location:index.php");
  exit;
}
// load Smarty template ...
$page = new Page();
$orderDetailsCell = "blank.tpl";
if (isset($_GET['OrderId']))
  $orderDetailsCell = "order_details_admin.tpl";
$page->assign("orderDetailsCell", $orderDetailsCell);
$page->display('orders_admin.tpl');
?>
```

How It Works: The orders_admin.php Page

The template of this page (orders_admin.tpl) has a simple structure. orders_list_admin.tpl is displayed in the upper part of the page, and order_details_admin.tpl appears in the bottom part of the page when OrderID exists in the query string (this happens when the administrator selects an order to see its details).

The PHP file (orders_admin.php) mainly deals with loading the template files, and with the login mechanism. If the administrator is not logged in, he or she is redirected to the admin_login.php page where he can authenticate himself just as you saw in Chapter 7:

```
// if admin is not logged in, redirect to admin_login.php page
if (!isset($_SESSION['AdminLogged']) || $_SESSION['AdminLogged'] != true)
{
  header('Location: admin_login.php?ReturnPage=orders_admin.php');
  exit;
}
```

The administrator login info (admin/admin) is kept inside the include/config.inc.php file.

Adding a Link to orders_admin.php on the First Page

Finally, let's add a link to the orders_admin.php page by updating the templates/first_page_contents.tpl file near the link to the catalog admin page, as in the following code snippet:

```
...
    Beginning PHP 5 E-Commerce: From Novice to Professional! <br /><br />
    Access the <a href="catalog_admin.php">catalog admin page</a>, the
    <a href="cart_admin.php">cart admin page</a> or the
    <a href="orders_admin.php">orders admin page</a>.
...
```

Displaying Pending Orders

In the following pages, you'll implement the orders_list_admin componentized template and its supporting data tier and business tier functionality. orders_list_admin is the componentized template that fills the first table cell in the orders administration page, and allows the administrator to view the orders that have been placed on the web site. Because the orders list will become very long, it is important to have a few well-chosen filtering options.

The administrator will be able to select the orders using the following criteria:

- Show the most recent orders.

- Show orders that took place in a certain period of time.

- Show pending orders that have not been canceled. This will show the recent orders that have been placed and for which payment confirmation from PayPal is still pending. The administrator will need to mark these orders as verified when the financial transaction is confirmed. Otherwise, if the payment is not confirmed in a reasonable amount of time, the administrator will probably want to cancel the order (marking it as canceled), so that it will not be listed again when the button is clicked again at a later time.

- Show orders that need to be shipped (they are verified, but not yet completed). These are the orders that have been paid for, but haven't shipped. After the products are shipped, the administrator will mark the order as completed.

Figure 9-9 shows how the control will look when first loaded in the orders administration page.

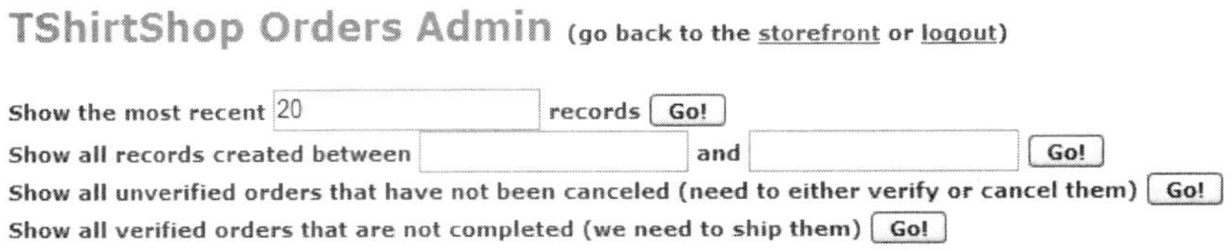

TShirtShop Orders Admin (go back to the storefront or logout)

Show the most recent 20   records Go!
Show all records created between   and   Go!
Show all unverified orders that have not been canceled (need to either verify or cancel them) Go!
Show all verified orders that are not completed (we need to ship them) Go!

Figure 9-9. *Orders filtering options*

Okay, now that you know what you want, let's start writing some code. You'll start with the data tier.

Implementing the Data Tier

First, create a new file named do_order_manager.php in the data_objects folder, and add the following code to it:

```php
<?php
// data tier class that supports order administration functionality
class DoOrderManager
{
  private $dbManager;
  // class constructor
  function __construct()
  {
    // get the global DbManager instance (created in app_top.php)
    $this->dbManager = $GLOBALS['gDbManager'];
  }
}
?>
```

The DoOrderManager class contains all the data tier functionality for orders administration. Next you'll add the methods in the newly created DoOrderManager class as described in the following sections.

GetMostRecentOrders

The GetMostRecentOrders method retrieves a list of the most recent orders. The SELECT SQL statement used in this method uses the LIMIT clause to limit the number of returned rows to $count rows.

```php
  // get the most recent $count orders
  public function GetMostRecentOrders($count)
  {
```

```
    $query_string =
      "SELECT order_id, total_amount, date_created, date_shipped,
             verified, completed, canceled, customer_name
      FROM orders
      ORDER BY date_created DESC
      LIMIT $count";
    $result = $this->dbManager->DbGetAll($query_string);
    return $result;
  }
```

The ORDER BY clause is used to sort the results. The default sorting mode is ascending, but by adding DESC, the descending sort mode is set (so the most recent orders will be listed first).

GetOrdersBetweenDates

This method returns all the records in which the current date is between the start and end dates that are supplied as parameters. The results are sorted descending by date.

```
  // get orders between two dates
  public function GetOrdersBetweenDates($startDate, $endDate)
  {
    $query_string =
      "SELECT order_id, total_amount, date_created, date_shipped,
             verified, completed, canceled, customer_name
      FROM orders
      WHERE date_created >= '$startDate' AND date_created <='$endDate'
      ORDER BY date_created DESC";
    $result = $this->dbManager->DbGetAll($query_string);
    return $result;
  }
```

GetUnverifiedUncanceledOrders

This method is used to return the orders that have not been verified yet, but have not been canceled either. In other words, we want to see the orders that need to be either verified (and then completed when the shipment is done), or canceled (if the payment isn't confirmed in a reasonable amount of time). The code is pretty straightforward:

```
  // gets pending orders that need to be either verified or canceled
  public function GetUnverifiedUncanceledOrders()
  {
    $query_string =
      "SELECT order_id, total_amount, date_created, date_shipped,
             verified, completed, canceled, customer_name
      FROM orders
      WHERE verified=0 AND canceled=0
      ORDER BY date_created DESC";
    $result=$this->dbManager->DbGetAll($query_string);
    return $result;
  }
```

GetVerifiedUncompletedOrders

The GetVerifiedUncompletedOrders method gets all the orders that have been verified, but not yet completed. The administrator will want to see these orders when an order has shipped and needs to be marked as completed. (When an order is marked as completed, the date_shipped field is also populated.)

```
// gets pending orders that need to be shipped
public function GetVerifiedUncompletedOrders()
{
  $query_string =
    "SELECT order_id, total_amount, date_created, date_shipped,
           verified, completed, canceled, customer_name
     FROM orders
     WHERE verified=1 AND completed=0
     ORDER BY date_created DESC";
  $result = $this->dbManager->DbGetAll($query_string);
  return $result;
}
```

Implementing the Business Tier

The business tier consists of a new class named BoOrderManager, whose methods call their data tier counterparts. This class is pretty straightforward with no special logic, so we'll just list the code. Create the business_objects/bo_order_manager.php file and add the following to it:

```
<?php
// reference data tier class
require_once SITE_ROOT . '/data_objects/do_order_manager.php';
// business tier class that supports order administration functionality
class BoOrderManager
{
  // private attributes
  private $mDoOrderManager;
  // class constructor
  function __construct()
  {
    $this->mDoOrderManager = new DoOrderManager();
  }
  // get the most recent $count orders
  public function GetMostRecentOrders($count)
  {
    $result = $this->mDoOrderManager->GetMostRecentOrders($count);
    return $result;
  }
  // get orders between two dates
  public function GetOrdersBetweenDates($startDate, $endDate)
  {
    $result =
```

```
     $this->mDoOrderManager->GetOrdersBetweenDates($startDate,$endDate);
     return $result;
   }
   // gets pending orders that need to be either verified or canceled
   public function GetUnverifiedUncanceledOrders()
   {
     $result = $this->mDoOrderManager->GetUnverifiedUncanceledOrders();
     return $result;
   }
   // gets pending orders that need to be shipped
   public function GetVerifiedUncompletedOrders()
   {
     $result = $this->mDoOrderManager->GetVerifiedUncompletedOrders();
     return $result;
   }
}//end class
?>
```

Implementing the Presentation Tier

Now it's time to implement the orders_list_admin componentized template. Follow these
steps to make the magic happen:

1. Create a new file named orders_list_admin.tpl in the templates folder with the
   following code in it:

   ```
   {load_orders_list_admin assign="orders_list_admin"}
   <form method="get" action="orders_admin.php">
   <span class="AdminPageText">Show the most recent</span>
   <input name="recordCountTextBox" type="text"
          value="{$orders_list_admin->mRecordCount}"/>
   <span class="AdminPageText">records</span>
   <input type="submit" name="mostRecentButton"
          value="Go!" class="AdminButtonText"/>
   </form>
   <form method="get" action="orders_admin.php">
   <span class="AdminPageText">Show all records created between</span>
   <input name="startDateTextBox" type="text"
          value='{$orders_list_admin->mStartDate}'/>
   <span class="AdminPageText">and</span>
   <input name="endDateTextBox" type="text"
          value='{$orders_list_admin->mEndDate}'/>
   <input type="submit" name="betweenDatesButton" value="Go!"
          class="AdminButtonText"/><br/>
   <span class="AdminPageText">
   Show all unverified orders that have not been canceled (need to either
   verify or cancel them)
   </span>
   ```

```
<input type="submit" name="unverifiedOrdersButton" value="Go!"
       class="AdminButtonText"/><br/>
<span class="AdminPageText">Show all verified orders that are not
completed (we need to ship them)</span>
<input type="submit" name="verifiedOrdersButton" value="Go!"
       class="AdminButtonText"/>
</form>
<br />
<span class="AdminErrorText">{$orders_list_admin->mErrorLabel}</span>
<br />
{if $orders_list_admin->mOrders}
<table cellspacing="0" border="1" width="100%">
  <tr bgcolor="Navy">
   <td><font face="Verdana" color="White" size="2">
       <b>Order ID</b></font></td>
   <td><font face="Verdana" color="White" size="2">
       <b>Date Created</b></font></td>
   <td><font face="Verdana" color="White" size="2">
       <b>Date Shipped</b></font></td>
   <td><font face="Verdana" color="White" size="2">
       <b>Verified</b></font></td>
   <td><font face="Verdana" color="White" size="2">
       <b>Completed</b></font></td>
   <td><font face="Verdana" color="White" size="2">
       <b>Canceled</b></font></td>
   <td><font face="Verdana" color="White" size="2">
       <b>Customer</b></font></td>
   <td><font face="Verdana" color="White" size="2">
       <b> </b></font></td>
  </tr>
  {section name=c_orders loop=$orders_list_admin->mOrders}
  <tr bgcolor="Gainsboro">
   <td><font face="Verdana" size="2">
{$orders_list_admin->mOrders[c_orders].order_id}</font></td>
   <td><font face="Verdana" size="2">
       {$orders_list_admin->mOrders[c_orders].date_created}</font></td>
   <td><font face="Verdana" size="2">
       {$orders_list_admin->mOrders[c_orders].date_shipped}</font></td>
   <td><font face="Verdana" size="2">
     <input type="checkbox" disabled="disabled"
{if $orders_list_admin->mOrders[c_orders].verified } checked="checked"
{/if} />
   </font></td>
   <td><font face="Verdana" size="2">
     <input type="checkbox"
           {if $orders_list_admin->mOrders[c_orders].completed}
           checked="checked" {/if} disabled="disabled"/>
```

```
        </font></td>
    <td><font face="Verdana" size="2">
      <input type="checkbox" disabled="disabled"
            {if $orders_list_admin->mOrders[c_orders].canceled }
            checked="checked" {/if} />
        </font></td>
    <td><font face="Verdana" size="2">
            {$orders_list_admin->mOrders[c_orders].customer_name}
        </font></td>
    <td><font face="Verdana" size="2">
     <input type="button" value="View Details" onclick="window.location='
orders_admin.php?OrderId={$orders_list_admin->mOrders[c_orders].order_id
}';"/>
        </font></td>
  </tr>
 {/section}
</table>
{/if}
```

> **Note** You must make sure the HTML code for the View Details button (which sets window.location to a new location by adding the OrderID query string parameter) is written in a single line, not split in multiple lines as shown in the code listing.

2. The plugin file for the orders_list_admin.tpl template is smarty_plugins/function.load_orders_list_admin.php:

```php
<?php
// plugin functions inside plugin files must be named: smarty_type_name
function smarty_function_load_orders_list_admin($params, $smarty)
{
  $orders_list_admin = new OrdersListAdmin();
  $orders_list_admin->init();
  // assign template variable
  $smarty->assign($params['assign'], $orders_list_admin);
}
// presentation tier class that supports order administration functionality
class OrdersListAdmin
{
  /* public variables available in smarty template */
  public $mOrders;
  public $mStartDate;
  public $mEndDate;
  public $mRecordCount = 20;
  public $mErrorLabel = "";
  /* private attributes */
```

```php
private $mOrderManager;
// constructor
function __construct()
{
  $this->mOrderManager = new BoOrderManager();
}
// init
function init()
{
  // if the "most recent x orders" filter is in action...
  if (isset($_GET['mostRecentButton']))
  {
    // if the record count value is not a valid integer, display error
    if ((string)(int)$_GET['recordCountTextBox'] ==
        (string)$_GET['recordCountTextBox'])
    {
      $this->mRecordCount = (int) $_GET['recordCountTextBox'];
      $this->mOrders = $this->mOrderManager->GetMostRecentOrders(
                                          $this->mRecordCount);
    }
    else
      $this->mErrorLabel = $_GET['recordCountTextBox'] .
                      " is not a number. <br />";
  }
  // if the "orders between d1 and d2" filter is in action...
  if (isset($_GET['betweenDatesButton']))
  {
    $this->mStartDate = $_GET['startDateTextBox'];
    $this->mEndDate = $_GET['endDateTextBox'];
    // check if the start date is in accepted format
    if (($this->mStartDate == "") ||
        ($timestamp = strtotime($this->mStartDate)) == -1)
      $this->mErrorLabel = "The start date is invalid. <br />";
    else
      // transform date to YYYY/MM/DD HH:MM:SS format
      $this->mStartDate =
          strftime("%Y/%m/%d %H:%M:%S", strtotime($this->mStartDate));
    // check if the end date is in accepted format
    if (($this->mEndDate == "") ||
        ($timestamp = strtotime($this->mEndDate)) == -1)
      $this->mErrorLabel .= "The end date is invalid. <br />";
    else
      // transform date to YYYY/MM/DD HH:MM:SS format
      $this->mEndDate =
          strftime("%Y/%m/%d %H:%M:%S", strtotime($this->mEndDate));
```

```
        // check if start date is more recent than the end date
        if ((empty($this->mErrorLabel)) &&
            (strtotime($this->mStartDate) > strtotime($this->mEndDate)))
          $this->mErrorLabel .=
            "The start date should be more recent than the end date.";
        // if there are no errors, get the orders between the two dates
        if (empty($this->mErrorLabel))
          $this->mOrders = $this->mOrderManager->GetOrdersBetweenDates(
                                  $this->mStartDate, $this->mEndDate);
      }
      // if "unverified orders" filter is in action...
      if (isset($_GET['unverifiedOrdersButton']))
        $this->mOrders =
            $this->mOrderManager->GetUnverifiedUncanceledOrders();
      // if "verified orders" filter is in action...
      if (isset($_GET['verifiedOrdersButton']))
        $this->mOrders =
            $this->mOrderManager->GetVerifiedUncompletedOrders();
    }
} //end class
?>
```

3. Load orders_admin.php into the browser and introduce the username/password combination in case you logged out. Click one of the Go! buttons and see the results that
   should be similar to those found in Figure 9-10.

TShirtShop Orders Admin (go back to the storefront or logout)

Show the most recent 20   records Go!
Show all records created between   and   Go!
Show all unverified orders that have not been canceled (need to either verify or cancel them) Go!
Show all verified orders that are not completed (we need to ship them) Go!

Order ID	Date Created	Date Shipped	Verified	Completed	Canceled	Customer	
9	2004-09-05 14:10:20	2004-09-05 14:14:32	✓	✓			View Details
8	2004-09-05 13:44:27	0000-00-00 00:00:00					View Details
7	2004-09-05 13:39:05	0000-00-00 00:00:00					View Details

Figure 9-10. *Selecting orders in the Orders Admin page*

How It Works: The orders_list_admin **Componentized Template**

Each of the Go! buttons calls one of the business tier methods (in the BoOrderManager class)
and populates the table with the returned orders information.

When processing the request, we test the data the visitor entered to make sure it's valid.
When the first Go! button is clicked, we verify that the entered value is a number (how many
records to show). We also verify whether the dates entered in start date and end date text
boxes are valid. We process them first with strtotime that parses a string and transforms it

into a Unix timestamp. This function is useful because it also accepts entries such as "now," "tomorrow," "last week," and so on as input values. The resulting timestamp is then processed with the strftime function, which transforms it into the YYYY/MM/DD HH:MM:SS format. Have a look at how these date/time values are parsed:

```
// check if the start date is in accepted format
if (($this->mStartDate == "") ||
    ($timestamp = strtotime($this->mStartDate)) == -1)
  $this->mErrorLabel = "The start date is invalid. <br />";
else
  // transform date to YYYY/MM/DD HH:MM:SS format
  $this->mStartDate =
      strftime("%Y/%m/%d %H:%M:%S", strtotime($this->mStartDate));
```

▪Note Check http://www.php.net/strtotime to see what input formats are supported by the strtotime function, and http://www.php.net/strftime for more details about strftime.

Apart from this detail, the orders_list_admin.tpl template file is pretty simple and doesn't introduce any new theoretical elements for you.

Displaying Order Details

In this section, you'll create the order_details_admin componentized template, which allows the administrator to edit the details of a particular order. The most common tasks are to mark an unverified order as either verified or canceled (it can't be directly marked as completed if it isn't verified yet), and to mark a verified order as completed when the shipment is dispatched.

Take a look at Figure 9-11 to see the order_details_admin template in action.

You provide the administrator with three very useful buttons: Mark this order as Verified, Mark this order as Completed, and Mark this order as Canceled. These buttons will be enabled or disabled, depending on the status of the order. The site administrator marks an order as verified when the payment for that order is confirmed by PayPal, and marks the order as completed when the order is assembled, addressed, and mailed to the purchaser. The administrator can mark an order as canceled if, for example, PayPal does not confirm the payment in a reasonable amount of time (the exact meaning of "reasonable" is up to the administrator).

The other buttons—Edit, Update, and Cancel—allow the administrator to manually edit any of the details of an order. When the Edit button is clicked, all of the check boxes and text boxes become editable.

Now that you have an idea of what this control will do, let's implement it in the usual style by starting with the data tier.

Order ID: 8

Total Amount:	$45.85
Date Created:	2004-09-05 13:44:27
Date Shipped:	0000-00-00 00:00:00
Verified:	☐
Completed:	☐
Canceled:	☐
Comments:	
Customer Name:	
Shipping Address:	
Customer Email:	

Edit   Update   Cancel
Mark this order as Verified
Mark this order as Completed
Mark this order as Canceled

Order contains these products:

Product ID	Product Name	Quantity	Unit Cost	Subtotal
12	Norway Post	1	15.95	15.95
14	Swedish Horse	1	14.95	14.95
23	Danish Locomotive	1	14.95	14.95

Figure 9-11. *The* order_details_admin *componentized template in action*

Implementing the Data Tier

Here you'll implement the data tier logic that supports the functionality required by the UI. You'll enable the administrator to do six operations, and you'll implement them with the following stored procedures:

- GetOrderInfo gets back the data needed to populate the text boxes of the form with general order information, such as the total amount, date created, date shipped, and so on. You can see the complete list in Figure 9-11, shown previously.

- GetOrderDetails returns all the products that belong to the selected order, and its return data is used to fill the grid at the bottom of the form.

- UpdateOrder is called when the administrator updates an order in edit mode.

- MarkOrderAsVerified is called to set the verified bit of the selected order to 1.

- MarkOrderAsCompleted sets the completed bit of the order to 1.

- MarkOrderAsCanceled sets the canceled bit of the order to 1.

Now implement each of these methods in the earlier created DoOrderManager class.

GetOrderInfo

This method returns the information necessary to fill the long list of text boxes in the order_details_admin componentized template. Add the GetOrderInfo method to the DoOrderManager class:

```
// gets the details of a specific order
public function GetOrderInfo($orderId)
{
  $query_string =
    "SELECT order_id, total_amount, date_created, date_shipped,
            verified, completed, canceled, comments,
            customer_name, shipping_address, customer_email
     FROM orders
     WHERE order_id = $orderId";
     $result = $this->dbManager->DbGetRow($query_string);
   return $result;
}
```

GetOrderDetails

The GetOrderDetails method returns the list of products that belong to a specific order. This will be used to populate the table containing the order details, situated at the bottom of the page. Add this method to the DoOrderManager class:

```
// gets the products that belong to a specific order
public function GetOrderDetails($orderId)
{
  $query_string =
    "SELECT orders.order_id, product_id, product_name, quantity,
            unit_cost, quantity*unit_cost AS subtotal
     FROM order_detail JOIN orders
     ON orders.order_id = order_detail.order_id
     WHERE orders.order_id = $orderId";
  $result = $this->dbManager->DbGetAll($query_string);
  return $result;
}
```

UpdateOrder

The UpdateOrder method updates the details of an order. Add this method to the DoOrderManager class:

```
// updates order details
public function UpdateOrder ($orderId, $dateCreated, $dateShipped,
                            $verified, $completed, $canceled,
                            $comments, $customerName,
                            $shippingAddress, $customerEmail)
{
```

```
$query_string =
  "UPDATE orders
   SET date_created = '$dateCreated',
       date_shipped = '$dateShipped',
       verified = $verified,
       completed = $completed,
       canceled = $canceled,
       comments = '$comments',
       customer_name = '$customerName',
       shipping_address = '$shippingAddress',
       customer_email = '$customerEmail'
   WHERE order_id = $orderId";
$result = $this->dbManager->DbQuery($query_string);
return $result;
}
```

Note that unlike the numerical values that are set in the UPDATE query, strings must be delimited by single quotation marks.

MarkOrderAsVerified

The MarkOrderAsVerified method is called when the "Mark this order as Verified" button is clicked.

```
// sets the verified bit of an order to 1
public function MarkOrderAsVerified($orderId)
{
  $query_string = "UPDATE orders
                   SET verified = 1
                   WHERE order_id = $orderId";
  $result = $this->dbManager->DbQuery($query_string);
  return $result;
}
```

MarkOrderAsCompleted

The MarkOrderAsCompleted method is called when the administrator clicks the "Mark this order as Completed" button. It not only sets the completed bit to 1, but also updates the date_shipped field because an order is completed just after the shipment has been done.

```
// sets the completed bit of an order to 1 and populates shipped_date
public function MarkOrderAsCompleted($orderId)
{
  $query_string = "UPDATE orders
                   SET completed = 1, date_shipped = NOW()
                   WHERE order_id = $orderId";
  $result = $this->dbManager->DbQuery($query_string);
  return $result;
}
```

MarkOrderAsCanceled

The `MarkOrderAsCancelled` method is called when the "Mark this order as Canceled" button is clicked.

```
// sets the canceled bit of an order to 1
public function MarkOrderAsCanceled($orderId)
{
  $query_string="UPDATE orders
                 SET canceled = 1
                 WHERE order_id = $orderId";
  $result = $this->dbManager->DbQuery($query_string);
  return $result;
}
```

Implementing The Business Tier

The business tier part of the order details admin component is very simple and consists of the following methods that you need to add to the BoOrderManager class:

```
// gets the details of a specific order
public function GetOrderInfo($orderId)
{
  $result = $this->mDoOrderManager->GetOrderInfo($orderId);
  return $result;
}
// gets the products that belong to a specific order
public function GetOrderDetails($orderId)
{
  $result = $this->mDoOrderManager->GetOrderDetails($orderId);
  return $result;
}
// updates order details
public function UpdateOrder($orderId, $dateCreated, $dateShipped,
                           $verified, $completed, $canceled,
                           $comments, $customerName,
                           $shippingAddress, $customerEmail)
{
  $result = $this->mDoOrderManager->UpdateOrder ($orderId,
       $dateCreated, $dateShipped, $verified=="on"?1:0,
       $completed=="on"?1:0, $canceled=="on"?1:0, $comments,
       $customerName, $shippingAddress, $customerEmail);
  return $result;
}
// marks an order as verified
public function MarkOrderAsVerified($orderId)
{
  $result = $this->mDoOrderManager->MarkOrderAsVerified($orderId);
  return $result;
```

```
}
// marks an order as completed and sets the order's ship_date
public function MarkOrderAsCompleted($orderId)
{
  $result = $this->mDoOrderManager->MarkOrderAsCompleted($orderId);
  return $result;
}
// marks an order as canceled
public function MarkOrderAsCanceled($orderId)
{
  $result = $this->mDoOrderManager->MarkOrderAsCanceled($orderId);
  return $result;
}
```

Implementing the Presentation Tier

Once again, you've reached the stage where you wrap up all the data tier and business tier functionality and package it into a nice-looking UI. The presentation tier consists of the order_details_admin componentized template. Let's create this componentized template in the following exercise.

Exercise: Creating the order_details_admin Componentized Template

Follow these steps to create the order_details_admin componentized template:

1. Create a new template file named order_details_admin.tpl in the templates folder and add the following code to it:

```
{load_order_details_admin assign="order_details_admin"}
<form method="get" action="orders_admin.php" >
 <input type="hidden" name="OrderId"
        value="{$order_details_admin->mOrderInfo.order_id}"/>
 <span class="ListDescription">
  Order ID:
  {$order_details_admin->mOrderInfo.order_id}</span><br/><br/>
 <table>
  <tr>
   <td width="130" class="AdminPageText">
    Total Amount:
   </td>
   <td class="ProductPrice">
    ${$order_details_admin->mOrderInfo.total_amount}</span><br/>
  </tr>
  <tr>
   <td width="130" class="AdminPageText">
    Date Created:
   </td>
   <td>
    <input name="dateCreatedTextBox" type="text"
```

```
              value="{$order_details_admin->mOrderInfo.date_created}"
           {if ! $order_details_admin->mDateCreatedTextBoxEnabled}
              disabled="disabled"{/if}/>
  </td>
 </tr>
 <tr>
  <td width="130" class="AdminPageText">
   Date Shipped:
  </td>
  <td>
   <input name="dateShippedTextBox" type="text"
           value="{$order_details_admin->mOrderInfo.date_shipped}"
        {if ! $order_details_admin->mDateShippedTextBoxEnabled}
           disabled="disabled" {/if}/><br/>
  </td>
 </tr>
 <tr>
  <td width="130" class="AdminPageText">
   Verified:
  </td>
  <td>
   <input type="checkbox" name="verifiedCheckBox"
        {if ! $order_details_admin->mVerifiedTextBoxEnabled}
           disabled="disabled" {/if}
        {if  $order_details_admin->mOrderInfo.verified}
           checked="checked" {/if} />
  </td>
 </tr>
 <tr>
  <td width="130" class="AdminPageText">
   Completed:
  </td>
  <td>
   <input type="checkbox" name="completedCheckBox"
        {if ! $order_details_admin->mCompletedTextBoxEnabled}
           disabled="disabled" {/if}
        {if $order_details_admin->mOrderInfo.completed}
           checked="checked" {/if}/>
  </td>
 <tr>
  <td width="130" class="AdminPageText">
   Canceled:
  </td>
  <td>
   <input type="checkbox" name="canceledCheckBox"
        {if ! $order_details_admin->mCanceledTextBoxEnabled}
           disabled="disabled" {/if}
```

```
      {if  $order_details_admin->mOrderInfo.canceled}
          checked="checked" {/if} />
 </td>
<tr>
 <td width="130" class="AdminPageText">
  Comments:
 </td>
 <td>
  <input name="commentsTextBox" type="text"
         value="{$order_details_admin->mOrderInfo.comments}"
      {if ! $order_details_admin->mCommentsTextBoxEnabled}
          disabled="disabled" {/if} />
 <td>
</tr>
<tr>
 <td width="130" class="AdminPageText">
  Customer Name:
 </td>
 <td>
  <input name="customerNameTextBox" type="text"
         id="customerNameTextBox"
         value="{$order_details_admin->mOrderInfo.customer_name}"
      {if ! $order_details_admin->mCustomerNameTextBoxEnabled}
          disabled="disabled" {/if} />
 <td>
</tr>
<tr>
 <td width="130" class="AdminPageText">
  Shipping Address:
 </td>
 <td>
  <input name="shippingAddressTextBox" type="text"
         value="{$order_details_admin->mOrderInfo.shipping_address}"
      {if ! $order_details_admin->mShippingAddressTextBoxEnabled}
          disabled="disabled" {/if} />
 </td>
</tr>
<tr>
 <td width="130" class="AdminPageText">
  Customer Email:
 </td>
 <td>
  <input name="customerEmailTextBox" type="text"
         value="{$order_details_admin->mOrderInfo.customer_email}"
      {if ! $order_details_admin->mCustomerEmailTextBoxEnabled}
          disabled="disabled" {/if} />
 </td>
```

```
    </tr>
  </table>
  <input type="submit" name="editButton" value="Edit"
      {if ! $order_details_admin->mEditButtonEnabled}
          disabled="disabled" {/if} class="AdminButtonText" />
  <input type="submit" name="updateButton" value="Update"
      {if ! $order_details_admin->mUpdateButtonEnabled}
          disabled="disabled" {/if} class="AdminButtonText" />
  <input type="submit" name="cancelButton" value="Cancel"
      {if ! $order_details_admin->mCancelButtonEnabled}
          disabled="disabled" {/if} class="AdminButtonText" /><br/>
  <input type="submit" name="markAsVerifiedButton" width="100%"
          value="Mark this order as Verified"
      {if ! $order_details_admin->mMarkAsVerifiedButtonEnabled}
          disabled="disabled" {/if} class="AdminButtonText" /><br/>
  <input type="submit" name="markAsCompletedButton" width="100%"
          value="Mark this order as Completed"
      {if ! $order_details_admin->mMarkAsCompletedButtonEnabled}
          disabled="disabled" {/if} class="AdminButtonText" /><br/>
  <input type="submit" name="markAsCanceledButton" width="100%"
          value="Mark this order as Canceled"
      {if ! $order_details_admin->mMarkAsCanceledButtonEnabled}
          disabled="disabled" {/if} class="AdminButtonText" />
  <br/><br/>
  <span class="ListDescription">
   Order contains these products:
  </span><br/><br/>
  <table cellspacing="0" border="1" width="100%">
  <tr bgcolor="Navy">
   <td>
    <font face="Verdana" color="White" size="2"><b>Product ID
    </b></font></td>
   <td>
    <font face="Verdana" color="White" size="2"><b>Product Name
    </b></font></td>
   <td><font face="Verdana" color="White" size="2"><b>Quantity
    </b></font></td>
   <td><font face="Verdana" color="White" size="2"><b>Unit Cost
    </b></font></td>
   <td><font face="Verdana" color="White" size="2"><b>Subtotal
    </b></font></td>
  </tr>
  {section name=item_no loop=$order_details_admin->mOrderDetails}
    <tr bgcolor="Gainsboro">
      <td><font face="verdana" size="2">
      {$order_details_admin->mOrderDetails[item_no].product_id}
      </font></td>
      <td><font face="verdana" size="2">
```

```
    {$order_details_admin->mOrderDetails[item_no].product_name}
    </font></td>
  <td><font face="verdana" size="2">
    {$order_details_admin->mOrderDetails[item_no].quantity}
    </font></td>
  <td><font face="verdana" size="2">
    {$order_details_admin->mOrderDetails[item_no].unit_cost}
    </font></td>
  <td><font face="verdana" size="2">
    {$order_details_admin->mOrderDetails[item_no].subtotal}
    </font></td>
 </tr>
 {/section}
 </table>
</form>
```

2. Create a new file named function.load_order_details_admin.php in the smarty_plug-ins folder, and write the following code in it:

```php
<?php
// plugin functions inside plugin files must be named: smarty_type_name
function smarty_function_load_order_details_admin($params, $smarty)
{
  $order_details_admin = new OrderDetailsAdmin();
  $order_details_admin->init();
  // assign template variable
  $smarty->assign($params['assign'], $order_details_admin);
}
// presentation tier class that deals with administering order details
class OrderDetailsAdmin
{
  /* public variables available in smarty template */
  public $mOrderId;
  public $mOrderInfo;
  public $mOrderDetails;
  public $mEditButtonEnabled;
  public $mUpdateButtonEnabled;
  public $mCancelButtonEnabled;
  public $mDateCreatedTextBoxEnabled;
  public $mVerifiedTextBoxEnabled;
  public $mCompletedTextBoxEnabled;
  public $mCanceledTextBoxEnabled;
  public $mCommentsTextBoxEnabled;
  public $mCustomerNameTextBoxEnabled;
  public $mShippingAddressTextBoxEnabled;
  public $mCustomerEmailTextBoxEnabled;
  public $mMarkAsVerifiedButtonEnabled;
  public $mMarkAsCompletedButtonEnabled;
```

```php
public $mMarkAsCanceledButtonEnabled;
/* private attributes */
private $mOrderManager;

// class constructor
function __construct()
{
  // we receive the order ID in the query string
  if (isset($_GET['OrderId']))
   $this->mOrderId = (int) $_GET['OrderId'];
  else
   trigger_error("OrderId paramater is required");
  // initialize instance of business tier class
  $this->mOrderManager = new BoOrderManager;
}

// initializes class members
function init()
{
  if (isset($_GET['markAsVerifiedButton']))
    $this->mOrderManager->MarkOrderAsVerified($this->mOrderId);
  if (isset($_GET['markAsCompletedButton']))
    $this->mOrderManager->MarkOrderAsCompleted($this->mOrderId);
  if (isset($_GET['markAsCanceledButton']))
    $this->mOrderManager->MarkOrderAsCanceled($this->mOrderId);
  if (isset($_GET['updateButton']))
  {
    $this->mOrderManager->UpdateOrder(
      $this->mOrderId,
      $_GET['dateCreatedTextBox'],
      $_GET['dateShippedTextBox'],
      isset($_GET['verifiedCheckBox']) ? "on" : "off",
      isset($_GET['completedCheckBox']) ? "on" : "off",
      isset($_GET['canceledCheckBox']) ? "on" : "off",
      $_GET['commentsTextBox'],
      $_GET['customerNameTextBox'],
      $_GET['shippingAddressTextBox'],
      $_GET['customerEmailTextBox']);
  }
  $this->PopulatePage();
  if (isset($_GET['editButton']))
    $this->SetEditMode(true);
  else
    $this->SetEditMode(false);
}

// fills the order details form with data
public function PopulatePage()
```

```php
  {
    $this->mOrderInfo = $this->mOrderManager->GetOrderInfo($this->mOrderId);
    $this->mEditButtonEnabled = true;
    $this->mUpdateButtonEnabled = false;
    $this->mCancelButtonEnabled = false;
    if (($this->mOrderInfo['canceled'] == 1)
     || ($this->mOrderInfo['completed'] == 1))
    {
      $this->mMarkAsVerifiedButtonEnabled = false;
      $this->mMarkAsCompletedButtonEnabled = false;
      $this->mMarkAsCanceledButtonEnabled = false;
    }
    elseif ($this->mOrderInfo['verified'] == 1)
    {
      $this->mMarkAsVerifiedButtonEnabled = false;
      $this->mMarkAsCompletedButtonEnabled = true;
      $this->mMarkAsCanceledButtonEnabled = true;
    }
    else
    {
      $this->mMarkAsVerifiedButtonEnabled = true;
      $this->mMarkAsCompletedButtonEnabled = false;
      $this->mMarkAsCanceledButtonEnabled = true;
    }
    $this->mOrderDetails =
          $this->mOrderManager->GetOrderDetails($this->mOrderId);
  }

  // input value is boolean value which specifies whether to
  // enable or disable edit mode
  public function SetEditMode($value)
  {
    $this->mDateCreatedTextBoxEnabled = $value;
    $this->mDateShippedTextBoxEnabled = $value;
    $this->mVerifiedTextBoxEnabled = $value;
    $this->mCompletedTextBoxEnabled = $value;
    $this->mCanceledTextBoxEnabled = $value;
    $this->mCommentsTextBoxEnabled = $value;
    $this->mCustomerNameTextBoxEnabled = $value;
    $this->mShippingAddressTextBoxEnabled = $value;
    $this->mCustomerEmailTextBoxEnabled = $value;
    $this->mEditButtonEnabled = !$value;
    $this->mUpdateButtonEnabled = $value;
    $this->mCancelButtonEnabled = $value;
  }
} //end class
?>
```

3. Add some fictional orders to the database, and then load the `orders_admin.php` file in your browser, click on a Go! button to show some orders, and click the "Show Details" button for one of the orders. The order details admin page will show up allowing you to edit the order's details, as advertised earlier in this chapter.

How It Works: The order_details_admin Componentized Template

The two long files you just wrote, `order_details_admin.tpl` and `function.load_order_details_admin.php`, allow you to view and update the details of a particular order.

The function plugin is loaded from the template file using the usual mechanism. The constructor of the `OrderDetailsAdmin` class (the `__construct` method) ensures that there's an `OrderId` parameter in the query string because without it this componentized template doesn't make sense:

```
// class constructor
function __construct()
{
  // we receive the order ID in the query string
  if (isset($_GET['OrderId']))
   $this->mOrderId = (int) $_GET['OrderId'];
  else
   trigger_error("OrderId paramater is required");
  // initialize instance of business tier class
  $this->mOrderManager = new BoOrderManager();
}
```

The `init()` method reacts to user's actions and calls various business tier methods to accomplish the user's requests. For example, when the "Mark this order as Verified" button is clicked, the following piece of code calls the `MarkOrderAsVerified()` business tier method to do the job:

```
if (isset($_GET['markAsVerifiedButton']))
  $this->mOrderManager->MarkOrderAsVerified($this->mOrderId);
```

It also calls the `PopulatePage()` method, which populates the form with data it gets from the `GetOrderInfo()` and `GetOrderDetails()` business tier methods.

The `SetEditMode()` method enters or exits edit mode depending on the value of the Boolean parameter it receives. When entering edit mode, all text boxes and the Update and Cancel buttons become enabled, while the Edit button is disabled. The reverse happens when exiting edit mode, which happens when either the Cancel or Update button is clicked.

Summary

We covered a lot of ground in this chapter. In two separate stages, you implemented a system for taking orders and manually administering them. You added a Place Order button to the shopping cart control to allow the visitor to order the products in the shopping cart. You implemented a simple orders administration page, in which the site administrator can view and handle pending orders.

Because order data is now stored in the database, you can do various statistics and calculations based on the items sold. In the next chapter, you'll learn how to implement a "Visitors who bought this also bought…" feature, which wouldn't have been possible without the order data stored in the database.

CHAPTER 10

Product Recommendations

One of the most important advantages of an Internet store compared to a brick-and-mortar location is the capability to customize the web site for each visitor based on his or her preferences, or based on data gathered from other visitors with similar preferences. If your web site knows how to suggest additional products to your visitor in a clever way, he or she might end up buying more than initially planned.

In this chapter, you'll implement a simple, but efficient, product recommendations system in your TShirtShop web store. You can implement a product recommendations system in several ways, depending on your kind of store. Here are a few popular ones:

- *Up-Selling*: Up-selling is defined as the strategy of offering consumers the opportunity to purchase an "upgrade" or a little extra based on their requested purchase. Perhaps the most famous example of up-selling—"Would you like to super-size that?"—is mentioned to someone when they order a value meal at McDonalds. This seemingly innocent request greatly increases the profit margin.

- *Cross-Selling*: Cross-selling is defined as the practice of offering customers complementary products. Continuing with the McDonalds analogy, you'll always hear the phrase "Would you like fries with that?" when someone orders a hamburger, because it's widely acknowledged that fries go with burgers, and because the consumer is ordering a burger, then its likely that they also like french fries—the mere mention of it is likely to generate a new sale.

- *Featured products on the home page*: TShirtShop permits the site administrator to choose the products featured on the main page and on the department pages.

In this chapter, you'll implement a dynamic recommendations system with both up-selling and cross-selling strategies. This system has the advantage of not needing manual maintenance. Because at this point TShirtShop retains what products were sold, in this chapter you will implement a "customers who bought this product also bought …" feature.

Let's have a look at what we are heading for (see Figure 10-1).

Figure 10-1. *Displaying product recommendations*

Implementing the Data Tier

You need to find out what other products were bought by customers that also bought the product for which you're calculating the recommendations. Let's develop the SQL logic to achieve the list of product recommendations step by step.

■**Note** After you understand the logic that makes this work, it'll be easy for you to change or extend the system for your particular purposes. For example, you can add product recommendations to the customer's shopping cart, in a "customers who bought the products in your shopping cart also bought:" list.

To find what other products were ordered together with a specific product, you need to join two instances of the order_detail table on their order_id fields. Feel free to review the "Joining Data Tables" section in Chapter 4 for a quick refresher about table joins. Joining multiple instances of a single table is just like joining different data tables, which contain the same data.

You join two instances of order_detail—called od1 and od2—on their order_id fields, while filtering the product_id value in od1 for the ID of the product you're looking for. This way you'll get in the od2 side of the relationship all the products that were ordered in the orders that contain the product you're looking for.

The SQL code that gets all the products that were ordered together with the product identified by a product_id of 4 is

```
SELECT od2.product_id
FROM order_detail od1 JOIN order_detail od2
ON od1.order_id = od2.order_id
WHERE od1.product_id = 4
```

This code returns a long list of products, which includes the product with the product_id of 4, such as this one:

```
product_id
----------
         4
         5
        10
        80
         4
         5
        10
        23
        25
        28
         4
        10
        12
        14
        80
```

Starting from this list of results, you need to get the products that are most frequently bought along with this product. The first problem with this list of products is that it includes the product with the product_id of 4. To eliminate it from the list (because, of course, you can't put it in the recommendations list), you simply add one more rule to the WHERE clause:

```
SELECT od2.product_id
FROM order_detail od1
JOIN order_detail od2 ON od1.order_id = od2.order_id
WHERE od1.product_id = 4 and od2.product_id != 4
```

Not surprisingly, you get a list of products that is similar to the previous one, except it doesn't contain the product with a `product_id` of 4 any more:

```
product_id
----------
         5
        10
        80
         5
        10
        23
        25
        28
        10
        12
        14
        80
```

Now the list of returned products is much shorter, but it contains multiple entries for the products that were ordered more than once in the orders that contain the product identifier 4. To get the most relevant recommendations, you need to see which products appear more frequently in these orders. You do this by grouping the results of the previous query by `product_id`, and sorting in descending order by how many times each product appears in the list (this number is given by the `rank` calculated column in the following code snippet):

```
SELECT od2.product_id, COUNT(od2.product_name) AS rank
FROM order_detail od1
JOIN order_detail od2 ON od1.order_id = od2.order_id
WHERE od1.product_id = 4 AND od2.product_id != 4
GROUP BY od2.product_id
ORDER BY rank DESC
```

■**Tip** Placing a space between COUNT and the expression that follows makes MySQL generate an error, so be careful.

This query now returns a list such as the following:

```
product_id    rank
----------    ----
        10       3
         5       2
        80       2
        23       1
        25       1
        28       1
        12       1
        14       1
```

Because you want to display both the name and the description of the recommended products, you also need to join the list of recommended product IDs with the product table. The following query returns the data you need:

```
SELECT od2.product_id, COUNT(od2.product_name) AS rank, p.description
FROM order_detail od1
JOIN order_detail od2 ON od1.order_id = od2.order_id
JOIN product p ON od2.product_id = p.product_id
WHERE od1.product_id = 4 AND od2.product_id != 4
GROUP BY od2.product_id
ORDER BY rank DESC
```

Based on the data from the previous fictional results, this query would return something like this:

```
product_id    rank    description
----------    ----    -----------
        10       3    Norse American - (USA - 1925). This classic shirt ...
         5       2    Canada Goose (Canada - 1952). Being on a major fly...
        80       2    Congo Rhino (Belgian Congo - 1959). Among land mam...
        23       1    Dane Train (1947). One hundred years of the Danis...
        25       1    Mali Soccer (1964). This T-shirt remembers the 196...
        28       1    Mexico Soccer #2 (1969). This is the companion T-s...
        12       1    Norway Post (1947). This is part of a series comme...
        14       1    Swede Horse (1972). Taken from a very old (Viking ...
```

Okay, you get the idea. Now add the GetRecommendations method in the DoCatalog class (in data_objects/do_catalog.php). The SQL code executed by this method has an additional LIMIT 5 bit at the end, which ensures that you only get a maximum of five recommended products (it would be counter-productive to list half of the product catalog):

```
// get product recommendations
public function GetRecommendations($productId)
{
  $len = SHORT_PRODUCT_DESCRIPTION_LENGTH;
  $query_string =
  "SELECT COUNT(p.name) AS rank, p.product_id, p.name,
          CONCAT(LEFT(description,$len),'...') AS description
    FROM order_detail od1
    JOIN order_detail od2 ON od1.order_id = od2.order_id
    JOIN product p ON od2.product_id = p.product_id
  WHERE od1.product_id = $productId AND od2.product_id != $productId
  GROUP BY p.product_id
  ORDER BY rank DESC LIMIT 5";
  return $this->dbManager->DbGetAll($query_string);
}
```

Alternatively, you might want to calculate the product recommendations only using data from the orders that happened in the last *n* days. For this you would need an additional join with the orders table, which contains the date_created field. The following version of GetRecommendations calculates product recommendations based on orders that happened in the last 30 days:

```
// get product recommendations
public function GetRecommendations($productId)
{
  $len = SHORT_PRODUCT_DESCRIPTION_LENGTH;
  $query_string =
  "SELECT COUNT(p.name) AS rank, p.product_id, p.name,
       CONCAT(LEFT(description,$len),'...') AS description
     FROM order_detail od1
     JOIN orders o ON od1.order_id = o.order_id
     JOIN order_detail od2 ON o.order_id = od2.order_id
     JOIN product p ON od2.product_id = p.product_id
   WHERE od1.product_id = $productId
     AND od2.product_id != $productId
     AND DATE_SUB(CURDATE(), INTERVAL 30 DAY) < o.date_created
   GROUP BY p.product_id
   ORDER BY rank DESC LIMIT 5";
  return $this->dbManager->DbGetAll($query_string);
}
```

Implementing the Business Tier

Create the GetRecommendations method in the BoCatalog class (in bo_catalog.php). This method calls the GetRecommendations function of the data tier:

```
// get product recommendations
public function GetRecommendations($productId)
{
  $result=$this->mDoCatalog->GetRecommendations($productId);
  return $result;
}
```

Implementing the Presentation Tier

This section shows you how to update the product componentized template to display the product recommendations in the products' details pages. Follow these steps to complete the task:

1. Open the smarty_plugins/function.load_product.php file, and add the $mRecommendation member to the Product class:

```
class Product
{
  // public variables to be used in Smarty template
  public $mProduct;
  public $mPageLink = "index.php";
  public $mRecommendations;
```

2. Now you have to get the recommended products data in $mRecommendations and create links to their home pages. Modify the init() method of the Product class like this:

```
// init
function init()
{
  // get product details from business tier
  $this->mProduct =
    $this->mBoCatalog->GetProductDetails($this->mProductId);
  if (isset($_SESSION['PageLink']))
    $this->mPageLink = $_SESSION['PageLink'];
  $this->mAddToCartLink = "index.php?CartAction=" . ADD_PRODUCT .
                          "&ProductID=" . $this->mProductId;
  // get product recommendations
  $this->mRecommendations =
    $this->mBoCatalog->GetRecommendations($this->mProductId);
  // create recommended product links
  $url = $this->mPageLink;
  if (count($_GET)>0)
    $url = $url . "&ProductID=";
  else
    $url = $url . "?ProductID=";
  for ($i=0; $i<count($this->mRecommendations); $i++)
    $this->mRecommendations[$i]['onclick'] =
              $url . $this->mRecommendations[$i]['product_id'];
}
```

3. Now update the `product` template to display the list of recommendations. Add the following lines at the end of `product.tpl`:

```
<br /><br />
{if $product->mRecommendations}
  <span class="ListDescription">Customers who bought this also bought:</span>
  {section name=m loop=$product->mRecommendations}
  <br />
  <a class="ProductName"
            href="{$product->mRecommendations[m].onclick|escape:"html"}">
    {$product->mRecommendations[m].name}
  </a> -
  <span class="ProductDescription">
    {$product->mRecommendations[m].description}
  </span>
  {/section}
{/if}
```

Now you can admire your work. The list of product recommendations contains links to the recommended product's details pages as shown in Figure 10-2.

Customers who bought this also bought:

Norwegian Flag - Norwegian Flag (1943). This is part of a series honoring those countries overrun by the Axis powers in WWII. This T-shirt won't le...
Brennerbahn - Brennerbahn (Austria - 1967). This T-shirt celebrates the first locomotive to haul a train over the Brenner Pass. That's an accomp...
Danish Locomotive - Dane Train (1947). One hundred years of the Danish State Railway are commemorated right here when you wear this beautiful "retro" ...
Dutch Sea Horse - Dutch Sea Horse (Netherlands - 1943). I think this T-shirt is destined to be one of our most popular simply because it is one of o...
Swedish Horse - Swede Horse (1972). Taken from a very old (Viking days?) carving, this image will last forever. Your T-shirt probably won't, howev...

Figure 10-2. *Product recommendations list*

Summary

Showing product recommendations is a great way to encourage sales, and we succeeded to implement this functionality throughout this short chapter. The greatest challenge was to build the SQL query that gets the list of recommended products, and we analyzed how to create it, step by step.

In the next chapter, you'll enter the third stage of development by adding customer accounts functionality.

PART 3

Phase III
of Development

CHAPTER 11

■ ■ ■

Customer Details

So far in this book you've built a basic (but functional) site, and hooked it into PayPal for taking payments and confirming orders. In this section of the book, you'll take things a little further. By cutting out PayPal from your ordering process, you can obtain much better control—as well as reduce overhead costs. It isn't as complicated as you might think, but we do have to be careful to do things right.

In this chapter, we'll be laying out the groundwork for this by implementing a customer account system.

To make e-commerce sites more user friendly, you usually store details such as credit card numbers in a database, so that users don't have to re-type this information each time they place an order. The customer account system you'll implement will store this information, and include all of the web pages required for the entry of such details.

As well as implementing these web pages, we'll need to take several other factors into account. First, simply placing credit card numbers, expiry dates, and so on into a database in plain text isn't ideal because we may unwittingly expose this data to unscrupulous people with access to the database. This could occur remotely or be perpetrated by individuals within our organization. Rather than (or in addition to) enforcing a prohibitively restrictive access policy to such data, it can be a lot easier simply to encrypt sensitive information, and retrieve it programmatically when required. We'll create a security library to ease this functionality.

Secondly, secure communications are important because you'll be capturing sensitive information such as credit card details via the web. We can't just put a form up for people to access via HTTP and allow them to send it to us, because the information could be intercepted. Instead, we'll use SSL over HTTPS connections. You'll take the TShirtShop application to the point where you can move on and implement your own back-end order pipeline in the next chapter.

In this chapter, you'll learn how to

- Store customer accounts

- Implement the security classes

- Add customer accounts functionality to TShirtShop

- Create the checkout page

- Use secure connections

Let's deal with these one by one.

Storing Customer Accounts

You can handle customer account functionality in web sites in many ways. In general, however, the methods share the following features:

- Customers log in via a login page or dialog box to get access to secured areas of the web site.

- Once logged in, the web application remembers the customer until they log out (either manually via a Log Out button, or automatically if their session times out or a server error occurs).

- All secure pages in a web application need to check whether a customer is logged in before allowing access.

First, let's look at the general implementation details for the TShirtShop e-commerce site.

The TShirtShop Customer Account Scheme

One simple way of enabling a check for a logged in customer is to store the customer ID in the session state. You can then check to see whether a value is present at the start of the secured pages, and warn the user if not. The login form itself can then authenticate the user and store a value in the session state if successful, ready for later retrieval. To log a user out, you simply remove the ID from the session state.

To log in, a customer needs to supply a username (we'll use their email address here, since it is guaranteed to be unique) and a password. Sending this information over the Internet is a sensitive issue because third parties can eavesdrop and capture it. Later in this chapter, we'll look at how to enable secure communications over the Internet. For now, though, we'll concentrate on the authentication side of things, which is unaffected by the type of connection used to transmit the email address and password of the customer.

Another issue related to security is about storing user passwords. It isn't a good idea to store user passwords in your database in plain text because this information is a potential target for attack. Instead, you should store what is known as the **hash** of the password. A hash is a unique string that represents the password, but cannot be converted back into the password itself. To validate the password entered by the user, then, you simply need to generate a hash for the password entered and compare it with the hash stored in your database. If the hashes match, then the passwords entered match as well, so you can be sure that the customer is genuine.

This leads to another important task—you need to supply a way for new users to register. The result of registration is to add a new customer to your database, including username and password hash information.

To implement this scheme in your application, you'll complete the following tasks:

- Create a new database table called `customer` to hold customer details.

- Implement the associated methods in data and business tiers that add, modify, and retrieve information from `customer`.

- Modify the `shopping_cart` componentized template, which will now redirect the user to a checkout page called `checkout.php`.

- Create a componentized template for customer login called `customer_login`.

- Create a componentized template for customer registration or for editing account basic details called `customer_details`.

- Create a componentized template named `customer_credit_card` that allows customers to enter credit card details.

- Create a componentized template named `customer_address` for customers to enter a shipping address.

Creating the customer Table

Now you can build the `customer` data table. Once again, you can download the MySQL script in the Downloads section of the Apress web site (`http://www.apress.com`) for this chapter that will build this table for you, or you can build it yourself in `phpMyAdmin` manually. Create the `customer` table (with 12 fields) in the tshirtshop database as described in Table 11-1.

Table 11.1. *The* `customer` *Table*

Column Name	Column Type	Description
customer_id	int	Primary key, `auto_increment`; this column should not `allow nulls`
name	varchar(50)	Customer name; should not allow nulls
email	varchar(100)	Customer email address; should not allow nulls, and should be unique
password	varchar(50)	Customer password stored as a hash; should not allow nulls
credit_card	Text	Customer credit card details; should allow nulls
address1	varchar(100)	First line of customer address; should allow nulls
address2	varchar(100)	Second line of customer address; should allow nulls
city	varchar(100)	Customer address town/city information; should allow nulls
region	varchar(100)	Customer address region/state information; should allow nulls
postal_code	varchar(100)	Customer address postal code/ZIP information; should allow nulls
country	varchar(100)	Customer address country information; should allow nulls
phone	varchar(100)	Customer phone number; should allow nulls

The SQL code that builds this table is as follows:

```
CREATE TABLE customer (
  customer_id int(10) unsigned NOT NULL auto_increment,
  name varchar(50) NOT NULL default '',
  email varchar(100) NOT NULL default '',
  password varchar(50) NOT NULL default '',
  credit_card text,
  address1 varchar(100) default NULL,
  address2 varchar(100) default NULL,
  city varchar(100) default NULL,
  region varchar(100) default NULL,
  postal_code varchar(100) default NULL,
  country varchar(100) default NULL,
```

```
  phone varchar(100) default NULL,
  PRIMARY KEY  (customer_id),
  UNIQUE KEY email (email)
) TYPE=INNODB;
```

Setting the table type to INNODB is not necessary, but it opens up the possibility to link the table to the orders and reviews tables later in this book through FOREIGN KEY constraints.

Customer's credit card information will be stored in an encrypted format so that no one will be able to access this information. However, unlike with passwords, you need to be able to retrieve this credit card information when required by the order pipeline, so you can't simply use a hash (the hash algorithm is one-way). You'll implement credit card data encryption functionality using a number of business tier classes, which you'll see next.

Implementing the Security Classes

So far, two areas need security functionality:

- Password hashing

- Credit card encryption

Both these tasks are carried out by business tier classes that you'll save in the business_objects directory, in the following files:

- password_hasher.php: Contains the PasswordHasher class, containing the static method Hash() that returns the hash value for the password supplied.

- secure_card.php: Contains the SecureCard class, which represents a credit card. This class can be supplied with credit card information, which is then accessible in encrypted format. This class can also take encrypted credit card data, and supply access to the decrypted information.

- symmetric_crypt.php: The class contained in this file, SymmetricCrypt, is used by SecureCard to encrypt and decrypt data. This means that if you ever want to change the encryption method, you only need to modify the code here, leaving the SecureCard class untouched.

We'll look at the code for hashing first, followed by encryption.

Implementing Hashing Functionality in the Business Tier

Hashing, as has already been noted, is a means by which you can obtain a unique value that represents an object. The algorithm used to convert the source byte array into a hashed byte array varies. The most used hashing algorithm is called MD5 (Message Digest, another name for the hash code generated), which generates a 128-bit hash value. Unfortunately, many kinds of attacks are based on word dictionaries constructed against MD5 hashes. Another popular hashing algorithm is called SHA1 (Secure Hash Algorithm), which generates a 160-bit hash value. SHA1 is generally agreed to be more secure (although slower) than MD5.

In the TShirtShop implementation, you'll use SHA1, although it is easy to change this if you require another type of security. Now, you'll implement the PasswordHasher class in the following exercise.

■**Note** PHP doesn't come by default with support for mhash and mcrypt, the libraries we're using in this chapter for hashing and encryption. If you're using Unix, please see Appendix A to learn how to compile PHP with support for mhash and mcrypt. If you're running Windows, first uncomment the lines extension=php_mhash.dll and extension=php_mcrypt.dll from php.ini by removing the leading semicolons. Then copy libmhash.dll from the dlls folder of your PHP folder, and libmcrypt.dll from http://ftp.emini.dk/pub/php/win32, to the Windows System32 folder. Finally, restart Apache.

Exercise: Implementing the PasswordHasher Class

To implement the PasswordHasher class, follow these steps:

1. Add the following line at the end of the config.inc.php file. This defines a random value (feel free to change it) to add to the passwords before hashing them.

```
// random value used for hashing
define("HASH_PREFIX", "K1-");
```

2. Create a new file named password_hasher.php in the business_objects directory, and write the PasswordHasher class in it:

```php
<?php
class PasswordHasher
{
  static public function Hash($password, $withPrefix = true)
  {
    if ($withPrefix)
      $hashed_password = sha1(HASH_PREFIX . $password);
    else
      $hashed_password = sha1($password);
    return $hashed_password;
  }
} //end class
?>
```

3. Next, write a simple test page to test the PasswordHasher class. Create a new file named test_hasher.php in the tshirtshop folder with the following code in it:

```php
<?php
if (isset($_GET['to_be_hashed']))
{
  require_once 'include/config.inc.php';
  require_once SITE_ROOT . '/business_objects/password_hasher.php';
  $original_string = $_GET['to_be_hashed'];
  $test = new PasswordHasher();
  echo "The hash of '" . $original_string . "' is "
      . $test->Hash($original_string, false);
  echo "<br/>";
```

```
      echo "... and the hash of '" . HASH_PREFIX . $original_string
          . "' (secret prefix concateneted with password) is "
          . $test->Hash($original_string, true);
    }
    ?>
    <br/><br/><br/>
    <form action="test_hasher.php">
      Write your password:
      <input type="text" name="to_be_hashed"> <br/><br/>
      <input type="submit" value="Hash it">
    </form>
```

4. Load the test_hasher.php file in your favorite browser, enter a password to hash, and admire the results as shown in Figure 11-1.

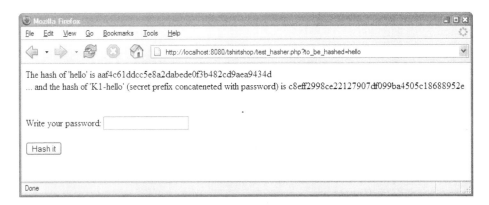

Figure 11-1. *Testing the password hashing functionality*

How It Works: The Hashing Functionality

The code in the PasswordHasher class is pretty simple. By default, the static Hash() method returns the hash of a string representing the secret prefix concatenated with the password.

You might be wondering what the secret prefix is all about. As you might have already guessed, it has to do with security. If someone managed to steal your database, they could try to match the hashed password values with a large dictionary of hashed values that looks something like this:

```
    word1      .... sha1(word1)
    word2      .... sha1(word2)
    ...
    word10000 .... sha1(word10000)
```

If two hash values match, it means the original strings (which in our case are the customers' passwords) also match.

Appending a secret prefix to the password before hashing it reduces the risk of dictionary attacks on the hashed passwords database, because the resulting string being hashed (secret prefix + password) is less likely to be found in a large dictionary of "password – hash value" pairs.

The `test_hasher.php` page tests your newly created `PasswordHasher` class.

Note You can also handle hashing at the database level by using MySQL hashing functions. Execute the following MySQL statement to see the `SHA1` MySQL function in action:

```
SELECT SHA1("freedom");
```

Of course, when relying on MySQL's hashing functionality, the passwords travel in "plain format" to your MySQL server, so if the MySQL server is on another machine, you must secure the connection between your web server and the MySQL server by using SSL connections. This can be avoided by handling hashing in the PHP code, which also offers better portability because it doesn't rely on MySQL specific functions. Remember that for the same portability reason we chose to use PEAR DB instead of using PHP MySQL-specific functions.

Implementing Encryption Functionality in the Business Tier

Encryption comes in many shapes and sizes, and continues to be a hot topic. There is no definitive solution to encrypting data, although there is plenty of advice on the subject. In general, the two forms of encryption are

- Symmetric encryption: A single key is used both to encrypt and decrypt data.

- Asymmetric encryption: Separate keys are used to encrypt and decrypt data. The encryption key is commonly known as the public key, and anyone can use it to encrypt information. The decryption key is known as the private key, because it can only be used to decrypt data that has been encrypted using the public key. The encryption key (public key) and the decryption key (private key) are mathematically related, and are always generated in pairs. The public key and private key can't be obtained one from another. If you have a public key – private key pair, you can send the public key to parties that need to encrypt information from you. You will be the only one who knows the private key associated with that public key, thus the only one able to decrypt the information.

Although asymmetric encryption is more secure, it also requires much more processing power. Symmetric encryption is faster, but can be less secure because both the encryptor and decryptor have knowledge of a single key. With symmetric encryption, the encryptor needs to send the key to the decryptor. With Internet communications, there is often no way of ensuring that this key remains a secret from third parties when it is sent to the encryptor.

Asymmetric encryption gets around this by using key pairs. There is never a need for the decryption key to be divulged, so it's much more difficult for a third party to break the encryption. Because it requires a lot more processing power, however, the practical method of operation is to use asymmetric encryption to exchange a symmetric key over the Internet, which is then used for symmetric encryption safe in the knowledge that this key has not been exposed to third parties.

In the TShirtShop application, things are much simpler than with Internet communications. You just need to encrypt data for storage in the database and decrypt it again when required, so you can use a symmetric encryption algorithm.

■**Note** Behind the scenes some asymmetric encryption is also going on, though, because that is the method implemented by HTTPS communications. You, however, don't need to worry about the internal details, because the web server and the visitor's web browser handle everything, as you'll see in the "Using Secure Connections" section later in this chapter.

As with hashing, several algorithms can be used for both symmetric and asymmetric encryption. PHP's mcrypt library contains implementations of the most important symmetric algorithms. There is no library in PHP that deals with asymmetric encryption, but in case you ever need to do asymmetric encryption, you can use the PGP (Pretty Good Privacy) family of software (for more information, see http://www.pgp.com) and GnuPG (http://www.gnupg.com).

The two most used asymmetric algorithms are DSA (Digital Signature Algorithm) and RSA (Rivest-Shamir-Adleman, from the names of its inventors, Ronald Rivest, Adi Shamir, and Leonard Adleman). Of these, DSA can only be used to "sign" data so that its authenticity can be verified, while RSA is more versatile (although slower than DSA when used to generate digital signatures). DSA is the current standard for digital authentication used by the U.S. government. Both the DSA and the RSA asymmetric algorithms are implemented in the PGP family of software (PGP and GnuPG).

Some popular symmetric algorithms found in the mcrypt library are DES (Data Encryption Standard), Triple DES (3DES), RC2 (Ron's Code, or Rivest's Cipher depending on who you ask, also from Ronald Rivest), and Rijndael (from the names of its inventors, Joan Daemen and Vincent Rijmen).

DES has been the standard for some time now, although this is gradually changing. It uses a 64-bit key, although in practice only 56 of these bits are used (8 bits are "parity" bits), which are not strong enough to avoid being broken using today's computers.

Both Triple DES and RC2 are variations of DES. Triple DES effectively encrypts data using three separate DES encryptions with three keys totaling 168 bits when parity bits are subtracted. The RC2 variant can have key lengths up to 128 bits (longer keys are also possible using RC3, RC4, and so on), so it can be made weaker or stronger than DES depending on the key size.

Rijndael is a completely separate encryption method, and has now been accepted as the new AES (Advanced Encryption Standard) standard (several competing algorithms were considered before Rijndael was chosen). This standard is intended to replace DES and is gradually becoming the most used (and secure) symmetric encryption algorithm.

The tasks associated with encrypting and decrypting data are a little more involved than hashing. The mcrypt functions are optimized to work with raw data, so you have some work to do with data conversion. You also have to define both a key and an initialization vector (IV) to perform encryption and decryption. The IV is required due to the nature of encryption: calculating the encrypted values for one sequence of bits involves using the encrypted values of the immediately preceding sequence of bits. Because there are no such values at the start of encryption, an IV is used instead. In the case of AES encryption (Rijndael_128), the IV and the key must be 32 bytes long.

The general steps required for encrypting a string are as follows:

1. Convert the IV (which you keep as a hexadecimal string) into a byte array.

2. Encrypt the string using AES encryption by supplying the IV in byte array format.

3. Convert the resulting encrypted data from a byte array into a hexadecimal string.

Decryption follows a similar scheme:

1. Convert the IV (which you keep as a hexadecimal string) into a byte array (the same with the encryption first step).

2. Convert the string to decrypt into a byte array.

3. Decrypt the binary string from the previous step by supplying the IV in byte array.

In your code, you'll use AES, but the code in the SymmetricCrypt class can be modified to use any of the supported encryption algorithms.

Exercise: Implementing the SymmetricCrypt Class

To implement the SymmetricCrypt class, follow these steps:

1. Add a new file in the business_objects directory called symmetric_crypt.php with the following code in it:

```php
<?php
class SymmetricCrypt
{
  // Encryption/decryption key
  private static $msSecretKey = "From Dusk Till Dawn";
  // The initialization vector
  private static $msHexaIv = "c7098adc8d6128b5d4b4f7b2fe7f7f05";
  // Use the Rijndael Encryption Algorithm
  private static $msCipherAlgorithm = MCRYPT_RIJNDAEL_128;
```

```php
  // Function encrypts plain-text string received as parameter
  // and returns the result in hexadecimal format
  public static function Encrypt($plainString)
  {
    // pack $hexaIV into a binary string
    $binary_iv = pack("H*", SymmetricCrypt::$msHexaIv);
    // encrypt $source
    $binary_encrypted_string = mcrypt_encrypt(
                       SymmetricCrypt::$msCipherAlgorithm,
                       SymmetricCrypt::$msSecretKey,
                       $plainString,
                       MCRYPT_MODE_CBC,
                       $binary_iv);
    // Convert $binaryEncryptedString to hexadecimal format
    $hexa_encrypted_string = bin2hex($binary_encrypted_string);
    return $hexa_encrypted_string;
  }

  // Function decrypts hexadecimal string received as parameter
  // and returns the result in hexadecimal format
  public static function Decrypt($encryptedString)
  {
    // pack $hexaIV into a binary string
    $binary_iv = pack("H*", SymmetricCrypt::$msHexaIv);
    // convert string in hexadecimal to byte array
    $binary_encrypted_string = pack("H*", $encryptedString);
    // Decrypt $binaryEncryptedString
    $decrypted_string = mcrypt_decrypt(
                           SymmetricCrypt::$msCipherAlgorithm,
                           SymmetricCrypt::$msSecretKey,
                           $binary_encrypted_string,
                           MCRYPT_MODE_CBC,
                           $binary_iv);
    return $decrypted_string;
  }
} //end class
?>
```

2. Add a test file in the tshirtshop folder called test_encryption.php with the following code:

```php
<?php
if (isset($_GET['mystring']))
{
```

```php
require_once 'include/config.inc.php';
require_once SITE_ROOT . '/business_objects/symmetric_crypt.php';
$string = $_GET['mystring'];
echo "The string is: <br/>" . $string;
echo"<br/><br/>";
$sc = new SymmetricCrypt();
$encrypted_string = $sc->Encrypt($string);
echo "Encrypted string: <br/>" . $encrypted_string;
echo "<br/><br/>";
$decrypted_string = $sc->Decrypt($encrypted_string);
Print "Decrypted string:<br/>" . $decrypted_string . "<br/>";
}

?>
<br/>
<form action="test_encryption.php">
Enter string to encrypt: <input type="text" name="mystring"><br/>
<input type="submit" value="Encrypt">
</form>
```

3. Load the newly created test_encryption.php file in your favorite browser and give a string to encrypt/decrypt (see Figure 11-2).

Figure 11-2. *Testing the password hashing functionality*

■Caution As you might have noticed after running the test page, the decrypted string always has a length that is a multiple of 32 bytes. If the original string is less than 32 bytes, null characters are appended until the string's length becomes a multiple of 32 bytes. You need to be careful with this detail because it means the decrypted value of the string may not be identical to the encrypted value. Because you'll encrypt XML data, you won't need to worry about having additional void characters at the end of the string.

How It Works: Encryption Functionality in the Business Tier

The SymmetricCrypt class has two static methods, Encrypt() and Decrypt(), which encrypt and decrypt data, and a number of encryption configurations parameters stored as static members:

```
// Encryption/decryption key
private static $msSecretKey = "From Dusk Till Dawn";
// The initialization vector for added security.
private static $msHexaIv = "c7098adc8d6128b5d4b4f7b2fe7f7f05";
// Use the Rijndael Encryption Algorithm
private static $msCipherAlgorithm = MCRYPT_RIJNDAEL_128;
```

The secret key is 16 characters (bytes) long for AES algorithms. Using a smaller key is allowed by the mcrypt library, but will reduce the encryption security. The IV should be exactly 16 bytes long for AES and will be kept as a hexadecimal string (2x16=32 chars long). Both $msSecretKey and $msHexaIv variables are set to temporary values here. They could just as easily take any other values, depending on the key you want to use.

Encrypt() starts by converting the IV from its hexadecimal value to a byte array, because this is the format expected by the mcrypt_encrypt function (the one that does the actual encryption):

```
// pack $hexaIV into a binary string
$binary_iv = pack("H*", SymmetricCrypt::$msHexaIv);
```

The conversion is done using PHP's pack function (learn more about it at http://www.php.net/pack).

The call to mcrypt_encrypt follows:

```
// encrypt $source
$binary_encrypted_string = mcrypt_encrypt(
                SymmetricCrypt::$msCipherAlgorithm,
                SymmetricCrypt::$msSecretKey,
                $plainString,
                MCRYPT_MODE_CBC,
                $binary_iv);
```

This is the call that performs the actual encryption. Its parameters are obvious, and you can find more detail about the mcrypt_encrypt function at http://www.php.net/mcrypt. The

MCRYPT_MODE_CBC specifies the "cipher block chaining" encryption method; this method uses a chaining mechanism in which the encryption of each block of data depends on the encryption results of preceding blocks, except for the first block in which the IV is used instead.

■**Note** At http://www.fact-index.com/b/bl/block_cipher_modes_of_operation.html. you can learn more about the various modes of operation.

At the end, the encrypted string is transformed into hexadecimal format, which is easier to work with (for example, to save in the database or in a configuration file):

```
// Convert $binaryEncryptedString to hexadecimal format
$hexa_encrypted_string = bin2hex($binary_encrypted_string);
```

The Decrypt() method is very similar to the Encrypt() method. First, you need the IV to be in a binary form (the same first step you took in the Encrypt() method).

As the Encrypt() method returns the encrypted string as a hexadecimal string, the input parameter of Decrypt() is also a hexadecimal string. You must convert this string to a byte array, which is the format mcrypt_decrypt() needs:

```
// convert string in hexadecimal to byte array
$binary_encrypted_string = pack("H*", $encryptedString);
// Decrypt $binaryEncryptedString
$decrypted_string = mcrypt_decrypt(
                         SymmetricCrypt::$msCipherAlgorithm,
                         SymmetricCrypt::$msSecretKey,
                         $binary_encrypted_string,
                         MCRYPT_MODE_CBC,
                         $binary_iv);
return $decrypted_string;
```

The test_encryption.php test file for this class simply encrypts and decrypts data, demonstrating that things are working properly. The code for this is very simple, so we won't detail it here.

Now that you have the SymmetricCrypt class code, the last step in creating the security-related classes is to add the SecureCard class.

Storing Credit Cart Information Using the SecureCard Class

In the following exercise, you'll build the SecureCard class, which represents the credit card of a customer. This class will use the functionality you implemented in the previous two exercises to ensure its data will be stored securely in the database.

Exercise: Implementing the SecureCard Class

To build the SecureCard class, follow these steps:

1. Create a new file named secure_card.php in the business_objects folder and add the following code to it:

```php
<?php
require_once 'symmetric_crypt.php';

// represents a credit card
class SecureCard
{
  // private members containing credit card's details
  private $mIsDecrypted = false;
  private $mIsEncrypted = false;
  private $mCardHolder;
  private $mCardNumber;
  private $mIssueDate;
  private $mExpiryDate;
  private $mIssueNumber;
  private $mCardType;
  private $mEncryptedData;
  private $mXmlCardData;

  // class constructor
  function __construct()
  {
    //nothing here
  }

  // decrypt data
  public function LoadEncryptedDataAndDecrypt($newEncryptedData)
  {
    $this->mEncryptedData = $newEncryptedData;
    $this->DecryptData();
  }

  // encrypt data
  public function LoadPlainDataAndEncrypt($newCardHolder, $newCardNumber,
        $newIssueDate, $newExpiryDate, $newIssueNumber, $newCardType)
  {
    // constructor for use with decrypted data
    $this->mCardHolder = $newCardHolder;
    $this->mCardNumber = $newCardNumber;
    $this->mIssueDate = $newIssueDate;
    $this->mExpiryDate = $newExpiryDate;
    $this->mIssueNumber = $newIssueNumber;
    $this->mCardType = $newCardType;
    $this->EncryptData();
  }
```

```php
// create XML with credit card information
private function CreateXml()
{
  // encode card details as XML document
  $xml_card_data = &$this->mXmlCardData;
  $xml_card_data = new DOMDocument();
  $document_root = $xml_card_data->createElement("CardDetails");
  $child = $xml_card_data->createElement("CardHolder");
  $child = $document_root->appendChild($child);
  $value = $xml_card_data->createTextNode($this->mCardHolder);
  $value = $child->appendChild($value);
  $child = $xml_card_data->createElement("CardNumber");
  $child = $document_root->appendChild($child);
  $value = $xml_card_data->createTextNode($this->mCardNumber);
  $value = $child->appendChild($value);
  $child = $xml_card_data->createElement("IssueDate");
  $child = $document_root->appendChild($child);
  $value = $xml_card_data->createTextNode($this->mIssueDate);
  $value = $child->appendChild($value);
  $child = $xml_card_data->createElement("ExpiryDate");
  $child = $document_root->appendChild($child);
  $value = $xml_card_data->createTextNode($this->mExpiryDate);
  $value = $child->appendChild($value);
  $child = $xml_card_data->createElement("IssueNumber");
  $child = $document_root->appendChild($child);
  $value = $xml_card_data->createTextNode($this->mIssueNumber);
  $value = $child->appendChild($value);
  $child = $xml_card_data->createElement("CardType");
  $child = $document_root->appendChild($child);
  $value = $xml_card_data->createTextNode($this->mCardType);
  $value = $child->appendChild($value);
  $document_root = $xml_card_data->appendChild($document_root);
}

// extract information from XML credit card data
private function ExtractXml($decryptedData)
{
  $xml = simplexml_load_string($decryptedData);
  $this->mCardHolder = (string)$xml->CardHolder;
  $this->mCardNumber = (string)$xml->CardNumber;
  $this->mIssueDate = (string)$xml->IssueDate;
  $this->mExpiryDate = (string)$xml->ExpiryDate;
  $this->mIssueNumber = (string)$xml->IssueNumber;
  $this->mCardType = (string)$xml->CardType;
}

// encrypts the XML credit card data
private function EncryptData()
```

```php
{
  // stuff data into XML doc
  $this->CreateXml();
  $this->mEncryptedData = SymmetricCrypt::Encrypt(
                              $this->mXmlCardData->saveXML());
  $this->mIsEncrypted = true;
}

// decrypts XML credit card data
private function DecryptData()
{
  // decrypt data
  $decrypted_data = SymmetricCrypt::Decrypt($this->mEncryptedData);
  // extract data from XML
  $this->ExtractXml($decrypted_data);
  // set decrypted flag
  $this->mIsDecrypted = True;
}

// returns credit card holder
public function GetCardHolder()
{
  if ($this->mIsDecrypted)
    return $this->mCardHolder;
  else
    throw new Exception("Data not decrypted");
}

// returns credit card number
public function GetCardNumber()
{
  if ($this->mIsDecrypted)
    return $this->mCardNumber;
  else
    throw new Exception("Data not decrypted");
}

// returns credit card number with only the last 4 digits
public function GetCardNumberX()
{
  if ($this->mIsDecrypted)
    return "XXXX-XXXX-XXXX-" . substr($this->mCardNumber,
                                  strlen($this->mCardNumber) - 4, 4);
  else
    throw new Exception("Data not decrypted");
}
```

```php
  // returns credit card issued date
  public function GetIssueDate()
  {
    if ($this->mIsDecrypted)
      return $this->mIssueDate;
    else
      throw new Exception("Data not decrypted");
  }

  // returns credit card expiry date
  public function GetExpiryDate()
  {
    if ($this->mIsDecrypted)
      return $this->mExpiryDate;
    else
      throw new Exception("Data not decrypted");
  }

  // returns credit card issue number
  public function GetIssueNumber()
  {
    if ($this->mIsDecrypted)
      return $this->mIssueNumber;
    else
      throw new Exception("Data not decrypted");
  }

  // returns credit card type
  public function GetCardType()
  {
    if ($this->mIsDecrypted)
      return $this->mCardType;
    else
      throw new Exception("Data not decrypted");
  }

  // returns encrypted version of cc details for database storage
  public function GetEncryptedData()
  {
    if ($this->mIsEncrypted)
      return $this->mEncryptedData;
    else
      throw new Exception("Data not encrypted");
  }
} //end class
?>
```

2. Create a new file named test_card.php file in the tshirtshop folder:

```php
<?php
require_once 'include/config.inc.php';
require_once SITE_ROOT . '/business_objects/secure_card.php';
$card_holder = "Mihai Bucica";
$card_number = "123456789";
$expiry_date = "01/04";
$issue_date = "01/01";
$issue_number = 100;
$card_type = "MasterVisa";
echo "<br/>Credit card data:<br/>"
     . $card_holder . ", "
     . $card_number . ", "
     . $issue_date  . ", "
     . $expiry_date . ", "
     . $issue_number . ", "
     . $card_type;
echo "<br/>";
$credit_card = new SecureCard();
try
{
  $credit_card->LoadPlainDataAndEncrypt(
                  $card_holder, $card_number, $issue_date,
                  $expiry_date, $issue_number, $card_type);
  $encrypted_data = $credit_card->GetEncryptedData();
}
catch(Exception $e)
{
  echo "<font color='red'>Exception: "
       . $e->getMessage() . "</font>";
  exit;
}
echo "<br/>Encrypted data:<br/>" . $encrypted_data . "<br/>";
$our_card = new SecureCard();
try
{
  $our_card->LoadEncryptedDataAndDecrypt($encrypted_data);
  echo "<br/>Decrypted data:<br/>"
       . $our_card->GetCardHolder() . ", "
       . $our_card->GetCardNumber() . ", "
       . $our_card->GetIssueDate() . ", "
       . $our_card->GetExpiryDate() . ", "
       . $our_card->GetIssueNumber() . ", "
       . $our_card->GetCardType();
}
catch(Exception $e)
{
```

```
    echo "<font color='red'>Exception: "
        . $e->getMessage() . "</font>";
    exit;
  }
  ?>
```

3. Load test_card.php file in your favorite browser to see the results (see Figure 11-3). You may change the data from this file as you want.

Figure 11-3. *Encrypting and decrypting credit card information*

How It Works: The SecureCard Class

There's a bit more code here than in previous examples, but it's all quite simple. First you have the private member variables to hold the card details as individual strings, as an encrypted string, and in an intermediate XML document. You also have Boolean flags indicating whether the data has been successfully encrypted or decrypted:

```
<?php
require_once 'symmetric_crypt.php';

// represents a credit card
class SecureCard
{
  // private members containing credit card's details
  private $mIsDecrypted = false;
  private $mIsEncrypted = false;
  private $mCardHolder;
  private $mCardNumber;
  private $mIssueDate;
  private $mExpiryDate;
  private $mIssueNumber;
  private $mCardType;
  private $mEncryptedData;
  private $mXmlCardData;
```

Next you have two important public methods. Public members are part of the public interface of the class, which provides the functionality for external clients. LoadEncryptedDataAndDecrypt receives an encrypted string and performs the decryption, and LoadPlainDataAndEncrypt receives the credit card data in plain format and encrypts it:

```
// decrypt data
public function LoadEncryptedDataAndDecrypt($newEncryptedData)
{
  $this->mEncryptedData = $newEncryptedData;
  $this->DecryptData();
}

// encrypt data
public function LoadPlainDataAndEncrypt($newCardHolder, $newCardNumber,
        $newIssueDate, $newExpiryDate, $newIssueNumber, $newCardType)
{
  // constructor for use with decrypted data
  $this->mCardHolder = $newCardHolder;
  $this->mCardNumber = $newCardNumber;
  $this->mIssueDate = $newIssueDate;
  $this->mExpiryDate = $newExpiryDate;
  $this->mIssueNumber = $newIssueNumber;
  $this->mCardType = $newCardType;
  $this->EncryptData();
}
```

The main work is carried out by the private EncryptData() and DecryptData() methods, which you'll come to shortly. First you have two utility methods for packaging and unpackaging data in XML format (which makes it easier to get at the bits you want when exchanging data with the encrypted format).

XML is a very powerful, tag-based format in which you can store various kinds of information. The SecureCard class stored a customer's credit card data in a structure like the following:

```
<?xml version="1.0"?>
<CardDetails>
   <CardHolder>Mihai Bucica</CardHolder>
   <CardNumber>123456789</CardNumber>
   <IssueDate>01/01</IssueDate>
   <ExpiryDate>01/04</ExpiryDate>
   <IssueNumber>100</IssueNumber>
   <CardType>MasterVisa</CardType>
</CardDetails>
```

The DOMDocument class is used to work with XML data; this class knows how to create, read, and manipulate XML documents without much effort from the developer. DOM (Document Object Model) is the most important and versatile tree model XML parsing API (Application Programming Interface).

Tip The World Wide Web Consortium manages the DOM standard; its official web page is
http://www.w3.org/DOM/.

With the new PHP 5 DOM, reading, creating, editing, saving, and searching XML documents from PHP has never been easier. The DOM extension in PHP 5 was entirely rewritten
from scratch to fully comply with the DOM specifications. You can see this extension in action
in the CreateXml() method, which creates an XML document with the structure shown earlier
by creating nodes and setting their values:

```
// create XML with credit card information
private function CreateXml()
{
  // encode card details as XML document
  $xml_card_data = &$this->mXmlCardData;
  $xml_card_data = new domDocument();
  $document_root = $xml_card_data->createElement("CardDetails");
  $child = $xml_card_data->createElement("CardHolder");
  $child = $document_root->appendChild($child);
  $value = $xml_card_data->createTextNode($this->mCardHolder);
  $value = $child->appendChild($value);
  ...
  $document_root = $xml_card_data->appendChild($document_root);
}
```

For reading the XML document, you can use the DOMDocument object, but in the
ExtractXml() method, we preferred to use a new and unique feature of PHP 5 called SimpleXML. Although less complex and powerful than DOMDocument, the SimpleXML extension
makes parsing XML data a piece of cake by transforming it into a data structure you can simply iterate through:

```
// extract information from XML credit card data
private function ExtractXml($decryptedData)
{
  $xml = simplexml_load_string($decryptedData);
  $this->mCardHolder = (string)$xml->CardHolder;
  $this->mCardNumber = (string)$xml->CardNumber;
  $this->mIssueDate = (string)$xml->IssueDate;
  $this->mExpiryDate = (string)$xml->ExpiryDate;
  $this->mIssueNumber = (string)$xml->IssueNumber;
  $this->mCardType = (string)$xml->CardType;
}
```

The EncryptData() method starts by using the CreateXml() method to package the details
supplied in the SecureCard constructor into XML format:

```
// encrypts the XML credit card data
private function EncryptData()
```

```
{
  // stuff data into XML doc
  $this->CreateXml();
```

Next, the XML string contained in the resultant XML document is encrypted into a single string and stored in the mEncryptedData member:

```
$this->mEncryptedData = SymmetricCrypt::Encrypt(
                        $this->mXmlCardData->saveXML());
```

Finally, the mIsEncrypted flag is set to True to indicate that the credit card data has been encrypted:

```
  $this->mIsEncrypted = true;
}
```

The DecryptData() method gets the XML credit card data from its encrypted form, decrypts it, and populates class attributes with the ExtractXml() method:

```
// decrypts XML credit card data
private function DecryptData()
{
  // decrypt data
  $decrypted_data = SymmetricCrypt::Decrypt($this->mEncryptedData);
  // extract data from XML
  $this->ExtractXml($decrypted_data);
  // set decrypted flag
  $this->mIsDecrypted = True;
}
```

Next up are the publicly accessible methods of the class. There are quite a few of these so we won't show them all. Several are for reading card detail data, such as mCardHolder:

```
// returns credit card holder
public function GetCardHolder()
{
  if ($this->mIsDecrypted)
    return $this->mCardHolder;
  else
    throw new Exception("Data not decrypted");
}
```

Note that the data is only accessible when mIsDecrypted is True, otherwise an exception is thrown.

Note What was that? An **exception**? Exception to what? Exceptions represent the modern way of intercepting and handling runtime errors in your code, and are much more powerful and flexible than intercepting PHP errors. Exceptions are a very important part of the OO (Object Oriented) model, and PHP 5 introduces an exception model resembling that of other object-oriented programming languages such as Java and C#. However, exceptions in PHP co-exist with the standard PHP errors in a strange combination, and you can't solely rely on exceptions for dealing with runtime problems. In future versions of PHP, it's likely that at least the object-oriented extensions will throw exceptions instead of generating errors; in TShirtShop, we decided to use exceptions for the customer accounts and credit card transactions code, and rely only on errors for the other kinds of problems. A PHP 5 exception is represented by the Exception class; you can generate (throw) an exception using the throw keyword, and the Exception object that you throw (which contains the exception's details) is propagated through the call stack until it is intercepted using the catch keyword. In our code, we throw exceptions from many places. We'll intercept all of them from code you'll write in the following chapters. This code will react to the exceptions by generating an error that is treated by the already-existing error-handling code.

Also, note that the data isn't accessible after encryption—the data used to initialize a SecureCard object is only accessible in encrypted form. This is more a use-case decision than anything else because this class is only really intended for encryption and decryption, not for persistently representing credit card details. After a SecureCard instance has been used to encrypt card details, we shouldn't subsequently need access to the unencrypted data, only the encrypted string.

One interesting property here is GetCardNumberX(), which displays only a portion of the number on a credit card. This is handy when showing a user existing details, and is becoming standard practice because it lets the customer know what card they have stored without exposing the details to prying eyes:

```
// returns credit card number with only the last 4 digits
public function GetCardNumberX()
{
  if ($this->mIsDecrypted)
    return "XXXX-XXXX-XXXX-" . substr($this->mCardNumber,
                                strlen($this->mCardNumber) - 4, 4);
  else
    throw new Exception("Data not decrypted");
}
```

The last property worth looking at is EncryptedData, used when extracting the encrypted credit card details for database storage:

```
// returns encrypted version of cc details for database storage
public function GetEncryptedData()
{
  if ($this->mIsEncrypted)
    return $this->mEncryptedData;
  else
    throw new Exception("Data not encrypted");
}
```

The structure here is much like the other properties, although this time the mIsEncrypted flag restricts access rather than the mIsDecrypted flag.

■Note Before moving on to the client code, it is worth explaining and justifying one important design consideration that you have probably already noticed. At no point are any of the card details validated. In fact, this class will work perfectly well with empty strings for any properties. This is so the class can remain as versatile as possible. It is more likely that credit card details will be validated as part of the UI used to enter them, or even not at all. This isn't at all dangerous—if invalid details are used, then the credit card transaction will simply fail, and we handle that using very similar logic to that required to deal with lack of funds (that is, we notify the customer of failure and ask them to try another card). Of course, there are also simple data formatting issues (dates are usually MM/YY for example), but as noted, these can be dealt with externally to the SecureCard class.

The test page (test_cart.php) for this class simply allows you to see how an encrypted card looks. As you can see, quite a lot of data is generated, hence the rather large column size in the customer database. You can also see that both encryption and decryption are working perfectly, so you can now move on to the customer account section of this chapter.

Adding Customer Accounts Functionality to TShirtShop

Before implementing the visual bits of the customer accounts functionality, let's preview what we're going to do in the final part of this chapter.

First, we want to have a login form on the front of the site. We also want to let users register on the site and edit their profiles. You'll create a componentized template for the login form and place it just on top of the departments list, as shown in Figure 11-4.

Figure 11-4. *TShirtShop with a login box*

The new user registration page looks like Figure 11-5.

Figure 11-5. *The new user registration page in TShirtShop*

After the user logs in to the site, a new componentized template appears on top of the departments list to display the logged user's name and a number of links for manipulating his or her account (see Figure 11-6).

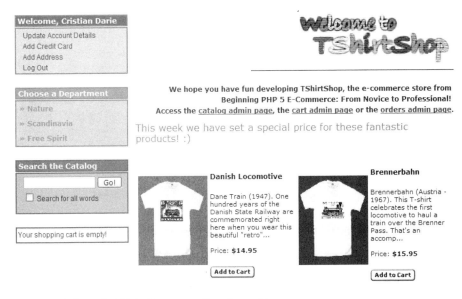

Figure 11-6. *Sample TShirtShop page for a logged in user*

Clicking the `Add Credit Card` link leads you to the page shown in Figure 11-7.

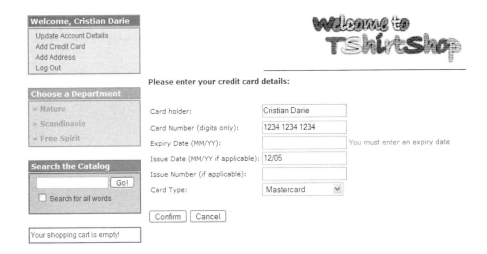

Figure 11-7. *Adding credit card information*

A similar form will be shown to you when clicking the `Add Address` link. When the user already has a credit card and an address listed, the `Add` links in the Welcome box change into `Change` links, as shown in Figure 11-8.

Figure 11-8. *Adding credit card information*

You'll start implementing the new functionality by writing the data tier code that will finally support the UI.

Implementing the Data Tier

You'll write the data tier code supporting customer accounts functionality in a new class named DoCustomer. Create a new file named do_customer.php in the data_objects folder, and add the following code to it:

```php
<?php
// data tier class that supports customer details functionality
class DoCustomer
{
  // contains the global instance of the DbManager class
  private $dbManager;

  // class constructor
  function __construct()
  {
    // get the global DbManager instance (created in app_top.php)
    $this->dbManager = $GLOBALS['gDbManager'];
  }
} //end class
?>
```

Next, add the methods in the following sections to the DoCustomer class.

GetCustomerIdPassword

When a user logs in to the site, you must check his or her password. The GetCustomerIdPassword() method returns the customer ID and the hashed password for a user with a specific email:

```
// returns customer_id and password for customer with email $email
public function GetCustomerIdPassword($email)
{
  $query_string="SELECT customer_id,password
                 FROM customer
                 WHERE email= '$email'";
  $result = $this->dbManager->DbGetRow($query_string);
  return $result;
}
```

AddCustomer

The AddCustomer() method is called when a user registers on the site. This method returns the customer ID for that user to be saved in the session:

```
// create a new customer and get his or her ID
public function AddCustomer($name,$email,$password,$phone)
{
  $query_string = "INSERT INTO customer (name,email,password,phone)
                   VALUES ('$name','$email','$password','$phone')";
  $this->dbManager->DbQuery($query_string);
  $query_string = "SELECT LAST_INSERT_ID()";
  $result = $this->dbManager->DbGetOne($query_string);
  return $result;
}
```

GetCustomer

The GetCustomer() method retrieves full customer details from the database:

```
// get customer details
public function GetCustomer($customerId)
{
  $query_string = "SELECT customer_id, name, password, email,
                          credit_card, address1, address2,
                          city, region, postal_code, country, phone
                   FROM customer
                   WHERE customer_id = $customerId";
  $result = $this->dbManager->DbGetRow($query_string);
  return $result;
}
```

UpdateCustomerDetails

The UpdateCustomerDetails() method updates the customer's account details in the database:

```
// update customer account details
public function UpdateCustomerDetails($customerId, $name,
                                 $email, $password, $phone)
{
  $query_string = "UPDATE customer
                   SET name = '$name', email = '$email',
                       password='$password', phone='$phone'
                   WHERE customer_id = $customerId";
  $result = $this->dbManager->DbQuery($query_string);
  return $result;
}
```

UpdateAddress

The UpdateAddress() method updates the customer's address in the database:

```
// update customer's address
public function UpdateAddress($customerId, $address1, $address2,
                             $city, $region, $postalCode, $country)
{
  $query_string = "UPDATE customer
                   SET address1='$address1', address2='$address2',
                       city='$city', region='$region',
                       postal_code='$postalCode', country='$country'
                   WHERE customer_id=$customerId";
   $result = $this->dbManager->DbQuery($query_string);
   return $result;
}
```

UpdateCreditCard

The UpdateCreditCard() method updates the customer's credit card information in the database. It only updates the credit_card column for the customer, which contains the encrypted version of the XML document containing the customer's complete credit card details.

```
// update credit_card column for a customer
public function UpdateCreditCard($customerId,$creditCard)
{
  $query_string = "UPDATE customer
                   SET credit_card='$creditCard'
                   WHERE customer_id=$customerId";
  $result=$this->dbManager->DbQuery($query_string);
  return $result;
}
```

Implementing the Business Tier

In the `business_objects` folder, create a new file named `bo_customer.php` that will contain the `PlainCreditCard` and `BoCustomer` classes. The `PlainCreditCard` class is simple and is used when communicating with the presentation tier to transfer plain credit card data. The `BoCustomer` class is a little longer, and it mainly accesses the data tier functionality to respond to requests that come from the presentation tier. Write the following code in the `business_objects/bo_customer.php` file: .

```php
<?php
// references required external functionality
require_once SITE_ROOT . '/data_objects/do_customer.php';
require_once SITE_ROOT . '/business_objects/password_hasher.php';
require_once SITE_ROOT . '/business_objects/secure_card.php';

// represents credit card details in unencrypted format
class PlainCreditCard
{
  public $mCardHolder="";
  public $mCardNumber="";
  public $mIssueDate="";
  public $mExpiryDate="";
  public $mIssueNumber="";
  public $mCardType="";
  public $mCardNumberX="";
}

// business tier class that manages customer accounts functionality
class BoCustomer
{
  /* private stuff */
  private $mDoCustomer;
  //class constructor
  function __construct()
  {
    $this->mDoCustomer = new DoCustomer();
  }
  public function IsAuthenticated()
  {
    if (!(isset($_SESSION['tshirtshop_customer_id'])))
      return 0;
    else
      return 1;
  }
  public function GetCustomerIdPassword($email)
  {
    $result = $this->mDoCustomer->GetCustomerIdPassword($email);
    return $result;
```

```php
}
public function AddCustomerAndLogin($name, $email, $password, $phone)
{
  $customer_id = $this->AddCustomer($name, $email, $password, $phone);
  $_SESSION['tshirtshop_customer_id'] = $customer_id;
}
public function AddCustomer($name, $email, $password, $phone)
{
  $hashed_password = PasswordHasher::Hash($password);
  $customer_id = $this->mDoCustomer->AddCustomer($name, $email,
                                    $hashed_password, $phone);
  return $customer_id;
}
public function IsValidUser($email, $password)
{
  $result = $this->GetCustomerIdPassword($email);
  if (empty($result)) return 2;
  $customer_id = $result['customer_id'];
  $hashed_password = $result['password'];
  if (PasswordHasher::Hash($password) != $hashed_password)
    return 1;
  else
  {
    $_SESSION['tshirtshop_customer_id'] = $customer_id;
    return 0;
  }
}
public function GetCurrentCustomerId()
{
  if ($this->IsAuthenticated())
    return $_SESSION['tshirtshop_customer_id'];
  else
    return 0;
}
public function DestroyCustomerSession()
{
  unset($_SESSION['tshirtshop_customer_id']);
}
public function UpdateCustomerDetails($customerId, $name, $email,
                                    $password, $phone)
{
  $hashed_password = PasswordHasher::Hash($password);
  $this->mDoCustomer->UpdateCustomerDetails($customerId, $name, $email,
                                    $hashed_password, $phone);
}
public function UpdateCurrentCustomerDetails($name, $email,
                                    $password, $phone)
```

```php
{
  $customer_id = $this->GetCurrentCustomerId();
  $this->UpdateCustomerDetails($customer_id, $name,
                               $email, $password, $phone);
}
public function GetCurrentCustomer()
{
  $customer_id = $this->GetCurrentCustomerId();
  $result = $this->GetCustomer($customer_id);
  return $result;
}
public function GetCustomer($customerId)
{
  $result = $this->mDoCustomer->GetCustomer($customerId);
  return $result;
}
public function UpdateCurrentAddress($address1, $address2, $city,
                                     $region, $postalCode, $country)
{
  $customer_id = $this->GetCurrentCustomerId();
  return $this->mDoCustomer->UpdateAddress($customer_id, $address1,
                   $address2, $city, $region, $postalCode, $country);
}
public function GetPlainCreditCardForCurrentUser()
{
  $customer_data = $this->GetCurrentCustomer();
  if (!(empty($customer_data['credit_card'])))
    return $this->DecryptCreditCard($customer_data['credit_card']);
  else
    return new PlainCreditCard();
}
public function DecryptCreditCard($encryptedCreditCard)
{
  $secure_card = new SecureCard();
  $secure_card->LoadEncryptedDataAndDecrypt($encryptedCreditCard);
  $credit_card = new PlainCreditCard();
  $credit_card->mCardHolder = $secure_card->GetCardHolder();
  $credit_card->mCardNumber = $secure_card->GetCardNumber();
  $credit_card->mIssueDate = $secure_card->GetIssueDate();
  $credit_card->mExpiryDate = $secure_card->GetExpiryDate();
  $credit_card->mIssueNumber = $secure_card->GetIssueNumber();
  $credit_card->mCardType = $secure_card->GetCardType();
  $credit_card->mCardNumberX = $secure_card->GetCardNumberX();
  return $credit_card;
}
```

```
  public function UpdateAddress($customerId, $address1, $address2,
                               $city, $region, $postalCode, $country)
  {
    return $this->mDoCustomer->UpdateAddress($customerId, $address1,
                     $address2, $city, $region, $postalCode, $country);
  }
  public function UpdateCurrentCreditCard($plainCreditCard)
  {
    $customer_id = $this->GetCurrentCustomerId();
    $this->UpdateCreditCard($customer_id, $plainCreditCard);
  }
  public function UpdateCreditCard($customerId, $plainCreditCard)
  {
    $secure_card = new SecureCard();
    $secure_card->LoadPlainDataAndEncrypt($plainCreditCard->mCardHolder,
      $plainCreditCard->mCardNumber, $plainCreditCard->mIssueDate,
      $plainCreditCard->mExpiryDate, $plainCreditCard->mIssueNumber,
      $plainCreditCard->mCardType);
    $encrypted_card = $secure_card->GetEncryptedData();
    $this->mDoCustomer->UpdateCreditCard($customerId, $encrypted_card);
  }
} //end class
?>
```

Implementing the Presentation Tier

The presentation tier for the TShirtShop customer account system consists of the following componentized templates:

- customer_login: The login box.

- customer_logged: After a user is logged, this componentized template takes the place of the customer_login componentized template to show the currently logged in user and displays account management and logout links.

- customer_details: For registering a new user or for editing the basic details of an existing user.

- customer_address: Allows a user to add/edit address information.

- customer_credit_card: Allows a user to add/edit credit card information.

These componentized templates can be used from the index.php page and the checkout.php script that you'll create in the next section.

Because at this point it is certainly easier to use the code download at the Apress web site, please follow these steps to have these new componentized templates work for you:

1. Copy the following files from the templates folder from this chapter's Downloads section (http://www.apress.com) to the templates folder of your working tshirtshop folder: customer_address.tpl, customer_credit_card.tpl, customer_details.tpl, customer_logged.tpl, and customer_login.tpl.

2. Copy the following files from the smarty_plugins folder from this chapter's code download to the smarty_plugins folder of your working tshirtshop folder: function.load_customer_address.php, function.load_customer_credit_card.php, function.load_customer_details.php, function.load_customer_logged.php, and function.load_customer_login.php.

3. Update index.php by adding a reference to the customer accounts business tier class:

```php
// Load Business Tier
require_once SITE_ROOT . '/business_objects/bo_catalog.php';
require_once SITE_ROOT . '/business_objects/bo_shopping_cart.php';
require_once SITE_ROOT . '/business_objects/bo_customer.php';
```

4. Update index.php by adding the new interface elements:

```php
// load department details if visiting a department
if (isset($_GET['DepartmentID']))
{
  $pageContentsCell = "department.tpl";
  $categoriesCell = "categories_list.tpl";
}
if (isset($_GET['Search']))
  $pageContentsCell="search_results.tpl";
if (isset($_GET['ProductID']))
  $pageContentsCell = "product.tpl";
if (isset($_GET['CartAction']))
{
  $pageContentsCell = "shopping_cart.tpl";
  $cartSummaryCell = "blank.tpl";
}
  else $cartSummaryCell="cart_summary.tpl";

// customer accounts functionality
$bo_customer = new BoCustomer();
if ($bo_customer->IsAuthenticated())
  $customerLoginOrLogged="customer_logged.tpl";
else
  $customerLoginOrLogged="customer_login.tpl";
if (isset($_GET['RegisterCustomer']) || isset($_GET['ChangeDetails']))
  $pageContentsCell="customer_details.tpl";
if (isset($_GET['AddOrChangeAddress']))
  $pageContentsCell="customer_address.tpl";
```

```
if (isset($_GET['AddOrChangeCreditCard']))
  $pageContentsCell="customer_credit_card.tpl";
$page->assign("customerLoginOrLogged",$customerLoginOrLogged);
$page->assign("cartSummaryCell",$cartSummaryCell);
$page->assign("pageContentsCell", $pageContentsCell);
$page->assign("categoriesCell", $categoriesCell);
$page->display('index.tpl');
```

5. Update templates/index.tpl by adding the following:

```
{include file="$customerLoginOrLogged"}
{include file="departments_list.tpl"}
{include file="$categoriesCell"}
{include file="search_box.tpl"}
{include file="$cartSummaryCell"}
```

6. Add the following styles to tshirtshop.css:

```
.Login
{
  font-family: Verdana, Helvetica, sans-serif;
  font-size: 9pt
}
.LoginHead
{
  border-right: #cc6666 2px solid;
  border-top: #cc6666 2px solid;
  border-left: #cc6666 2px solid;
  border-bottom: #cc6666 2px solid;
  background-color: #dc143c;
  font-family: Verdana, Arial;
  font-weight: bold;
  font-size: 10pt;
  color: #f5f5dc;
  padding-left: 3px
}
.LoginContent
{
  border-right: #cc6666 2px solid;
  border-top: #cc6666 2px solid;
  border-left: #cc6666 2px solid;
  border-bottom: #cc6666 2px solid;
  background-color: #ffcccc;
  font-family: Arial, Verdana;
  font-size: 9pt;
  color: brown;
  padding-top: 3px;
  padding-left: 12px;
```

```
    margin-top: 3px
}
.SubmitLogin
{
  border-right: #cc6666 1px solid;
  border-top: #cc6666 1px solid;
  border-left: #cc6666 1px solid;
  border-bottom: #cc6666 1px solid;
  background-color: #ffcccc;
  font-family: Arial, Verdana;
  font-size: 9pt;
  color: #a52a2a;
  margin-top: 3px;
  margin-bottom: 5px
}
.SimpleText
{
  color: Black;
  font-family: Verdana, Helvetica, sans-serif;
  font-size: 11px;
}
.ErrorText
{
  color: Red;
  font-family: Verdana, Helvetica, sans-serif;
  font-size: 11px;
}
a.RegisterLink
{
  color: blue;
  text-decoration: none;
  line-height: 25px;
}
```

Creating the Checkout Page

You are now ready to add the checkout page. This page will look similar to the shopping_cart componentized template, because you are displaying the items ordered, but it will also display additional information such as the shipping address or the type of the credit card. For new customers, neither address nor credit card information will be available yet, so you can also disable the order button until this information has been added.

Let's take a look now at what you'll be doing (see Figure 11-9).

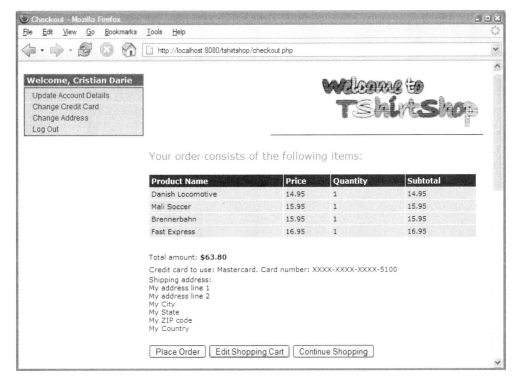

Figure 11-9. *The* checkout_info *componentized template in action*

At this point, the customer also has the option to change the credit card or address details, using the functionality you implemented earlier.

Let's implement the checkout_info componentized template that you saw in Figure 11-9.

Exercise: Implementing the checkout_info Componentized Template

Follow these steps to implement the checkout_info componentized template:

1. Create a new file named checkout_info.tpl in the templates folder and add the following code to it:

```
{load_checkout_info assign="checkout_info"}
<form action="checkout.php" method="post">
<br/>
<span class="ListDescription">
 Your order consists of the following items:
</span>
<br/><br/>
<table cellpadding="3" cellspacing="1" border="0" width="98%">
```

```
<tr class="TableHeader">
 <td>Product Name</td>
 <td>Price</td>
 <td>Quantity</td>
 <td>Subtotal</td>
</tr>
{section name=c_shoppingCartItems loop=$checkout_info->mShoppingCartItems}
 <tr class="TableRow">
  <td>{$checkout_info->mShoppingCartItems[c_shoppingCartItems].name}
  </td>
  <td>{$checkout_info->mShoppingCartItems[c_shoppingCartItems].price}
  </td>
  <td>{$checkout_info->mShoppingCartItems[c_shoppingCartItems].quantity}
  </td>
  <td>{$checkout_info->mShoppingCartItems[c_shoppingCartItems].subtotal}
  </td>
 </tr>
{/section}
</table>
<br/>
<span class="SimpleText">Total amount:</span>
 <span class="ProductPrice">${$checkout_info->mTotalAmountLabel}</span>
 <br/>
 <span class="SimpleText">{$checkout_info->mLblCreditCardNote}</span>
 <br/>
{if $checkout_info->mNoShippingAddress == "yes"}
<span class="ErrorText">Shipping address required to place order.</span>
{else}
<span class="SimpleText">
 Shipping address: <br/>
 {$checkout_info->mCustomerData.address1} <br/>
 {$checkout_info->mCustomerData.address2} <br/>
 {$checkout_info->mCustomerData.city} <br/>
 {$checkout_info->mCustomerData.region} <br/>
 {$checkout_info->mCustomerData.postal_code} <br/>
 {$checkout_info->mCustomerData.country} <br/>
</span>
{/if}
<br/>
<input type="submit" name="sended" value="Place Order"
  {$checkout_info->mOrderButtonVisible}/>
<input type="button" value="Edit Shopping Cart"
onclick="window.location='{$checkout_info->mEditShoppingCart}';"/>
<input type="button" value="Continue Shopping"
onclick="window.location='{$checkout_info->mContinueShopping}';"/>
</form>
```

2. Create the smarty_plugins/function.load_checkout_info.php file and fill it with the following code:

```php
<?php
/* smarty plugin function that gets called when the
load_checkout_info function plugin is loaded from a template */

function smarty_function_load_checkout_info($params, $smarty)
{
  $checkout_info = new CheckoutInfo();
  $checkout_info->init();
  // assign template variable
  $smarty->assign($params['assign'], $checkout_info);
}

// class that supports the checkout page
class CheckoutInfo
{
  // public attributes
  public $mShoppingCartItems;
  public $mTotalAmountLabel;
  public $mLblCreditCardNote;
  public $mEditShoppingCart = "index.php?CartAction";
  public $mOrderButtonVisible;
  public $mNoShippingAddress = "no";
  public $mContinueShopping;
  public $mPlainCreditCard;
  // private attributes
  private $mPlaceOrder = 0;
  // constructor
  function __construct()
  {
    $this->mBoCustomer = new BoCustomer();
    if (isset($_POST['sended'])) $this->mPlaceOrder=1;
  }
  // init
  public function init()
  {
    // create business tier object
    $cart = new BoShoppingCart();
    // if the Place Order button was clicked, save the order to database
    if ($this->mPlaceOrder == 1)
    {
      $order_id = $cart->CreateOrder();
      header("Location:index.php");
      exit;
    }
```

```
        // set members for use in the Smarty template
        $this->mShoppingCartItems=$cart->GetCartProducts(GET_CART_PRODUCTS);
        $this->mTotalAmountLabel = $cart->GetTotalAmount();
        $this->mContinueShopping = $_SESSION['PageLink'];
        $this->mCustomerData = $this->mBoCustomer->GetCurrentCustomer();
        // we allow placing orders only if we have complete customer details
        if (empty($this->mCustomerData))
        {
          header("Location:checkout.php");
          exit;
        }
        if (empty($this->mCustomerData['credit_card']))
        {
          $this->mLblCreditCardNote = "No credit card details stored.";
          $this->mOrderButtonVisible = "disabled='disabled'";
        }
        else
        {
          $this->mPlainCreditCard = $this->mBoCustomer->DecryptCreditCard(
                                  $this->mCustomerData['credit_card']);
          $this->mLblCreditCardNote = "Credit card to use: "
                                  . $this->mPlainCreditCard->mCardType
                                  . ". Card number: "
                                  . $this->mPlainCreditCard->mCardNumberX;
        }
        if (empty($this->mCustomerData['address1']))
        {
          $this->mOrderButtonVisible = "disabled";
          $this->mNoShippingAddress = "yes";
        }
      }
    }//end class
    ?>
```

How It Works: The checkout_info Componentized Template

In the init() method of the Checkout class, you start by checking whether the customer clicked the Place Order button. If so, you save the order into the database and redirect the customer to the home page:

```
    // if the Place Order button was clicked, save the order to database
    if ($this->mPlaceOrder == 1)
    {
      $order_id = $cart->CreateOrder();
      header("Location:index.php");
      exit;
    }
```

You then need to set up some variables for the template to use:

```
// set members for use in the Smarty template
$this->mShoppingCartItems=$cart->GetCartProducts(GET_CART_PRODUCTS);
$this->mTotalAmountLabel = $cart->GetTotalAmount();
$this->mContinueShopping = $_SESSION['PageLink'];
$this->mCustomerData = $this->mBoCustomer->GetCurrentCustomer();
```

If the customer didn't enter his credit card information or shipping address yet, a notice is displayed and the Place Order button is disabled. If credit card information exists for the customer, you decrypt it and prepare to display the credit card type and the last four digits of its number:

```
// we allow placing orders only if we have complete customer details
if (empty($this->mCustomerData))
{
  header("Location:checkout.php");
  exit;
}
if (empty($this->mCustomerData['credit_card']))
{
  $this->mLblCreditCardNote = "No credit card details stored.";
  $this->mOrderButtonVisible = "disabled='disabled'";
}
else
{
  $this->mPlainCreditCard = $this->mBoCustomer->DecryptCreditCard(
                           $this->mCustomerData['credit_card']);
  $this->mLblCreditCardNote = "Credit card to use: "
                           . $this->mPlainCreditCard->mCardType
                           . ". Card number: "
                           . $this->mPlainCreditCard->mCardNumberX;
}
if (empty($this->mCustomerData['address1']))
{
  $this->mOrderButtonVisible = "disabled";
  $this->mNoShippingAddress = "yes";
}
```

Finalizing the Checkout Page

To complete the checkout functionality, follow these steps:

1. Copy checkout.php, templates/checkout.tpl and templates/checkout_not_logged.tpl from the Downloads section of this chapter (http://www.apress.com) to your project and look them over to understand their functionality (this should be easy for you at this point in the book).

2. Modify your `templates/shopping_cart.tpl` file to redirect the user to the `checkout.php` page instead of PayPal. The Place Order button becomes the Checkout button:

```
<input type="button" value="Checkout"
{if $shopping_cart->mTotalAmount eq 0} "disabled" {/if}
onclick="window.location='checkout.php';">
...
   <td>
    <span class="ProductDescription">Total amount:</span> 
    <span class="ProductPrice">${$shopping_cart->mTotalAmount}</span>
   </td>
   <td align="right">
    <input type="submit" name="update" value="Update"/>
    <input type="button" value="Checkout"
           {if $shopping_cart->mTotalAmount eq 0} "disabled" {/if}
           onclick="window.location='checkout.php';">
   </td>
...
```

3. Now everything is in its place and you can see the results. Log in to your site, add some products to your shopping cart, and then click the Checkout button on your shopping cart page. Your page will look something like Figure 11-9 shown earlier.

Using Secure Connections

Customers can now register on the site, log in, and change details. However, the current system involves sending potentially sensitive information over HTTP. This protocol isn't secure, and data could be intercepted and stolen. To avoid this, you need to set up the application to work with SSL (Secure Socket Layer) connections, using the HTTPS protocol (Hypertext Transport Protocol [Secure]).

To do this, you have a bit of groundwork to get through first. Unless you have already been using an SSL connection on your web server, you are unlikely to have the correct configuration to do so. This configuration involves obtaining a security certificate for your server and installing it on your Apache web server.

Security certificates are basically public-private key pairs similar to those used in asynchronous encryption algorithms. You can generate these if your domain controller is configured as a certification authority, but this method is problematic. Digitally signed SSL certificates may cause browsers that use these certificates to be unable to verify the identity of your certification authority and therefore doubt your security. This isn't disastrous, but might affect consumer confidence, because visitors will be presented with a warning message when they attempt to establish a secure connection.

The alternative is to obtain SSL certificates from a known and respected organization that specializes in web security, such as VeriSign. Web browsers such as Internet Explorer have built-in root certificates from organizations such as this, and are able to authenticate the digital signature of SSL certificates supplied by them. This means that no warning message will appear, and a SSL secured connection will be available with a minimum of fuss.

In this section, we assume that you take this latter option, although if you want to create your own certificates that won't affect the end result.

Obtaining an SSL Certificate from VeriSign

Obtaining a certificate from VeriSign is a relatively painless experience, and full instructions are available on the VeriSign web site (`http://www.verisign.com/`). You can also get test certificates from VeriSign, which are free to use for a trial period. The basic steps are as follows:

1. Sign up for a trial certificate on the VeriSign web site.

2. Generate a Certificate Signing Request (CSR) on your web server. This involves filling out various personal information, including the name of your web site, and so on. For this to work, you need to install an SSL module in your web server, as described in Appendix A.

3. Copy the contents of the generated CSR into the VeriSign request system.

4. Shortly afterwards, you will receive a certificate from VeriSign that you copy into your web server to install the certificate.

There is a little more to it than that, but as noted previously, detailed instructions are available on the VeriSign web site, and you shouldn't run into any difficulties.

Enforcing SSL Connections

Once installed, you can access any web pages on your web server using an SSL connection, simply by replacing the `http://` part of the URL used to access the page with `https://` (assuming that your firewall is set up to allow an SSL connection, which by default uses port 443, if you use a firewall—this doesn't apply to local connections). Obviously, you don't need SSL connections for all areas of the site, and shouldn't enforce it in all places because that reduces performance. However, you *do* want to make sure that the checkout, customer login, customer registration, and customer detail modification pages are accessible only via SSL.

If you already have installed an SSL certificate into your web server, the steps to upgrade your web site to use HTTPS connections for transferring sensitive data are very simple:

1. Add the following lines at the start of `checkout.php` to ensure this page will be accessed just with SSL:

```
// ensures that checkout.php is only accessible via SSL connection
if ( !isset($_SERVER['HTTPS']) || strtolower($_SERVER['HTTPS']) != 'on' )
{
   header ('Location:
https://'.$_SERVER['HTTP_HOST'].$_SERVER['REQUEST_URI']);
   exit();
}
```

2. Also add the following code at the beginning of index.php to force client browsers to use SSL when accessing sensitive pages and also to get rid of SSL when accessing regular web pages:

```
// is the page being accessed through an HTTPS connection?
if ( !isset($_SERVER['HTTPS']) || strtolower($_SERVER['HTTPS']) != 'on' )
  $is_https = false;
else
  $is_https = true;
// visiting a sensitive page?
if (isset($_GET['RegisterCustomer']) ||
    isset($_GET['ChangeDetails']) ||
    isset($_GET['AddOrChangeAddress']) ||
    isset($_GET['AddOrChangeCreditCard']) ||
    isset($_POST['Login']))
  $is_sensitive_page = true;
else
  $is_sensitive_page = false;
// use HTTPS when accessing sensitive pages
if ($is_sensitive_page && $is_https==false)
 {
   header ('Location: https://' . $_SERVER['HTTP_HOST'] .
           $_SERVER['REQUEST_URI']);
   exit();
 }
// don't use HTTPS for nonsensitive pages
if (!$is_sensitive_page && $is_https == true)
 {
   header ('Location: http://' . $_SERVER['HTTP_HOST'] .
           $_SERVER['REQUEST_URI']);
   exit();
 }
```

3. Modify smarty_plugins/function.load_customer_login.php to pass customer login data over SSL:

```
public function init()
{
  $this->mActionTarget = "https://" . $_SERVER['SERVER_NAME'] .
        $_SERVER['REQUEST_URI'];
  $this->mRegisterUser = $_SERVER['REQUEST_URI'] .
        (empty($_GET) ? "?" : "&") . "RegisterCustomer";
```

4. As homework, we'll leave you to modify admin_login.php to use secure connections.

Summary

In this chapter, you've implemented a customer account system that customers can use to store their details for use during order processing. You've looked at many aspects of the customer account system, including encrypting sensitive data, and securing web connections for obtaining it.

You started by looking at a new table in your database, `customer`, with fields for storing customer information.

Next, you created the security classes in your business tier, that handle hashing and encrypting strings, and a secure credit card representation that makes it easy to exchange credit card details between the encrypted and decrypted format.

After this, you used these classes to create the login, registration, and customer detail editing web pages. This required a bit more code, but the result turned out to be simple to understand.

Finally, we looked at how to secure data passing over the Internet using secure SSL connections. This involved obtaining a certificate from a known certification authority (VeriSign, for example), installing it, restricting access to SSL where appropriate, and modifying the redirection code slightly to use SSL connections.

In the next chapter, we'll be looking at how to create the framework for the order-processing pipeline, enabling you to automate even more of the supply process.

CHAPTER 12

███

Implementing the
Order Pipeline:
Part I

Your e-commerce application is shaping up nicely. You have added customer account functionality, and you are keeping track of customer addresses and credit card information, which is stored securely. However, you are not currently using this information—instead, you are delegating responsibility for this to PayPal.

In this and the next chapter, you'll build your own order-processing pipeline that deals with credit card authorization, stock checking, shipping, email notification, and so on. We'll leave the credit card processing specifics until Chapter 14, but in this chapter we'll show you where this process fits into the picture.

Order pipeline functionality is an extremely useful capability for an e-commerce site. Order pipeline functions let you keep track of orders at every stage in the process, and provide auditing information that you can refer to later, or if something goes wrong during the order processing. You can do all this without relying on a third-party accounting system, which can also reduce costs. The first section of this chapter discusses what an order pipeline is and the specifics that apply to the TShirtShop application.

The bulk of this chapter deals with constructing the order pipeline system, which also involves a small amount of modification to the way things currently work, and some additions to the database you've been using. However, the code in this chapter isn't much more complicated than the code you've already been using. The real challenges are in designing your system.

By the end of the next chapter, customers will be able to place orders into your pipeline, and you'll be able to follow the progress of these orders as they pass through various stages. Although no real credit card processing will take place, you'll end up with a fairly complete system, including a new administration web page that can be used by suppliers to confirm that they have items in stock and to confirm that orders have been shipped. To start with, however, you need a bit more background about what you're actually trying to achieve.

What Is an Order Pipeline?

Any commercial transaction, whether in a shop on the street, over the Internet, or anywhere else, has several related tasks that must be carried out before it can be considered complete. For example, you can't simply remove an item of clothing from a fashion boutique (without paying) and say that you've bought it—remuneration is (unfortunately!) an integral part of any purchase. In addition, a transaction only completes successfully if each of the tasks carried out completes successfully. If a customer's credit card is rejected, for example, then no funds can be taken from it, so a purchase can't be made.

The sequence of tasks in a transaction is often thought of in terms of a pipeline. In this analogy, orders start at one end of the pipe and come out of the other end when they are completed. Along the way, they must pass through several pipeline sections, each of which is responsible for a particular task, or a related group of tasks. If any pipeline section fails to complete, then the order "gets stuck," and might require outside interaction before it can move further along the pipeline or it might be canceled completely.

For example, the simple pipeline shown in Figure 12-1 applies to transactions in a brick and mortar store.

Figure 12-1. *Transactions for a brick and mortar store*

The last section might be optional, and might involve additional tasks such as gift-wrapping. The payment stage might also take one of several methods of operation, because the customer could pay using cash, credit card, gift certificates, and so on.

When you consider e-commerce purchasing, the pipeline becomes longer, but isn't really any more complicated.

Implementing the Order Pipeline

In the TShirtShop e-commerce application, the pipeline will look like the one in Figure 12-2.

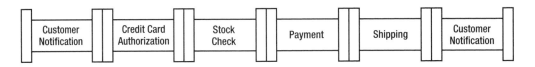

Figure 12-2. *The TShirtShop order pipeline*

The tasks carried out in these pipeline sections are as follows:

- *Customer Notification*: An email is sent to the customer notifying them that order processing has started, and confirming the items to be sent and the address that goods will be sent to.

- *Credit Card Authorization*: The credit card used for purchasing is checked, and the total order amount is set aside (although no payment is taken at this stage).

- *Stock Check*: An email is sent to the supplier with a list of the items that have been ordered. Processing continues when the supplier confirms that the goods are available.

- *Payment*: The credit card transaction is completed using the funds set aside earlier.

- *Shipping*: An email is sent to the supplier confirming that payment for the items ordered has been taken. Processing continues when the supplier confirms that the goods have been shipped.

- *Customer Notification*: An email is sent to the customer notifying them that the order has been shipped, and thanking them for using the TShirtShop web site.

Note In terms of implementation, as you'll see shortly, there are more stages than this because the stock check and shipping stages actually consist of two pipeline sections—one for sending the email and one that waits for confirmation.

As orders flow through this pipeline, entries are added to a new database table called `audit`. These entries can be examined to see what has happened to an order, and are an excellent way to identify problems if they occur. Each entry in the `orders` table is also flagged with a status, identifying which point in the pipeline it has reached.

Building the TShirtShop Pipeline

To process the pipeline, you'll create classes representing each stage. These classes carry out the required processing and then modify the status of the order in the `orders` table to advance the order. You'll also need a coordinating class (or processor), which can be called for any order and executes the appropriate pipeline stage class. This processor is called once when the order is placed, and in normal operation is called twice more—once for stock confirmation and once for shipping confirmation.

To make life easier, you'll also define a common interface supported by each pipeline stage class. This enables the order processor class to access each stage in a standard way. You'll also define several utility functions and expose several common properties in the order processor class, which will be used as necessary by the pipeline stages. For example, the ID of the order should be accessible to all pipeline stages, so to save code duplication, you'll put that information in the order processor class.

Now, let's get on to the specifics. You'll build a number of files in the `commerce_lib` directory (a subdirectory of the `business_objects` folder) containing all the new classes, which you'll reference from `TShirtShop`. The files in the `commerce_lib` directory will contain the following:

- *OrderProcessor*: Main class for processing orders

- *OrderProcessorConfiguration*: Class containing various configuration details for the `OrderProcessor` class, including administrator email address, supplier email address, and so on

- *IPipelineSection*: Interface definition for pipeline sections

- *Customer, OrderDetails, OrderDetail*: Classes used to store data extracted from the database, for ease of access

- *PsInitialNotification, PsCheckFunds, PsCheckStock, PsStockOk, PsTakePayment, PsShipGoods, PsShipOk, PsFinalNotification*: Pipeline section classes

The progress of an order through the pipeline as mediated by the order processor relates to the pipeline shown earlier (see Figure 12-3).

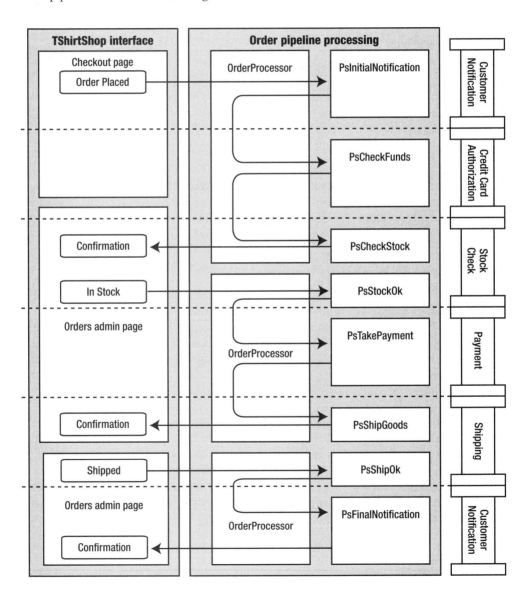

Figure 12-3. *Pipeline processing*

The process shown in this diagram is divided into three sections:

- Customer places order.
- Supplier confirms stock.
- Supplier confirms shipping.

The first stage is as follows:

1. When the customer confirms an order, checkout.php creates the order in the database and calls OrderProcessor to begin order processing.

2. OrderProcessor detects that the order is new and calls PsInitialNotification.

3. PsInitialNotification sends an email to the customer confirming the order, and advances the order stage. It also instructs OrderProcessor to continue processing.

4. OrderProcessor detects the new order status and calls PsCheckFunds.

5. PsCheckFunds checks that funds are available on the customer's credit card, and stores the details required to complete the transaction if funds are available. If this is successful, then the order stage is advanced and OrderProcessor is told to continue.

6. OrderProcessor detects the new order status and calls PsCheckStock.

7. PsCheckStock sends an email to the supplier with a list of the items ordered, instructs the supplier to confirm via orders_admin.php, and advances the order status.

8. OrderProcessor terminates.

The second stage:

1. When the supplier logs in to the orders admin page (orders_admin.php) to confirm that stock is available, orders_admin.php calls OrderProcessor to continue order processing.

2. OrderProcessor detects the new order status and calls PsStockOk.

3. PsStockOk advances the order status and tells OrderProcessor to continue.

4. OrderProcessor detects the new order status and calls PsTakePayment.

5. PsTakePayment uses the transaction details stored earlier by PsCheckFunds to complete the transaction, then advances the order status and tells OrderProcessor to continue.

6. OrderProcessor detects the new order status and calls PsShipGoods.

7. PsShipGoods sends an email to the supplier with a confirmation of the items ordered, instructs the supplier to ship these goods to the customer, and advances the order status.

8. OrderProcessor terminates.

The third stage:

1. When the supplier confirms that the goods have been shipped, `orders_admin.php` calls `OrderProcessor` to continue order processing.

2. `OrderProcessor` detects the new order status and calls `PsShipOk`.

3. `PsShipOk` enters the shipment date in the database, advances the order status, and tells `OrderProcessor` to continue.

4. `OrderProcessor` detects the new order status and calls `PsFinalNotification`.

5. `PsFinalNotification` sends an email to the customer confirming that the order has been shipped and advances the order stage.

6. `OrderProcessor` terminates.

If anything goes wrong at any point in the pipeline processing, such as a credit card being declined, an email is sent to an administrator. The administrator then has all the information necessary to check what has happened, get in contact with the customer involved, and cancel or replace the order if necessary.

No point in this process is particularly complicated; it's just that quite a lot of code is required to put this into action!

Laying the Groundwork

Before you start building the components just described, you need to make a few modifications to the `TShirtShop` database and web application.

Creating the audit Table

During order processing, one of the most important functions of the pipeline is to maintain an up-to-date audit trail. The implementation of this audit trail involves adding records to a new database table called `audit`.

Create the `audit` table (preferably using InnoDB), like this:

Column Name	Column Type	Description
`audit_id`	int (unsigned, auto_increment)	Primary key
`order_id`	int	The ID of the order that the audit entry applies to
`datestamp`	datetime	The date and time that the audit entry was created
`message`	text	The text of the audit entry
`message_number`	int	An identifying number for the audit entry type

The SQL query that builds this table is

```
CREATE TABLE audit (
  audit_id INT UNSIGNED NOT NULL AUTO_INCREMENT ,
  order_id INT NOT NULL ,
  datestamp DATETIME NOT NULL ,
  message TEXT NOT NULL ,
  message_number INT NOT NULL ,
  PRIMARY KEY ( audit_id )
) TYPE = InnoDB;
```

Entries will be added by OrderProcessor and by individual pipeline stages to indicate successes and failures. These entries can then be examined to see what has happened to an order, an important function when it comes to error checking.

The message number column is interesting because it allows you to associate specific messages with an identifying number. You can have another database table that matched these message numbers with descriptions, although this isn't really necessary because the scheme used for numbering (as you'll see later in the chapter) is quite descriptive. In addition, you have the message column, which already provides human-readable information.

Updating the orders Table

Currently, the orders table doesn't allow for as much information as you'll need to implement the order-processing pipeline. You need to add the following new columns to the orders table:

Column Name	Column Type	Description
status	int	The current status of the order, which is equivalent to what pipeline section the order has reached
customer_id	unsigned int	The ID of the customer that placed the order
auth_code	varchar(50)	The authentication code used to complete the customer credit card transaction
reference	varchar(50)	The unique reference code of the customer credit card transaction

The SQL script that adds these fields to the orders table is

```
ALTER TABLE orders
ADD status INT NOT NULL,
ADD customer_id INT UNSIGNED NOT NULL,
ADD auth_code VARCHAR(50) NOT NULL,
ADD reference VARCHAR(50) NOT NULL;
```

The first two of these new columns are self-explanatory, but the next two are related to credit card transactions, which we'll look at in Chapter 14.

■**Note** From now on, you won't be using a number of columns from the `orders` table. Feel free to remove the columns related to the status of the order (which is now handled by the `status` field you just added), and the columns related to customer data (which is now stored in a separate table and linked to using the `customer_id` field you just added). The columns you can safely remove from the `orders` table are `verified`, `completed`, `canceled`, `customer_name`, `shipping_address`, and `customer_email`.

You should also enforce the new relationship you have between the `orders` and `customer` tables by adding a `FOREIGN KEY` constraint to the `orders` table. The new relationship links the `customer_id` field in `orders` to the `customer_id` field in `customer`.

Before adding the foreign key, you need to take care of one more detail first. MySQL requires indexes to be created on the columns linked through a foreign key constraint. The `customer_id` field in `customer` is the primary key of the table, so it's indexed by default (remember that MySQL automatically creates indexes on primary key columns). However, at this moment, you don't have an index on the `customer_id` field in `orders`. Add the index using the following SQL query:

```
ALTER TABLE orders
ADD INDEX idx_customer_id (customer_id)
```

Now that you have the index in place, create the `FOREIGN KEY` constraint using this query:

```
ALTER TABLE orders
ADD CONSTRAINT fk_customer_id
    FOREIGN KEY (customer_id)
    REFERENCES customer(customer_id)
```

Updating the Data Tier Code

You need to update the `CreateOrder()` method in the data tier `ShoppingCart` class (in the `data_objects/do_shopping_cart.php` file) to reflect the changes in the database. The new version of this file must include a `customer_id` value with the order, and set the `status` value to 0.

Replace your version of the `CreateOrder()` method with this one:

```
// creates a new order
public function CreateOrder($cartId, $customerId)
{
  // insert the new order
  $query_string =
    "INSERT INTO orders
        (date_created, status, customer_id)
     VALUES
        (NOW(), 0, $customerId)";
  $this->dbManager->DbQuery($query_string);
  // gets the id of the inserted order
  $query_string="SELECT LAST_INSERT_ID()";
  $order_id = $this->dbManager->DbGetOne($query_string);
  // get order's items
  $query_string =
```

```
  "SELECT product.product_id, product.name,
         shopping_cart.quantity, product.price
   FROM product JOIN shopping_cart
     ON product.product_id = shopping_cart.product_id
   WHERE shopping_cart.cart_id = '$cartId'";
$order_items = $this->dbManager->DbGetAll($query_string);
// Insert order items in order_detail table and calculate total amount
$total_amount=0;
for ($i=0; $i<count($order_items); $i++)
{
  $total_amount += $order_items[$i]['price']*$order_items[$i]['quantity'];
  $query_string =
    "INSERT INTO order_detail
         (order_id, product_id, product_name, quantity, unit_cost)
     VALUES
         ($order_id, {$order_items[$i]['product_id']},
          '" . $order_items[$i]['name'] . "',
          {$order_items[$i]['quantity']},
          {$order_items[$i]['price']})";
  $this->dbManager->DbQuery($query_string);
}
// set order's total amount
$query_string =
  "UPDATE orders
   SET total_amount = $total_amount
   WHERE customer_id = $customerId AND order_id = $order_id";
$this->dbManager->DbQuery($query_string);
//delete shopping cart
$this->EmptyShoppingCart($cartId);
return $order_id;
}
```

The two new bits here are the following:

- Including a customer_id value with the order

- Setting the status column to 0, signifying that the order needs processing from the start of the order pipeline

Updating the Business Tier Code

To use the new CreateOrder() method of the data tier, you must add the corresponding method in the BoShoppingCart class. Modify the CreateOrder() method in business_objects/bo_shopping_cart.php:

```
// create a new order from the shopping cart
public function CreateOrder()
{
  $bo_customer = new BoCustomer();
```

```php
$customer_id = $bo_customer->GetCurrentCustomerId();
return $this->mDoShoppingCart->CreateOrder($this->GetCartId(), $customer_id);
}
```

This method is called when you place an order in the checkout page.

Implementing the Utility Classes

The first classes to consider are the utility classes for database objects—Customer, OrderDetail, and OrderDetails—which you'll save into a subfolder of the business_objects folder, named commerce_lib. We're looking at these first because the other classes use them, so having the types defined makes entering the code for later classes easier.

To implement the utility classes, follow these steps:

1. Add the following lines at the end of your include/config.inc.php file:

```php
// constant definitions for commerce lib classes
define("COMMERCELIB_DIR", SITE_ROOT . "/business_objects/commerce_lib/");
define("NEWLINE", "\n");
```

2. Create a subdirectory named commerce_lib in the business_objects folder. Add a new file named commerce_lib.all.php in the commerce_lib folder, and write the following code in it:

```php
<?php
require_once SITE_ROOT . '/business_objects/secure_card.php';
require_once COMMERCELIB_DIR . 'customer.php';
require_once COMMERCELIB_DIR . 'order_detail.php';
require_once COMMERCELIB_DIR . 'order_details.php';
?>
```

3. Add the following customer.php file to your commerce_lib directory. This file contains the Customer class, which represents a customer record from the customer table.

```php
<?php
// represents a customer
class Customer
{
  public $mCustomerId;
  public $mName;
  public $mEmail;
  public $mCreditCard;
  public $mAddress1;
  public $mAddress2;
  public $mCity;
  public $mRegion;
  public $mPostalCode;
  public $mCountry;
  public $mPhone;
  public $mAddressAsString;
  // constructor receives customer data from the database as parameter
```

```php
function __construct($customer)
{
  // simple test to check we didn't receive void parameter
  if (empty($customer)) throw new Exception("No customer data");
  // save customer data in class members
  $this->mCustomerId = $customer['customer_id'];
  $this->mName = $customer['name'];
  $this->mEmail = $customer['email'];
  $this->mAddress1 = $customer['address1'];
  $this->mAddress2 = $customer['address2'];
  $this->mCity = $customer['city'];
  $this->mRegion = $customer['region'];
  $this->mPostalCode = $customer['postal_code'];
  $this->mCountry = $customer['country'];
  $this->mPhone = $customer['phone'];
  // decrypt credit card data
  $this->mCreditCard = new SecureCard();
 $this->mCreditCard->LoadEncryptedDataAndDecrypt($customer['credit_card']);
  $this->mSddressAsString = $this->mName . NEWLINE .
                            $this->mAddress1 . NEWLINE;
  if (!(empty($this->mAddress2)))
    $this->mAddressAsString .= $this->mAddress2 . NEWLINE;
  $this->mAddressAsString .= $this->mCity . NEWLINE .
                             $this->mRegion . NEWLINE .
                             $this->mPostalCode . NEWLINE .
                             $this->mCountry . NEWLINE;
  }
}
?>
```

4. Create a new file named order_detail.php in the commerce_lib folder and write the following code in it. The OrderDetail class represents the details of an ordered product (ID, name, quantity, unit cost).

```php
<?php
// an instance of this class represents an ordered product
class OrderDetail
{
  public $mProductId;
  public $mProductName;
  public $mQuantity;
  public $mUnitCost;
  public $mItemAsString;
  public $mCost;
  // constructor receives item's details and saves them to class members
  function __construct($newProductId, $newProductName,
                       $newQuantity, $newUnitCost)
  {
```

```php
        $this->mProductId = $newProductId;
        $this->mProductName = $newProductName;
        $this->mQuantity = $newQuantity;
        $this->mUnitCost = $newUnitCost;
        $this->mCost = $this->mUnitCost * $this->mQuantity;
        $this->mItemAsString = $this->mQuantity . " " .
                               $this->mProductName . " $" .
                               $this->mUnitCost . " each, total cost $" .
                               $this->mCost . NEWLINE;
    }
}
?>
```

5. Implement the OrderDetails class in the order_details.php file in the commerce_lib folder:

```php
<?php
// represents array of order detail objects
class OrderDetails
{
  public $mList; // array of OrderDetail objects
  public $mTotalCost;
  public $mListAsString = "";
  // retrieves a number of records and stores them as OrderDetail instances
  function __construct($orderDetails)
  {
    // simple test to guard against void input data
    if (empty($orderDetails))
      throw new Exception("Empty Order Details");
    // populates the mList array
    for ($i = 0; $i < count($orderDetails); $i++)
    {
      // creates a new OrderDetail instance
      $new_order_detail = new OrderDetail($orderDetails[$i]['product_id'],
        $orderDetails[$i]['product_name'], $orderDetails[$i]['quantity'],
        $orderDetails[$i]['unit_cost']);
      // saves the new OrderDetail instance into the mList array
      $this->mList[$i] = $new_order_detail;
      // builds output string
      $this->mListAsString .= $new_order_detail->mItemAsString . NEWLINE;
      // adds product cost to total cost
      $this->mTotalCost += $new_order_detail->mCost;
    }
    // finishes building the output string
    $this->mListAsString .= NEWLINE . "Total order cost: $" .
                            $this->mTotalCost;
  }
}
?>
```

6. Create the `test_commerce_lib.php` in your site root folder (the `tshirtshop` folder), replacing the values for `$customer_id` and `$order_id` with IDs of existing items in the tshirtshop database.

```php
<?php
require_once 'include/config.inc.php';
require_once SITE_ROOT . '/include/app_top.php';
require_once COMMERCELIB_DIR . 'commerce_lib.all.php';
require_once SITE_ROOT . '/business_objects/bo_customer.php';
require_once SITE_ROOT . '/business_objects/bo_order_manager.php';
$order_id = 55;
$customer_id = 7;
$bo_customer = new BoCustomer();
$order_manager = new BoOrderManager();
$customer_data = $bo_customer->GetCustomer($customer_id);
try
{
  $customer = new Customer($customer_data);
}
catch(Exception $e)
{
  echo'Exception: ' . $e->getMessage();
  exit;
}
echo "Customer found. Address:<br/>";
echo "<pre>";
echo $customer->mAddressAsString;
echo "</pre>";
echo "Customer credit card number: " .
    $customer->mCreditCard->GetCardNumberX() . "<br/>";
$order_command = $order_manager->GetOrderDetails($order_id);
try
{
  $order_object = new OrderDetails($order_command);
}
catch(Exception $e)
{
  Echo 'Exception :' . $e->getMessage() ;
  exit;
}
echo "<br/>Order found. Details:<br/>";
echo "<pre>";
echo $order_object->mListAsString;
echo "</pre>";
echo "<br/>";
echo "List of items names:<br/>";
for ($i = 0; $i < count($order_object->mList); $i++)
  echo $order_object->mList[$i]->mProductName."<br/>";
?>
```

7. Load your `test_commerce_lib.php` file in your favorite browser and see the results, as shown in Figure 12-4.

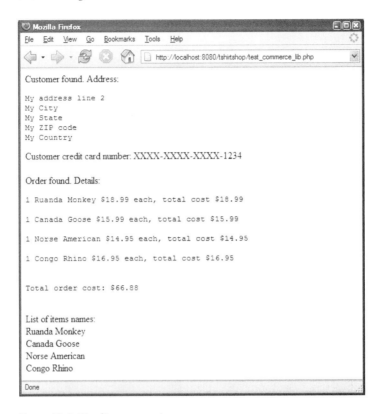

Figure 12-4. *Pipeline processing*

How It Works: The New Code

You've added quite a lot of code here, but much of it is similar to code you've already seen. The `Customer` class is simply a wrapper around a row of data from the `customer` table. To initialize a `Customer` object, you pass an associative array with customer info to the class constructor. This associative array contains the fields in the `customer` table as keys, and is retrieved in the test code using the `GetCustomer` business tier method from the last chapter.

The constructor of the `Customer` class starts by checking if it received an initialized object, and an exception is thrown if no data is encountered:

```
// simple test to check we didn't receive void parameter
if (empty($customer)) throw new Exception("No customer data");
```

When reading credit card data from the database, it is first decrypted using the `Secure-Card` class you implemented in the previous chapter:

```
// decrypt credit card data
$this->mCreditCard = new SecureCard();
$this->mCreditCard->LoadEncryptedDataAndDecrypt($customer['credit_card']);
```

The Customer class has one extra public field that is not read directly from the database: $mAddressAsString. This field provides direct access to a formatted string representing the address of the customer, which will be very useful later on when you need to notify your supplier of the address to send an order to! This string is built up from the data already stored. The test_commerce_lib.php file that is used to test the Customer class displays the value of this field to show typical output.

The OrderDetail class is similar to Customer in that it doesn't have much functionality apart from storing data. The OrderDetail class represents one ordered item in an order, so the data it needs to store is the ordered item's ID, name, quantity, and cost. The constructor of the class retrieves this data, saves it in individual class members, calculates the product's total cost as the product's quantity ($mQuantity) multiplied by the product's cost ($mUnitCost), and creates a string representation of the item (the $mItemAsString member), which is a formatted string suitable for displaying item properties to a human reader.

OrderDetails keeps an array of OrderDetail objects in its $mList member. The constructor for the OrderDetails class starts in a similar way to that of Customer, as it checks for existing data before progressing:

```
// simple test to guard against void input data
if (empty($orderDetails))
   throw new Exception("Empty Order Details");
```

The remainder of the constructor reads each item from the $orderDetails associative array received as a parameter, which contains a list of records from the order_detail table. The constructor adds each record in $mOrderDetails to the $mList member as OrderDetail objects (so $mList will be an array of OrderDetail objects), and builds another handy public field: mListAsString. This public field is a combination of the $mItemAsString fields of each OrderDetail, and a "Total order cost" string. This will come in handy when confirming orders with customers, and passing lists of items to suppliers. The code to achieve this is as follows:

```
// populates the mList array
for ($i = 0; $i < count($orderDetails); $i++)
{
  // creates a new OrderDetail instance
  $new_order_detail = new OrderDetail($orderDetails[$i]['product_id'],
    $orderDetails[$i]['product_name'], $orderDetails[$i]['quantity'],
    $orderDetails[$i]['unit_cost']);
  // saves the new OrderDetail instance into the mList array
  $this->mList[$i] = $new_order_detail;
  // builds output string
  $this->mListAsString .= $new_order_detail->mItemAsString . NEWLINE;
  // adds product cost to total cost
  $this->mTotalCost += $new_order_detail->mCost;
}
// finishes building the output string
$this->mListAsString .= NEWLINE . "Total order cost: $" .
                        $this->mTotalCost;
```

The code consists mainly of a single for loop, which executes for every item found in the $mOrderDetails variable.

The `test_commerce_lib.php` page uses the `GetOrderDetails` method of the business tier to initialize an instance of `OrderDetails`. The `GetOrderDetails` method simply gets all the rows in the `order_detail` table that have a specific `order_id` value, and returns this data in the form of an associative array. This gets all the information required for the `OrderDetails` constructor to carry out its data extraction.

In `test_commerce_lib.php`, if you want to make sure an exception is thrown in case of an error, simply choose a value for `customer_id` or `order_id` that doesn't have associated data in the database.

Implementing the OrderProcessor Class

As is probably apparent now, the `OrderProcessor` class (which is the class responsible for moving an order through the pipeline) contains a lot of code. However, you can start simply, and build up additional functionality as you need it. To start with, you'll create a version of the `OrderProcessor` class with the following functionality:

- Includes full configuration, in which information—such as the connection string to use, the mail server to send mail with, the required email addresses, and so on—is loaded into the order processor when it is instantiated

- Dynamically selects a pipeline section supporting the `IPipelineSection` interface

- Adds basic auditing data

- Gives access to the current order details

- Gives access to the customer for the current order

- Gives access to administrator mailing

- Mails the administrator in case of error

The configuration is carried out via a class called `OrderProcessorConfiguration`. You'll also create a single pipeline section, `PsDummy`, which uses some of this functionality. `PsDummy` is used in the code of this chapter in place of the real pipeline section classes, which you'll implement in the next chapter.

To implement the functionality just described, you'll also need to add three new methods to the `DoOrderManager` class:

- *GetOrderStatus*: Returns the status of an order with the given order ID

- *AddAudit*: Adds an entry to the `audit` table

- *GetCustomerByOrderId*: Returns customer data associated with an order with a given order ID

The code for these methods is shown in the next exercise.

Exercise: Implementing the OrderProcessor Class

To implement the OrderProcessor class, follow these steps:

1. Add a new file called order_processor_configuration.php in your commerce_lib directory with the following in it:

```php
<?php
class OrderProcessorConfiguration
{
  public $mAdminEmail;
  public $mAdminEmailParams;
  public $mCustomerServiceEmail;
  public $mCustomerServiceEmailParams;
  public $mOrderProcessorEmail;
  public $mOrderProcessorEmailParams;
  public $mSupplierEmail;
  // constructor initializes class members
  function __construct($newAdminEmail, $newAdminEmailParams,
    $newCustomerServiceEmail, $newCustomerServiceEmailParams,
    $newOrderProcessorEmail, $newOrderProcessorEmailParams, $newSupplierEmail)
  {
    $this->mAdminEmail = $newAdminEmail;
    $this->mAdminEmailParams = $newAdminEmailParams;
    $this->mCustomerServiceEmail = $newCustomerServiceEmail;
    $this->mCustomerServiceEmailParams = $newCustomerServiceEmailParams;
    $this->mOrderProcessorEmail = $newOrderProcessorEmail;
    $this->mOrderProcessorEmailParams = $newOrderProcessorEmailParams;
    $this->mSupplierEmail = $newSupplierEmail;
  }
}
?>
```

2. Add the following three methods to the DoOrderManager class from
   data_objects/do_order_manager.php:

```php
// gets status of an order
public function GetOrderStatus($orderId)
{
  $query_string = "SELECT status FROM orders WHERE order_id=$orderId";
  $result = $this->dbManager->DbGetOne($query_string);
  return $result;
}

// adds audit record
public function AddAudit($orderId, $message, $messageNumber)
{
  $query_string = "INSERT INTO audit (order_id, datestamp,
                                  message, message_number)
                  VALUES ($orderId, NOW(), '$message', $messageNumber)";
```

```php
    $result = $this->dbManager->DbQuery($query_string);
    return $result;
  }

  // gets the data of a customer that made a particular order
  public function GetCustomerByOrderId($orderId)
  {
    $query_string = "SELECT customer.customer_id, customer.name,
                            customer.email, customer.password,
                            customer.credit_card, customer.address1,
                            customer.address2, customer.city,
                            customer.region, customer.postal_code,
                            customer.country, customer.phone
                     FROM customer INNER JOIN orders
                       ON customer.customer_id = orders.customer_id
                     WHERE orders.order_id = $orderId";
    $result=$this->dbManager->DbGetRow($query_string);
    return $result;
  }
```

3. Add a new file to the commerce_lib directory called order_processor.php with the following code:

```php
<?php
// reference the Mail PEAR library
require_once 'Mail.php';
// Main class, used to obtain order information,
// run pipeline sections, audit orders, etc.
class OrderProcessor
{
  public $mOrderId;
  public $mOrderStatus;
  public $mConnection;
  public $mConfiguration;
  public $mContinueNow;
  private $mCurrentCustomer;
  private $mCurrentOrderDetails;
  private $mOrderManager;
  private $mReference;
  private $mAuthCode;
  // constructor creates DoOrderManager instance
  function __construct()
  {
    $this->mOrderManager = new DoOrderManager();
  }
  // Process is called from checkout.php and orders_admin.php to process an
  // order; the first parameter is the ID of the order, and the second
  // parameter is an OrderProcessorConfiguration instance.
```

```php
public function Process($newOrderId, $newConfiguration)
{
  // set order ID
  $this->mOrderId = $newOrderId;
  // configure processor
  $this->mConfiguration = $newConfiguration;
  $this->mContinueNow = true;
  // log start of execution
  $this->AddAudit("Order Processor started.", 10000);
  // obtain status of order
  $this->mOrderStatus = $this->mOrderManager->GetOrderStatus($this->mOrderId);
  // process pipeline section
  try
  {
    while ($this->mContinueNow)
    {
      $this->GetCurrentPipelineSection();
      $this->mCurrentPipelineSection->Process($this);
    }
  }
  catch(Exception $e)
  {
    trigger_error('Exception "' . $e->getMessage() . '" on ' .
                  $e->getFile() . " line " . $e->getLine());
    $this->MailAdmin("Order Processing error ocured.", $e->getMessage());
    $this->AddAudit("Order Processing error ocured.", 10002);
    throw new Exception("processor error");
  }
  $this->AddAudit("Order Processor finished.", 10001);
}
// gets current pipeline section
private function GetCurrentPipelineSection()
{
  return new PsDummy();
}
// sends email
public function Mail($params, $to, $headers, $message)
{
  // Create the mail object using the Mail::factory method
  $mail_object = Mail::factory('smtp', $params);
  // Test the mail object is valid
  if (PEAR::isError($mail_object))
    throw new Exception($mail_object->getMessage());
  // sends email
  $result = $mail_object->send($to, $headers, $message);
  // Test if mail was sent successfully
```

```php
      if (PEAR::isError($result))
        throw new Exception("Unable to send e-mail to $to. " .
                            $result->getMessage());
    }
    // builds email message
    public function MailAdmin($subject, $message)
    {
      // usually you are not allowed to set the 'From' header
      $headers['From'] = $this->mConfiguration->mOrderProcessorEmail;
      $headers['Subject'] = $subject;
      $headers['To'] = $this->mConfiguration->mAdminEmail;
      $this->Mail($this->mConfiguration->mOrderProcessorEmailParams,
                  $this->mConfiguration->mAdminEmail,
                  $headers,
                  $message);
    }
    // gets the customer that made the order
    public function GetCurrentCustomer()
    {
      if (empty($this->mCurrentCustomer))
      {
        $this->mCurrentCustomer = new
         Customer($this->mOrderManager->GetCustomerByOrderId($this->mOrderId));
        if (empty($this->mCurrentCustomer))
          throw new Exception($this->mOrderId . " order doesn't have a
customer");
      }
      return $this->mCurrentCustomer;
    }
    // gets the details of the current order
    public function GetCurrentOrderDetails()
    {
      if (empty($this->mCurrentOrderDetails))
      {
        $this->mCurrentOrderDetails = new
          OrderDetails($this->mOrderManager->GetOrderDetails($this->mOrderId));
        if (empty($this->mCurrentOrderDetails))
          throw new Exception($this->mOrderId .
                              " doesn't have order details entry");
      }
      return $this->mCurrentOrderDetails;
    }
    // adds audit message
    public function AddAudit($message, $messageNumber)
    {
      $this->mOrderManager->AddAudit($this->mOrderId, $message, $messageNumber);
    }
```

```
// updates order status
public function UpdateOrderStatus($newStatus)
{
  $this->mOrderManager->UpdateOrderStatus($this->mOrderId, $newStatus);
  $this->mOrderStatus = $newStatus;
}
}
?>
```

4. Create the IPipelineSection interface in the commerce_lib/i_pipeline_section.php file as follows:

```php
<?php
interface IPipelineSection
{
  public function Process($processor);
}
?>
```

5. Add a new file in the commerce_lib directory called ps_dummy.php with the following code. The PsDummy class is used in this chapter for testing purposes in place of the real pipeline sections that you'll implement in the next chapter.

```php
<?php
class PsDummy implements IPipelineSection
{
  public function Process($processor)
  {
    $processor->AddAudit("PsDoNothing started.",99999);
    $processor->AddAudit("Customer: " .
                         $processor->GetCurrentCustomer()->mName, 99999);
    $processor->AddAudit("First item in order: " .
    $processor->GetCurrentOrderDetails()->mList[0]->mItemAsString, 99999);
    $processor->MailAdmin("Test.", "Test mail from PsDummy.", 99999);
    $processor->AddAudit("PsDoNothing finished", 99999);
  }
}
?>
```

6. Uncomment the following line in the php.ini configuration file by removing the leading ";". This is required for the email-sending functionality.

```
extension=php_sockets.dll
```

7. Add the following code at the start of the tss_error_handler() function in include/tss_error_handler.php:

```
// error handler function
function tss_error_handler($errNo, $errStr, $errFile, $errLine)
{
```

```
// '@'-prepended expressions from the Mail class of the PEAR library
// generate irrelevant warning messages that we choose to ignore
// (errors_reporting() is set to 0 when such warnings are generated)
if (error_reporting() == 0) return;
```

8. Add the following code to include/config.inc.php, customizing the data with your own email addresses and SMTP login info:

```
// constant definitions for order handling related messages
define("ADMIN_EMAIL", "mihai_bucica@netpost.ro");
$admin_email_params = array('host' => 'netpost.ro',
                            'auth' => true,
                            'username' => 'mihai_bucica',
                            'password' => 'secretpassword');
define("CUSTOMER_SERVICE_EMAIL", "mihai_bucica@netpost.ro");
$customer_service_email_params = array('host' => 'netpost.ro',
                                       'auth' => true,
                                       'username' => 'mihai_bucica',
                                       'password' => 'secretpassword');
define("ORDER_PROCESSOR_EMAIL", "mihai_bucica@netpost.ro");
$order_processor_email_params = array('host' => 'netpost.ro',
                                      'auth' => true,
                                      'username' => 'mihai_bucica',
                                      'password' => 'secretpassword');
define("SUPPLIER_EMAIL", "mihai_bucica@netpost.ro");
```

9. Add the highlighted lines to commerce_lib.all.php, which should now contain the following code:

```
<?php
require_once SITE_ROOT . '/business_objects/secure_card.php';
require_once SITE_ROOT . '/data_objects/do_order_manager.php';
require_once COMMERCELIB_DIR . 'customer.php';
require_once COMMERCELIB_DIR . 'order_detail.php';
require_once COMMERCELIB_DIR . 'order_details.php';
require_once COMMERCELIB_DIR . 'i_pipeline_section.php';
require_once COMMERCELIB_DIR . 'ps_dummy.php';
require_once COMMERCELIB_DIR . 'order_processor_configuration.php';
require_once COMMERCELIB_DIR . 'order_processor.php';
?>
```

10. Create a new file named test_commerce_dummy.php in your site root (the tshirtshop folder) and add the following code to it, customizing the $order_id with one from your database:

```
<?php
// reference configuration files
require_once 'include/config.inc.php';
require_once SITE_ROOT . '/include/app_top.php';
require_once COMMERCELIB_DIR . 'commerce_lib.all.php';
```

```
// sets an order id
$order_id = 23;
//
$configuration = new OrderProcessorConfiguration
    (ADMIN_EMAIL,
      $GLOBALS['admin_email_params'],
      CUSTOMER_SERVICE_EMAIL,
      $GLOBALS['customer_service_email_params'],
      ORDER_PROCESSOR_EMAIL,
      $GLOBALS['order_processor_email_params'],
      SUPPLIER_EMAIL);
$processor = new OrderProcessor();
try
{
  $processor->Process($order_id, $configuration);
}
catch (Exception $e)
{
  echo $e->getMessage() . ' on ' . $e->getFile() . " line " . $e->getLine();
  exit;
}
echo "Finished";
?>
```

11. Modify the customer_id field in the tshirtshop database for the order selected in the previous code, giving it the value of a valid customer in the customers table (this is necessary because you haven't yet modified checkout.php to place orders that include this information).

12. Load the newly created test_commerce_dummy.php file in your browser.

13. Check your inbox for a new mail that should say "Test mail from PsDummy."

14. Examine the audit table in the database to see the new entries (see Figure 12-5).

audit_id	order_id	datestamp	message	message_number
56	14	2004-09-20 00:02:31	Order Processor started.	10000
57	14	2004-09-20 00:02:31	PsDoNothing started.	99999
58	14	2004-09-20 00:02:31	Customer: Cristian Darie	99999
59	14	2004-09-20 00:02:31	First item in order: 1 Ruanda Monkey $18.99 each, ...	99999
60	14	2004-09-20 00:02:31	PsDoNothing finished	99999
61	14	2004-09-20 00:02:31	Order Processor finished.	10001

Figure 12-5. *Audit table entries from* PsDummy

How It Works: The Skeleton of the Order-Processing Functionality

The first code added in the exercise was for the OrderProcessorConfiguration class. This is a simple class for grouping together the various pieces of information required to allow the OrderProcessor class to function. There are alternatives to this, such as storing this data in a config file or in a database, but this method works fine and keeps your code simple. It also allows the same component library to be used in multiple e-commerce applications, because it is dynamically configured.

The following list describes the information stored in the OrderProcessorConfiguration class:

- *Administrator email (with SMTP login info)*: The email address to send mail to if something goes wrong during order processing. This includes messages concerning lack of funds available, allowing the administrator to take corrective action, and maybe contact the customer directly.

- *Customer service email (with SMTP login info)*: The return address for email sent to customers and suppliers.

- *Order processor email (with SMTP login info)*: The return address for emails sent to the administrator.

- *Supplier email*: The address for email sent to the supplier.

For demonstration purposes, we set the administrator and supplier email addresses to our own email address, which should also be the address of the customer used to generate test orders. You should do this to check that everything is working properly before sending mail to the outside world.

Let's now look at the OrderProcessor class. The main body of the OrderProcessor class is the Process() method, which is called from function.load_checkout_info.php and function.load_order_details_admin.php to process an order. The order to be processed is indicated by its ID, and the configuration to use is set via an OrderProcessorConfiguration parameter:

```
public function Process($newOrderId, $newConfiguration)
{
  // set order ID
  $this->mOrderId = $newOrderId;
  // configure processor
  $this->mConfiguration = $newConfiguration;
  $this->mContinueNow = true;
```

Next you used the AddAudit() method (which we'll come to shortly) to add an audit entry indicating that the OrderProcessor has started:

```
// log start of execution
$this->AddAudit("Order Processor started.", 10000);
```

Note 10000 is the message number to store for the audit entry. We'll look at these codes in more detail shortly.

As detailed earlier, processing an order depends on its status, so the first thing to do is to get the status of the order using the new GetOrderStatus data tier method:

```
// obtain status of order
$this->mOrderStatus = $this->mOrderManager->GetOrderStatus($this->mOrderId);
```

The status is stored in the order_status field you saw earlier.

Next you come to the order processing itself. The model used here is to check the Boolean $mContinueNow field before processing a pipeline section. This allows sections to specify either that processing should continue when they're finished with the current task (by setting $mContinueNow to true) or that processing should pause (by setting $mContinueNow to false). This is necessary because you need to wait for external input at certain points along the pipeline when checking if the products are in stock and if the funds are available on the customer's credit card.

The pipeline section to process is selected by the private GetCurrentPipelineSection() method, which eventually returns a pipeline section class (you'll build these classes in the next chapter) corresponding to the current status of the order. However, at this moment, the GetCurrentPipelineSection() just has the job of returning an instance of PsDummy. In the next chapter, you'll implement classes representing each pipeline section, and you'll return one of those classes instead of PsDummy.

```
// gets current pipeline section
private function GetCurrentPipelineSection()
{
  return new PsDummy();
}
```

Back to Process(), you see this method being called in a try block:

```
// process pipeline section
try
{
  while ($this->mContinueNow)
  {
    $this->mContinueNow = false;
    $cps = $this->GetCurrentPipelineSection();
    $cps->Process($this);
  }
}
```

Note that $mContinueNow is set to false in the while loop—the default behavior is to stop after each pipeline section. However, the call to the Process() method of the current pipeline section class (which receives a parameter of the current OrderProcessor instance, thus having access to the $mContinueNow member) changes the value of $mContinueNow back to true, in case processing should go to the next pipeline section without waiting for user interaction.

Note that in the previous code snippet, the Process method is called without knowing what kind of object $cps references. Each pipeline section is represented by a different class, but all these classes need to expose a method named Process. When such behavior is needed, the standard technique is to create an *interface* that defines the common behavior you need in that set of classes.

All order pipeline section classes support the simple IPipelineSection interface, defined as follows:

```php
<?php
interface IPipelineSection
{
  public function Process($processor);
}
?>
```

■**Note** An interface is a set of method signatures, and serves as a contract for classes that implement it. When a class implements an interface, it guarantees that it will implement every signature defined in that interface. An interface cannot be instantiated like a normal class because it doesn't contain any method implementations, only their signatures. By implementing IPipelineSection in all order pipeline section classes (you'll write them in the next chapter), you guarantee that they all will export a public method named Process. This way, you can safely call the Process method on any pipeline section class from your OrderProcessor class without the risk of generating an error.

All pipeline sections use a Process() method to perform their work. This method requires an OrderProcessor reference as a parameter because the pipeline sections need access to the public fields and methods exposed by the OrderProcessor class.

The last part of the Process() method in OrderProcessor involves catching exceptions. Here you catch any exceptions that may be thrown by the order pipeline section classes, and react to them by sending an email to the administrator using the MailAdmin() method, adding an audit entry, and throwing a new exception that can be caught by PHP pages that use the OrderProcessor class:

```php
catch(Exception $e)
{
  trigger_error('Exception "' . $e->getMessage() . '" on ' .
              $e->getFile() . " line " . $e->getLine());
  $this->MailAdmin("Order Processing error ocured.", $e->getMessage());
  $this->AddAudit("Order Processing error ocured.", 10002);
  throw new Exception("Processor error");
}
```

Regardless of whether processing is successful, you add a final audit entry saying that the processing has completed:

```php
$this->AddAudit("Order Processor finished.",10001);
```

Let's now look at the `Mail()` method that simply takes a few parameters for the basic email properties. This emailing code is the `PEAR::Mail` way of sending email using an SMTP server.

```
// sends email
public function Mail($params, $to, $headers, $message)
{
  // Create the mail object using the Mail::factory method
  $mail_object = Mail::factory('smtp', $params);
  // Test the mail object is valid
  if (PEAR::isError($mail_object))
    throw new Exception($mail_object->getMessage());
  // sends email
  $result = $mail_object->send($to, $headers, $message);
  // Test if mail was sent successfully
  if (PEAR::isError($result))
    throw new Exception("Unable to send e-mail to $to. " .
                        $result->getMessage());
}
```

You also have a `MailAdmin()` method that uses the `Mail()` method to send an email message to the administrator.

The `AddAudit()` method is also a simple one, and calls the `AddAudit` data tier method shown earlier:

```
public function AddAudit($message, $messageNumber)
{
 $this->mOrderManager->AddAudit($this->orderId, $message, $messageNumber);
}
```

At this point, it's worth examining the message number scheme we've chosen for order processing audits. In all cases, the audit message number will be a five-digit number. The first digit of this number is either 1 if an audit is being added by `OrderProcessor` or 2 if the audit is added by a pipeline section. The next two digits are used for the pipeline stage that added the audit (which maps directly to the status of the order when the audit was added). The final two digits uniquely identify the message within this scope. For example, so far you've seen the following message numbers:

- *10000*: Order processor started

- *10001*: Order processor finished

- *10002*: Order processor error occurred

Later you'll see a lot of these numbers that start with 2, as you get on to pipeline sections, and include the necessary information for identifying the pipeline section as noted previously. Hopefully, you'll agree that this scheme allows for plenty of flexibility, although you can, of course, use whatever numbers you see fit. As a final note, numbers ending in 00 and 01 are used for starting and finishing messages for both the order processor and pipeline stages, while 02 and above are for other messages. There is no real reason for this apart from consistency between the components.

The last part of the OrderProcessor class is the code for the GetCurrentCustomer (which returns an instance of the Customer class representing the customer of the current order) and GetCurrentOrderDetails (which returns an OrderDetails object containing the products of the current order) methods. These methods get the data from the database and cache it in the $mCurrentCustomer and $mCurrentOrderDetails private members. This way, on every subsequent call, these methods will return the cached data instead of accessing the database once again.

▓Note As an aside, this method of only getting information when needed is often known as "lazy initialization," which is one of those bits of computer programming terminology that always makes me grin.

The code for both methods is simple, using the new GetCustomerByOrderID for Current-Customer, and the GetOrderDetails stored procedure from earlier in the chapter in CurrentOrderDetails:

```
// gets the customer that made the order
public function GetCurrentCustomer()
{
  if (empty($this->mCurrentCustomer))
  {
    $this->mCurrentCustomer = new
     Customer($this->mOrderManager->GetCustomerByOrderId($this->mOrderId));
    if (empty($this->mCurrentCustomer))
      throw new Exception($this->mOrderId . " order doesn't have a customer");
  }
  return $this->mCurrentCustomer;
}
// gets the details of the current order
public function GetCurrentOrderDetails()
{
  if (empty($this->mCurrentOrderDetails))
  {
    $this->mCurrentOrderDetails = new
     OrderDetails($this->mOrderManager->GetOrderDetails($this->mOrderId));
    if (empty($this->mCurrentOrderDetails))
      throw new Exception($this->mOrderId .
                         " doesn't have order details entry");
  }
  return $this->mCurrentOrderDetails;
}
```

The PsDummy class that is used in this skeleton processor performs some basic functions to check that things are working correctly:

```php
<?php
class PsDummy implements IPipelineSection
{
  public function Process($processor)
  {
    $processor->AddAudit("PsDoNothing started.",99999);
    $processor->AddAudit("Customer: " .
                         $processor->GetCurrentCustomer()->mName, 99999);
    $processor->AddAudit("First item in order: " .
    $processor->GetCurrentOrderDetails()->mList[0]->mItemAsString, 99999);
    $processor->MailAdmin("Test.", " Test mail from PsDummy.", 99999);
    $processor->AddAudit("PsDoNothing finished", 99999);
  }
}
?>
```

The code here uses the AddAudit() and MailAdmin() methods of OrderProcessor to generate something to show that the code has executed correctly. Note that the numbering schemes outlined previously aren't used there because this isn't a real pipeline section!

That was quite a lot of code to get through, but it did make the client code very simple. All you needed to do to test the skeleton of the order pipeline functionality was create a new OrderProcessorConfiguration instance, supply it as parameter for the OrderProcessor class, and call the Process method on the OrderProcessor instance:

```php
$configuration = new OrderProcessorConfiguration
    (ADMIN_EMAIL,
     $GLOBALS['admin_email_params'],
     CUSTOMER_SERVICE_EMAIL,
     $GLOBALS['customer_service_email_params'],
     ORDER_PROCESSOR_EMAIL,
     $GLOBALS['order_processor_email_params'],
     SUPPLIER_EMAIL);
$processor = new OrderProcessor();
try
{
  $processor->Process($order_id, $configuration);
}
```

Short of setting all the configuration details, there is very little to do because OrderProcessor does a *lot* of work for you. Note that the code you have ended up with is for the most part a consequence of the design choices made earlier. This is an excellent example of how a strong design can lead you straight to powerful and robust code.

Adding More Functionality to OrderProcessor

You need to add a few more bits and pieces to the OrderProcessor class, but it hardly seems worth going through another "Exercise" section to do so. Instead, we'll simply go through the code briefly.

We need to look at

- Updating the status of an order

- Setting and getting credit card authentication details

- Setting the order shipment date

Updating the Status of an Order

Each pipeline section needs the capability to change the status of an order, advancing it to the next pipeline section. Rather than simply incrementing the status, this functionality is kept flexible, just in case you end up with a more complicated branched pipeline. This requires a new data tier method, UpdateOrderStatus, which you need to add to the DoOrderManager class (located in data_objects/do_order_manager.php):

```
// updates the order pipeline status of an order
public function UpdateOrderStatus($orderId, $status)
{
  $query_string = "UPDATE orders SET status=$status WHERE order_id=$orderId";
  $result = $this->dbManager->DbQuery($query_string);
  return $result;
}
```

The method in OrderProcessor that calls this data tier method is also called UpdateOrder-Status.

Setting and Getting Credit Card Authentication Details

In the next chapter, when we deal with credit card usage, you'll need to set and retrieve data in the auth_code and reference fields in the orders table.

To support that functionality, add the SetOrderAuthCodeAndReference method to your DoOrderManager class:

```
// sets order's authorization code
public function SetOrderAuthCodeAndReference($orderId, $authCode, $reference)
{
  $query_string = "UPDATE orders
               SET auth_code='$authCode', reference='$reference'
               WHERE order_id=$orderId";
  $result=$this->dbManager->DbQuery($query_string);
  return $result;
}
```

The authorization and reference codes are stored in private fields of the DoOrderManager class because you'll use a similar method of access to that of the Customer and OrderDetails information covered earlier:

```
private $mReference;
private $mAuthCode;
```

The code to set these values in the database is the SetOrderAuthCodeAndReference method, which you need to add to your OrderProcessor class:

```
// set order's authorization code and reference code
public function SetOrderAuthCodeAndReference($newAuthCode, $newReference)
{
  $this->mOrderManager->SetOrderAuthCodeAndReference($this->mOrderId,
                                               $newAuthCode,
                                               $newReference);

  $this->mAuthCode = $newAuthCode;
  $this->mReference = $newReference;
}
```

This code also sets the private fields, just in case they are required before the OrderProcessor terminates. In this situation, it wouldn't make much sense to get these values from the database when we already know what the result will be.

Getting this data also requires a new data tier method, GetOrderAuthCodeAndReference. Add the following method to the DoOrderManager class:

```
// gets order's authorization code
public function GetOrderAuthCodeAndReference($orderId)
{
  $query_string = "SELECT auth_code, reference
                   FROM orders
                   WHERE order_id=$orderId";
  $result = $this->dbManager->DbGetRow($query_string);
  return $result;
}
```

$mAuthCode and $mReference are available through methods that only perform a database read if no data is currently available. Because the values of these items are linked, we supply the data-access code in one place. Add the following methods to your OrderProcessor class:

```
// gets order authorization code and reference code
private function GetOrderAuthCodeAndReference()
{
  $result = $this->mOrderManager->GetOrderAuthCodeAndReference(
                                              $this->mOrderId);
  if (empty($result)) throw Exception($this->mOrderId." doesn't exist");
  $this->mAuthCode = $result['auth_code'];
  $this->mReference = $result['reference'];
}
// gets order authorization code
```

```php
public function GetAuthCode()
{
  if (empty($this->mAuthCode)) $this->GetOrderAuthCodeAndReference();
  return $this->mAuthCode;
}
// gets order reference code
public function GetReference()
{
  if (empty($this->mReference)) $this->GetOrderAuthCodeAndReference();
  return $this->mReference;
}
```

Setting the Order Shipment Date

When an order is shipped, you should update the shipment date in the database, which can simply be the current date. Add the new data tier method, SetDateShipped, to your DoOrder-Manager class as follows:

```php
// set order's ship date
public function SetDateShipped($orderId)
{
  $query_string = "UPDATE orders
                   SET date_shipped=NOW()
                   WHERE order_id=$orderId";
  $result = $this->dbManager->DbQuery($query_string);
  return $result;
}
```

Add the following method to the OrderProcessor class:

```php
// set order's ship date
public function SetDateShipped()
{
  $this->mOrderManager->SetDateShipped($this->mOrderId);
}
```

Summary

You've begun to build the backbone of the application, and prepared it for the lion's share of the order pipeline processing functionality, which you'll implement in the next chapter.

Specifically, we've covered

- Modifications to the TShirtShop application to enable your own pipeline processing

- The basic framework for your order pipeline

- The database additions for auditing data and storing additional required data in the orders table

In the next chapter, you'll go on to fully implement the order pipeline.

■ ■ ■

CHAPTER 13

Implementing the Pipeline: Part II

In the last chapter, you completed the basic functionality of the OrderProcessor class, which is responsible for moving orders through the pipeline stages. You've seen a quick demonstration of this using a dummy pipeline section, but you haven't yet implemented the pipeline discussed at the beginning of the last chapter.

In this chapter, you'll add the required pipeline sections so that you can process orders from start to finish, although you won't be adding full credit card transaction functionality until the next chapter.

We'll also look at the web administration of orders by modifying the order admin pages added earlier in the book to take into account the new order-processing system.

Implementing the Pipeline Sections

In the previous chapter, you completed the OrderProcessor class, except for one important section—the pipeline stage selection. Rather than forcing the processor to use PsDummy (the class you used instead of the real pipeline section classes that you'll build in this chapter), you actually want to select one of the pipeline stages outlined in Chapter 12, depending on the status of the order.

Let's run through the code for each of the pipeline sections in turn, which will take you to the point where the order pipeline will be complete, apart from actual credit card authorization that you'll implement in Chapter 14. You'll implement eight new classes with the following names:

- PsInitialNotification
- PsCheckFunds
- PsCheckStock
- PsStockOK
- PsTakePayment
- PsShipGoods
- PsShipOK
- PsFinalNotification

We'll discuss the classes you're creating as we go. Before moving on, remember that this code is available in the Downloads section on the Apress web site (http://www.apress.com).

PsInitialNotification

This is the first pipeline stage, and is responsible for sending an email to the customer confirming that the order has been placed. Create a new file named ps_initial_notification.php in the commerce_lib folder, and start adding code to it as shown here. This class starts off in what will soon become a very familiar fashion:

```php
<?php
class PsInitialNotification implements IPipelineSection
{
  private $mProcessor;
  private $mCurrentCustomer;
  private $mCurrentOrderDetails;
  public function Process($processor)
  {
    $this->mProcessor = $processor;
    $processor->AddAudit("PsInitialNotification started.", 20000);
```

The class implements the IPipelineSection interface, then some private fields for storing important references, and finally the Process() method implementation. This method starts by storing the reference to OrderProcessor, which all your pipeline sections will do because using the methods it exposes (either in the Process() method or in other methods) is essential. We also add an audit entry, using the numbering scheme introduced in Chapter 12 (the initial 2 indicates it's coming from a pipeline section, the next 00 shows that it's the first pipeline section, and the final 00 means that it's the start message for the pipeline section).

Next, you get the customer and order details required by the pipeline section by using the appropriate properties of OrderProcessor:

```php
    $this->mCurrentCustomer = $processor->GetCurrentCustomer();
    $this->mCurrentOrderDetails = $processor->GetCurrentOrderDetails();
```

The remainder of the Process() method sends the notification email. This requires information from the customer and configuration data, which you have easy access to. You also use a private method to build a message body, which we'll look at shortly:

```php
    $headers['From'] = $processor->mConfiguration->mCustomerServiceEmail;
    $headers['To'] = $this->mCurrentCustomer->mEmail;
    $headers['Subject'] = "Order received.";
    $processor->Mail($processor->mConfiguration->mCustomerServiceEmailParams,
                     $this->mCurrentCustomer->mEmail,
                     $headers,
                     $this->GetMailBody());
```

After the mail is sent, you add an audit message to change the status of the order, and tell the order processor that it's okay to move straight on to the next pipeline section:

```
$processor->AddAudit("Notification email sent to customer.", 20002);
$processor->UpdateOrderStatus(1);
$processor->mContinueNow = true;
```

If all goes according to plan, the Process() method finishes by adding a final audit entry:

```
$processor->AddAudit("PsInitialNotification finished.", 20001);
  }
```

The GetMailBody() method is used to build up an email body to send to the customer. The text uses customer and order data, but follows a generally accepted e-commerce email format:

```
private function GetMailBody()
  {
    $body = "Thank you for your order! " .
            "The products you have ordered are as follows:";
    $body.= NEWLINE;
    $body.= NEWLINE;
    $body.= $this->mCurrentOrderDetails->mListAsString;
    $body.= NEWLINE;
    $body.= NEWLINE;
    $body.= "Your order will be shipped to:";
    $body.= NEWLINE;
    $body.= NEWLINE;
    $body.= $this->mCurrentCustomer->mAddressAsString;
    $body.= NEWLINE;
    $body.= NEWLINE;
    $body.= "Order reference number: ";
    $body.= $this->mProcessor->mOrderId;
    $body.= NEWLINE;
    $body.= NEWLINE;
    $body.= "You will receive a confirmation email when this order has been " .
            "dispatched. Thank you for shopping at TShirtShop.com!";
    return $body;
  }
}
?>
```

When this pipeline stage finishes, processing moves straight on to PsCheckFunds.

PsCheckFunds

This pipeline stage is responsible for making sure that the customer has the required funds available on a credit card. For now, you'll provide a dummy implementation of this, and just assume that these funds are available. You'll implement the real functionality in the next chapter, which deals with credit card transactions.

Add the following code to a new file in the commerce_lib folder named ps_check_funds.php. The code of the Process() method starts in the same way as PsInitialNotification:

```php
<?php
class PsCheckFunds implements IPipelineSection
{
  private $mProcessor;
  public function Process($processor)
  {
    $this->mProcessor = $processor;
    $processor->AddAudit("PSCheckFunds started.", 20100);
```

Even though you aren't actually performing a check, set the authorization and reference codes for the transaction to make sure that the code in OrderProcessor works properly:

```php
    $processor->SetOrderAuthCodeAndReference("DummyAuthCode", "DummyReference");
```

You finish up with some auditing and the code required for continuation:

```php
    $processor->AddAudit("Funds available for purchase.", 20102);
    $processor->UpdateOrderStatus(2);
    $processor->mContinueNow = true;
    $processor->AddAudit("PSCheckFunds finished.", 20101);
  }
} //end class
?>
```

When this pipeline stage finishes, processing moves straight on to PsCheckStock.

PsCheckStock

This pipeline stage sends an email to the supplier instructing them to check stock availability. Add the following code to a new file in the commerce_lib folder named ps_check_stock.php:

```php
<?php
class PsCheckStock implements IPipelineSection
{
  private $mProcessor;
  private $mCurrentOrderDetails;
  public function Process($processor)
  {
    $this->mProcessor = $processor;
    $processor->AddAudit("PSCheckStock started.", 20200);
```

This time, you need access to order details, although you don't need to get the customer details because the supplier isn't interested in who has placed the order at this stage:

```
$this->mCurrentOrderDetails = $processor->GetCurrentOrderDetails();
```

Mail is sent in a similar way to PsInitialNotification, using a private method to build up the body:

```
$headers['From'] = $processor->mConfiguration->mAdminEmail;
$headers['To'] = $processor->mConfiguration->mSupplierEmail;
$headers['Subject'] = "Stock check.";
$processor->Mail($processor->mConfiguration->mAdminEmailParams,
                 $processor->mConfiguration->mSupplierEmail,
                 $headers,
                 $this->GetMailBody());
```

As before, you finish by auditing and updating the status, although this time you don't tell the order processor to continue straight away:

```
$processor->AddAudit("Notification email sent to supplier.", 20202);
$processor->UpdateOrderStatus(3);
$processor->AddAudit("PSCheckStock finished.", 20201);
}
```

The code for building the message body is simple; it just lists the items in the order and tells the supplier to confirm via the TShirtShop web site (using the order administration page orders_admin_page.php, which you'll modify later):

```
  private function GetMailBody()
  {
    $body = "The following goods have been ordered:";
    $body .= NEWLINE;
    $body .= NEWLINE;
    $body .= $this->mCurrentOrderDetails->mListAsString;
    $body .= NEWLINE;
    $body .= NEWLINE;
    $body .= "Please check availability and confirm via " .
             "http://www.tshirtshop.com/orders_admin_page.php";
    $body .= NEWLINE;
    $body .= NEWLINE;
    $body .= "Order reference number: ";
    $body .= $this->mProcessor->mOrderId;
    return $body;
  }
} //end class
?>
```

When this pipeline stage finishes, processing pauses. Later, when the supplier confirms that stock is available, processing moves on to PsStockOK.

PsStockOK

This pipeline section just confirms that the supplier has the product in stock and moves on. Its Process() method is called for orders whose stock was confirmed and that need to move on to the next pipeline section. Add the following code to a new file in the commerce_lib folder named ps_stock_ok.php:

```php
<?php
class PsStockOK implements IPipelineSection
{
  private $mProcessor;
  public function Process($processor)
  {
    $this->mProcessor = $processor;
    $processor->AddAudit("PSStockOk started.", 20300);
    $processor->AddAudit("Stock confirmed by supplier.", 20302);
    $processor->UpdateOrderStatus(4);
    $processor->mContinueNow = true;
    $processor->AddAudit("PSStockOK finished.", 20301);
  }
}
?>
```

When this pipeline stage finishes, processing moves straight on to PsTakePayment.

PsTakePayment

This pipeline section completes the transaction started by PsCheckFunds. As with that section, you only provide a dummy implementation here, although you do retrieve the authorization and reference codes to check that part of OrderProcessor. Add the following code to a new file in the commerce_lib folder named ps_take_payment.php:

```php
<?php
class PsTakePayment implements IPipelineSection
{
  private $mProcessor;
  private $mAuthCode;
  private $mReference;
  public function Process($processor)
  {
    $this->mProcessor = $processor;
    $processor->AddAudit("PSTakePayment started.", 20400);
    $this->mAuthCode = $processor->GetAuthCode();
    $this->mReference = $processor->GetReference();
    $processor->AddAudit("Funds deducted from customer credit card account.",
                         20402);
    $processor->UpdateOrderStatus(5);
    $processor->mContinueNow = true;
    $processor->AddAudit("PSTakePayment finished.", 20401);
```

```
  }
}
?>
```

When this pipeline stage finishes, processing moves straight on to PsShipGoods.

PsShipGoods

This pipeline section is remarkably similar to PsCheckStock, as it sends an email to the supplier and stops the pipeline until the supplier has confirmed that stock has shipped. This time you do need customer information, however, because the supplier needs to know where to ship the order! Add the following code to a new file in the commerce_lib folder named ps_ship_goods.php:

```php
<?php
class PsShipGoods implements IPipelineSection
{
  private $mProcessor;
  private $mCurrentCustomer;
  private $mCurrentOrderDetails;
  public function Process($processor)
  {
    $this->mProcessor = $processor;
    $processor->AddAudit("PSShipGoods started.", 20500);
    $this->mCurrentCustomer = $processor->GetCurrentCustomer();
    $this->mCurrentOrderDetails = $processor->GetCurrentOrderDetails();
    $headers['From'] = $processor->mConfiguration->mAdminEmail;
    $headers['To'] = $processor->mConfiguration->mSupplierEmail;
    $headers['Subject'] = "Ship goods.";
    $processor->Mail($processor->mConfiguration->mAdminEmailParams,
                     $processor->mConfiguration->mSupplierEmail,
                     $headers,
                     $this->GetMailBody());
    $processor->AddAudit("Ship goods email sent to supplier.", 20502);
    $processor->UpdateOrderStatus(6);
    $processor->AddAudit("PSShipGoods finished.", 20501);
  }
```

As before, a private method called GetMailBody() is used to build the message body for the email sent to the supplier:

```php
  private function GetMailBody()
  {
    $body = "Payment has been received for the following goods:";
    $body.= NEWLINE;
    $body.= NEWLINE;
    $body.= $this->mCurrentOrderDetails->mListAsString;
    $body.= NEWLINE;
    $body.= NEWLINE;
    $body.= "Please ship to:";
```

```
      $body.= NEWLINE;
      $body.= NEWLINE;
      $body.= $this->mCurrentCustomer->mAddressAsString;
      $body.= NEWLINE;
      $body.= NEWLINE;
      $body.= "When goods have been shipped, please confirm via " .
              "http://www.tshirtshop.com/orders_admin_page.php";
      $body.= NEWLINE;
      $body.= NEWLINE;
      $body.= "Order reference number: ";
      $body.= $this->mProcessor->mOrderId;
      return $body;
    }
  }
?>
```

When this pipeline stage finishes, processing pauses. Later, when the supplier confirms that the order has been shipped, processing moves on to PsShipOK.

PsShipOK

This pipeline section is very similar to PsStockOK, although it has slightly more to do. Because you know that items have shipped, you can add a shipment date value to the orders table. Technically, this isn't really necessary, because all audit entries are dated. However, this method means that you have all the information easily accessible in one database table. Add the following code to a new file in the commerce_lib folder named ps_ship_ok.php:

```
<?php
class PsShipOk implements IPipelineSection
{
  private $mProcessor;
  public function Process($processor)
  {
    $this->mProcessor = $processor;
    $processor->AddAudit("PSShipOk started.", 20600);
    $processor->SetDateShipped();
    $processor->AddAudit("Order dispatched by supplier.", 20602);
    $processor->UpdateOrderStatus(7);
    $processor->mContinueNow = true;
    $processor->AddAudit("PSShipOK finished.", 20601);
  }
}
?>
```

When this pipeline stage finishes, processing moves straight on to PsFinalNotification.

PsFinalNotification

This last pipeline section is very similar to the first, as it sends an email to the customer. This time you're confirming that the order has shipped. Add the following code to a new file in the commerce_lib folder named ps_final_notification.php:

```php
<?php
class PsFinalNotification implements IPipelineSection
{
  private $mProcessor;
  private $mCurrentCustomer;
  private $mCurrentOrderDetails;
  public function Process($processor)
  {
    $this->mProcessor = $processor;
    $processor->AddAudit("PSFinalNotification started.", 20700);
    $this->mCurrentCustomer = $processor->GetCurrentCustomer();
    $this->mCurrentOrderDetails = $processor->GetCurrentOrderDetails();
    $headers['From'] = $processor->mConfiguration->mCustomerServiceEmail;
    $headers['To'] = $this->mCurrentCustomer->mEmail;
    $headers['Subject'] = "Order dispatched.";
    $processor->Mail($processor->mConfiguration->mCustomerServiceEmailParams,
                     $this->mCurrentCustomer->mEmail,
                     $headers,
                     $this->GetMailBody());
    $processor->AddAudit("Dispatch email send to customer.", 20702);
    $processor->UpdateOrderStatus(8);
    $processor->AddAudit("PSFinalNotification finished.", 20701);
  }
```

It uses a familiar-looking GetMailBody() method to build the body of the email:

```php
private function GetMailBody()
{
  $body = "Your order has now been dispatched! " .
          "The following products have been shipped:";
  $body .= NEWLINE;
  $body .= NEWLINE;
  $body .= $this->mCurrentOrderDetails->mListAsString;
  $body .= NEWLINE;
  $body .= NEWLINE;
  $body .= "Your order has been shipped to : ";
  $body .= NEWLINE;
  $body .= NEWLINE;
  $body .= $this->mCurrentCustomer->mAddressAsString;
  $body .= NEWLINE;
  $body .= NEWLINE;
  $body .= "Order reference number: ";
  $body .= $this->mProcessor->mOrderId;
```

```
    $body .= NEWLINE;
    $body .= NEWLINE;
    $body .= "Thank you for shopping at TshirtShop.com!";
    return $body;
  }
}
?>
```

When this pipeline section finishes, the order status is changed to 8, which represents a completed order. Further attempts to process the order using OrderProcessor will result in an exception being thrown.

Testing the Pipeline

Now let's do a simple test to make sure the code you just wrote is working as expected.

Exercise: Testing the Pipeline

To test the pipeline, follow these steps:

1. Add the following lines at the end of your commerce_lib.all.php file, which is located in the commerce_lib folder:

```
require_once COMMERCELIB_DIR . 'ps_initial_notification.php';
require_once COMMERCELIB_DIR . 'ps_check_funds.php';
require_once COMMERCELIB_DIR . 'ps_check_stock.php';
require_once COMMERCELIB_DIR . 'ps_stock_ok.php';
require_once COMMERCELIB_DIR . 'ps_take_payment.php';
require_once COMMERCELIB_DIR . 'ps_ship_goods.php';
require_once COMMERCELIB_DIR . 'ps_ship_ok.php';
require_once COMMERCELIB_DIR . 'ps_final_notification.php';
```

2. Modify the code of the GetCurrentPipelineSection() method in OrderProcessor as follows:

```
// gets an object instance representing the current pipeline section
private function GetCurrentPipelineSection()
{
  switch ($this->mOrderStatus)
  {
    case 0:
      $this->mCurrentPipelineSection = new PsInitialNotification(); break;
    case 1:
      $this->mCurrentPipelineSection = new PsCheckFunds(); break;
    case 2:
      $this->mCurrentPipelineSection = new PsCheckStock(); break;
    case 3:
      $this->mCurrentPipelineSection = new PsStockOk(); break;
```

```
    case 4:
      $this->mCurrentPipelineSection = new PsTakePayment(); break;
    case 5:
      $this->mCurrentPipelineSection = new PsShipGoods(); break;
    case 6:
      $this->mCurrentPipelineSection = new PsShipOK(); break;
    case 7:
      $this->mCurrentPipelineSection = new PsFinalNotification(); break;
    case 8:
      throw new Exception("Order has already been completed."); break;
    default:
      throw new Exception("Unknown pipeline section requested.");
  }
}
```

3. Add a new file named test_processor.php file in your tshirtshop folder as follows, using the same values you used in the last example for the configuration:

```php
<?php
require_once 'include/config.inc.php';
require_once SITE_ROOT . '/include/app_top.php';
require_once COMMERCELIB_DIR . 'commerce_lib.all.php';
// change this to reflect one of your orders
$order_id = 6;
// initial step is 1
if (isset($_GET['step']))
  $step = (int)$_GET['step'];
else
  $step=0;
$step++;
// if the Execute! button was clicked...
if ($step!=1)
{
  // step == 2 -> 1st call to OrderProcessor, normally from checkout.php
  // step == 3 -> 2nd call to OrderProcessor, normally from
orders_admin_page.php
  // step == 4 -> 3rd call to OrderProcessor, normally from
orders_admin_page.php
  $configuration = new OrderProcessorConfiguration(
                        ADMIN_EMAIL,
                        $GLOBALS['admin_email_params'],
                        CUSTOMER_SERVICE_EMAIL,
                        $GLOBALS['customer_service_email_params'],
                        ORDER_PROCESSOR_EMAIL,
                        $GLOBALS['order_processor_email_params'],
                        SUPPLIER_EMAIL);
```

```php
// creates new OrderProcessor instance and uses it
$processor = new OrderProcessor();
try
{
  $processor->Process($order_id, $configuration);
}
catch (Exception $e)
{
  echo $e->getMessage();
  exit;
}
}
if ($step==4)
{
 echo "Finished.";
 exit;
}
?>
<form action="test_processor.php">
<input type="hidden" name="step" value="<?php echo $step; ?>">
Execution number <?php echo $step; ?> of Process() method
<input type=submit value="Execute!">
</form>
```

4. Execute the code by loading test_processor.php in your favorite browser and clicking the Execute button, as shown in Figure 13-1.

Figure 13-1. *The first step in testing the order pipeline*

5. Assuming you entered the ID of an existing order in the test_processor.php script, you should get a customer notification email (see Figure 13-2).

6. Check your supplier email for the stock check email (see Figure 13-3).

7. Continue processing in the test_processor.php file by clicking the Execute! button again, calling the Process() method of the OrderProcessor class for the second time.

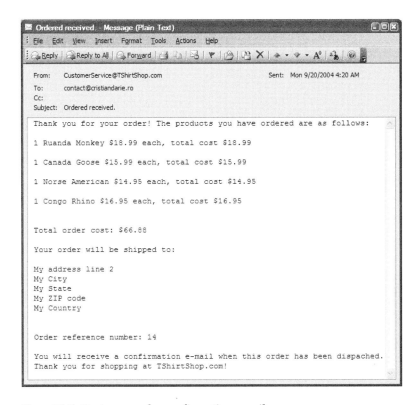

Figure 13-2. *Customer order confirmation email*

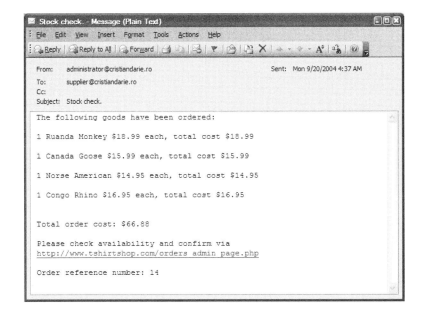

Figure 13-3. *Stock check email*

8. Check your email for the ship goods email (see Figure 13-4).

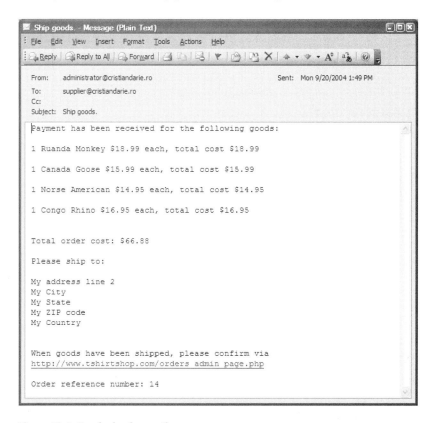

Figure 13-4. *Stock check email*

9. Continue processing in the test_processor.php file by clicking Execute!, and calling the Process() method of the OrderProcessor class for the third and last time.

10. Check your email for the shipping confirmation email (see Figure 13-5).

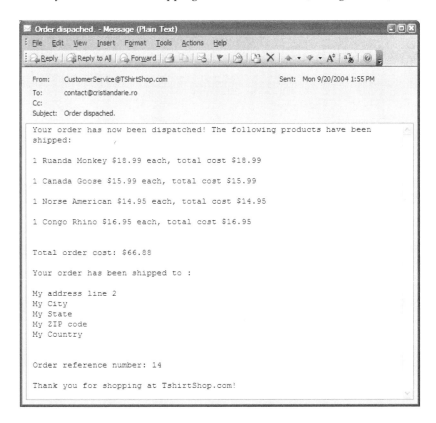

Figure 13-5. *Customer shipping notification email*

11. Examine the new audit entries for the order as shown in Figure 13-6.

audit_id	order_id	datestamp	message	message_number
3049	14	2004-10-05 23:59:55	Order Processor started.	10000
3050	14	2004-10-05 23:59:55	PsInitialNotification started.	20000
3051	14	2004-10-05 23:59:56	Notification email sent to customer.	20002
3052	14	2004-10-05 23:59:56	PsInitialNotification finished.	20001
3053	14	2004-10-05 23:59:56	PSCheckFunds started.	20100
3054	14	2004-10-06 00:00:02	Funds available for purchase.	20102
3055	14	2004-10-06 00:00:02	PSCheckFunds finished.	20101
3056	14	2004-10-06 00:00:02	PSCheckStock started.	20200
3057	14	2004-10-06 00:00:03	Notification email sent to supplier.	20202
3058	14	2004-10-06 00:00:03	PSCheckStock finished.	20201
3059	14	2004-10-06 00:00:03	Order Processor finished.	10001
3060	14	2004-10-06 00:00:15	Order Processor started.	10000
3061	14	2004-10-06 00:00:15	PSStockOk started.	20300
3062	14	2004-10-06 00:00:15	Stock confirmed by supplier.	20302
3063	14	2004-10-06 00:00:15	PSStockOK finished.	20301
3064	14	2004-10-06 00:00:15	PSTakePayment started.	20400
3065	14	2004-10-06 00:00:20	Funds deducted from customer credit card.	20403
3066	14	2004-10-06 00:00:20	PSTakePayment finished.	20401
3067	14	2004-10-06 00:00:20	PSShipGoods started.	20500
3068	14	2004-10-06 00:00:21	Ship goods email sent to supplier.	20502
3069	14	2004-10-06 00:00:21	PSShipGoods finished.	20501
3070	14	2004-10-06 00:00:21	Order Processor finished.	10001
3071	14	2004-10-06 00:00:23	Order Processor started.	10000
3072	14	2004-10-06 00:00:23	PSShipOk started.	20600
3073	14	2004-10-06 00:00:23	Order dispatched by supplier.	20602
3074	14	2004-10-06 00:00:23	PSShipOK finished.	20601
3075	14	2004-10-06 00:00:23	PSFinalNotification started.	20700
3076	14	2004-10-06 00:00:24	Dispatch email sent to customer.	20702
3077	14	2004-10-06 00:00:24	PSFinalNotification finished.	20701
3078	14	2004-10-06 00:00:24	Order Processor finished.	10001

Figure 13-6. *Audit entries for completed order*

How It Works: The Order Pipeline

We've covered how the order pipeline works, so now we only need to explain the new code added to OrderProcessor. We changed the code in the GetCurrentPipelineSection() method, which is responsible for selecting the pipeline section that needs to be executed.

The change is simply a switch block that assigns a pipeline section to the $Current-PipelineSection member:

```
// gets an object instance representing the current pipeline section
private function GetCurrentPipelineSection()
{
  switch ($this->mOrderStatus)
  {
```

```
case 0:
  $this->mCurrentPipelineSection = new PsInitialNotification(); break;
case 1:
  $this->mCurrentPipelineSection = new PsCheckFunds(); break;
case 2:
  $this->mCurrentPipelineSection = new PsCheckStock(); break;
case 3:
  $this->mCurrentPipelineSection = new PsStockOk(); break;
case 4:
  $this->mCurrentPipelineSection = new PsTakePayment(); break;
case 5:
  $this->mCurrentPipelineSection = new PsShipGoods(); break;
case 6:
  $this->mCurrentPipelineSection = new PsShipOK(); break;
case 7:
  $this->mCurrentPipelineSection = new PsFinalNotification(); break;
case 8:
  throw new Exception("Order has already been completed."); break;
default:
  throw new Exception("Unknown pipeline section requested.");
  }
}
```

If the order has been completed or an unknown section is requested, then you generate an exception.

The test code gives you the additional opportunity of testing this exception generation, because if you run it again, you'll be processing an already completed order. Execute the test page again and you should get an error email as shown in Figure 13-7.

Figure 13-7. *Order completion error email*

The error message mailed to the administrator should be enough to get started on your way to finding out what happened.

Updating the Checkout Page

In the last example, you were forced to call the OrderProcessor.Process() method three times in a row from the test code. In practice this won't happen—it will be called once by checkout.php when a customer places an order, and twice more by the supplier in orders_admin_page.php. You'll need to modify these web pages to enable the web interface.

   You also need to add a reference to your new commerce_lib folder in the checkout.php page. Follow the steps to have checkout.php work with the new order pipeline:

1. Add a reference to your new commerce_lib folder in checkout.php:

```
require_once 'include/config.inc.php';
require_once SITE_ROOT.'/include/app_top.php';
require_once SITE_ROOT . '/business_objects/bo_shopping_cart.php';
require_once SITE_ROOT . '/business_objects/bo_customer.php';
require_once COMMERCELIB_DIR.'commerce_lib.all.php';
```

2. Modify the first if statement in smarty_plugins/function.load_checkout_info.php as follows:

```
public function init()
{
  // create business tier object
  $cart = new BoShoppingCart();
  // if the Place Order button was clicked, save the order to database
  if ($this->mPlaceOrder == 1)
  {
    // Create the order and store the order ID
    $order_id=$cart->CreateOrder();
    // Get configuration for order processor
    $processor_configuration = new OrderProcessorConfiguration
                               (ADMIN_EMAIL,
                                $GLOBALS['admin_email_params'],
                                CUSTOMER_SERVICE_EMAIL,
                                $GLOBALS['customer_service_email_params'],
                                ORDER_PROCESSOR_EMAIL,
                                $GLOBALS['order_processor_email_params'],
                                SUPPLIER_EMAIL);
    // Create new OrderProcessor instance
    $processor = new OrderProcessor();
    try
    {
      $processor->Process($order_id, $processor_configuration);
    }
    catch (Exception $e)
    {
      // If an error occurs, head to an error page
      header("Location: checkout.php?OrderError");
      exit;
```

```
    }
    // On success head to an order successful page
    header("Location:checkout.php?OrderDone");
    exit;
  }
  // set members for use in the Smarty template
  $this->mShoppingCartItems=$cart->GetCartProducts(GET_CART_PRODUCTS);
  $this->mTotalAmountLabel = $cart->GetTotalAmount();
  $this->mContinueShopping = $_SESSION['PageLink'];
  $this->mCustomerData = $this->mBoCustomer->GetCurrentCustomer();
......
```

This used the values from config.inc.php to initialize an OrderProcessor instance and process the order in the same way as earlier in this chapter.

3. Create a new file named order_done.tpl in the templates folder and add the following code to its body:

```
{* smarty *}
<br/>
<span class="ListDescription">Thank you for your order!</span>
<br/><br/>
<span class="SimpleText">A confirmation email should arrive shortly.</span>
<br/><br/>
<a href="index.php">Back to shop</a>
```

4. If an error occurs, redirect to another page. Create templates/order_error.tpl with the following in it:

```
{* smarty *}
<br/>
<span class="ListDescription">
An error has occured during the processing of your order.</span>
<br/><br/>
<span class="SimpleText">
If you have an enquiry regarding this message please email
<a href="mailto:customerservice@TShirtShop.com">
customerservice@TShirtShop.com</a></span>
<br/><br/>
<a href="index.php">Back to shop</a>
```

5. Modify checkout.php to load either order_done.tpl or order_error.tpl, depending on whether the order processed successfully or not:

```
if (isset($_GET['OrderDone']))
  $checkout_body = "order_done.tpl";
if (isset($_GET['OrderError']))
  $checkout_body = "order_error.tpl";
$page->assign("checkout_body", $checkout_body);
$page->assign("customerLoginOrLogged", $customerLoginOrLogged);
```

You can now use the TShirtShop web store to place orders, but they will pause when it gets to stock confirmation. To continue, you'll implement the interface for suppliers and administrators to use to force orders to continue processing.

Updating the Orders Admin Page

The basic functionality of this page is to allow suppliers and administrators to view a list of orders that need attention, and advance them in the pipeline manually. This is simply a case of calling the OrderProcess.Process() method as described earlier.

This page could be implemented in many ways. In fact, in some setups it might be better to implement this as a standalone application, for example, if your suppliers are in-house and on the same network. Or it might be better to combine this approach with web services.

To simplify things in this section, you'll supply a single page for both administrators and suppliers. This might not be ideal in all situations because you might not want to expose all order details and audit information to external suppliers. However, for demonstration purposes this reduces the amount of code you have to get through. You'll also tie in the security for this page with the administrator forms-based security used earlier in the book, assuming that people with permission to edit the site data will also have permission to administer orders. In a more advanced setup, you could modify this slightly, providing roles for different types of users, and restricting the functionality available to users in different roles.

As a starting point, you'll take the existing orders_admin.php page and associated componentized templates, and rewrite them to provide the functionality you need. In fact, you can simplify the code slightly to achieve this because you won't need to update order data in such a complete way as you did before. However, you must get through quite a lot of code modifications. The first thing to do is to add a new database table.

Adding the status Data Table

The status data table contains human-readable strings describing the status of orders. When filtering orders, it's a lot better to filter by an order stage description than by a status number, because it's easier to remember "Order Completed" than to remember the number 8, for example. Placing this data in your database allows for future extensibility.

The new table, status, has columns as shown in Table 13-1.

Table 13-1. status *Table Columns*

Column Name	Column Type	Description
status_id	int	Primary key. Corresponds to a status number.
description	varchar(50)	The human-readable description of the status.

Add data to this table as shown in Table 13-2.

Table 13-2. status *Table Contents*

StatusId	Value
0	Order placed, notifying customer
1	Awaiting confirmation of funds
2	Notifying supplier - stock check
3	Awaiting stock confirmation
4	Awaiting credit card payment
5	Notifying supplier - shipping
6	Awaiting shipment confirmation
7	Sending final notification
8	Order completed

Implementing the Data Tier

You need to add several data tier methods in the DoOrderManager class to get the data required for displaying order information.

Note that many of these data tier methods are used in place of some already existing data tier methods that were previously used by the older version of this page (or, more specifically, by the BoOrderManager class). Different columns are important now because the order data storage system has changed a little.

First, remove these obsolete methods from the DoOrderManager class: GetMostRecentOrders, GetOrdersBetweenDates, GetUnverifiedUncanceledOrders, GetVerifiedUncompletedOrders, GetOrderInfo, UpdateOrder, MarkOrderAsVerified, MarkOrderAsCompleted, and MarkOrderAsCanceled.

Now add the following new methods to the DoOrderManager class:

```
// retrieves all data from the status table
public function GetStatuses()
{
  $query_string = "SELECT status_id, description FROM status";
  $result = $this->dbManager->DbGetAll($query_string);
  return $result;
}
// gets the
details of a specific order
public function GetOrder($orderId)
{
  $query_string =
    "SELECT orders.order_id, orders.date_created, orders.date_shipped,
          orders.status, orders.customer_id, orders.auth_code,
          orders.reference, status.description, customer.name
     FROM orders INNER JOIN customer
       ON customer.customer_id = orders.customer_id
     INNER JOIN status
       ON status.status_id = orders.status
```

```php
      WHERE orders.order_id = $orderId";
  $result = $this->dbManager->DbGetRow($query_string);
  return $result;
}
// gets all
orders
public function GetOrders()
{
  $query_string =
    "SELECT orders.order_id, orders.date_created, orders.date_shipped,
            orders.status, orders.customer_id, status.description, customer.name
     FROM orders INNER JOIN customer
       ON customer.customer_id = orders.customer_id
     INNER JOIN status
       ON status.status_id = orders.status";
  $result = $this->dbManager->DbGetAll($query_string);
  return $result;
}
// gets specified number of most recent orders
public function GetOrdersByRecent($count)
{
  $query_string =
    "SELECT orders.order_id, orders.date_created, orders.date_shipped,
            orders.status, orders.customer_id, status.description, customer.name
     FROM orders INNER JOIN customer
       ON customer.customer_id = orders.customer_id
     INNER JOIN status
       ON status.status_id = orders.status
     ORDER BY date_created DESC LIMIT $count";
  $result = $this->dbManager->DbGetAll($query_string);
  return $result;
}
// gets all orders placed by a specified customer
public function GetOrdersByCustomer($customerId)
{
  $query_string =
    "SELECT orders.order_id, orders.date_created, orders.date_shipped,
            orders.status, orders.customer_id, status.description, customer.name
     FROM orders INNER JOIN customer
       ON customer.customer_id = orders.customer_id
     INNER JOIN status
       ON status.status_id = orders.status
     WHERE orders.customer_id = $customerId";
  $result = $this->dbManager->DbGetAll($query_string);
  return $result;
}
// gets orders between two specified dates
```

```php
public function GetOrdersByDate($startDate, $endDate)
{
  $query_string =
    "SELECT orders.order_id, orders.date_created, orders.date_shipped,
            orders.status, orders.customer_id, status.description, customer.name
     FROM orders INNER JOIN customer
       ON customer.customer_id = orders.customer_id
     INNER JOIN status
       ON status.status_id = orders.status
     WHERE orders.date_created > '$startDate'
       AND orders.date_created < '$endDate'";
  $result = $this->dbManager->DbGetAll($query_string);
  return $result;
}
// gets all orders with a specific status
public function GetOrdersByStatus($status)
{
  $query_string =
    "SELECT orders.order_id, orders.date_created, orders.date_shipped,
            orders.status, orders.customer_id, status.description, customer.name
                   FROM orders INNER JOIN customer
                   ON customer.customer_id = orders.customer_id
                   INNER JOIN status
                   ON status.status_id = orders.status
                   WHERE orders.status = $status";
  $result=$this->dbManager->DbGetAll($query_string);
  return $result;
}
// gets the audit table entries associated with a specific order
public function GetGetAuditTrail($orderId)
{
  $query_string = "SELECT datestamp, message_number, message
                   FROM audit
                   WHERE order_id = $orderId";
  $result = $this->dbManager->DbGetAll($query_string);
  return $result;
}
```

Implementing the Business Tier

You also have to add several new methods to the BoOrderManager class from business_objects/
bo_order_manager.php to cater to the data tier methods listed in the previous section. Optionally,
you can remove these methods that you no longer need: GetMostRecentOrders, GetOrders-
BetweenDates, GetUnverifiedUncanceledOrders, GetVerifiedUncompletedOrders, GetOrderInfo,
UpdateOrder, MarkOrderAsVerified, MarkOrderAsCompleted, and MarkOrderAsCanceled. :

Your new BoOrderManager class should look like this:

```php
<?php
// reference data tier class
require_once SITE_ROOT . '/data_objects/do_order_manager.php';
// business tier class that supports order administration functionality
class BoOrderManager
{
  // private attributes
  private $mDoOrderManager;
  // class constructor
  function __construct()
  {
    $this->mDoOrderManager = new DoOrderManager();
  }
  // gets order details for the order details admin page
  public function GetOrderDetails($orderId)
  {
    $result = $this->mDoOrderManager->GetOrderDetails($orderId);
    return $result;
  }
  // gets the customer that made a particular order
  public function GetCustomerByOrderId($orderId)
  {
    $result = $this->mDoOrderManager->GetCustomerByOrderId($orderId);
    return $result;
  }
  // retrieves all possible order statuses
  public function GetStatuses()
  {
    $result = $this->mDoOrderManager->GetStatuses();
    return $result;
  }
  // gets the details of a specific order
  public function GetOrder($orderId)
  {
    $result = $this->mDoOrderManager->GetOrder($orderId);
    return $result;
  }
  // gets all orders
  public function GetOrders()
  {
    $result = $this->mDoOrderManager->GetOrders();
    return $result;
  }
  // gets specified number of most recent orders
  public function GetOrdersByRecent($count)
```

```
{
    $result = $this->mDoOrderManager->GetOrdersByRecent($count);
    return $result;
}
// gets all orders placed by a specified customer
public function GetOrdersByCustomer($customerId)
{
    $result = $this->mDoOrderManager->GetOrdersByCustomer($customerId);
    return $result;
}
// gets orders between two specified dates
public function GetOrdersByDate($startDate, $endDate)
{
    $result = $this->mDoOrderManager->GetOrdersByDate($startDate, $endDate);
    return $result;
}
// gets all orders with a specific status
public function GetOrdersByStatus($status)
{
    $result = $this->mDoOrderManager->GetOrdersByStatus($status);
    return $result;
}
// gets the audit table entries associated with a specific order
public function GetAuditTrail($orderId)
{
    $result = $this->mDoOrderManager->GetGetAuditTrail($orderId);
    return $result;
}
}//end class
?>
```

Implementing the Presentation Tier

You need to update two componentized templates here: orders_list_admin and order_details_admin. Let's deal with them one by one.

Administering the Orders List

The next task is to update orders__list_admin, the componentized template that displays a list of orders meeting certain criteria, such as orders placed between certain dates. Now that you have changed the way orders are processed, you no longer need some of these filters, such as searching for unverified or uncanceled orders. Instead, you add filters that take into account the new structure of your data, such as filtering orders by status or by customer ID. You also need to change what data is displayed in the table. This requires a lot of modifications to the code for this componentized template. Let's preview the new orders_list_admin componentized template (see Figure 13-8).

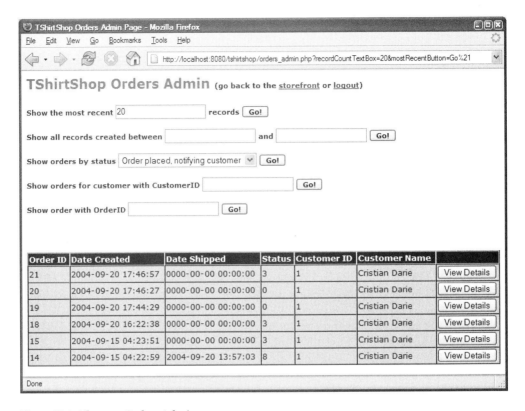

Figure 13-8. *The new Orders Admin page*

Implement the new functionality by following the steps:

1. Update the `orders_list_admin.tpl` file in the `templates` folder. Here is the complete code for the file:

```
{load_orders_list_admin assign="orders_list_admin"}
<form method="get" action="orders_admin.php">
<span class="AdminPageText">Show the most recent</span>
<input name="recordCountTextBox" type="text"
       value="{$orders_list_admin->mRecordCount}">
<span class="AdminPageText">records</span>
<input type="submit" name="mostRecentButton"
       value="Go!" class="AdminButtonText"/>
</form>

<form method="get" action="orders_admin.php">
<span class="AdminPageText">Show all records created between</span>
<input name="startDateTextBox" type="text"
       value='{$orders_list_admin->mStartDate}'/>
<span class="AdminPageText">and</span>
<input name="endDateTextBox" type="text"
       value='{$orders_list_admin->mEndDate}'/>
```

```
<input type="submit" name="betweenDatesButton" value="Go!"
       class="AdminButtonText"/><br/>
</form>

<form method="get" action="orders_admin.php">
<span class="AdminPageText">Show orders by status</span>
<select name=status>
{html_options options=$orders_list_admin->mStatuses
               selected=$orders_list_admin->mStatus}
</select>
<input type="submit" name="ordersByStatusButton" value="Go!"
        class="AdminButtonText"/><br/>
</form>

<form method="get" action="orders_admin.php">
<span class="AdminPageText">Show orders for customer with CustomerID </span>
<input name="customerIDTextBox" type="text"
       value='{$orders_list_admin->mCustomerId}'/>
<input type="submit" name="ordersByCustomerButton" value="Go!"
       class="AdminButtonText"/><br/>
</form>

<form method="get" action="orders_admin.php">
<span class="AdminPageText">Show order with OrderID</span>
<input name="OrderId" type="text" value='{$orders_list_admin->mOrderId}'/>
<input type="submit" name="orderByIDButton" value="Go!"
       class="AdminButtonText"/><br/>
</form>

<br/>
<span class="AdminErrorText">{$orders_list_admin->mErrorLabel}</span>
<br/>

{if $orders_list_admin->mOrders}
  <tr>
   <td>
    <table cellspacing="0" border="1" width="100%">
     <tr class="TableHeader">
      <td><font face="Verdana" color="White" size="2">Order ID
          </font></td>
      <td><font face="Verdana" color="White" size="2">Date Created
          </font></td>
      <td><font face="Verdana" color="White" size="2">Date Shipped
          </font></td>
      <td><font face="Verdana" color="White" size="2">Status
          </font></td>
      <td><font face="Verdana" color="White" size="2">Customer ID
          </font></td>
```

```
    <td><font face="Verdana" color="White" size="2">Customer Name
        </font></td>
    <td> </td>
   </tr>
   {section name=c_orders loop=$orders_list_admin->mOrders}
   <tr bgcolor="Gainsboro">
    <td><font face="Verdana" size="2">
        {$orders_list_admin->mOrders[c_orders].order_id}</font></td>
    <td><font face="Verdana" size="2">
        {$orders_list_admin->mOrders[c_orders].date_created}</font></td>
    <td><font face="Verdana" size="2">
        {$orders_list_admin->mOrders[c_orders].date_shipped}</font></td>
    <td><font face="Verdana" size="2">
        {$orders_list_admin->mOrders[c_orders].status}</font></td>
    <td><font face="Verdana" size="2">
        {$orders_list_admin->mOrders[c_orders].customer_id}</font></td>
    <td><font face="Verdana" size="2">
        {$orders_list_admin->mOrders[c_orders].name}</font></td>
    <td>
      <input type="button" value="View Details"
onclick="window.location='orders_admin.php?
OrderId={$orders_list_admin->mOrders[c_orders].order_id}';"/>
      </td>
    </tr>
    {/section}
   </table>
  </td>
 </tr>
 {/if}
</table>
```

■**Note** Ensure the window.location call (highlighted with bold code) is not split in multiple lines as in this code listing, otherwise the View Details buttons won't work.

As you can see, you have the template code for your five filters from the top of the page:

- The most recent X orders

- Orders created between Date1 and Date2

- Orders with a certain status

- Orders for a specific customer

- A specific order

2. Next, you have to update the smarty function plugin file (smarty_plugins/ function.load_orders_list_admin.php). Clear the file and start by adding the following code to it:

```php
<?php
// plugin functions inside plugin files must be named: smarty_type_name
function smarty_function_load_orders_list_admin($params, $smarty)
{
  $orders_list_admin = new OrdersListAdmin();
  $orders_list_admin->init();
  // assign template variable
  $smarty->assign($params['assign'], $orders_list_admin);
}
// presentation tier class that supports order administration functionality
class OrdersListAdmin
{
  /* public variables available in smarty template */
  public $mOrders;
  public $mStartDate;
  public $mEndDate;
  public $mStatus;
  public $mCustomerId;
  public $mOrderId;
  public $mRecordCount = 20;
  public $mErrorLabel = "";
  /* private attributes */
  private $mOrderManager;
  //constructor
  function __construct()
  {
    $this->mOrderManager = new BoOrderManager();
  }
```

3. Continue by adding the init() method and add the code that deals with the first two filters of your page (the most recent n orders, and orders created between two dates):

```php
// init
function init()
{
  // if the "most recent x orders" filter is in action...
  if (isset($_GET['mostRecentButton']))
  {
    // if the record count value is not a valid integer, display error
    if ((string)(int)$_GET['recordCountTextBox'] ==
        (string)$_GET['recordCountTextBox'])
    {
      $this->mRecordCount = (int) $_GET['recordCountTextBox'];
      $this->mOrders = $this->mOrderManager->GetOrdersByRecent(
                                        $this->mRecordCount);
```

```
      }
      else
        $this->mErrorLabel = $_GET['recordCountTextBox'] .
                             " is not a number. <br />";
  }

  // if the "orders between d1 and d2" filter is in action...
  if (isset($_GET['betweenDatesButton']))
  {
    $this->mStartDate = $_GET['startDateTextBox'];
    $this->mEndDate = $_GET['endDateTextBox'];
    // check if the start date is in accepted format
    if (($this->mStartDate == "") ||
        ($timestamp = strtotime($this->mStartDate)) == -1)
      $this->mErrorLabel = "The start date is invalid. <br />";
    else
      // transform date to YYYY/MM/DD HH:MM:SS format
      $this->mStartDate =
          strftime("%Y/%m/%d %H:%M:%S", strtotime($this->mStartDate));
    // check if the end date is in accepted format
    if (($this->mEndDate == "") ||
        ($timestamp = strtotime($this->mEndDate)) == -1)
      $this->mErrorLabel .= "The end date is invalid. <br />";
    else
      // transform date to YYYY/MM/DD HH:MM:SS format
      $this->mEndDate =
          strftime("%Y/%m/%d %H:%M:%S", strtotime($this->mEndDate));
    // check if start date is more reccent than the end date
    if ((empty($this->mErrorLabel)) &&
        (strtotime($this->mStartDate) > strtotime($this->mEndDate)))
      $this->mErrorLabel .=
        "The start date should be more recent than the end date.";
    // if there are no errors, get the orders between the two dates
    if (empty($this->mErrorLabel))
      $this->mOrders = $this->mOrderManager->GetOrdersByDate(
                              $this->mStartDate, $this->mEndDate);
  }
```

This is exactly the same piece of code in the orders_list_admin.php file from Chapter 9 except here you get your new data with the earlier created GetOrdersByRecent and GetOrdersByDate business tier methods.

4. The following lines deal with the last three filters (orders with a certain status, orders for a specific customer, and a specific order) from this page and are very easy to understand:

```php
    // if the "get order by id" filter is in action...
    if (isset($_GET['orderByIDButton']))
    {
      if (empty($_GET['OrderId']))
        $this->mErrorLabel = "You must enter an order ID.";
      else
        $this->mOrderId = $_GET['OrderId'];
    }
    $statuses = $this->mOrderManager->GetStatuses();
    for ($i=0;$i<count($statuses);$i++)
      $temp[$statuses[$i]['status_id']] = $statuses[$i]['description'];
    $this->mStatuses = $temp;

    // if the "get orders by status" filter is in action...
    if (isset($_GET['ordersByStatusButton']))
    {
      $this->mStatus = (int) $_GET['status'];
      $this->mOrders = $this->mOrderManager->GetOrdersByStatus($this->mStatus);
      if (empty($this->mOrders))
        $this->mErrorLabel = "No orders with this status";
    }

    // if the "get orders by customer" filter is in action...
    if (isset($_GET['ordersByCustomerButton']))
    {
      if (empty($_GET['customerIDTextBox']))
        $this->mErrorLabel = 'Customer ID must be set';
      else
      {
        $this->mCustomerId = $_GET['customerIDTextBox'];
        if ((string)(int)$_GET['customerIDTextBox'] ==
            (string)$_GET['customerIDTextBox'])
        {
          $this->mOrders =
              $this->mOrderManager->GetOrdersByCustomer($this->mCustomerId);
          if (empty($this->mOrders))
            $this->mErrorLabel = "No orders for " .
                                 $this->mCustomerId . " customer id";
        }
        else
          $this->mErrorLabel = $this->mCustomerId . " is not an integer value";
      }
    }
  }
} //end class
?>
```

5. You can now load `orders_admin.php`, log in with your administrator credentials, and see the results of your work (see Figure 13-9).

TShirtShop Orders Admin (go back to the storefront or logout)

Show the most recent [5] records [Go!]

Show all records created between [ ] and [ ] [Go!]

Show orders by status [Order placed, notifying customer ▼] [Go!]

Show orders for customer with CustomerID [ ] [Go!]

Show order with OrderID [ ] [Go!]

Order ID	Date Created	Date Shipped	Status	Customer ID	Customer Name	
21	2004-09-20 17:46:57	0000-00-00 00:00:00	3	1	Cristian Darie	View Details
20	2004-09-20 17:46:27	0000-00-00 00:00:00	0	1	Cristian Darie	View Details
19	2004-09-20 17:44:29	0000-00-00 00:00:00	0	1	Cristian Darie	View Details
18	2004-09-20 16:22:38	0000-00-00 00:00:00	3	1	Cristian Darie	View Details
15	2004-09-15 04:23:51	0000-00-00 00:00:00	3	1	Cristian Darie	View Details

Figure 13-9. *The new Orders Admin page*

Administering Order Details

The second componentized template to modify is `order_details_admin`, which shows the details of an order. Earlier in the book, this componentized template also included the capability to modify order data, but we're removing this here. Instead, you'll provide the capability for orders to be pushed along the pipeline when they are stuck at the `Awaiting confirmation of stock` and `Awaiting confirmation of shipment` stages.

You also need to make a few other modifications. Now that you have more detailed customer information, you can display all available data (apart from credit card and password information) for the customer who placed the order in a new table. You can also display all the audit information for the order in another new table. Because of these new sources of information, you can also cut back a little on the other information displayed for the order, which is displayed in read-only text boxes above the tables. Let's look at what you're going to achieve, as shown in Figure 13-10.

You can split the Orders Admin page into four sections:

- In the first section, read-only text boxes display the date when the order was created, the date when it was shipped, and then its status, Authentification Code, and Reference Code.

- In the second section, a table is filled with the items data from the order.

- In the third section, a table displays customer information.

- In the fourth section, a table shows the audit trail for the order.

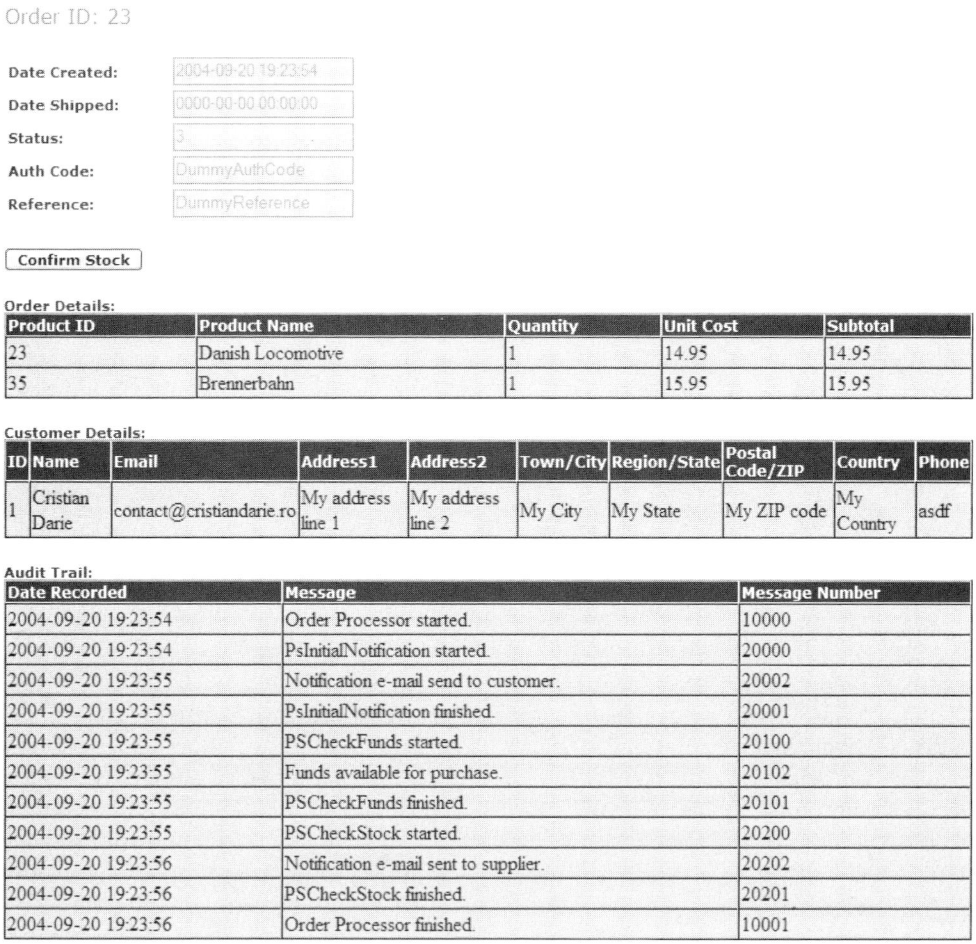

Order ID: 23

Date Created:	2004-09-20 19:23:54
Date Shipped:	0000-00-00 00:00:00
Status:	3
Auth Code:	DummyAuthCode
Reference:	DummyReference

[Confirm Stock]

Order Details:

Product ID	Product Name	Quantity	Unit Cost	Subtotal
23	Danish Locomotive	1	14.95	14.95
35	Brennerbahn	1	15.95	15.95

Customer Details:

ID	Name	Email	Address1	Address2	Town/City	Region/State	Postal Code/ZIP	Country	Phone
1	Cristian Darie	contact@cristiandarie.ro	My address line 1	My address line 2	My City	My State	My ZIP code	My Country	asdf

Audit Trail:

Date Recorded	Message	Message Number
2004-09-20 19:23:54	Order Processor started.	10000
2004-09-20 19:23:54	PsInitialNotification started.	20000
2004-09-20 19:23:55	Notification e-mail send to customer.	20002
2004-09-20 19:23:55	PsInitialNotification finished.	20001
2004-09-20 19:23:55	PSCheckFunds started.	20100
2004-09-20 19:23:55	Funds available for purchase.	20102
2004-09-20 19:23:55	PSCheckFunds finished.	20101
2004-09-20 19:23:55	PSCheckStock started.	20200
2004-09-20 19:23:56	Notification e-mail sent to supplier.	20202
2004-09-20 19:23:56	PSCheckStock finished.	20201
2004-09-20 19:23:56	Order Processor finished.	10001

Figure 13-10. *The new Orders Details Admin page*

You implement the new functionality by writing new versions of order_details_admin.tpl and function.load_order_details_admin.php. The new code for order_details_admin.tpl is listed here:

```
{load_order_details_admin assign="order_details_admin"}
<span class="AdminErrorText">{$order_details_admin->mErrorLabel}</span>
{if $order_details_admin->mErrorLabel==""}
{* SECTION 1 *}
<form method="get" action="orders_admin.php">
<input type="hidden" name="OrderId" value="{$order_details_admin-
>mOrderInfo.order_id}"/>
<span class="ListDescription">Order ID:
{$order_details_admin->mOrderInfo.order_id}</span><br/><br/>
 <table>
  <tr>
```

```
  <td width="130" class="AdminPageText">
   Date Created:
  </td>
  <td>
   <input type="text" value="{$order_details_admin->mOrderInfo.date_created}"
disabled="disabled"/>
  </td>
 </tr>
 </tr>
  <td width="130" class="AdminPageText">
   Date Shipped:
  </td>
  <td>
   <input type="text" value="{$order_details_admin->mOrderInfo.date_shipped}"
disabled="disabled"/>
  </td>
 </tr>
 </tr>
  <td width="130" class="AdminPageText">
   Status:
  </td>
  <td>
   <input type="text" value="{$order_details_admin->mOrderInfo.status}"
disabled="disabled"/>
  </td>
 </tr>
 </tr>
  <td width="130" class="AdminPageText">
   Auth Code:
  </td>
  <td>
   <input type="text" value="{$order_details_admin->mOrderInfo.auth_code}"
disabled="disabled"/>
  </td>
 </tr>
 </tr>
  <td width="130" class="AdminPageText">
   Reference:
  </td>
  <td>
   <input type="text" value="{$order_details_admin->mOrderInfo.reference}"
disabled="disabled"/>
  </td>
 </tr>
</table>
<br/>
{if $order_details_admin->mProcessButtonText}
```

```
<input class="AdminButtonText" type="submit" name="process"
value='{$order_details_admin->mProcessButtonText}'/>
 {/if}
 <br/>
{* SECTION 2 *}
 <br/>
 <span class="AdminPageText"> Order Details:</span>
 <table cellspacing="0" border="1" width="100%">
 <tr class="TableHeader">
  <td>Product ID</td>
  <td>Product Name</td>
  <td>Quantity</td>
  <td>Unit Cost</td>
  <td>Subtotal</td>
 </tr>
 {section name=item_no loop=$order_details_admin->mOrderDetails}
 <tr bgcolor="Gainsboro">
  <td>{$order_details_admin->mOrderDetails[item_no].product_id}</td>
  <td>{$order_details_admin->mOrderDetails[item_no].product_name}</td>
  <td>{$order_details_admin->mOrderDetails[item_no].quantity}</td>
  <td>{$order_details_admin->mOrderDetails[item_no].unit_cost}</td>
  <td>{$order_details_admin->mOrderDetails[item_no].subtotal}</td>
 </tr>
 {/section}
</table>
<br/>
{* SECTION 3 *}
<span class="AdminPageText"> Customer Details:</span>
<table cellspacing="0" border="1" width="100%">
 <tr class="TableHeader">
  <td>ID</td>
  <td>Name</td>
  <td>Email</td>
  <td>Address1</td>
  <td>Address2</td>
  <td>Town/City</td>
  <td>Region/State</td>
  <td>Postal Code/ZIP</td>
  <td>Country</td>
  <td>Phone</td>
 </tr>
 <tr bgcolor="Gainsboro">
  <td>{$order_details_admin->mCustomerDetails.customer_id}</td>
  <td>{$order_details_admin->mCustomerDetails.name}</td>
  <td>{$order_details_admin->mCustomerDetails.email}</td>
  <td>{$order_details_admin->mCustomerDetails.address1}</td>
  <td>{$order_details_admin->mCustomerDetails.address2}</td>
```

```
 <td>{$order_details_admin->mCustomerDetails.city}</td>
 <td>{$order_details_admin->mCustomerDetails.region}</td>
 <td>{$order_details_admin->mCustomerDetails.postal_code}</td>
 <td>{$order_details_admin->mCustomerDetails.country}</td>
 <td>{$order_details_admin->mCustomerDetails.phone}</td>
 </tr>
</table>
<br/>
{* SECTION 4 *}
<span class="AdminPageText">Audit Trail:</span>
<table cellspacing="0" border="1" width="100%">
 <tr class="TableHeader">
  <td>Date Recorded</td>
  <td>Message</td>
  <td>Message Number</td>
 </tr>
 {section name=audit_no loop=$order_details_admin->mAudit}
 <tr bgcolor="Gainsboro">
  <td>{$order_details_admin->mAudit[audit_no].datestamp}</td>
  <td>{$order_details_admin->mAudit[audit_no].message}</td>
  <td>{$order_details_admin->mAudit[audit_no].message_number}</td>
 </tr>
 {/section}
</table>
</form>
{/if}
```

The code in the Smarty plugin used by this template file is pretty straightforward. The only user interaction that is now possible for an order is clicking on the Process button. Clicking this button calls code very similar to that in `smarty_plugins/function.load_checkout_info.php`, because `OrderProcessor` is used to push an order along the pipeline.

To ensure that you have access to the `ecommerce_lib` functionality, add the highlighted line in `orders_admin.php`:

```
<?php
// load config files
require_once 'include/app_top.php';
// load business objects
require_once COMMERCELIB_DIR . 'commerce_lib.all.php';
require_once 'business_objects/bo_order_manager.php';
```

Next, let's create the Smarty function plugin file `function.load_order_details_admin.php`, which is loaded from `order_details_admin.tpl`. The function plugin implements its functionality using the `OrderDetailsAdmin` class, which retrieves the data to be displayed on the administration page. In the following code, the `init()` method found in `OrderDetailsAdmin` advances the pipeline to the next section if the process button is clicked; the presence of this button on the page is decided by the `PopulatePage` function, which sets the text of the button to "Confirm Stock" if the current pipeline section is 3 (awaiting for stock confirmation), or to

"Confirm Shipment" if the current pipeline section is 6 (awaiting for shipment confirmation). If the current pipeline section is not set to 3 or 6, it means that either the order has been completed successfully, or that an error occurred while processing, in which case it isn't possible to advance to the next pipeline section. The administrator can always check what happened to the order for checking the audit trail that gets displayed on the page.

Write the following code to function.load_order_details_admin.php:

```php
<?php
// plugin functions inside plugin files must be named: smarty_type_name
function smarty_function_load_order_details_admin($params, $smarty)
{
  $order_details_admin = new OrderDetailsAdmin();
  $order_details_admin->init();
  // assign template variable
  $smarty->assign($params['assign'], $order_details_admin);
}

// presentation tier class that deals with administering order details
class OrderDetailsAdmin
{
  /* public variables avaible in smarty template */
  public $mOrderId;
  public $mOrderInfo;
  public $mOrderDetails;
  public $mCustomerDetails;
  public $mAudit;
  public $mErrorLabel = "";
  public $mProcessButtonText;
  /* private stuff */
  private $mOrderManager;
  function __construct()
  {
    $this->mOrderManager = new BoOrderManager();
    // we receive the order ID in the query string
    $this->mOrderId = (int)$_GET['OrderId'];
  }
  function init()
  {
    if (empty($_GET['OrderId']))
      trigger_error("OrderId parameter is required", E_USER_ERROR);
    // we check order ID to be integer
    if ((string)(int)$_GET['OrderId'] == (string)$_GET['OrderId'])
      $this->mOrderId = (int)$_GET['OrderId'];
    else
    {
      $this->mErrorLabel = $_GET['OrderId']." is not integer";
      return ;
    }
```

```php
    if (isset($_GET['process']))
    {
      // Get configuration for order processor
      $processor_configuration = new OrderProcessorConfiguration(
                  ADMIN_EMAIL,
                  $GLOBALS['admin_email_params'],
                  CUSTOMER_SERVICE_EMAIL,
                  $GLOBALS['customer_service_email_params'],
                  ORDER_PROCESSOR_EMAIL,
                  $GLOBALS['order_processor_email_params'],
                  SUPPLIER_EMAIL);
      $processor = new OrderProcessor();
      try
      {
        $processor->Process($this->mOrderId, $processor_configuration);
      }
      catch (Exception $e)
      {
        echo $e->getMessage();
        exit;
      }
    }
    $this->PopulatePage();
  }
  public function PopulatePage()
  {
    /* SECTION 1 */
    $this->mOrderInfo = $this->mOrderManager->GetOrder($this->mOrderId);
    if (empty($this->mOrderInfo))
      $this->mErrorLabel = $this->mOrderId." is not a valid order id";
    // Name or hide Process button
    if ($this->mOrderInfo['status'] == 3)
      $this->mProcessButtonText = "Confirm Stock";
    elseif ($this->mOrderInfo['status'] == 6)
      $this->mProcessButtonText = "Confirm Shipment";
    /* get data for SECTION 2 table */
    $this->mOrderDetails =
        $this->mOrderManager->GetOrderDetails($this->mOrderId);
    /* get data for SECTION 3 table */
    $this->mCustomerDetails =
        $this->mOrderManager->GetCustomerByOrderID($this->mOrderId);
    /* get data for SECTION 4 table */
    $this->mAudit =
        $this->mOrderManager->GetAuditTrail($this->mOrderId);
  }
} //end class
?>
```

Testing the Order Administration Page

All that remains now is to check that everything is working properly. To do this, use the web interface to place an order, and then check it out via the orders admin link in the main page. You should see that the order is awaiting confirmation of stock, as shown in Figure 13-11.

Order ID: 23

Date Created:	2004-09-20 19:23:54
Date Shipped:	0000-00-00 00:00:00
Status:	3
Auth Code:	DummyAuthCode
Reference:	DummyReference

Confirm Stock

Order Details:

Product ID	Product Name	Quantity	Unit Cost	Subtotal
23	Danish Locomotive	1	14.95	14.95
35	Brennerbahn	1	15.95	15.95

Customer Details:

ID	Name	Email	Address1	Address2	Town/City	Region/State	Postal Code/ZIP	Country	Phone
1	Cristian Darie	contact@cristiandarie.ro	My address line 1	My address line 2	My City	My State	My ZIP code	My Country	asdf

Audit Trail:

Date Recorded	Message	Message Number
2004-09-20 19:23:54	Order Processor started.	10000
2004-09-20 19:23:54	PsInitialNotification started.	20000
2004-09-20 19:23:55	Notification e-mail send to customer.	20002
2004-09-20 19:23:55	PsInitialNotification finished.	20001
2004-09-20 19:23:55	PSCheckFunds started.	20100
2004-09-20 19:23:55	Funds available for purchase.	20102
2004-09-20 19:23:55	PSCheckFunds finished.	20101
2004-09-20 19:23:55	PSCheckStock started.	20200
2004-09-20 19:23:56	Notification e-mail sent to supplier.	20202
2004-09-20 19:23:56	PSCheckStock finished.	20201
2004-09-20 19:23:56	Order Processor finished.	10001

Figure 13-11. *The new Orders Admin page*

Click the Confirm Stock button and the order is processed. Because this happens very quickly, you are soon presented with the next stage, where the Confirm Stock button is replaced by a new button named Confirm Shipment and the audit trail shows a new set of data.

Finally, clicking the Confirm Shipment button completes the order. If you scroll down the page, you can see all audit trail messages that have been stored in the database concerning this order, as shown in Figure 13-12.

Audit Trail:

Date Recorded	Message	Message Number
2004-10-05 23:24:59	Order Processor started.	10000
2004-10-05 23:24:59	PsInitialNotification started.	20000
2004-10-05 23:25:00	Notification email sent to customer.	20002
2004-10-05 23:25:00	PsInitialNotification finished.	20001
2004-10-05 23:25:00	PSCheckFunds started.	20100
2004-10-05 23:25:06	Funds available for purchase.	20102
2004-10-05 23:25:06	PSCheckFunds finished.	20101
2004-10-05 23:25:06	PSCheckStock started.	20200
2004-10-05 23:25:07	Notification email sent to supplier.	20202
2004-10-05 23:25:07	PSCheckStock finished.	20201
2004-10-05 23:25:07	Order Processor finished.	10001
2004-10-05 23:27:36	Order Processor started.	10000
2004-10-05 23:27:36	PSStockOk started.	20300
2004-10-05 23:27:36	Stock confirmed by supplier.	20302
2004-10-05 23:27:36	PSStockOK finished.	20301
2004-10-05 23:27:36	PSTakePayment started.	20400
2004-10-05 23:27:41	Funds deducted from customer credit card.	20403
2004-10-05 23:27:41	PSTakePayment finished.	20401
2004-10-05 23:27:41	PSShipGoods started.	20500
2004-10-05 23:27:42	Ship goods email sent to supplier.	20502
2004-10-05 23:27:42	PSShipGoods finished.	20501
2004-10-05 23:27:42	Order Processor finished.	10001
2004-10-05 23:27:44	Order Processor started.	10000
2004-10-05 23:27:44	PSShipOk started.	20600
2004-10-05 23:27:44	Order dispatched by supplier.	20602
2004-10-05 23:27:44	PSShipOK finished.	20601
2004-10-05 23:27:44	PSFinalNotification started.	20700
2004-10-05 23:27:45	Dispatch email sent to customer.	20702
2004-10-05 23:27:45	PSFinalNotification finished.	20701
2004-10-05 23:27:45	Order Processor finished.	10001

Figure 13-12. *The new Orders Admin page*

Summary

You've taken giant strides toward completing the TShirtShop e-commerce application in this chapter. Now you have a fully audited, secure backbone for the application.

Specifically, we've covered:

- Modifications to the TShirtShop application to enable your own pipeline processing

- The basic framework for your order pipeline

- The database additions for auditing data and storing additional required data in the orders table

- The implementation of most of the order pipeline, apart from those sections that deal with credit cards

- A simple implementation of an order administration web page

The only thing missing that you need to add before delivering this application to the outside world is credit card processing functionality, which we'll look at in the next chapter.

■ ■ ■

CHAPTER 14

Credit Card Transactions

The last thing you need to do before launching the e-commerce site is to enable credit card processing. In this chapter, we examine how you can build this into the pipeline you created in the previous chapter.

We'll start by looking at the theory behind credit card transactions, the sort of organizations that help you achieve credit card processing, and the sort of transactions that are possible. Moving on, we'll take two example organizations and discuss the specifics of their transaction APIs (Application Program Interfaces, the means by which you access credit card transaction functionality). After this, you'll build a new class library that helps you use one of these transaction APIs via some simple test code.

Finally, you'll integrate the API with the TShirtShop e-commerce application and order-processing pipeline.

Credit Card Transaction Fundamentals

Banks and other financial institutions use secure networks for their transactions based on the X.25 protocol rather than TCP/IP (Transmission Control Protocol/Internet Protocol, the primary means by which data is transmitted across the Internet). X.25 isn't something you need to know anything about, apart from the fact that it's a different protocol for networking and isn't compatible with TCP/IP. As such, X.25 networks are completely separate from the Internet, and although it's possible to get direct access to them, this isn't likely to be a reasonable option. To do so, you might have to enter into some serious negotiation with the owner of the network you want to use. The owner will want to be completely sure that you are a reliable customer who is capable of enforcing the necessary safeguards to prevent an attack on their system. The owner of the network won't be handing out these licenses to just anyone, because most people can't afford the security measures required (which include locking your servers in a cage, sending daily backup tapes down a secure chute, having three individuals with separate keys to access these tapes, and so on).

The alternative is to access these networks via a gateway provider. This enables you to perform your side of the credit card transaction protocol over the Internet (using a secure protocol), while relying on your chosen gateway to communicate with X.25 networks. Although there is likely to be a cost involved with this, the provider should have a deal with financial institutions to keep costs low and pass the savings on to you (after the gateway takes its share), so it's likely to be much cheaper than having your own X.25 connection. This method is also likely to be cheaper than using a third party such as PayPal, because you only need the minimum functionality when you are handling your own order pipeline. There is no need, for example, to use all the order-auditing functionality offered by a company such as PayPal, because in the previous chapter, you already built all this functionality.

Working with Credit Card Payment Gateways

To work with a gateway organization, you first need to open a merchant bank account. This can be done at most banks, and will get you a merchant ID that you can use when signing up with the gateway. The next step is to find a suitable gateway. Unfortunately, this can be a lot of hard work!

It isn't hard to find a gateway; but it *is* hard to find the right one. Literally hundreds of companies are eager to take a cut of your sales. A quick search on the Internet for "credit card gateway" will produce a long list. The web sites of these companies are for the most part pure brochureware—you'll find yourself reading through pages of text about how they are the best and most secure at what they do, only to end up with a form to fill in so that a customer service representative can call you to "discuss your needs." In the long run, you can rest assured that at least you will probably only have to go through the procedure once.

You'll probably find that most of the organizations offering this service offer similar packages. However, key points to look for include the banks they do business with (your merchant bank account will have to be at one of these), the currencies they deal in, and, of course, the costs.

In this chapter, we'll look at two of the few organizations that are easy to deal with—DataCash and VeriSign Payflow Pro.

Table 14-1 shows some of the gateway services available.

Table 14-1. *Gateway Services*

United States	URL	United Kingdom	URL
CyberCash	http://www.cybercash.com/	Arcot	http://www.arcot.com
First Data	http://www.firstdata.com/	WorldPay	http://www.worldpay.com/
Cardservice International	http://www.cardservice.com/	DataCash	http://www.datacash.com/
VeriSign Payflow Pro	http://www.verisign.com/ products/payflow/pro/	ICVerify	http://www.icverify.com/

DataCash

DataCash is a UK-based credit card gateway organization. Unfortunately, this means that you'll need a UK merchant bank account if you want to use it in your final application, but you don't have to worry about this for now. The reason for using DataCash in this chapter is that you don't have to do very much to get access to a rather useful test account—you don't even need a merchant bank account. As you'll see later in this chapter, you'll be able to perform test transactions using so-called "magic" credit card numbers supplied by DataCash, which will accept or decline transactions without performing any actual financial transactions. This is fantastic for development purposes, because you don't want to use your own credit cards for testing!

The important point to remember is that the techniques covered in this chapter apply to every credit card gateway. The specifics might change slightly if you switch to a different organization, but you'll have done most of the hard work already.

■**Note** Before you ask, no, we're not sales representatives for DataCash. It's just that we've spent many hours (days?) looking into credit card transactions, and so far we've yet to find a more developer-friendly way of getting started.

Payflow Pro

Payflow Pro is a service supplied by the globally recognized Internet company VeriSign. This company has established itself as an excellent resource for Internet security and e-commerce applications, so it's not surprising that VeriSign has an entry in the competitive credit card gateway arena.

This is particularly relevant to US-based developers, who might find that experimenting with and choosing Payflow Pro could be just the solution they need.

■**Note** The authors of this book are in no way affiliated with VeriSign or DataCash.

Understanding Credit Card Transactions

Whichever gateway you use, the basic principles of credit card transactions are the same. First, the sort of transactions you'll be dealing with in an e-commerce web site are known as Card Not Present (CNP) transactions, which means you don't have the credit card in front of you, and you can't check the customer signature. This isn't a problem; after all you've probably been performing CNP transactions for some time now online, over the phone, by mail, and so on. It's just something to be aware of should you see the CNP acronym.

Several advanced services are offered by various gateways, including cardholder address verification, security code checking, fraud screening, and so on. Each of these adds an additional layer of complexity to your credit card processing, and we're not covering those details here. Rather, this chapter provides a starting point from which you can add these services if required. Whether to choose these optional extra services depends on how much money is passing through your system, and the trade off between the costs of implementing the services and the potential costs if something goes wrong that could have been prevented by these extra services. If you are interested in these services, the "customer service representative" mentioned previously will be happy to explain things.

You can perform several types of transactions, including

- *Authorization*: Basic type checks card for funds and deducts them.

- *Pre-authorization*: Checks cards for funds and allocates them if available, but doesn't deduct them immediately.

- *Fulfillment*: Completes a pre-authorization transaction, deducting the funds already allocated.

- *Refund*: Refunds a completed transaction, or simply puts money on a credit card.

Again, the specifics vary, but these are the basic types.

In this chapter, you'll use the pre/fulfill model, which means you don't take payment until just before you instruct your supplier to ship goods. This has been hinted at previously by the structure of the pipeline you created in the previous chapter.

Implementing Credit Card Processing

Now that we've covered the basics, let's consider how you'll get things working in the TShirtShop application using the DataCash system. The first thing to do is to get a test account with DataCash by following these steps:

1. Go to `http://www.datacash.com/`.

2. Head to the Support ➤ Integration Info section of the web site.

3. Enter your details and submit.

4. From the e-mail you receive, make a note of your account username and password, as well as the additional information required for accessing the DataCash reporting system.

Normally, the next step would be to download one of DataCash's toolkits for easy integration. However, because DataCash doesn't provide a PHP-compatible implementation, you need to use the XML API for performing transactions. Basically, this involves sending XML requests to a certain URL using an SSL connection, and then deciphering the XML result. This is easy to do in PHP if you have the CURL (Client URL Library Functions) library installed on your computer and PHP is aware of it (see Appendix A).

Working with DataCash

You'll be doing a lot of XML manipulation when communicating with DataCash, because you'll need to create XML documents to send to DataCash, and to extract data from XML responses. In this section, we'll take a quick look at the XML required for the operations you'll be performing and the responses you can expect.

Pre-authentication Request

When you send a pre-authentication request to DataCash, you need to include the following information:

- DataCash username (known as the DataCash Client)

- DataCash password

- A unique transaction reference number (explained later in this section)

- The amount of money to be debited

- The currency used for the transaction (USD, GBP, and so on)

- The type of transaction (the code `pre` for pre-authentication, and the code `fulfil` for fulfillment)

- The credit card number

- The credit card expiry date

- The credit card issue date (if applicable to the type of credit card being used)

- The credit card issue number (if applicable to the type of credit card being used)

The unique transaction reference number must be a number between 6 and 12 digits long, which you choose to uniquely identify the transaction with an order. Because you can't use a short number, you can't just use the order ID values you've been using until now for orders. However, you can use this order ID as the starting point for creating a reference number simply by adding a high number, such as 1,000,000. You can't duplicate the reference number in any future transactions, so you can be sure that after a transaction is completed, it won't execute again, which might otherwise result in charging the customer twice. This does mean, however, that if a credit card is rejected, you might need to create a whole new order for the customer, but that shouldn't be a problem if required.

The XML request is formatted in the following way, with the values detailed previously shown in bold:

```
<?xml version="1.0" encoding="UTF-8"?>
<Request>
  <Authentication>
    <password>DataCash password</password>
    <client>DataCash client</client>
  </Authentication>
  <Transaction>
    <TxnDetails>
      <merchantreference>Unique reference number</merchantreference>
      <amount currency='Currency Type'>Cash amount</amount>
    </TxnDetails>
    <CardTxn>
      <method>pre</method>
      <Card>
        <pan>Credit card number</pan>
        <expirydate>Credit card expiry date</expirydate>
      </Card>
    </CardTxn>
  </Transaction>
</Request>
```

Response to Pre-authentication Request

The response to a pre-authentication request includes the following information:

- A status code number indicating what happened; 1 if the transaction was successful, or one of several other codes if something else happens. For a complete list of return codes for a DataCash server, see `https://testserver.datacash.com/software/returncodes.html`.

- A reason for the status, which is basically a string explaining the status in English. For a status of 1, this string is `ACCEPTED`.

- An authentication code and a reference number that will be used to fulfill the transaction in the fulfillment request stage (discussed next).

- The time that the transaction was processed.

- The mode of the transaction, which is `TEST` when using the test account.

- Confirmation of the type of credit card used.

- Confirmation of the country that the credit card was issued in.

- The authorization code used by the bank (for reference only).

The XML for this is formatted as follows:

```
<?xml version="1.0" encoding="utf-8"?>
<Response>
  <status>Status code</status>
  <reason>Reason</reason>
  <merchantreference>Authentication code</merchantreference>
  <datacash_reference>Reference number</datacash_reference>
  <time>Time</time>
  <mode>TEST</mode>
  <CardTxn>
    <card_scheme>Card Type</card_scheme>
    <country>Country</country>
    <authcode>Bank authorization code</authcode>
  </CardTxn>
</Response>
```

Fulfillment Request

For a fulfillment request, you need to send the following information:

- DataCash username (the DataCash Client)

- DataCash password

- The type of the transaction (for fulfillment, the code `fulfil`)

- The authentication code received earlier

- The reference number received earlier

Optionally, you can include additional information, such as a confirmation of the amount to be debited from the credit card, although this isn't really necessary.

This is formatted as follows:

```
<?xml version="1.0" encoding="UTF-8"?>
<Request>
  <Authentication>
    <password>DataCash password</password>
    <client>DataCash client</client>
  </Authentication>
  <Transaction>
    <HistoricTxn>
      <reference>Reference Number</reference>
      <authcode>Authentication code</authcode>
      <method>fulfil</method>
    </HistoricTxn>
  </Transaction>
</Request>
```

Fulfillment Response

The response to a fulfillment request includes the following information:

- A status code number indicating what happened; 1 if the transaction was successful, or one of several other codes if something else happens. Again, for a complete list of the codes, see https://testserver.datacash.com/software/returncodes.html.

- A reason for the status, which is basically a string explaining the status in English. For a status of 1, this string is FULFILLED OK.

- Two copies of the reference code for use by DataCash.

- The time that the transaction was processed.

- The mode of the transaction, which is TEST when using the test account.

The XML for this is formatted as follows:

```
<?xml version="1.0" encoding="utf-8"?>
<Response>
  <status>Status code</status>
  <reason>Reason</reason>
  <merchantreference>Reference Code</merchantreference>
  <datacash_reference>Reference Code</datacash_reference>
  <time>Time</time>
  <mode>TEST</mode>
</Response>
```

Exchanging XML Data with DataCash

Because the XML data you need to send to DataCash has a simple and standard structure, we'll build it manually in a string, without using the XML support offered by PHP 5. We will, however, take advantage of PHP 5's new SimpleXML extension, which makes reading simple XML data a piece of cake.

Although less complex and powerful than DOMDocument, the SimpleXML extension makes parsing XML data easy by transforming it into a data structure you can simply iterate through. You first met the SimpleXML extension in Chapter 11.

■**Note** For the code that communicates with DataCash, we use the CURL library (http://curl.haxx.se/). Please read Appendix A for complete installation instructions. Under Linux, the process can be more complicated, but if you are running PHP under Windows, you just need to copy libeay32.dll and ssleay32.dll from the PHP package to the System32 folder of your Windows installation, and uncomment the following line in php.ini (by default located in your Windows installation folder) by removing the leading semicolon, and then restarting Apache: extension=php_curl.dll.

For more details about the CURL library, check the excellent tutorial at http://www.zend.com/zend/tut/tutorial-thome3.php. The official documentation of PHP's CURL support is located at http://www.php.net/curl.

Exercise: Communicating with DataCash

To communicate with DataCash, follow these steps:

1. Create a new folder named datacash_lib in the business_objects folder.

2. Create a new file named datacash_request.php in the datacash_lib folder, and add the following code to it:

```php
<?php
class DataCashRequest
{
  // DataCash Server URL
  private $mUrl;
  // Will hold the current XML document to be sent to DataCash
  private $mXml;

  // constructor initializes the class with URL of DataCash
  function __construct($url)
  {
    //Datacash URL
    $this->mUrl = $url;
  }
```

```php
// compose the XML structure for the pre-authentication request to DataCash
public function MakeXmlPre($dataCashClient,
                          $dataCashPassword,
                          $merchantReference,
                          $amount,
                          $currency,
                          $method,
                          $cardNumber,
                          $expiryDate,
                          $startDate = "",
                          $issueNumber = "")
{
  $this->mXml =
      "<?xml version=\"1.0\" encoding=\"UTF-8\"\x3F>
      <Request>
      <Authentication>
        <password>$dataCashPassword</password>
        <client>$dataCashClient</client>
      </Authentication>
      <Transaction>
      <TxnDetails>
       <merchantreference>$merchantReference</merchantreference>
       <amount currency='$currency'>$amount</amount>
      </TxnDetails>
      <CardTxn>
       <method>pre</method>
       <Card>
        <pan>$cardNumber</pan>
        <expirydate>$expiryDate</expirydate>
        <startdate>$startDate</startdate>
        <issuenumber>$issueNumber</issuenumber>
       </Card>
      </CardTxn>
      </Transaction>
      </Request>";
}

// Compose the XML structure for the fulfillment request to DataCash
public function MakeXmlFulfill($dataCashClient,
                              $dataCashPassword,
                              $method,
                              $authCode,
                              $reference)
```

```php
      {
        $this->mXml =
              "<?xml version=\"1.0\" encoding=\"UTF-8\"\x3F>
               <Request>
                <Authentication>
                 <password>$dataCashPassword</password>
                 <client>$dataCashClient</client>
                </Authentication>
                <Transaction>
                 <HistoricTxn>
                  <reference>$reference</reference>
                  <authcode>$authCode</authcode>
                  <method>$method</method>
                 </HistoricTxn>
                </Transaction>
               </Request>";
      }

      // get the current XML
      public function GetRequest()
      {
        return $this->mXml;
      }

      // send an HTTP POST request to DataCash using CURL
      public function GetResponse()
      {
        // initialize a CURL session
        $ch = curl_init();
        // prepare for an HTTP POST request
        curl_setopt($ch, CURLOPT_POST, 1);
        // prepare the XML document to be POSTed
        curl_setopt($ch, CURLOPT_POSTFIELDS,$this->mXml);
        // set the URL where we want to POST our XML structure
        curl_setopt($ch, CURLOPT_URL, $this->mUrl);
        // do not verify the Common name of the peer certificate in the SSL
        // handshake
        curl_setopt($ch, CURLOPT_SSL_VERIFYHOST, 0);
        // prevent CURL from verifying the peer's certificate
        curl_setopt($ch, CURLOPT_SSL_VERIFYPEER, 0);
        // we want CURL to directly return the transfer instead of
        // printing it
        curl_setopt($ch, CURLOPT_RETURNTRANSFER, 1);
        // perform a CURL session
        $result = curl_exec($ch);
        // close a CURL session
        curl_close ($ch);
```

```
    // return the response
    return $result;
  }
}//end class
?>
```

3. Add the following line at the end of the include/config.inc.php file:

```
// constant that stores the path to the datacash_lib folder
define("DATACASH_DIR", SITE_ROOT . "/business_objects/datacash_lib/");
```

4. Create the test_datacash.php file in your project's home (the tshirtshop folder) and add the following in it:

```php
<?php
session_start();
if (empty($_GET['step']))
{
  require_once 'include/config.inc.php';
  require_once DATACASH_DIR . 'datacash_request.php';
  $data_cash_url = "https://testserver.datacash.com/Transaction";
  $data_cash_client = "99265300";
  $data_cash_password = "4SXmkzM8h";
  $request = new DataCashRequest($data_cash_url);
  $request->MakeXmlPre($data_cash_client,
                       $data_cash_password,
                       8880000+rand(0,10000),
                       49.99,
                       "GBP",
                       "pre",
                       "3528000000000007",
                       "10/04");
  $request_xml = $request->GetRequest();
  $_SESSION['pre_request'] = $request_xml;
  $response_xml = $request->GetResponse();
  $_SESSION['pre_response'] = $response_xml;
  $xml = simplexml_load_string($response_xml);
  $request->MakeXmlFulfill($data_cash_client,
                           $data_cash_password,
                           "fulfill",
                           $xml->merchantreference,
                           $xml->datacash_reference);
  $response_xml = $request->GetResponse();
  $_SESSION['fulfill_response'] = $response_xml;
}
else
{
  header('Content-type: text/xml');
  switch ($_GET['step'])
```

```
    {
    case 1:
      print $_SESSION['pre_request'];
      break;
    case 2:
      print $_SESSION['pre_response'];
      break;
    case 3:
      print $_SESSION['fulfill_response'];
      break;
    }
  exit;
}
?>
<frameset cols="33%, 33%, 33%">
<frame src="test_datacash.php?step=1">
<frame src="test_datacash.php?step=2">
<frame src="test_datacash.php?step=3">
</frameset>
```

5. Load the test_datacash.php file in your browser and see the results. It should look like
    Figure 14-1.

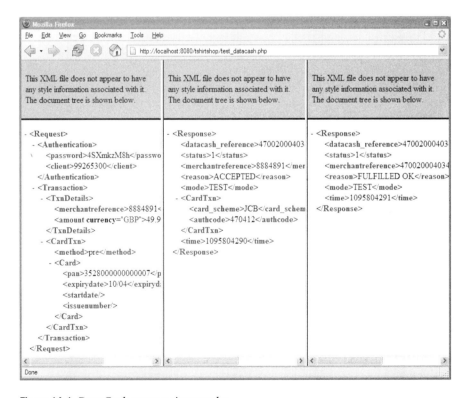

Figure 14-1. *DataCash transaction results*

6. Log on to https://testserver.datacash.com/reporting2 to see the transaction log for your DataCash account (note that this view takes a while to update, so you might not see the transaction right away). This report is shown in Figure 14-2.

Figure 14-2. *DataCash transaction report details*

How It Works: The code that communicates with DataCash

The DataCashRequest class is quite simple. First the constructor sets the HTTPS address where you send your requests:

```
// constructor initializes the class with URL of DataCash
function __construct($url)
{
  // DataCash URL
  $this->mUrl = $url;
}
```

When you want to make a pre-authentication request, you first need to call the MakeXmlPre() method to create the required XML for this kind of request. Some XML elements are optional (such as startdate or issuenumber, which get default values in case you don't provide your own—have a look at the definition of the MakeXmlPre() method), but the others are mandatory.

■**Note** If you want to see exactly which elements are mandatory and which are optional for each kind of request, check the XML API FAQ document from DataCash at `https://testserver.datacash.com/software/XML_API_FAQ.html`.

The next kind of request you must be able to make to the DataCash system is a fulfill request. The XML for this kind of request is prepared in the `MakeXmlFulfill()` method.

You then have the `GetRequest()` method that returns the last XML document built by either `MakeXmlPre()` or `MakeXmlFulfill()`:

```
// get the current XML
public function GetRequest()
{
    return $this->mXml;
}
```

Finally, the `GetResponse()` method actually sends the latest XML request file, built by a call to either `MakeXmlPre()` or `MakeXmlFulfill()`, and returns the response XML. Let's take a closer look at this method.

`GetResponse()` starts by initializing a CURL session and setting the `POST` method to send your data:

```
// send an HTTP POST request to DataCash using CURL
public function GetResponse()
{
    // initialize a CURL session
    $ch = curl_init();
    // prepare for an HTTP POST request
    curl_setopt($ch, CURLOPT_POST, 1);
    // prepare the XML document to be POSTed
    curl_setopt($ch, CURLOPT_POSTFIELDS,$this->mXml);
    // set the URL where we want to POST our XML structure
    curl_setopt($ch, CURLOPT_URL, $this->mUrl);
    // do not verify the Common name of the peer certificate in the SSL
    // handshake
    curl_setopt($ch, CURLOPT_SSL_VERIFYHOST, 0);
    // prevent CURL from verifying the peer's certificate
    curl_setopt($ch, CURLOPT_SSL_VERIFYPEER, 0);
```

To return the transfer into a PHP variable, we set the `CURLOPT_RETURNTRANSFER` parameter to 1 and then send the request and close the CURL session:

```
    // we want CURL to directly return the transfer instead of
    // printing it
    curl_setopt($ch, CURLOPT_RETURNTRANSFER, 1);
    // perform a CURL session
    $result = curl_exec($ch);
    // close a CURL session
```

```
    curl_close ($ch);
    // return the response
    return $result;
}
```

The datacash_test.php file acts like this:

1. The first time (when you load it in the browser) the script makes a pre-authentication request and a fulfill request and saves the pre-authentication request XML, the pre-authentication response XML, and the fulfill response XML data in session:

```
if (empty($_GET['step']))
{
    require_once 'include/config.inc.php';
    require_once DATACASH_DIR . 'datacash_request.php';
    $data_cash_url = "https://testserver.datacash.com/Transaction";
    $data_cash_client = "99265300";
    $data_cash_password = "4SXmkzM8h";
    $request = new DataCashRequest($data_cash_url);
    $request->MakeXmlPre($data_cash_client,
                         $data_cash_password,
                         8880000+rand(0,10000),
                         49.99,
                         "GBP",
                         "pre",
                         "3528000000000007",
                         "10/04");
    $request_xml = $request->GetRequest();
    $_SESSION['pre_request'] = $request_xml;
    $response_xml = $request->GetResponse();
    $_SESSION['pre_response'] = $response_xml;
    $xml = simplexml_load_string($response_xml);
    $request->MakeXmlFulfill($data_cash_client,
                             $data_cash_password,
                             "fulfill",
                             $xml->merchantreference,
                             $xml->datacash_reference);
    $response_xml = $request->GetResponse();
    $_SESSION['fulfill_response'] = $response_xml;
}
```

2. The datacash_test.php page will be loaded three more times because you have three frames that you want to fill with data:

```
<frameset cols="33%, 33%, 33%">
<frame src="test_datacash.php?step=1">
<frame src="test_datacash.php?step=2">
<frame src="test_datacash.php?step=3">
</frameset>
```

Depending on the step value, you decide which of the previously saved in session XMLs are displayed in the current frame:

```
else
{
  header('Content-type: text/xml');
  switch ($_GET['step'])
    {
    case 1:
      print $_SESSION['pre_request'];
      break;
    case 2:
      print $_SESSION['pre_response'];
      break;
    case 3:
      print $_SESSION['fulfill_response'];
      break;
  }
  exit;
}
```

Integrating DataCash with TShirtShop

Now that you have a new class that performs credit card transactions, all you need to do is integrate its functionality into the order pipeline you built in the previous chapters. To fully integrate DataCash with TShirtShop, you'll need to update the existing OrderProcessor, PsCheckFunds, and PsTakePayments classes. Let's deal with these one at a time.

Updating the OrderProcessor class

Update the existing OrderProcessor functionality by following these steps:

1. The classes from commerce_lib directory require three new pieces of information to operate:

   - DataCash client

   - DataCash password

   - DataCash URL

   You'll place all this information into the OrderProcessorConfiguration class that is used to initialize OrderProcessor. Update the OrderProcessorConfiguration class, situated in business_objects/commerce_lib/order_processor_configuration.php, as highlighted in the following code listing:

```
<?php
class OrderProcessorConfiguration
{
  public $mAdminEmail;
  public $mAdminEmailParams;
```

```
    public $mCustomerServiceEmail;
    public $mCustomerServiceEmailParams;
    public $mOrderProcessorEmail;
    public $mOrderProcessorEmailParams;
    public $mSupplierEmail;
    public $mDataCashClient;
    public $mDataCashPwd;
    public $mDataCashUrl;

    function __construct($newAdminEmail, $newAdminEmailParams,
      $newCustomerServiceEmail, $newCustomerServiceEmailParams,
      $newOrderProcessorEmail, $newOrderProcessorEmailParams, $newSupplierEmail,
      $newDataCashUrl, $newDataCashClient, $newDataCashPwd)
    {
      $this->mAdminEmail = $newAdminEmail;
      $this->mAdminEmailParams = $newAdminEmailParams;
      $this->mCustomerServiceEmail = $newCustomerServiceEmail;
      $this->mCustomerServiceEmailParams = $newCustomerServiceEmailParams;
      $this->mOrderProcessorEmail = $newOrderProcessorEmail;
      $this->mOrderProcessorEmailParams = $newOrderProcessorEmailParams;
      $this->mSupplierEmail = $newSupplierEmail;
      $this->mDataCashUrl=$newDataCashUrl;
      $this->mDataCashClient=$newDataCashClient;
      $this->mDataCashPwd=$newDataCashPwd;
    }
}
?>
```

2. Add your own DataCash login data at the end of your include/config.inc.php file:

```
// DataCash login info
define("DATACASH_URL", "https://testserver.datacash.com/Transaction");
define("DATACASH_CLIENT", "99265300");
define("DATACASH_PWD", "4SXmkzM8h");
```

3. Add the following line at the end of the
   business_objects/commerce_lib/commerce_lib.all.php file:

```
require_once DATACASH_DIR . 'datacash_request.php';
```

4. To add DataCash login info, update the code that builds a new OrderProcessorConfiguration object in smarty_plugins/function.load_checkout_info.php as shown here,:

```
        // Get configuration for order processor
        $processor_configuration = new OrderProcessorConfiguration
                                    (ADMIN_EMAIL,
                                     $GLOBALS['admin_email_params'],
                                     CUSTOMER_SERVICE_EMAIL,
```

```
$GLOBALS['customer_service_email_params'], ORDER_PROCESSOR_EMAIL,

$GLOBALS['order_processor_email_params'], SUPPLIER_EMAIL,
                                          DATACASH_URL,
                                          DATACASH_CLIENT,
                                          DATACASH_PWD);
```

5. Change the `smarty_plugins/function.load_order_details_admin.php` file to add Data-Cash login info:

```
// Get configuration for order processor
$processor_configuration = new OrderProcessorConfiguration(
        ADMIN_EMAIL,
        $GLOBALS['admin_email_params'],
        CUSTOMER_SERVICE_EMAIL,
        $GLOBALS['customer_service_email_params'],
        ORDER_PROCESSOR_EMAIL,
        $GLOBALS['order_processor_email_params'],
        SUPPLIER_EMAIL,
        DATACASH_URL,
        DATACASH_CLIENT,
        DATACASH_PWD);
```

■**Note**   Making this change will break any code that uses the `commerce_lib` classes, including `test_commerce_lib.php`. Don't worry about this for now though; by the time you'll use those classes, you'll have corrected things.

Implementing the Order Pipeline Classes

Finally, you need to modify the pipeline section classes that deal with credit card transactions. We've already included the infrastructure for storing and retrieving authentication codes and reference information, via the `OrderProcessor::SetOrderAuthCodeAndReference()` method.

1. First modify `commerce_lib/ps_check_funds.php` to work with DataCash:

```php
<?php
class PsCheckFunds implements IPipelineSection
{
  public function Process($processor)
  {
    $processor->AddAudit("PSCheckFunds started.",20100);
    $currentCustomer = $processor->GetCurrentCustomer();
    $currentOrderDetails = $processor->GetCurrentOrderDetails();
    $request = new DataCashRequest($processor->mConfiguration->mDataCashUrl);
```

```php
    $request->MakeXmlPre($processor->mConfiguration->mDataCashClient,
                        $processor->mConfiguration->mDataCashPwd,
                        $processor->mOrderId+1000006,
                        $currentOrderDetails->mTotalCost,
                        "GBP",
                        "pre",
                        $currentCustomer->mCreditCard->GetCardNumber(),
                        $currentCustomer->mCreditCard->GetExpiryDate(),
                        $currentCustomer->mCreditCard->GetIssueDate(),
                        $currentCustomer->mCreditCard->GetIssueNumber());
    $responseXML = $request->GetResponse();
    $xml = simplexml_load_string($responseXML);
    if ($xml->status == 1)
    {
      $processor->SetOrderAuthCodeAndReference($xml->merchantreference,
                                              $xml->datacash_reference);
      $processor->AddAudit("Funds available for purchase.", 20102);
      $processor->UpdateOrderStatus(2);
      $processor->mContinueNow = true;
    }
    else
    {
      $processor->AddAudit("Funds not available for purchase.", 20103);
      throw new Exception("Credit card check funds failed for order " .
                          $processor->mOrderId . ".\n\n" .
                          "Data exchanged:\n" .
                          $request->GetRequest(). "\n". $responseXML);
    }
    $processor->AddAudit("PSCheckFunds finished.", 20101);
  }
} //end class
?>
```

2. Modify ps_take_payment.php as follows:

```php
<?php
class PsTakePayment implements IPipelineSection
{
  public function Process( $processor)
  {
    $processor->AddAudit("PSTakePayment started.",20400);
    $request = new DataCashRequest($processor->mConfiguration->mDataCashUrl);
    $request->MakeXmlFulfill($processor->mConfiguration->mDataCashClient,
                            $processor->mConfiguration->mDataCashPwd,
                            "fulfill",
                            $processor->GetAuthCode(),
                            $processor->GetReference());
    $responseXML = $request->GetResponse();
```

```
$xml = simplexml_load_string($responseXML);
if ($xml->status == 1)
{
  $processor->AddAudit("Funds deducted from customer credit card.",
                       20403);
  $processor->UpdateOrderStatus(5);
  $processor->mContinueNow = true;
}
else
{
  $processor->AddAudit("Could not deduct funds from credit card.",
                       20403);
  throw new Exception("Credit card take payment failed for order " .
                      $processor->mOrderId. ".\n\n" .
                      "Data exchanged:\n" .
                      $request->GetRequest() . "\n" . $responseXML);
}
$processor->UpdateOrderStatus(5);
$processor->mContinueNow = true;
$processor->AddAudit("PSTakePayment finished.", 20401);
  }
}
?>
```

Testing DataCash Integration

Now that you have all this in place, it's important to test with a few orders. You can do this easily by making sure you create a customer with "magic" credit card details. As mentioned earlier in the chapter, DataCash supplies these numbers for testing purposes and to obtain specific responses from DataCash. A sample of these numbers is shown in Table 14-2; a full list is available on the DataCash web site.

Table 14-2. *DataCash Credit Card Test Numbers*

Card Type	Card Number	Return Code	Description	Sample Message
Switch	4936000000000000001	1	Authorized with random auth code.	AUTH CODE ??????
	4936000000000000019	7	Decline the transaction.	DECLINED
	6333000000000005	1	Authorized with random auth code.	AUTH CODE ??????
	6333000000000013	7	Decline the transaction.	DECLINED
	6333000000123450	1	Authorized with random auth code.	AUTH CODE ??????
Visa	4242424242424242	7	Decline the transaction.	DECLINED
	4444333322221111	1	Authorized with random auth code.	AUTH CODE ??????
	4546389010000131	1	Authorized with random auth code.	AUTH CODE ??????

At this moment, you can experiment with your new fully featured e-commerce web site by placing orders with the test credit card numbers, checking the emails the web site sends, and finding out how it reacts in certain situation, such as how it logs errors, how orders are administered using the orders administration page, and so on.

Going Live

Moving from the test account to the live one is now simply a matter of replacing the DataCash login info in `include/config.inc.php`. After you set up a merchant bank account, you can use the new details to set up a new DataCash account, obtaining new client and password data along the way. You also need to change the URL for the DataCash server that you send data to, because it needs to be the production server instead of the testing server (the address of the production server is `https://transaction.datacash.com/Transaction`). Other than removing the test user accounts from the database and moving your web site to an Internet location (see Appendix B for more details), this is all you need to do before exposing your newly completed e-commerce application to customers.

Working with VeriSign Payflow Pro

To use Payflow Pro you need to sign up for a trial account via its web site (`http://www.verisign.com/products/payflow/pro/`). After you register, you can log on to the VeriSign Manager web site and download the appropriate SDK (Software Developer Kit) for your platform and documentation necessary to use Payflow Pro.

Integrating Payflow Pro with PHP in Linux has the advantage of using an existent PHP extension named `pfpro`. Because we don't have the `pfpro` extension in Windows, we decided to install and use VeriSign's Payflow Pro COM integration object.

■**Note** Linux users should check Appendix A to learn more about installing the `pfpro` extension.

Communicating with Payflow Pro is different than with DataCash. Instead of sending and receiving XML files, you send and receive strings consisting of name-value pairs, separated by ampersands. Effectively, you use a similar syntax to query strings appended to URLs.

The simplest transaction type is `Sale`, where you request and deduct the funds from the credit card in real time. We'll write a simple test with this transaction type before implementing any modifications to TShirtShop. Because integration is implemented differently under Windows and Linux, we'll cover them separately.

■**Note** Your main documentation for interacting with VeriSign Payflow Pro should be the *PayFlow Pro Developers Guide*, which you can download from the Downloads section in the VeriSign Manager page.

When doing test transactions with VeriSign, you'll send an array similar to the one shown here to `test-payflow.verisign.com`:

```
$transaction = array('USER'     => 'your_user_name', // username
                     'PWD'      => 'your_password', // password
                     'PARTNER'  => 'VeriSign', // Partner
                     'TRXTYPE'  => 'S', // Type Sale
                     'TENDER'   => 'C', // Credit Card
                     'AMT'      => 50.50, // Amount to charge
                     'ACCT'     => '378282246310005', // CC #
                     'EXPDATE'  => '0905' // Expiry (MMYY)
```

In our site, instead of processing the payment in one step with a Sale transaction (`'TRXTYPE' => 'S'`), we'll do a pre/fulfill type transaction using two actual transactions. First, an Authorization transaction (`'TRXTYPE' => 'A'`) is used in the `PsCheckFunds` pipeline section to reserve the needed amount of money on the customer's credit card. At the moment of shipping (after the stock has been confirmed), a Delayed Capture transaction (`'TRXTYPE' => 'D'`) is used in `PsTakePayment` to deduct the reserved amount of money from the customer's credit card.

Please check *PayFlow Pro Developers Guide* for the most accurate and up-to-date explanation of the parameters you send to the Payflow Pro system for each transaction.

Exchanging Data with VeriSign Payflow Pro

If your solution works under Linux, you package the transaction data into an array and pass it to the VeriSign Payflow Pro system using the `pfpro` library. If you're working under Windows, you'll build a string consisting of name-value pairs similar to a URL query string and send it to VeriSign using the Payflow Pro COM object.

Before implementing the VeriSign Payflow Pro functionality into TShirtShop, let's first do a short test of interacting with the Payflow Pro system. We'll deal with this separately for Windows and Linux.

Testing Payflow Pro Under Linux

To test Payflow Pro under Linux, follow these steps:

1. First, install the `pfpro` library, which allows access to the Payflow Pro system from your PHP script. After you register for your trial Payflow Pro account, log in to `https://manager.verisign.com/` and get the Linux SDK from the Downloads section. Unpack the SDK and copy the header file `pfpro.h` to `/usr/local/include` and the library file `libpfpro.so` to `/usr/local/lib`. See Appendix A to learn how to compile PHP to work with the `pfpro` library.

2. Copy the `certs` directory from the Payflow Pro SDK in the `commerce_lib` directory.

3. Add the following line at the end of the `include/config.inc.php` file:

```
putenv("PFPRO_CERT_PATH=" . COMMERCELIB_DIR . "certs");
```

4. Add the following `test_payflow_pro.php` test file in your site root folder, changing the USER, PWD, and even ACCT fields (if that credit card number is no longer valid for testing):

```php
<?php
require_once 'include/config.inc.php';
 $transaction = array('USER'    => 'misu200', // username
                      'PWD'     => 'misu992', // password
                      'PARTNER' => 'VeriSign', // Partner
                      'TRXTYPE' => 'S', // Type Sale
                      'TENDER'  => 'C', // Credit Card
                      'AMT'     => 50.50, // Amount to charge
                      'ACCT'    => '378282246310005', // CC #
                      'EXPDATE' => '0905' // Expiry (MMYY)
                     );

$result = pfpro_process($transaction,"test-payflow.verisign.com");

if ($result['RESULT'] == 0)
 {
    echo "<b>Success!</b><br/><br/>";
 }
 else
 {
    echo "<b>Failure!</b><br/><br/>";
 }
echo "<pre>";
print_r($result);
echo "</pre>";
?>
```

5. Load the `test_payflow_pro.php` page in your favorite browser and see the results (see Figure 14-3).

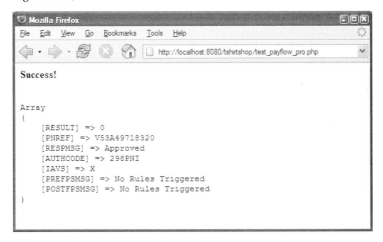

Figure 14-3. *Payflow Pro transaction results*

> ▥**Note** If instead of success you get a failed transaction with "Under review by Fraud Service" or a similar error message, you need go to your VeriSign Manager page, go to Security ➤ Test Setup ➤ Edit Filters, and disable the filters that your transaction has problems with. Specifically, most test transactions fail due to no transaction amount ceiling being set and failure of address verification (AVS). If you set a suitably high amount ceiling and disable AVS, you should be able to carry out successful transactions.

Testing Payflow Pro Under Windows

To test Payflow Pro under Windows, follow these steps:

1. Go to the VeriSign Manager at `https://manager.verisign.com`, go to the Downloads section, and download the Windows SDK. Unzip the file somewhere on your hard drive.

2. Copy `lib/pfpro.dll` from Payflow Pro SDK to your `Windows\System32` directory.

3. Execute the `com/PFProCOMSetup.exe` file from the Payflow Pro SDK to register VeriSign's Payflow Pro COM object in the Windows Registry, so it can be accessed from your code.

4. Copy the `certs` directory from the Payflow Pro SDK in `business_objects/commerce_lib/`.

5. Add the following lines at the end of the `include/config.inc.php` file:

```
/* Create the environment variable PFPRO_CERT_PATH to point to the certs
    directory from Payflow Pro SDK */
putenv("PFPRO_CERT_PATH=" . COMMERCELIB_DIR . "certs");
```

6. Create a new script in your project root, named `test_Payflow_pro.php`, changing of course the USER, PWD, and even ACCT fields (if that credit card number isn't a valid one for testing anymore):

```php
<?php
require_once 'include/config.inc.php';
// Create Payflow Pro COM Object
$objCOM = new COM("PFProCOMControl.PFProCOMControl.1");
// Initialize parameter list
$parmList = "TRXTYPE=S&TENDER=C";
$parmList .= "&ACCT=378282246310005";
$parmList .= "&EXPDATE=0905";
$parmList .= "&AMT=50.50";
$parmList .= "&PWD=misu992";
$parmList .= "&USER=misu201";
$parmList .= "&PARTNER=VeriSign";
// Process Transaction
```

```php
$ctx1 = $objCOM->CreateContext("test-payflow.verisign.com",
                               443, 30, "", 0, "", "");
$result = $objCOM->SubmitTransaction($ctx1, $parmList, strlen($parmList));
// Destroy Context
$objCOM->DestroyContext($ctx1);

$valArray = explode('&', $result);
foreach($valArray as $val)
{
  $valArray2 = explode('=', $val);
  $response[$valArray2[0]] = $valArray2[1];
}

if ($response['RESULT'] == 0)
{
  echo "<b>Success!</b><br/><br/>";
}
else
{
  echo "<b>Failure!</b><br/><br/>";
}
echo "<pre>";
print_r($response);
echo "</pre>";
?>
```

7. Load test_payflow_pro.php in your browser and you should see something similar to Figure 14-4.

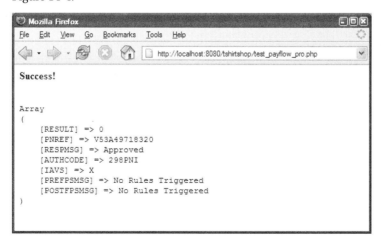

Figure 14-4. *Payflow Pro transaction results*

Note If instead of success you get a failed transaction with "Under review by Fraud Service" or a similar error message, you need go to your VeriSign Manager page, go to Security ➤ Test Setup ➤ Edit Filters, and disable the filters that your transaction has problems with. Specifically, most test transactions will fail due to no transaction amount ceiling being set and failure of address verification (AVS). If you set a suitably high amount ceiling and disable AVS, you should be able to carry out successful transactions.

---

8. Go to Payflow Pro, log in to VeriSign Manager (`https://manager.verisign.com/login/login.cfm?partner=VeriSign`) and you can see the transaction you just performed in the "Reports" section.

Integrating VeriSign Payflow Pro with TShirtShop

As with DataCash, there are two main steps you need to take to integrate Payflow Pro functionality into your web site:

1. You'll modify the `OrderProcessor` class to use Payflow Pro functionality. This will imply modifying a few other related classes (such as `OrderProcessorConfiguration`), and adding the Payflow Pro login connection information to `config.inc.php`.

2. You'll modify the `PsCheckFunds` and `PsTakePayment` classes to make use of the new Payflow Pro functionality.

The implementation for `PsCheckFunds` and `PsTakePayment` is different for the Linux and Windows versions of TShirtShop (under Linux the communication is done through the `pfpro` library, whereas under Windows, the Payflow Pro COM object is used).

Remember that you can use the files from the Downloads section of the Apress web site (`http://www.apress.com`) instead of typing the code yourself.

Updating the OrderProcessor Class: Windows and Linux

Update the existing `OrderProcessor` functionality by following these steps:

1. Place VeriSign account information into the `OrderProcessorConfiguration` class that is used to initialize `OrderProcessor`. Update the `OrderProcessorConfiguration` class, located in `business_objects/commerce_lib/order_processor_configuration.php`, as highlighted in the following code listing:

```php
<?php
class OrderProcessorConfiguration
{
  public $mAdminEmail;
  public $mAdminEmailParams;
  public $mCustomerServiceEmail;
  public $mCustomerServiceEmailParams;
```

```php
    public $mOrderProcessorEmail;
    public $mOrderProcessorEmailParams;
    public $mSupplierEmail;
    public $mPayflowProPartner;
    public $mPayflowProHost;
    public $mPayflowProUser;
    public $mPayflowProPwd;

    function __construct($newAdminEmail,
                         $newAdminEmailParams,
                         $newCustomerServiceEmail,
                         $newCustomerServiceEmailParams,
                         $newOrderProcessorEmail,
                         $newOrderProcessorEmailParams,
                         $newSupplierEmail,
                         $newPayflowProPartner,
                         $newPayflowProHost,
                         $newPayflowProUser,
                         $newPayflowProPwd)
  {
    $this->mAdminEmail = $newAdminEmail;
    $this->mAdminEmailParams = $newAdminEmailParams;
    $this->mCustomerServiceEmail = $newCustomerServiceEmail;
    $this->mCustomerServiceEmailParams = $newCustomerServiceEmailParams;
    $this->mOrderProcessorEmail = $newOrderProcessorEmail;
    $this->mOrderProcessorEmailParams = $newOrderProcessorEmailParams;
    $this->mSupplierEmail = $newSupplierEmail;
    $this->mPayflowProPartner = $newPayflowProPartner;
    $this->mPayflowProHost = $newPayflowProHost;
    $this->mPayflowProUser = $newPayflowProUser;
    $this->mPayflowProPwd = $newPayflowProPwd;
  }
}
?>
```

2. Add your own Payflow Pro login data at the end of your `include/config.inc.php` file:

```php
/* Create the environment variable PFPRO_CERT_PATH to
 point to the certs directory from Payflow Pro SDK */
putenv("PFPRO_CERT_PATH=" . COMMERCELIB_DIR . "certs");
// VeriSign Payflow Pro login info
define("PAYFLOW_PRO_PARTNER", "VeriSign");
define("PAYFLOW_PRO_HOST", "test-payflow.verisign.com");
define("PAYFLOW_PRO_USER", "<your username>");
define("PAYFLOW_PRO_PWD", "<your password>");
```

3. Update smarty_plugins/function.load_checkout_info.php as shown here to add Payflow Pro login info:

```
// Get configuration for order processor
$processor_configuration = new OrderProcessorConfiguration
                                (ADMIN_EMAIL,
                                 $GLOBALS['admin_email_params'],
                                 CUSTOMER_SERVICE_EMAIL,
                                 $GLOBALS['customer_service_email_params'],
                                 ORDER_PROCESSOR_EMAIL,
                                 $GLOBALS['order_processor_email_params'],
                                 SUPPLIER_EMAIL,
                                 PAYFLOW_PRO_PARTNER,
                                 PAYFLOW_PRO_HOST,
                                 PAYFLOW_PRO_USER,
                                 PAYFLOW_PRO_PWD);
```

4. Change the smarty_plugins/function.load_order_details_admin.php file to add Payflow Pro login info:

```
// Get configuration for order processor
$processor_configuration = new OrderProcessorConfiguration
                                (ADMIN_EMAIL,
                                 $GLOBALS['admin_email_params'],
                                 CUSTOMER_SERVICE_EMAIL,
                                 $GLOBALS['customer_service_email_params'],
                                 ORDER_PROCESSOR_EMAIL,
                                 $GLOBALS['order_processor_email_params'],
                                 SUPPLIER_EMAIL,
                                 PAYFLOW_PRO_PARTNER,
                                 PAYFLOW_PRO_HOST,
                                 PAYFLOW_PRO_USER,
                                 PAYFLOW_PRO_PWD);
```

■**Note**   Making this change will break any code that uses the commerce_lib classes, including test_commerce_lib.php. Don't worry about this for now though; by the time you'll use those classes, you'll have corrected things.

Implementing the Order Pipeline Classes

The final modifications involve changing the pipeline section classes that deal with credit card transactions (PsCheckFunds and PsTakePayment). We've already included the infrastructure for storing and retrieving authentication code and reference information, via the OrderProcessor::SetOrderAuthCodeAndReference() method.

The code is different for Windows and Linux, so we'll cover it separately.

Windows

First, modify `commerce_lib/ps_check_funds.php` to work with Payflow Pro:

```php
<?php
class PsCheckFunds implements IPipelineSection
{
  public function Process($processor)
  {
    $processor->AddAudit("PSCheckFunds started.",20100);
    $currentCustomer = $processor->GetCurrentCustomer();
    $currentOrderDetails=$processor->GetCurrentOrderDetails();
    /* Create Payflow Pro COM Object */
    $objCOM = new COM("PFProCOMControl.PFProCOMControl.1");
    $exp_date = str_replace("/", "",
                           $currentCustomer->mCreditCard->GetExpiryDate());
    $parmList = "TRXTYPE=A"; // Type Authorize
    $parmList .= "&TENDER=C"; // Credit Card
    $parmList .= "&ACCT=" . $currentCustomer->mCreditCard->GetCardNumber();
    $parmList .= "&PWD=" . $processor->mConfiguration->mPayflowProPwd;
    $parmList .= "&USER=" . $processor->mConfiguration->mPayflowProUser;
    $parmList .= "&PARTNER=VeriSign";   // Partner
    $parmList .= "&EXPDATE=" . $exp_date; // Expiry (MMYY)
    $parmList .= "&AMT=" . $currentOrderDetails->mTotalCost; // Amount to charge
    $parmList .= "&INVNUM=" . ($processor->mOrderId+1000000);
    /* Process Transaction */
    $ctx1 = $objCOM->CreateContext($processor->mConfiguration->mPayflowProHost,
                                  443,  30, "", 0, "", "");
    $result = $objCOM->SubmitTransaction($ctx1, $parmList,  strlen($parmList));
    /* Destroy Context */
    $objCOM->DestroyContext($ctx1);
    $valArray = explode('&', $result);
    foreach($valArray as $val)
    {
      $valArray2 = explode('=', $val);
      $response[$valArray2[0]] = $valArray2[1];
    }
    if ($response['RESULT']==0)
    {
      $reference = $response['PNREF'];
      $auth_code = $response['AUTHCODE'];
      $processor->SetOrderAuthCodeAndReference($auth_code, $reference);
      $processor->AddAudit("Funds available for purchase.", 20102);
      $processor->UpdateOrderStatus(2);
      $processor->mContinueNow = true;
    }
    else
    {
      $processor->AddAudit("Funds not available for purchase.", 20103);
```

```php
        ob_start();
        var_dump($response);
        $response_dump = ob_get_contents();
        ob_end_clean();
        throw new Exception("Credit card check funds failed for order " .
                            $processor->mOrderId . ".\n\n" .
                            "Data exchanged:\n" . $parmList .
                            "\n" . $response_dump);
      }
      $processor->AddAudit("PSCheckFunds finished.", 20101);
    }
  } //end class
?>
```

Second, modify ps_take_payment.php as follows:

```php
<?php
class PsTakePayment implements IPipelineSection
{
  public function Process($processor)
  {
    $processor->AddAudit("PSTakePayment started.", 20400);
    /* Create Payflow Pro COM Object */
    $objCOM = new COM("PFProCOMControl.PFProCOMControl.1");
    $parmList = "TRXTYPE=D"; // Type Delayed Capture
    $parmList .= "&TENDER=C"; // Credit Card
    $parmList .= "&PWD=" . $processor->mConfiguration->mPayflowProPwd;
    $parmList .= "&USER=" . $processor->mConfiguration->mPayflowProUser;
    $parmList .= "&PARTNER=VeriSign";
    $parmList .= "&ORIGID=" . $processor->GetReference();

    /* Process Transaction */
    $ctx1 = $objCOM->CreateContext($processor->mConfiguration->mPayflowProHost,
                                   443, 30, "", 0, "", "");
    $result = $objCOM->SubmitTransaction($ctx1, $parmList,   strlen($parmList));
    /* Destroy Context */
    $objCOM->DestroyContext($ctx1);
    $valArray = explode('&', $result);
    foreach($valArray as $val)
    {
      $valArray2 = explode('=', $val);
      $response[$valArray2[0]] = $valArray2[1];
    }
    if ($response['RESULT']==0)
    {
      $processor->AddAudit("Funds deducted from customer credit card.",
                           20403);
      $processor->UpdateOrderStatus(5);
```

```php
      $processor->mContinueNow=true;
    }
    else
    {
      $processor->AddAudit("Error taking funds from customer credit card.",
                           20403);
      ob_start();
      var_dump($response);
      $response_dump = ob_get_contents();
      ob_end_clean();
      throw new Exception("Credit card take payment failed for order ".
                          $processor->mOrderId. ".\n\n" .
                          "Data exchanged:\n" . $parmList . "\n" .
                          $response_dump);
    }
    $processor->UpdateOrderStatus(5);
    $processor->mContinueNow = true;
    $processor->AddAudit("PSTakePayment finished.",20401);
  }
}
?>
```

Linux

First modify commerce_lib/ps_check_funds.php to work with Payflow Pro:

```php
<?php
class PsCheckFunds implements IPipelineSection
{
  public function Process($processor)
  {
    $processor->AddAudit("PSCheckFunds started.", 20100);
    $currentCustomer = $processor->GetCurrentCustomer();
    $currentOrderDetails = $processor->GetCurrentOrderDetails();
    $exp_date = str_replace("/", "" ,
                            $currentCustomer->mCreditCard->GetExpiryDate());
    $transaction =
      array('USER'    => $processor->mConfiguration->mPayflowProUser, // username
            'PWD'     => $processor->mConfiguration->mPayflowProPwd, // password
            'PARTNER' => 'VeriSign', // Partner
            'TRXTYPE' => 'A', // Type Authorize
            'TENDER'  => 'C', // Credit Card
            'AMT'     => $currentOrderDetails->mTotalCost, // Amount to charge
            'ACCT'    => $currentCustomer->mCreditCard->GetCardNumber(), // CC #
            'EXPDATE' => $exp_date, // Expiry (MMYY)
            'INVNUM'  => ($processor->mOrderId + 1000000));
    $response =
        pfpro_process($transaction,$processor->mConfiguration->mPayflowProHost);
```

```php
    if ($response['RESULT']==0)
    {
      $reference = $response['PNREF'];
      $auth_code = $response['AUTHCODE'];
      $processor->SetOrderAuthCodeAndReference($auth_code, $reference);
      $processor->AddAudit("Funds available for purchase.", 20102);
      $processor->UpdateOrderStatus(2);
      $processor->mContinueNow = true;
    }
    else
    {
      $processor->AddAudit("Funds not available for purchase.", 20103);
      ob_start();
      var_dump($transaction);
      var_dump($response);
      $response_dump = ob_get_contents();
      ob_end_clean();
      throw new Exception("Credit card check funds failed for order " .
                          $processor->mOrderId . ".\n\n" .
                          "Data exchanged:" . $transaction .
                          "\n" . $response_dump);
    }
    $processor->AddAudit("PSCheckFunds finished.", 20101);
  }
} //end class
?>
```

Second, modify ps_take_payment.php as follows:

```php
<?php
class PsTakePayment implements IPipelineSection
{
  public function Process($processor)
  {
    $processor->AddAudit("PSTakePayment started.", 20400);
    $transaction =
        array('USER'     => $processor->mConfiguration->mPayflowProUser, //username
              'PWD'      => $processor->mConfiguration->mPayflowProPwd, // password
              'PARTNER' => 'VeriSign', // Partner
              'TRXTYPE' => 'D', // Type Delayed Capture
              'TENDER'   => 'C', // Credit Card
              'ORIGID' => $processor->GetReference());
    $response =
          pfpro_process($transaction,$processor->mConfiguration->mPayflowProHost);
    if ($response['RESULT']==0)
    {
      $processor->AddAudit("Funds deducted from customer credit card.", 20403);
      $processor->UpdateOrderStatus(5);
      $processor->mContinueNow=true;
```

```
    }
    else
    {
      $processor->AddAudit("Error taking funds from credit card.", 20403);
      ob_start();
      var_dump($transaction);
      var_dump($response);
      $response_dump = ob_get_contents();
      ob_end_clean();
      throw new Exception("Credit card take payment failed for order ".
                          $processor->mOrderId. ".\n\n" .
                          "Data exchanged:" . $transaction . "\n" .
                          $response_dump);
    }
    $processor->UpdateOrderStatus(5);
    $processor->mContinueNow = true;
    $processor->AddAudit("PSTakePayment finished.",20401);
  }
}
?>
```

Testing VeriSign Integration

All you have to do now is run some tests with your new web site. Retrieve the list of "magic" Payflow Pro credit card numbers from
`http://www.verisign.com/support/payflow/manager/selfHelp/testCardNum.html` and experiment doing transactions with them.

For more details about customizing this service for your particular needs and moving from the test server to a live server, check out the *Verisign Payflow Pro Developers Guide*, which is an excellent and complete resource.

Summary

In this chapter, you have completed your e-commerce application by integrating it with credit card authorization. Short of putting your own products in, hooking it up with your suppliers, getting a merchant bank account, and putting it on the web, you're ready to go. Okay, so that's still quite a lot of work, but none of it is particularly difficult. The hard work is behind you now.

Specifically, in this chapter we have looked at the theory behind credit card transactions on the web and looked at one full implementation—DataCash. We created a library that can be used to access DataCash and integrated it with our application. We also looked at Payflow Pro. The code required to use this credit card gateway is included in the Downloads section for this book on the Apress web site.

CHAPTER 15

■■■

Product Reviews

At this point, you have a complete and functional e-commerce web site. However, this doesn't stop you from adding even more features to it, making it more useful and pleasant for visitors.

By adding a product reviews system to your web site, you increase the chances that visitors will get back to your site, either to write a review for a product they bought, or to see what other people think about that product.

A review system can also help you learn your customers' tastes, which enables you to improve the product recommendations, and even make changes in the web site or the structure of the product catalog based on customer feedback.

To make things easy for both you and the customer, you'll add the list of product reviews and the form to add a new product review to the products' details pages. The form to add a new product review shows up only for registered users because we decided not to allow anonymous reviews (however, you can easily change this, if you want). You'll create the code for the new functionality in the usual way, starting from the database and finishing with the user interface (UI). The final result of your work in this chapter will look like Figure 15-1.

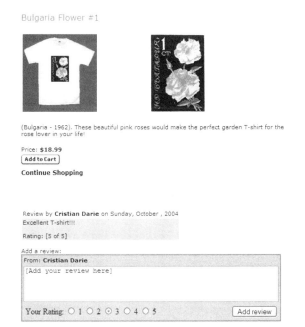

Bulgaria Flower #1

(Bulgaria - 1962). These beautiful pink roses would make the perfect garden T-shirt for the rose lover in your life!

Price: **$18.99**

[**Add to Cart**]

Continue Shopping

Review by **Cristian Darie** on Sunday, October , 2004
Excellent T-shirt!!!

Rating: [5 of 5]

Add a review:

From: **Cristian Darie**

[Add your review here]

Your Rating: ○ 1 ○ 2 ⊙ 3 ○ 4 ○ 5   [Add review]

Figure 15-1. *The product details page containing product reviews*

Storing Reviews in the Database

You'll have one new data table in the database that will store the reviews information. Add the review table to your database by executing the following SQL script. By now, the SQL script shouldn't be mysterious to you, and the column names are self-explanatory.

```
CREATE TABLE review (
  review_id INT UNSIGNED NOT NULL AUTO_INCREMENT,
  customer_id INT UNSIGNED NOT NULL DEFAULT '0',
  product_id INT UNSIGNED NOT NULL DEFAULT '0',
  review TEXT NOT NULL,
  rating TINYINT NOT NULL DEFAULT '0',
  date_added DATETIME NOT NULL,
  PRIMARY KEY (review_id)
) TYPE=MyISAM;
```

Note We could have enforced the relationship with the `customer` and `product` tables if all tables were of type INNO DB, but in this case, we won't enforce the relationship in any way. Also, depending on your preferences, you can choose to remove all reviews of a customer if the customer's account is deleted, or remove all reviews for a product if the product is removed from the database.

Implementing the Data Tier

For your review system, you only need two data tier methods in the `DoCatalog` class (in `data_objects/do_catalog.php`). The `GetProductReviews` method gets the reviews for a specific product, and the `AddProductReview` method adds a review to a product.

GetProductReviews

The `GetProductReviews` method retrieves the reviews for the product identified by the `$productId` parameter. You also need the name of the reviewer so we made an INNER JOIN with the customer table. Add the following method to your `DoCatalog` class:

```
  // gets the reviews for a specific product
  public function GetProductReviews($productId)
  {
    $query_string = "SELECT customer.name, review.review,
                            review.rating, review.date_added
                      FROM review INNER JOIN customer
                        ON customer.customer_id = review.customer_id
                      WHERE product_id = $productId";
    $result = $this->dbManager->DbGetAll($query_string);
    return $result;
  }
```

AddProductReview

When a registered visitor adds a product review, the AddProductReview method is called. Add the following method to your DoCatalog class:

```
// add a product review
public function AddProductReview($customerId, $productId, $review, $rating)
{
  $query_string =
     "INSERT INTO review (customer_id, product_id, review, rating, date_added)
       VALUES ($customerId, $productId, '$review', $rating, NOW())";
  $result = $this->dbManager->DbQuery($query_string);
  return $result;
}
```

Implementing the Business Layer

Add the corresponding business tier methods to the BoCatalog class:

```
// gets the reviews for a specific product
public function GetProductReviews($productId)
{
  $result = $this->mDoCatalog->GetProductReviews($productId);
  return $result;
}
// add a product review
public function AddProductReview($productId, $review, $rating)
{
  $bo_customer = new BoCustomer();
  $result = $this->mDoCatalog->AddProductReview(
                                $bo_customer->GetCurrentCustomerId(),
                                $productId,
                                $review,
                                $rating);
  return $result;
}
```

Implementing the User Interface

Now it's time to see the code you've written so far at work. The UI consists of the reviews componentized template that will be placed on the product details page. You'll create it in the following exercise.

Exercise: Creating the reviews Componentized Template

To create the reviews componentized template, follow these steps:

1. Create the file templates/reviews.tpl and add the following to it:

```
{* display reviews *}
{load_reviews assign = "reviews"}
{if $reviews->mTotalReviews !=0}
 <table>
  {section name=k loop=$reviews->mReviews}
  <tr>
   <td class="SimpleText">
    Review by <b>{$reviews->mReviews[k].name}</b>
    on {$reviews->mReviews[k].date_added|date_format:"%A, %B %e, %Y"}
   </td>
  </tr>
  <tr bgcolor="#ccddff">
   <td colspan=2 class="SimpleText">
    {$reviews->mReviews[k].review}
    <br/><br/>
    Rating: <img src="images/{$reviews->mReviews[k].rating}box.gif">
    [{$reviews->mReviews[k].rating} of 5]
   </td>
  </tr>
  {/section}
 </table>
{else}
 <span class="SimpleText">
   <b>Be the first person to voice your opinion!</b> <br/>
 </span>
{/if}

{if $reviews->mEnableAddProductReviewForm}
{* add review form*}
<span class="SimpleText">
<br/>Add a review:<br/></span>
<form action="index.php?ProductID={$reviews->mProductId}" method="post">
 <input type="hidden" name="ProductID" value="{$reviews->mProductId}"/>
 <input type="hidden" name="DisplayReviews"/>
 <table class="CategoryListContent" width="300">
  <tr>
   <td>
    <span class="SimpleText">
     From: <b>{$reviews->mReviewerName}<b/><br/>
   </td>
  </tr>
  <tr>
   <td>
```

```
<textarea name="review" rows="3" cols="60">[Add your review here]</textarea>
    </td>
   </tr>
   <tr>
    <td>
     <table>
      <tr>
       <td width="100%">
        Your Rating:
        <input type="radio" name="rating" value="1"/> 1
        <input type="radio" name="rating" value="2"/> 2
        <input type="radio" name="rating" value="3" checked="checked"/> 3
        <input type="radio" name="rating" value="4"/> 4
        <input type="radio" name="rating" value="5"/> 5
       </td>
       <td>
        <input type="submit" name="AddProductReview" value="Add review"/>
       </td>
      </tr>
     </table>
    </td>
   </tr>
  </table>
 </form>
 {else}
  <span class="SimpleText">
   <b>You must log in to add a review.<b/><br/>
  </span>
 {/if}
```

2. Create the smarty_plugins/function.load_reviews.php file and add the following in it:

```php
<?php
// plugin function for the reviews function plugin
function smarty_function_load_reviews($params, $smarty)
{
  $reviews = new Reviews();
  $reviews->init();
  $smarty->assign($params['assign'], $reviews);
}

// class that handles product reviews
class Reviews
{
  public $mProductId;
  public $mReviews;
  public $mTotalReviews;
  public $mRevieweName;
```

```php
  public $mEnableAddProductReviewForm = false;
  function __construct()
  {
    if (isset($_GET['ProductID']))
      $this->mProductId = (int)$_GET['ProductID'];
    else
      trigger_error("ProductID not set", E_USER_ERROR);
  }
  public function init()
  {
    $bo_catalog = new BoCatalog();
    $bo_customer = new BoCustomer();
    // if visitor is logged in....
    if ($bo_customer->IsAuthenticated())
    {
      // check if visitor is adding a review
      if (isset($_POST['AddProductReview']))
        $bo_catalog->AddProductReview($this->mProductId,
                                      $_POST['review'],
                                      $_POST['rating']);
      // display "add review" form because visitor is registered
      $this->mEnableAddProductReviewForm = true;
      // get visitor's (reviewer's) name
      $customer_data = $bo_customer->GetCurrentCustomer();
      $this->mReviewerName = $customer_data['name'];
    }
    // get reviews for this product
    $this->mReviews = $bo_catalog->GetProductReviews($this->mProductId);
    // get the number of the reviews
    $this->mTotalReviews = count($this->mReviews);
  }
}
?>
```

3. Open `templates/product.tpl` and add the following lines at the end of it:

```
<br/><br/>
{include file="reviews.tpl"}
```

4. Load `index.php` in your browser, click on a product to view its product details page, and admire the results (see Figure 15-2). You must be logged in to add new reviews.

Mali Soccer

Mali Soccer (1964). This T-shirt remembers the 1964 Olympic games in Tokyo - do you?
(Shown on Small T-shirt).

Price: **$15.95**

[**Add to Cart**]

Continue Shopping

Customers who bought this also bought:

Danish Locomotive - Dane Train (1947). One hundred years of the Danish State Railway are
commemorated right here when you wear this beautiful "retro"...

Fast Express - Fast Express (U.S. - 1901). This is one of my favorite images, not least
because of the babes celebrating this locomtive in their ...

Brennerbahn - Brennerbahn (Austria - 1967). This T-shirt celebrates the first locomotive to
haul a train over the Brenner Pass. That's an accomp...

Be the first person to voice your opinion!
Add a review:

From: **Cristian Darie**

Your Rating: ○ 1 ○ 2 ⊙ 3 ○ 4 ○ 5   [Add review]

Figure 15-2. *The new product details page that allows adding product reviews*

How It Works: The reviews Componentized Template

The reviews componentized template takes care of both displaying the reviews and adding a
new review. The first part of the reviews.tpl file determines whether you have any reviews to
display for the current product. If you don't, a short message appears encouraging your visitor
to write the first review.

```
{if $reviews->mTotalReviews !=0}
 [a table with reviews]
{else}
 <span class="SimpleText">
  <b>Be the first person to voice your opinion!</b> <br/>
 </span>
{/if}
```

The second part of the template displays a form to add a review or a message that invites your visitor to "log in" to be able to add a review:

```
{if $reviews->mEnableAddProductReviewForm}
 [add review form]
{else}
 You must log in to add a review.
{/if}
```

The code from the function plugin is pretty straightforward and should not be a problem for you.

Summary

Yep, it was that simple. Although you might want to add certain improvements for your own solution (for example, allow the visitors to edit their reviews, or forbid them from adding more reviews), the base is there and it works as expected.

You're now all set to proceed to the final chapter of this book, where you'll learn how to sell items to your customer from Amazon.com by using XML Web Services.

CHAPTER 16

■■■

Connecting to Web Services

In the dynamic world of the Internet, sometimes it isn't enough to just have an important web presence; you also need to interact with functionality provided by third parties to achieve your goals. So far in this book, you already saw how to integrate external functionality to process payments from your customers.

In this chapter, you'll learn how to use functionality from an external source through a web service. A **web service** is a piece of functionality that is exposed through a web interface using standard Internet protocols such as HTTP. The messages exchanged by the client and the server are encoded using an XML-based protocol named SOAP (Simple Object Access Protocol), or by using REST (Representational State Transfer). These messages are sent over HTTP. You'll learn more about these technologies a bit later.

The beauty of using web services is that the client and the server can use any technology, any language, and any platform. As long as they exchange information with a standard protocol such as SOAP over HTTP, there is no problem if the client is a cell phone, and the server is a Java application running on a SUN server, for example.

The possibilities are exciting, and we recommend you purchase a book that specializes in web services to discover more about their world. Have a look at the list of public web services at http://www.xmethods.net to get an idea of the kinds of external functionality you can integrate into your application. You can find a number of working examples involving interfacing with Xmethod's Web Services in *Beginning PHP 5 and MySQL: From Novice to Professional* (Apress, 2004).

In this chapter, you'll learn how to integrate Amazon E-Commerce Service (formerly known as Amazon Web Services—the Web Services interface provided by Amazon.com), to sell Amazon.com products through your TShirtShop web site. You already have an e-commerce web site and your visitors buy T-shirts with stamp images because they are probably stamp collectors. You can go further and make some more money from their passion by incorporating some postal stamp-related books from Amazon.com into your site. For free? Oh no . . . You'll display Amazon.com's book details on your site, but the final checkout will be processed by Amazon.com, and Amazon.com will deliver in our bank account a small commission fee for purchases made from our web site. Sounds like easy money, doesn't it?

The rest of this chapter is divided into two parts. In the first part, you'll learn how to access Amazon E-Commerce Service (ECS); in the second part, you'll implement this functionality in the TShirtShop web site.

■**Tip** Because the code in this chapter is independent of the rest of the site, you only need the code from the first four chapters (so you have a working product catalog) to add the Amazon functionality to your TShirtShop web site. Of course, with minor adjustments you can also adapt this code to your own personal solutions.

Using Web Services

Most service providers (including Amazon.com) use SOAP or REST (or both) to expose web services functionality to Internet client programs. You can choose to make a web service request by using either REST or SOAP, and you get the exact same results with both options. In this chapter, you'll learn how to access ECS 4.0 using both REST and SOAP.

REST uses carefully crafted URLs with specific name-value pairs to call specific methods on the servers. You can find two useful articles about REST at `http://www.xml.com/pub/a/2004/08/11/rest.html` and `http://www.onlamp.com/pub/a/php/2003/10/30/amazon_rest.html`.

REST is considered to be the easiest way to communicate with the web services that expose this interface. Non-official sources say that 85 percent of ECS clients went the REST way. When using REST, all you have to do for a search on Amazon is to make a classical HTTP GET request and you'll receive the response in XML format.

SOAP is an XML-based standard for encoding the information transferred in a web service request or response. The SOAP protocol is fostered by a number of organizations, including powerful companies such as Microsoft, IBM, and Sun. You'll query the Amazon SOAP server using the excellent NuSOAP library to retrieve the same information you'd get using the REST method.

Using ECS, you can send the request either through REST or by sending a SOAP message. The web service will return an XML response with the data you requested.

You'll learn about REST and SOAP by playing with ECS. You can reach the official documentation for ECS at `http://www.amazon.com/webservices`. To access ECS, you need a *subscription ID*, which is like a password that identifies your account in the ECS system. Every request you make to ECS contains your *subscription ID*.

Register at `http://www.amazon.com/gp/ecs/registration/registration-form.html` before moving on to get a subscription ID (which will look something like 1R4EY7DQY0ATN521XXX2).

Accessing Amazon E-Commerce Service Using REST

REST web services are accessed by requesting a properly formed URL. Try the following link in your browser (don't forget to replace the string [Your subscription ID] with your real *subscription ID* that you got earlier):

```
http://webservices.amazon.com/onca/xml?Service=ECSProductData&
SubscriptionId=[Your subscription ID]&Operation=ItemLookup&
IdType=ASIN&ItemId=1590593928
```

Your browser will display an XML structure with information about the book you are reading now (see Figure 16-1).

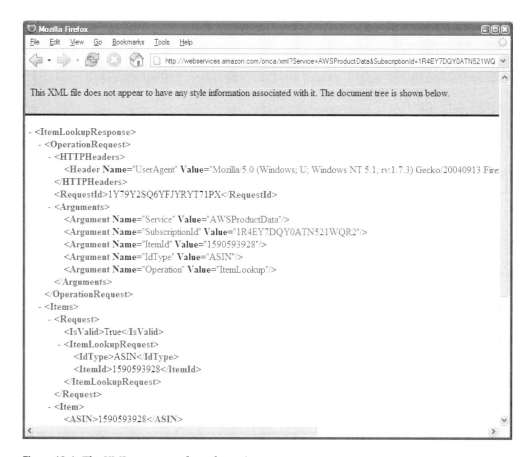

Figure 16-1. *The XML response of a web service request*

Pretty cool, huh? You have just seen REST in action. Every product in the Amazon database has a unique identifier called an ASIN (Amazon.com Standard Item Number). In case of books, the ASIN is the book's ISBN number (this book has the ASIN 1590593928).

The web service request you just made tells ECS the following: I have a subscription ID (SubscriptionId=[Your subscription ID]) and I want to make an item lookup operation (Operation=ItemLookup) to learn more about the product with the 1590593928 ASIN (IdType=ASIN&ItemId=1590593928).

You didn't get much information about this book in this example—no price or availability information and no links to the cover picture or customer reviews. ECS 4 introduces a finer control of the data you want to receive using Response Groups (a response group is a set of information about the product). At the end of your web service request link, add the following string to get more specific information about the book: &ResponseGroup=Request,Small, Images,OfferSummary. Go to the following address to get more specific data about the Amazon.com item:

```
http://webservices.amazon.com/onca/xml?Service=ECSProductData&
SubscriptionId=[Your subscription ID]&Operation=ItemLookup&
IdType=ASIN&ItemId=1590593928&ResponseGroup=Request,Small,Images,OfferSummary
```

The new XML response from Amazon.com includes more details about the Amazon.com item, as shown in Figure 16-2.

Figure 16-2. *The XML response of a web service request*

■**Note** Always remember to replace [Your subscription ID] with your subscription ID.

We have just mixed four response groups: Request, Small, Images, and OfferSummary. To learn more about the response groups, go to http://www.amazon.com/gp/ecs/sdk/main.html, click the API Reference link, and then click the Response Groups link. Here's the description for the four response groups used in the previous example:

- Request Response Group is a default response group in every kind of operation and it returns the list of name-value pairs you used to make the request.

- Small Response Group returns general item data (ASIN, item name, URL, and so on) about items included in the response. This is a default response group for an Item-Lookup operation (like we have in this example).

- Images Response Group gives you the addresses for the three pictures (small, medium, and large) for each item in the response.

- OfferSummary Response Group returns price information for each item in the response.

You can check the ECS 4 API's docs to see all the response groups you can use for an Item-Lookup operation.

Let's continue by learning how to make a REST request from PHP. One trivial way is to use the PHP file_get_contents() function, as you can see in the following little script:

```php
<?php
//tell the browser it is going to receive an XML document.
header('Content-type: text/xml');
/* DON'T FORGET to replace the string '[Your subscription ID]' with your
subscription ID in the following line */
$url = "http://webservices.amazon.com/onca/xml?Service=ECSProductData&" .
      "SubscriptionId=[Your subscription ID]&Operation=ItemLookup&" .
      "IdType=ASIN&ItemId=1590593928";
echo file_get_contents($url);
?>
```

To exercise and build more XML links, just study the examples in the "API Reference" section of the ECS 4 documentation. The material will show you how to do a variety of Amazon operations using REST.

Accessing Amazon E-Commerce Service Using SOAP

To access Amazon's SOAP server, you need a PHP SOAP library to compose correctly formed SOAP messages. Among the usual developer's choices are the following three PHP SOAP libraries: PHP-SOAP, PEAR SOAP, and NuSOAP. Because at the time this book was written the PHP-SOAP extension to PHP is still experimental and PEAR SOAP is buggy, we decided to use the popular NuSOAP library. Get nusoap.php from http://dietrich.ganx4.com/nusoap/index.php (click on the Download NuSOAP link) and place it in your data_objects directory.

To test accessing web services using SOAP, create the following test_soap.php file in your tshirtshop directory:

```php
<?php
// reference NuSOAP library
require_once 'data_objects/nusoap.php';
// initialize SOAP client object
$soap_client = new Soapclient
("http://webservices.amazon.com/AWSECommerceService/AWSECommerceService.wsdl", true);
// create a proxy so that WSDL methods can be accessed directly
$proxy = $soap_client->getProxy();
$proxy ->soap_defencoding = 'UTF-8';
$request =
  array('Keywords' => 'postal stamps',
        'SearchIndex' => 'Books');
$params['Request'] = $request;
$params['SubscriptionId'] = '[Your subscription ID]';
$result = $proxy->ItemSearch($params);
```

```
echo "<pre>";
print_r($result);
echo "</pre>";
?>
```

Load test_soap.php in your browser (don't forget to put your subscription ID in it). You'll get the first ten books' details as shown in Figure 16-3).

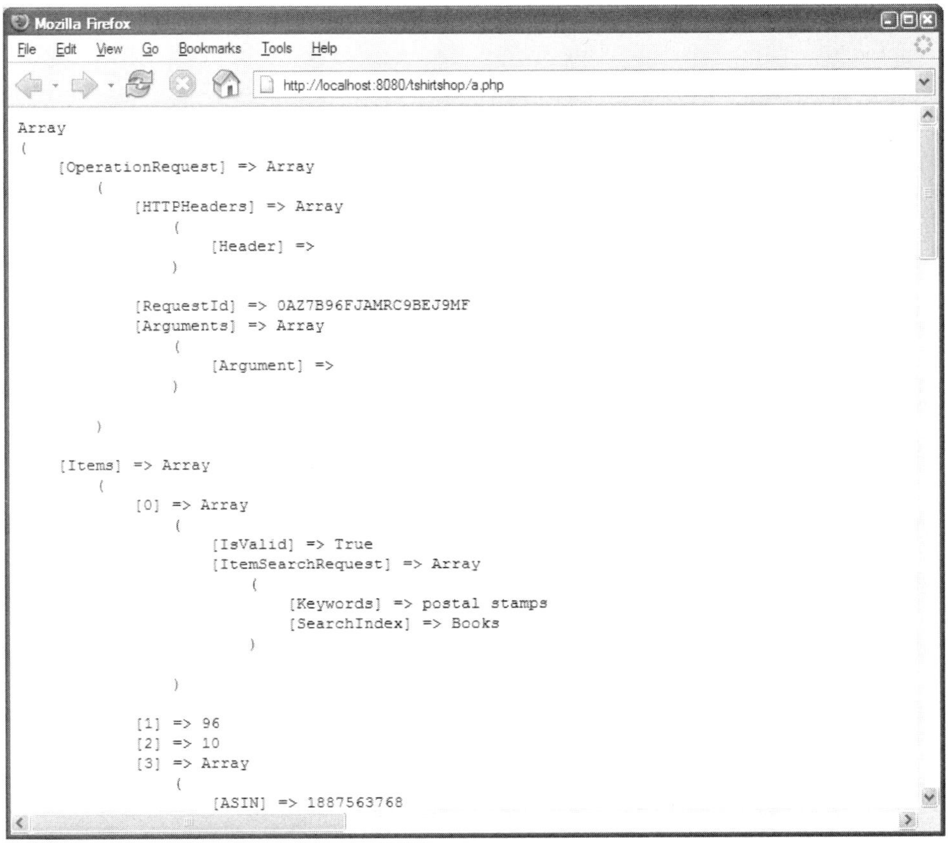

Figure 16-3. *The XML response of a web service request*

The code starts by creating a SOAP client object to the Amazon SOAP web service:

```
// initialize SOAP client object
$soap_client = new Soapclient
("http://webservices.amazon.com/AWSECommerceService/AWSECommerceService.wsdl", true);
```

The referenced WSDL (Web Services Definition Language) file describes all the functions and their parameters' types that Amazon SOAP server understands. The earlier created Amazon SOAP client object knows about all these functions and you can call them now using something like this:

```
$soap_client->call("method_name", ... parameters ...);
```

Although this way of accessing a web service method works, it's more convenient to create a proxy class that contains methods with the same names as the ones exposed by the web service, and that call their corresponding web service methods for you. You do this by creating a SOAP proxy object:

```
$proxy = $soap_client->getProxy();
```

Using this object, you can now call web service methods directly:

```
$result = $proxy->ItemSearch($params);
```

You needed the following line of code because NuSOAP encodes data by default using the ISO-8859-1 charset, and the ECS 4 SOAP Server needs UTF-8 encoding:

```
$proxy ->soap_defencoding = 'UTF-8';
```

The web service request does an `ItemSearch` operation on the "postal stamps" keywords in the "Books" store:

```
$request =
  array('Keywords' => 'postal stamps',
        'SearchIndex' => 'Books');
$params['Request'] = $request;
$params['SubscriptionId'] = '[Your subscription ID]';
$result = $proxy->ItemSearch($params);
```

Integrating Amazon E-Commerce Service with TShirtShop

The goal is to bring some books related to postal stamps from Amazon to your store. You'll build a special department with no categories that will display some book info (cover image, title, authors, and price). Each book will have a Buy from Amazon link that allows your visitor to buy the book from Amazon.com. If you apply for an Amazon Associates ID account, you'll get a small commission from this.

■**Note** An Amazon Associate ID gives you the possibility to get a small commission when someone buys a product via your interface. You can get an ID by visiting

http://associates.amazon.com/exec/panama/associates/apply/.

Let's look at what you're going to build, as shown in Figure 16-4.

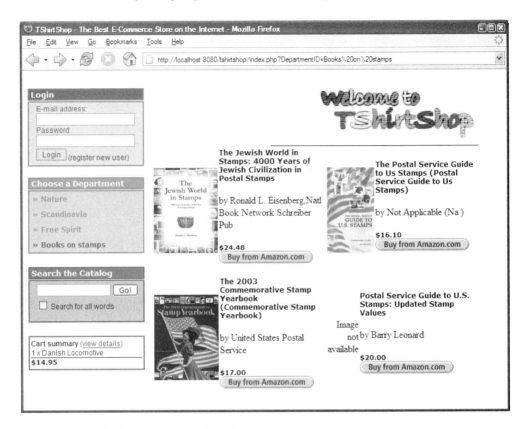

Figure 16-4. *Displaying Amazon products in TShirtShop*

The following link engages a REST search for Amazon Books on the "postal card" keywords and returns the first ten books data sorted by their sales rank:

```
http://webservices.amazon.com/onca/xml?Service=ECSProductData&
Operation=ItemSearch&SubscriptionId=[Your subscription ID]&
Keywords=postal+stamps&SearchIndex=Books&
ResponseGroup=Request%2CMedium%2CImages%2COffers&Sort=salesrank
```

From these ten books, we will place on our site only the ones available for purchase and with cover images. As you can see in the previous figure, when this book was written only three books (out of ten) managed to appear in our Amazon department.

There's one more problem we need to discuss. When you downloaded the ECS Developers' kit, you accepted a license agreement that I bet you didn't read very carefully. Among other things, it says that you must cache the data you receive from Amazon. It also says that you should not cache data for more than 1 hour and the images for more than 24 hours. So, you have to implement a caching mechanism. The simplest way to cache this data is by using the Cache_Lite class that comes with PEAR.

Note For more details about `Cache_Lite` than we provide in this chapter, visit its official intro tutorial at `http://pear.php.net/manual/en/package.caching.cache-lite.intro.php`.

It's possible that your PEAR installation doesn't include the `Cache_Lite` package, so you should get it from the official PEAR web site, at `http://pear.php.net/package/Cache_Lite`, unzip the archive into a directory, and then copy the `Lite.php` file from the archive into the `cache` subdirectory in the `PEAR` directory.

You need to install one more PEAR package called `XML_Serializer`, which you can get from `http://pear.php.net/package/XML_Serializer`. Unzip the archive and copy the `Serializer.php` and `Unserializer.php` files into the `Xml` subdirectory in the `PEAR` directory. The PEAR `XML_Serializer` class creates XML documents from complex data structures and vice-versa. You'll use the `Unserializer` class from the `XML_Serializer` package to generate an associative array from an XML input string.

Implementing the Data Tier

In the data tier, you'll add the code that accesses the ECS system.

Exercise: Adding ECS Communication Code to the Data Tier

Follow these steps to add the ECS communication code to the data tier:

1. Install the `Cache_Lite` and `XML Serializer` packages as explained earlier in this chapter.

2. Create the `amazon_data_cache` and `amazon_images_cache` subdirectories in your project root home (the `tshirtshop` folder). Make sure your web server has write permission in those newly created subdirectories.

3. Add the following code in your `include/config.inc.php` file:

```
/* AMAZON E-COMMERCE SERVICE */
//define("AMAZON_METHOD", "REST");
define("AMAZON_METHOD", "SOAP");
define("AMAZON_WSDL",
    "http://webservices.amazon.com/AWSECommerceService/AWSECommerceService.wsdl");
define("AMAZON_REST_BASE_URL",
    "http://webservices.amazon.com/onca/xml?Service=AWSECommerceService");
define("AMAZON_DATA_CACHE", SITE_ROOT . '/amazon_data_cache/');
define("AMAZON_IMAGES_CACHE", SITE_ROOT . '/amazon_images_cache/');
/* Set Amazon subscription ID - required */
define("AMAZON_SUBSCRIPTION_ID", "[Your subscription ID]");
/* Set Amazon associates tag - optional */
define("AMAZON_ASSOCIATES_TAG", "[Your amazon associates tag]");
define("AMAZON_SEARCH_KEYWORDS", "postal stamps");
define("AMAZON_SEARCH_NODE", "Books");
```

4. Create a new file named do_amazon.php in the data_objects folder, and add the following code to it. The single public method, which will be called from the upper tiers, is GetAmazonProducts, while the others are private methods for internal use that support the functionality of GetAmazonProducts.

```php
<?php
// data tier class for accessing ECS
class DoAmazon
{
  // retrieves Amazon products for sending to presentation tier
  public function GetAmazonProducts()
  {
    // retrieve XML data from Amazon or from cache
    $result = $this->CacheAndGetAmazonData();
    // retrieve new Amazon images every 24 hours
    $this->CacheAmazonImages($result);
    // initializes Array object
    $filtered_results = array();
    // filters results
    $filtered_results = $this->AmazonDataFilterAndFormat($result);
    // returns results
    return $filtered_results;
  }

  // returns Amazon data by calling ECS or by using cache
  private function CacheAndGetAmazonData()
  {
    // references Cache_Lite library
    require_once 'cache/Lite.php';
    // Set an id for amazon data cache (can be anything)
    $id_amazon_data = 'amazon_data_cache_id';
    // Set data cache options
    $options_amazon_data =
      array('cacheDir' => AMAZON_DATA_CACHE,
            'lifeTime' => 3600,
            'automaticSerialization' => true);
    // Create a Cache_Lite object
    $cache_lite_data = new Cache_Lite($options_amazon_data);
    // if the cache contains recent data do nothing
    if ($result = $cache_lite_data->get($id_amazon_data))
    {
      // do nothing
    }
    else
    // cache doesn't contain recent data, so get new data from ECS
    {
      // use SOAP to get data
      if (AMAZON_METHOD == "SOAP")
```

```
    $result = $this->GetAmazonDataWithSoap();
    // use REST to get data
    else
      $result = $this->GetAmazonDataWithRest();
    // save cache data
    $cache_lite_data->save($result);
  }
  // returns XML document
  return $result;
}

// retrieves product pictures if they are older than 24 hours
private function CacheAmazonImages($data)
{
  // references Cache_Lite library
  require_once 'cache/Lite.php';
  // Set an id for amazon images cache (can be anything)
  $id_amazon_images = 'amazon_images_cache_id';
  // Set images cache options
  $options_amazon_images =
    array('cacheDir' => AMAZON_DATA_CACHE,
          'lifeTime' => 3600*24);
  // Create a Cache_Lite object
  $cache_lite_images = new Cache_Lite($options_amazon_images);
  // Test if there is a valid cache for this id
  if ($cache_lite_images->get($id_amazon_images))
  {
    // do nothing
  }
  else
  {
    $this->DownloadAmazonImages($data);
    $cache_lite_images->save("amazon images");
  }
}

// call ECS using REST
private function GetAmazonDataWithRest()
{
  // Include PEAR::XML_Unserializer
  require_once 'XML/Unserializer.php';
  $params =
    array('Operation'      => 'ItemSearch',
          'SubscriptionId' => AMAZON_SUBSCRIPTION_ID,
          'Keywords'       => AMAZON_SEARCH_KEYWORDS,
          'SearchIndex'    => AMAZON_SEARCH_NODE,
          'ResponseGroup'  => 'Request,Medium,Images,Offers',
          'Sort'           => 'salesrank');
```

```php
      $query_string = '&';
      foreach ($params as $key => $value)
        $query_string .= "$key=" . urlencode($value) . "&";
      $amazon_url = AMAZON_REST_BASE_URL . $query_string;
      // Get the XML response using REST
      $amazon_xml = file_get_contents($amazon_url);
      // Create an instance of XML_Unserializer
      $unserializer = new XML_Unserializer();
      // Unserialize the XML
      $status = $unserializer->unserialize($amazon_xml);
      // Check for errors
      if (PEAR::isError($status))
        trigger_error($status->getMessage());
      // Get the PHP data structure from the XML
      $result = $unserializer->getUnserializedData();
      return $result;
    }

    // call ECS using SOAP
    private function GetAmazonDataWithSoap()
    {
      require_once 'nusoap.php';
      $soap_client = new soapclient(AMAZON_WSDL,true);
      // create a proxy so that WSDL methods can be accessed directly
      $proxy = $soap_client->getProxy();
      $proxy ->soap_defencoding = 'UTF-8';
      // set up an array containing input parameters to be
      // passed to the remote procedure
      $request =
        array('Keywords'       => AMAZON_SEARCH_KEYWORDS,
              'SearchIndex'    => AMAZON_SEARCH_NODE,
              'ResponseGroup' => 'Request,Medium,Images,Offers',
              'Sort'           => 'salesrank');
      $params['Request'] = $request;
      $params['SubscriptionId'] = AMAZON_SUBSCRIPTION_ID;
      // invoke the method
      $result = $proxy->ItemSearch($params);
      return $result;
    }

    // downloads Amazon product images into the cache
    private function DownloadAmazonImages($result)
    {
      // No valid cache found (you have to download product images)
      for ($i=0; $i<count($result['Items']['Item']); $i++)
      {
        $temp = $result['Items']['Item'][$i];
```

```
    if (!isset($temp['MediumImage']['URL'])
        || substr($temp['MediumImage']['URL'],
                strlen($temp['MediumImage']['URL'])-3) == "gif")
    {
      $result['Items']['Item'][$i]['MediumImage']['URL']="";
      continue;
    }
    $image_name = substr($temp['MediumImage']['URL'],
                        strripos($temp['MediumImage']['URL'],
                        "/") + 1);
    $image = file_get_contents($temp['MediumImage']['URL']);
    if (strlen($image)<1024)
    {
      $result['Items']['Item'][$i]['MediumImage']['URL'] = "";
      continue;
    }
    file_put_contents('amazon_images_cache/' . $image_name, $image);
  }
}


// places an "image not available" picture for products with no image,
// removes products that are not available for buying, and saves the
// results in an array with a simple structure for easier handling
// at the upper levels
private function AmazonDataFilterAndFormat($result)
{
  // variable k is the index of the $new_res array, which will contain
  // the Amazon products to be displayed in TShirtShop
  $k = 0;
  // analyze all products retrieved from ECS and save the ones that are
  // available for purchase into the $new_res array
  for ($i=0; $i<count($result['Items']['Item']); $i++)
  {
    $availability =
$result['Items']['Item'][$i]['Offers']['Offer']["OfferListing"]["Availability"];
    // test if the product is available
    if (strncmp($availability,
                "Usually ships",
                strlen("Usually ships")) == 0
    || (strncmp($availability,
                "Available",
                strlen("Available")) == 0 )
    || (strncmp($availability,
                "In stock",
                strlen("In stock")) == 0))
    {
      // if the product is available, save it into the $new_res array
```

```
            $temp = $result['Items']['Item'][$i];
            // save product's image, if it exists
            if (isset($temp['MediumImage']['URL']))
            {
              $image_url = $temp['MediumImage']['URL'];
              $image_name = substr($image_url, strripos($image_url, "/") + 1);
              if ($temp['MediumImage']['URL'] != '')
                $new_res[$k]['image'] = 'amazon_images_cache/' . $image_name;
              else
                $new_res[$k]['image'] = 'images/not_available.jpg';
            }
            // if product has no image, use generic "image not available" picture
            else
              $new_res[$k]['image'] = 'images/not_available.jpg';
            // save name, price, authors, and asin info into the $new_res array
            $new_res[$k]['item_name'] = $temp['ItemAttributes']['Title'];
            $new_res[$k]['price'] =
   $temp['Offers']["Offer"]["OfferListing"]["Price"]["FormattedPrice"];
          $new_res[$k]['Authors'] = isset($temp['ItemAttributes']['Author']) ?
                                    $temp['ItemAttributes']['Author'] : "";
            $new_res[$k]['Asin'] = $temp['ASIN'];
            $k++;
          }
        }
      return $new_res;
    }
  } //end DoAmazon
  ?>
```

How It Works: Communicating with ECS

The only public Amazon data-tier method is GetAmazonProducts() that takes care to cache
Amazon data and retrieve it to the business tier. Its functionality is quite clear, as it uses a
number of helper methods to get the work done:

```
// retrieves Amazon products for sending to presentation tier
public function GetAmazonProducts()
{
  // retrieve XML data from Amazon or from cache
  $result = $this->CacheAndGetAmazonData();
  // retrieve new Amazon images every 24 hours
  $this->CacheAmazonImages($result);
  // initializes Array object
  $filtered_results = array();
  // filters results
  $filtered_results = $this->AmazonDataFilterAndFormat($result);
  // returns results
  return $filtered_results;
}
```

The CacheAndGetAmazonData() and CacheAmazonImages() functions use Cache_Lite cache objects to cache data retrieved from Amazon.

CacheAndGetAmazonData() uses two other helper methods (GetAmazonDataWithSoap() and GetAmazonDataWithRest()) to get data from Amazon, and caches this data with a cache expiry time of one hour. When called, it checks whether the data is in cache, in which case it returns it from there. If the data is not in cache, it contacts ECS to get new data.

Every cache you create with the Cache_Lite library must have a unique ID because you can use as many caches as you want. You create two caches, one for data with a lifetime of one hour, and one for images with a lifetime of 24 hours. The data cache will contain the data retrieved from ECS, while the images data doesn't actually contain anything (you'll store the images fetched from Amazon to the file system instead of the cache object), but you'll use the images cache as a counter to decide when you need to get new sets of images from Amazon.

The Cache_Lite object is created by passing it an associative array that contains cache configuration options. The cacheDir option specifies the folder the Cache_Lite object should use to save its data. Amazon's data is cached for one hour (3,600 seconds), so the lifeTime option is set accordingly. Because the data you get from Amazon is kept in an associative array, you need to serialize this array into a string. That's why the automaticSerialization option is set to true here. The following code snip shows how the cache object is initialized, and then how the cached data is retrieved from the cache into the $result variable. Note the highlighted piece of code uses the assignment operator (=), not the equal operator (==), to do the required operation and check whether the result is not void:

```
// returns Amazon data by calling ECS or by using cache
private function CacheAndGetAmazonData()
{
  // references Cache_Lite library
  require_once 'cache/Lite.php';
  // Set an id for amazon data cache (can be anything)
  $id_amazon_data = 'amazon_data_cache_id';
  // Set data cache options
  $options_amazon_data =
    array('cacheDir' => AMAZON_DATA_CACHE,
          'lifeTime' => 3600,
          'automaticSerialization' => true);
  // Create a Cache_Lite object
  $cache_lite_data = new Cache_Lite($options_amazon_data);
  // if the cache contains recent data do nothing
  if ($result = $cache_lite_data->get($id_amazon_data))
  {
    // do nothing
  }
```

If no valid cache is found, you must get new data from Amazon. Depending on the AMAZON_METHOD value, you get the data using either the SOAP protocol or REST:

```
  else
  // cache doesn't contain recent data, so get new data from ECS
  {
```

```
    // use SOAP to get data
    if (AMAZON_METHOD == "SOAP")
      $result = $this->GetAmazonDataWithSoap();
    // use REST to get data
    else
      $result = $this->GetAmazonDataWithRest();
    // save cache data
    $cache_lite_data->save($result);
  }
  // returns XML document
  return $result;
}
```

Let's have a look now at `GetAmazonDataWithRest()` and `GetAmazonDataWithSoap()`, which are the methods that do the actual communication with ECS.

The `AMAZON_METHOD` constant you defined in `config.inc.php` instructs whether ECS will be contacted through REST or SOAP. The value of that constant (which should be REST or SOAP) decides whether `GetAmazonDataWithRest()` or `GetAmazonDataWithSoap()` will be used to contact Amazon. No matter which method you choose, the results should be the same.

`GetAmazonDataWithRest()` retrieves web service data using REST. It starts by constructing the required query string by joining the individual parameters you want to send to Amazon:

```
$params =
  array('Operation'     => 'ItemSearch',
        'SubscriptionId' => AMAZON_SUBSCRIPTION_ID,
        'Keywords'      => AMAZON_SEARCH_KEYWORDS,
        'SearchIndex'   => AMAZON_SEARCH_NODE,
        'ResponseGroup' => 'Request,Medium,Images,Offers',
        'Sort'          => 'salesrank');
$query_string = '&';
foreach ($params as $key => $value)
  $query_string .= "$key=" . urlencode($value) . "&";
```

The complete Amazon URL that you need to call is composed of the base URL (which you saved as a constant in `config.inc.php`) to which you append the query string you just built:

```
$amazon_url = AMAZON_REST_BASE_URL . $query_string;
```

Using the `file_get_contents()` function, you make a simple HTTP GET request to Amazon. It's just like typing the address in your browser:

```
// Get the XML response using REST
$amazon_xml = file_get_contents($amazon_url);
```

The `$amazon_xml` variable will contain a string with the returned XML data. To make further processing easier, you transform this data into an associative array using PEAR's `XML_Unserializer` class:

```
$amazon_xml = file_get_contents($amazon_url);
// Create an instance of XML_Unserializer
$unserializer = new XML_Unserializer();
```

```
// Unserialize the XML
$status = $unserializer->unserialize($amazon_xml);
// Check for errors
if (PEAR::isError($status))
  trigger_error($status->getMessage());
// Get the PHP data structure from the XML
$result = $unserializer->getUnserializedData();
return $result;
```

The GetAmazonDataWithSoap() method has similar functionality as GetAmazonDataWithRest(), but it makes the ItemSearch operation using the SOAP protocol. The logic this method uses to contact ECS is the same as in the page you wrote earlier in this chapter.

The data retrieved from Amazon is processed by GetAmazonProducts() with a call to a helper method named AmazonDataFilterAndFormat(). The AmazonDataFilterAndFormat() method takes the Amazon search results and builds a new array in the $new_res variable with the items that are available for purchase. At the time of this writing, the Availability field for items that are available for purchase starts with either "Usually ships", "Available", or "In stock" and also makes the item image address point to the local stored images.

Let's go back to GetAmazonProducts() now. After caching the data retrieved from Amazon, it continues by caching the image files.

You store the cached images using another cache id (you use another cache for images), because you need to cache them for a different period of time (24 hours). You save the images in the file system instead of the cache, but you use the cache object as a timer that tells you when to retrieve new sets of images from Amazon.

```
// retrieves product pictures if they are older than 24 hours
private function CacheAmazonImages($data)
{
  // references Cache_Lite library
  require_once 'cache/Lite.php';
  // Set an id for amazon images cache (can be anything)
  $id_amazon_images = 'amazon_images_cache_id';
  // Set images cache options
  $options_amazon_images =
    array('cacheDir' => AMAZON_DATA_CACHE,
          'lifeTime' => 3600*24);
  // Create a Cache_Lite object
  $cache_lite_images = new Cache_Lite($options_amazon_images);
  // Test if there is a valid cache for this id
  if ($cache_lite_images->get($id_amazon_images))
  {
    // do nothing
  }
  else
  {
    $this->DownloadAmazonImages($data);
    $cache_lite_images->save("amazon images");
  }
}
```

DownloadAmazonImages() is the method that will download valid cover images to the folder specified by the AMAZON_IMAGES_CACHE constant. The method searches through the results returned by ECS and detects the books that don't have valid cover images. Amazon keeps all the items images in JPEG format and it generates a 1 pixel by 1 pixel GIF file when there's no image available:

```
for ($i=0; $i<count($result['Items']['Item']); $i++)
{
  $temp = $result['Items']['Item'][$i];
  if (!isset($temp['MediumImage']['URL'])
      || substr($temp['MediumImage']['URL'],
              strlen($temp['MediumImage']['URL'])-3) == "gif")
  {
    $result['Items']['Item'][$i]['MediumImage']['URL']="";
    continue;
  }
```

The method then gets the book image into a binary variable:

```
$image_name = substr($temp['MediumImage']['URL'],
                    strripos($temp['MediumImage']['URL'],
                    "/") + 1);
$image = file_get_contents($temp['MediumImage']['URL']);
```

Images that are smaller than 1,024 bytes are not considered valid:

```
if (strlen($image)<1024)
{
  $result['Items']['Item'][$i]['MediumImage']['URL'] = "";
  continue;
}
```

The last thing you do is download the book image to your server:

```
file_put_contents(AMAZON_IMAGES_CACHE . $image_name, $image);
```

Implementing the Business Tier

Because all the hard work is done by the data tier, the business logic is very simple here. Create a new file named bo_amazon.php in the business_objects folder, and write the following code in it:

```
<?php
// reference the data tier
require_once SITE_ROOT . '/data_objects/do_amazon.php';
// business tier class for ECS interaction
class BoAmazon
{
```

```php
  public function GetAmazonProducts()
  {
    $mDoAmazon = new DoAmazon();
    $result = $mDoAmazon->GetAmazonProducts();
    return $result;
  }
}
// end BoAmazon
?>
```

Implementing the Presentation Tier

Let's have another look at what we want to achieve in Figure 16-5.

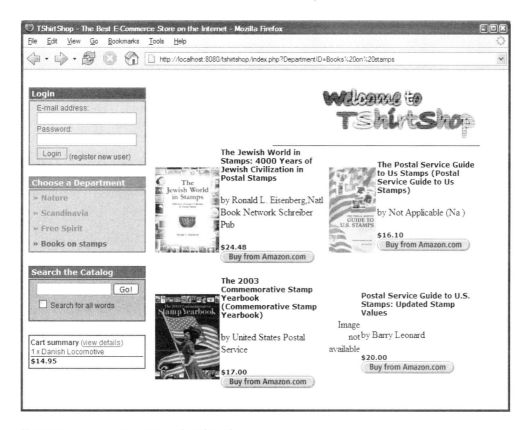

Figure 16-5. *Integrating ECS with TShirtShop*

As you can see, there are three books on this page and one of them doesn't have a picture. So another seven books from Amazon that we received info about are not available for purchase. This is true at the time of this writing and you are probably getting different results. Let's create the componentized template that will display the books and then modify the departments_list componentized template to include this new department.

Exercise: Displaying Amazon.com products in TShirtShop

To display Amazon.com products in TShirtShop, follow these steps:

1. Add a new file named `amazon_products_list.tpl` in the `templates` folder of your project:

```
{load_amazon_products_list assign="amazon_products_list"}
<table cellspacing="0" border="0">
  <tr>
  {section name=k2 loop=$amazon_products_list->mProducts}
  {if $smarty.section.k2.index % 2 == 0}
  </tr>
  <tr>
  {/if}
    <td>
     <table cellPadding="0" align="left">
      <tr>
       <td align="right">
         <img src="{$amazon_products_list->mProducts[k2].image}"
              border="0" alt="Image not available"/></a>
    </td>
     <td vAlign="middle" width="200">
      <span class="ProductName">
       {$amazon_products_list->mProducts[k2].item_name}
         </span>
         <br/><br/>
          by {$amazon_products_list->mProducts[k2].authors_string}
         <br/><br/>
         </span>
         <span class="ProductPrice">
          {$amazon_products_list->mProducts[k2].price}
         </span>
         <br/>
         <form method="post" action=
"http://buybox.amazon.com/o/dt/assoc/handle-buy-box=
{$amazon_products_list->mProducts[k2].Asin}">
             <input type="hidden" value="1"
                name="asin.{$amazon_products_list->mProducts[k2].Asin}"/>
             <input type="hidden" name="tag-value"
                value="{$amazon_products_list->mAssocTag}"/>
             <input type="hidden" name="tag_value"
                value="{$amazon_products_list->mAssocTag}"/>
             <input type="image" name="submit.add-to-cart"
                value="Buy from Amazon.com" border="0"
                alt="Buy from Amazon.com" src=
"http://rcm-images.amazon.com/images/G/01/associates/add-to-cart.gif"/>
         </form>
         </td>
```

```
        </tr>
      </table>
    </td>
  {/section}
 </tr>
</table>
```

2. Create a new file named function.load_amazon_products_list.php in the smarty_plugins folder and add the following code in it:

```php
<?php
// plugin functions inside plugin files must be named: smarty_type_name
function smarty_function_load_amazon_products_list($params, $smarty)
{
  $amazon_products_list = new AmazonProductsList();
  $amazon_products_list->init();
  // assign template variable
  $smarty->assign($params['assign'], $amazon_products_list);
}
// class that handles receiving ECS data
class AmazonProductsList
{
   /* public variables available in smarty template */
   public $mProducts;
   public $amAssocTag;
   /* private stuff */
   private $mBoAmazon;
   // constructor
   function __construct()
   {
     $this->mBoAmazon = new BoAmazon();
   }
   // init
   function init()
   {
     $this->mProducts = $this->mBoAmazon->GetAmazonProducts();
     for ($i=0;$i<count($this->mProducts);$i++)
       if (is_array($this->mProducts[$i]['Authors']))
         $this->mProducts[$i]['authors_string'] =
                 implode(',', $this->mProducts[$i]['Authors']);
       else
         $this->mProducts[$i]['authors_string'] =
                 $this->mProducts[$i]['Authors'];
       $this->mAssocTag=AMAZON_ASSOCIATES_TAG;
   } //end init
} //end class
?>
```

3. Add the following two configuration lines at the end of your `config.inc.php` file:

```
// Amazon.com department configuration options
define("AMAZON_DEPARTMENT_TITLE", "Books on stamps");
define("AMAZON_DEPARTMENT_DESCRIPTION", "Books on stamps from Amazon.com");
```

4. Modify the `departments_list.tpl` template file to add the "Amazon books" department. Add these lines at the end of the file:

```
      <br/>
    {/section}
     {if $departments_list->mAmazonSelected}
        {assign var=class_d value="DepartmentSelected"}
     {else}
        {assign var=class_d value="DepartmentUnselected"}
     {/if}
     <a class="{$class_d}"
        href="{$departments_list->mAmazonDepartmentOnClick}">
        &raquo; {$departments_list->mAmazonDepartment}</a>
    </td>
  </tr>
</table>
{* end departments list *}
```

5. Update `smarty_plugins/function.load_departments_list.php` as highlighted in this code snippet:

```
// Manages the departments list
class DepartmentsList
{
  /* public variables available in departments_list.tpl Smarty template */
  public $mDepartments;
  public $mSelectedDepartment;
  public $mAmazonSelected = false;
  /* private members */
  private $mBoCatalog;

  // constructor initializes business tier object
  // and reads query string parameter
  function __construct()
  {
    // creating the middle tier object
    $this->mBoCatalog = new BoCatalog();
    // if DepartmentID exists in the query string, we're visiting a department
    if (isset($_GET['DepartmentID']))
      $this->mSelectedDepartment = (int)$_GET['DepartmentID'];
    else
```

```
    $this->mSelectedDepartment = -1;
  // check if the Amazon department is selected
  if ((isset($_GET['DepartmentID'])) &&
      ((string)$_GET['DepartmentID']==AMAZON_DEPARTMENT_TITLE))
      $this->mAmazonSelected = true;
}
...
```

6. Add the following lines at the end of the init() method of the DepartmentsList class in function.load_departments_list.php:

```
// Amazon stuff
$this->mAmazonDepartment = AMAZON_DEPARTMENT_TITLE;
$this->mAmazonDepartmentOnClick =
          "index.php?DepartmentID=" . AMAZON_DEPARTMENT_TITLE;
```

7. Update index.php to reference the new business tier class:

```
// Load Business Tier
require_once SITE_ROOT . '/business_objects/bo_catalog.php';
require_once SITE_ROOT . '/business_objects/bo_shopping_cart.php';
require_once SITE_ROOT . '/business_objects/bo_customer.php';
require_once SITE_ROOT . '/business_objects/bo_amazon.php';
```

8. Modify index.php file to load the newly created componentized template:

```
...
$categoriesCell = "blank.tpl";
// load department details if visiting a department
if (isset($_GET['DepartmentID']))
{
  if ((string)$_GET['DepartmentID'] == AMAZON_DEPARTMENT_TITLE)
    $pageContentsCell = "amazon_products_list.tpl";
  else
  {
    $pageContentsCell = "department.tpl";
    $categoriesCell = "categories_list.tpl";
  }
}
if (isset($_GET['Search']))
  $pageContentsCell="search_results.tpl";
if (isset($_GET['ProductID']))
  $pageContentsCell = "product.tpl";
...
```

9. Load index.php in your browser and then click on your newly created "Amazon books" department.

How It Works: Displaying Amazon.com Products in TShirtShop

In this exercise, you simply updated TShirtShop to display Amazon.com products by employing the techniques you studied in the first part of the chapter. The new functionality isn't especially complex, but the possibilities are exciting. Feel free to play with the code and experiment with the whole area of functionality that Amazon.com (and other companies) offer you.

Summary

In this chapter, you learned how to access Amazon E-Commerce Service using REST and SOAP. You will be able to use the same techniques when accessing any kind of external functionality exposed through these protocols.

Congratulations, you have just finished your journey into learning about building e-commerce web sites with PHP 5 and MySQL. You have the knowledge to build your own customized solutions, perhaps even more interesting and powerful than what we showed you in this book. We hope you enjoyed reading this book, and we wish you good luck with your own personal PHP 5 and MySQL projects!

PART 4

Appendixes

■ ■ ■

Installing Apache, PHP, MySQL, and phpMyAdmin

In this appendix, you'll learn how to install

- Apache 2

- PHP 5 and the extra modules required for this book

- MySQL 4

- phpMyAdmin

Later in this chapter, we'll cover detailed installation instructions for Windows and Unix users. But first, let's see some general information about installing all the stuff on Windows and Unix.

Because highly sensitive data such as credit card information must travel safely over the Web, it's critical to host your application on an SSL-powered web server. The problem is that installing an SSL-enabled Apache on Windows is pretty tricky. In Linux, it's easier to configure an SSL-enabled Apache, but it's harder to configure PHP with all the features required for your site.

When hosting your application, you'll need to find a hosting company to supply you with the required software. In the development stage, the easiest way to solve these logistical problems is to use XAMPP, which is an Apache distribution with many useful applications, including the required PHP and MySQL modules for this project. You can get XAMPP from http://www.apachefriends.org/en/xampp.html. In a matter of minutes, you'll get an SSL-powered Apache with MySQL 4 and PHP 5 up and ready on your Windows or Unix system. If you feel comfortable installing all the required software manually instead of using XAMPP, then keep reading this appendix.

■**Note** Unix users should note that XAMPP doesn't contain the pfpro library used to access the VeriSign Payflow Pro system. If you want to use pfpro when you get to Chapter 14, you will still need to compile PHP manually even if you used XAMPP until that point.

Preparing your Windows Playground

In this section, you'll learn how to install Apache, PHP 5, and MySQL 4 on your development machine. Let's take them one by one.

Installing Apache 2

If you want to have an SSL-powered Apache, follow the steps shown in the excellent "Apache + SSL HOWTO" page at `http://raibledesigns.com/wiki/Wiki.jsp?page=ApacheSSL`. If you don't need SSL, just read on and you'll still be able to complete this book without an SSL-enabled Apache.

Download the latest Win32 Binary (MSI Installer) version of the Apache HTTP Server from `http://httpd.apache.org/download.cgi`. At the time of this writing, the .msi file corresponding to the latest version is `apache_2.0.52-win32-x86-no_ssl.msi`. Download the file and execute it.

At install time, you'll be given the option to choose the location your Apache web server should be installed. By default, this location is `C:\Program Files\Apache Group\Apache2\`, but you can choose a more convenient location (such as `C:\Apache`) that will make your life working with Apache a tad easier.

After accepting the license agreement and reading the introductory text, you're asked to enter your server's information (see Figure A-1).

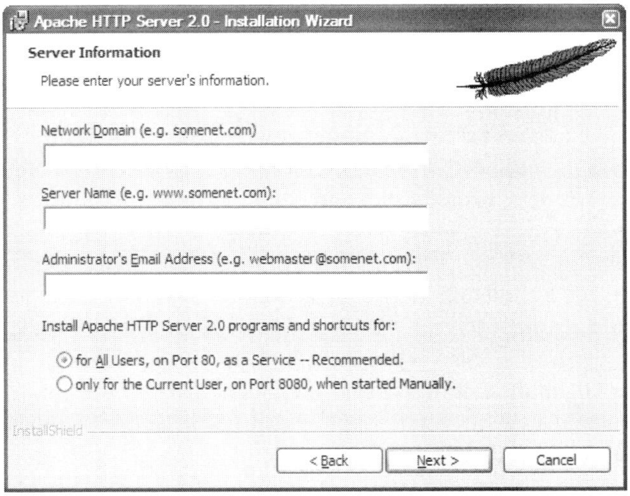

Figure A-1. *Apache HTTP Server 2.0 Installation Wizard*

If you're not sure about how to complete the form, just use "localhost" for the first two fields, and write an e-mail address for the last. You can change this information later by editing the `httpd.conf` file (located in `C:\Program Files\Apache Group\Apache2\conf\httpd.conf` by default.

If you already have a web server (such as IIS) working on port 80, you'll need to install Apache on a different port. During installation, you have an option that specifies Apache should work "only for Current User, on Port 8080, when started Manually." If you choose that option, you will need to start the Apache service manually by going to the folder you installed Apache to (probably \Program Files\Apache Group\Apache2\bin), and typing

```
apache -k install
```

■**Note** Because on our development machines we also have IIS working on Windows, in the book's figures you'll see TShirtShop web addresses that start with http://localhost:8080/tshirtshop.

After installing the Apache service, you'll be able to see it in the Apache Service Monitor program (which is accessible from the taskbar) as shown in Figure A-2, which also allows you to start, stop, or restart the Apache service. You'll need to restart (or stop and then start) the service after making changes to the httpd.conf configuration file.

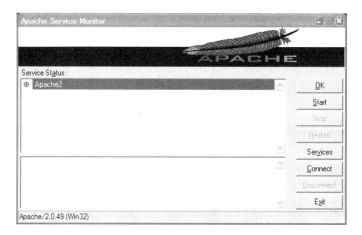

Figure A-2. *The Apache Service Monitor Window*

After making sure the Apache2 service is started and running, test to make sure it works okay. If you installed it on port 80, browse to http://localhost/. If you installed it on 8080, go to http://localhost:8080/. You should see an Apache welcome message.

Installing PHP 5

Start by downloading the latest PHP 5 Windows binaries from http://www.php.net/downloads.php. Don't use a PHP 5 installer because it won't include the external extensions needed for TShirtShop.

After you download the Windows binaries, follow these steps to install PHP:

1. Unzip the file (which should be named something like `php-5.0.2-win32.zip`) into a folder named `C:\PHP\`. You can choose another name or location for this folder if you want.

2. Copy `php5ts.dll` from `C:\PHP` to `C:\Windows\System32` (or to your `System32` folder, if it has a different location).

3. Copy `php.ini-recommended` from `C:\PHP` to your Windows folder (`C:\Windows`), renaming it as `php.ini`.

4. Uncomment the following lines from `C:\Windows\php.ini` to enable the `mhash`, `mcrypt`, and `curl` extensions:

   ```
   extension=php_mhash.dll
   extension=php_mcrypt.dll
   extension=php_curl.dll
   ```

5. Copy libmhash.dll, libeay32.dll and ssleay32.dll from your PHP folder, and `libmcrypt.dll` from `http://ftp.emini.dk/pub/php/win32/mcrypt/`, to the Windows System32 folder.

6. Open for editing, with any text editor (even Notepad), the Apache configuration file. The location of this file is `C:\Program Files\Apache Group\Apache2\conf\httpd.conf` by default.

7. In `httpd.conf`, find the portion with many `LoadModule` entries, and add the following lines:

   ```
   LoadModule php5_module c:/php/php5apache2.dll
   AddType application/x-httpd-php .php
   ```

8. Also in `httpd.conf`, find the `DirectoryIndex` entry, and add `index.php` at the end of the line, like this:

   ```
   DirectoryIndex index.html index.html.var index.php
   ```

9. Open the Apache Service Monitor by clicking its icon in the Notification Area of the taskbar, and restart the Apache 2 service.

10. To test that your PHP installation works, create a file named `test.php` in the `htdocs` folder (by default `C:\Program Files\Apache Group\Apache2\htdocs`) with a call to PHP's `phpinfo()` function:

    ```
    <?php
    phpinfo();
    ?>
    ```

11. Point your web browser to `http://localhost/test.php` (or `http://localhost:8080/test.php` if you installed Apache to work on port 8080) to test if everything went okay with the installation.

Installing MySQL 4

At the time of this writing, MySQL 4.1 was in gamma version, so we made our queries compatible with both MySQL 4.0 and MySQL 4.1. The most important (or at least most expected) new functionality MySQL 4.1 has over 4.0 is subqueries, so we highlighted in the book the places where the new functionality could make a difference. For advanced developers, MySQL 4.1 brings even more new exciting functionality such as the possibility to replicate over SSL, OpenGIS spatial types, and the new `CREATE TABLE` syntax.

You can download the Windows installer for MySQL 4.0 from `http://dev.mysql.com/downloads/mysql/4.0.html`, and for MySQL 4.1 from `http://dev.mysql.com/downloads/mysql/4.1.html`. After downloading the installer, simply execute it to install your MySQL Server.

After installing MySQL, it's good practice to change the MySQL administrator's password (the `root@localhost` user), which is blank by default, by executing the MySQL console program (or using a database administration tool such as phpMyAdmin or MySQL Control Center) and executing this command:

```
SET PASSWORD FOR root@localhost=PASSWORD('your_new_password');
```

To ensure you can access the MySQL 4 server from PHP programs, you need to

1. Open `php.ini` and uncomment the following line:

   ```
   extension=php_mysql.dll
   ```

2. Copy `libmysql.dll` from your PHP installation folder to the `Windows\System32` folder.

3. Restart Apache.

Preparing your Unix Playground

Depending on your Unix distribution, installing the needed software for this book may be more or less painful. Almost all the Linux distributions include Apache, PHP, and MySQL, however it's likely that you'll get slightly out-of-date versions of these programs, and this project has some special requirements. Before trying to download anything, you should check first whether you can find what you need on your system, online, or on the installation CDs of your Linux distribution. We don't have high requirements for Apache and MySQL, so you can do a binary installation for them, but you'll have to compile PHP from sources to enable all the libraries you need.

Installing Apache 2

The most common way to create an SSL-powered web server is to use Apache 2 (at least version 2.0.45) and OpenSSL. You probably have them installed on your system.

You should first check whether you have OpenSSL RPMs installed on your system with the following command:

```
rpm -qa | grep openssl
```

If you don't have OpenSSL, grab the following RPMs from a resource such as `http://www.rpmfind.net` and install them:

```
openssl-0.9.7a-2.i386.rpm
openssl-devel-0.9.7a-2.i386.rpm
```

We decided to build the latest Apache Web Server (version 2.0.52 at the moment of writing) from sources. First, you should download the latest Unix Apache source from `http://httpd.apache.org/download.cgi` and uncompress it with something like this:

```
tar -zxvf httpd-2.0.52.tar.gz
```

Note If you're running Red Hat, you should execute the following command to avoid a compilation bug (related to the `krb5.h` file), described at `http://bugzilla.redhat.com/bugzilla/show_bug.cgi?id=82369`:

```
export C_INCLUDE_PATH=/usr/kerberos/include;
```

Now you can move on to actually compile and install the Apache Web Server on your system. Go to the root of the Apache sources and execute the following commands, while logged in as root:

```
/configure --prefix=/usr/local/apache2 --enable-so --enable-ssl --with-ssl --enable-
auth-digest
make
make install
```

To enable SSL, you'll need to install an SSL certificate into Apache. In case you'll host your application with a hosting company that offers you SSL, you can do all testing on your development machine with a "fake" SSL certificate that you generate on your own. You can do this by making yourself a certificate authority. For testing purposes on your development machine, it's easier to install the XAMPP package on Windows, which takes only a matter of minutes and provides you with an SSL-enabled Apache. However, if you want to generate your own certificate, you should follow some excellent tutorials you can find on the Internet, such as the one at `http://www.linux.com/howtos/SSL-Certificates-HOWTO/index.shtml` (you can also find many more using a simple web search). Otherwise, if you want to install an SSL certificate for production, you'll need to get a "real" SSL certificate from a certification authority such as VeriSign, as explained in Chapter 11.

Make any changes you need in the `httpd.conf` configuration file, and then start your Apache server with

```
/usr/local/apache2/bin/apachectl start
```

Note If you get errors such as "module `access_module` is built in and can't be loaded," try to comment out the `LoadModule` line from the `httpd.conf` that corresponds to the module that generated the error. Even better, try to comment out every module that you don't need.

Now load `http://localhost/` in your browser to make sure your Apache Web Server is up and running, and then browse to `https://localhost/` to test that you can also access Apache through SSL.

Installing MySQL 4

Many of the Linux distributions contain a 3.23.x version of MySQL and you need at least a 4.x version. You should get a MySQL binary from `http://dev.mysql.com/downloads/mysql/4.0.html`, from the "Linux x86 RPM downloads" section. You need the following RPMs from there:

- Server

- Client programs

- Libraries and header files

After downloading, install these RPMs with commands such as

```
rpm -i MySQL-xxxx.rpm
```

The RPM automatically starts MySQL if the installation is successful (see `http://dev.mysql.com/doc/mysql/en/Linux-RPM.html`), and also creates the appropriate entries in `/etc/init.d` to start MySQL automatically.

Note Find more details about MySQL startup methods at `http://dev.mysql.com/doc/mysql/en/Automatic_start.html`.

After installing MySQL, you should change the MySQL administrator's password (the `root@localhost` user), which is blank by default. One way to change root's password is to execute:

```
mysqladmin -u root password 'your_new_password.'
```

Alternatively, you can access MySQL through a console program or by using a database administration tool such as phpMyAdmin or MySQL Control Center, and execute this command:

```
SET PASSWORD FOR root@localhost=PASSWORD('your_new_password');
```

See more about MySQL passwords at `http://dev.mysql.com/doc/mysql/en/Passwords.html`.
You can now test your MySQL server by executing the following command in your console:

```
#mysql -u root -p
Enter password:
mysql>show databases;
```

Installing PHP 5

Every time you want to get a new PHP library working on Linux, you need to recompile the PHP module. That's why it's recommended to make a "good" compilation, with all the needed libraries, from the start.

Go to `http://www.php.net/downloads.php` and get the complete source code archive of PHP 5.x and extract the contents in a directory. At the moment of writing, the latest PHP version was 5.0.2.

Before compiling PHP and making Apache aware of it (by updating Apache's configuration file `httpd.conf`), you need to install the extra modules you'll need to work under PHP. Let's deal with them one by one.

The mhash Library

`Mhash` is a free library that provides a uniform interface to a large number of hash algorithms. You used it to hash customers' passwords in Chapter 11. Refer to that chapter to learn more about hashing.

Download `mhash` from `http://mhash.sourceforge.net/`, unpack it (using `tar -zxvf`), and install it by executing the following commands:

```
./configure
./make
./make install
```

Alternatively, if you use Red Hat, you can download the RPMs from `http://www.ottolander.nl/opensource/mhash/libmhash.html` and install them. We installed both `libmhash-0.8.18-2a.i386.rpm` and `libmhash-devel-0.8.18-2a.i386.rpm` RPMs.

mcrypt Library

This library allows you to use a wide range of encryption functions. You'll need it to encrypt highly sensitive information such as credit card details as discussed in Chapter 11. (Refer to Chapter 11 for more details about this.)

Download `mcrypt` from `http://mcrypt.sourceforge.net/`, unpack it (using `tar -zxvf`), and install it by executing the following commands:

```
./configure
./make
./make install
```

Alternatively, you can find the RPMs for Red Hat at `http://www.ottolander.nl/open-source/mcrypt/mcrypt.html`. We installed both `libmcrypt-2.5.7-1a.i386.rpm` and `libmcrypt-devel-2.5.7-1a.i386.rpm` RPMs.

Alternatively, you can use the source code from `http://mcrypt.sourceforge.net`.

CURL (Client URL Library) Functions

You'll use `libcurl`, a library that allows you to connect and communicate to many different types of servers with many different types of protocols. You need it to communicate through

SSL with the payment gateways in Chapter 14. You can take a fresh version of the `curl` library from `http://curl.haxx.se/download.html`, but you can also use `http://www.rpmfind.net` to find the RPM packages for your system.

pfpro

`pfpro` is an extension from VeriSign that allows you to process credit cards and other financial transactions using VeriSign Payflow Pro. Refer to Chapter 14 for more details about working with VeriSign Payflow Pro.

To compile the `pfpro` extension under PHP, you need to get the Payflow Pro SDK from VeriSign. First, you'll need to go to `http://www.verisign.com/products/payflow/pro/index.html` and apply for a Free Payment Trial Account. After you have a valid account, you'll be able to get the SDK from the Downloads section of the VeriSign manager at `https://manager.verisign.com/`.

Copy the header file `pfpro.h` to `/usr/local/include` and the library file `libpfpro.so` to `/usr/local/lib`. Effective installation will happen when you compile PHP, as explained a bit later in this appendix.

libxml2

PHP 5 requires a `libxml2` library version 2.5.10 or greater. If your Unix or Linux system doesn't have a recent enough version, go get fresh RPMs of `libxml2` and `libxml2-devel` from `http://xmlsoft.org/` and install them.

You can check for your `libxml2` library with the following command:

```
rpm -qa | grep libxml2
```

Compiling and Installing PHP 5

To compile and install PHP 5, follow these steps:

1. Go to the folder where you extracted the PHP source and execute the following commands:

```
./configure --with-config-file-path=/etc --with-mysql=/usr/include/mysql
--with-apxs2=/usr/local/apache2/bin/apsx2 --with-mcrypt --with-mhash
--with-openssl-dir --with-pfpro --with-curl --with-zlib
make
make install
```

Note If you are compiling PHP for XAMPP, you need to use the following configure command instead:

```
./configure --with-config-file-path=/opt/lampp/etc --with-mysql=/opt/lampp
--with-apxs2=/opt/lampp/bin/apxs --with-mcrypt --with-mhash
--with-openssl-dir --with-pfpro --with-curl --with-zlib
```

After executing `make` and `make install`, you need to copy the newly created `php_src/libs/libphp5.so` to `/opt/lampp/modules/libphp5.so`.

---

2. Copy `php.ini-recommended` to `/etc/php.ini` by executing the following command:

```
cp php.ini-recommended /etc/php.ini
```

3. Open the Apache configuration file (`httpd.conf`), find the `DirectoryIndex` entry, and make sure you have `index.php` at the end of the line:

```
DirectoryIndex index.html index.html.var index.php
```

4. Restart your Apache Web Server and everything should be okay. To make sure your PHP installation works, create a file named `test.php` in the `htdocs` folder (by default `/usr/local/apache2/htdocs/`), with the following contents in it:

```
<?php
phpinfo();
?>
```

Finally, point your web browser to `http://localhost/test.php` to ensure PHP was correctly installed under Apache.

Installing phpMyAdmin

phpMyAdmin is the most well known tool for accessing MySQL databases from a web interface. phpMyAdmin is written in PHP so you first need to have a PHP-enabled web server to use it.

You should first download phpMyAdmin from `http://www.phpmyadmin.net/home_page/downloads.php`, and then follow the excellent installation instructions in its official documentation at `http://www.phpmyadmin.net/documentation/`.

In short, after uploading phpMyAdmin's files to the web server, you'll need to edit a few settings in its `config.inc.php` file, the most important being the ones used to connect to MySQL (the hostname of the machine on which MySQL runs, port, username, and password):

```
$cfg['PmaAbsoluteUri'] = "http://your-web-site.com/phpMyAdmin/";
$cfg['Servers'][$i]['host']
$cfg['Servers'][$i]['port']
$cfg['Servers'][$i]['user']
$cfg['Servers'][$i]['password']
```

For even more details about working with phpMyAdmin than the ones offered by its documentation, read *Mastering phpMyAdmin for Effective MySQL Management* (Packt Publishing, 2004).

Hosting the Web Site

In this appendix, you'll learn how to place your local e-commerce web site on the Internet. You need to follow four steps in this process:

1. Choose a web hosting company.

2. Install phpMyAdmin on the production web server, if the hosting company doesn't offer it by default. phpMyAdmin installation was covered in Appendix A.

3. Create the database on the hosting location. (We'll show you how to do it using phpMyAdmin.)

4. Copy your application from the development machine to the production server, updating the configuration files to accommodate the new environment (such as updating the database connection string, and so on).

In this appendix, we'll review these steps in detail.

Choosing a Web Hosting Company

Choosing the best company to host your web site is a critical step, because this choice determines the total cost of keeping your web site up and the features you will have.

The minimum set of technical features the web hosting company must offer includes

- PHP 5 (your web site contains features that are not compatible with PHP 4)

- MySQL 4 (the SQL queries in the web site are compatible with both MySQL 4.0 and MySQL 4.1)

- The mcrypt extension to encrypt credit card information (discussed in Chapter 11)

- The mhash extension for hashing customer passwords (discussed in Chapter 11)

- The curl extension if you choose DataCash or the Payflow Pro (pfpro) extension if you choose VeriSign Payflow Pro (for communicating with the payment gateway in Chapter 14)

Apart from these features, you should also compare the level of technical support they provide for you, server power, uptime guarantee, connection speed, transfer limits, and so on. It's also important to find out whether the hosting company is flexible about the features they offer you in case your requirements change over time.

Another difference between web hosting companies that offer hosting for PHP and MySQL is the platform they use. I recommend hosting your web site on Unix platforms because they usually offer better performance, stability, and security for applications that work with Apache, PHP, and MySQL.

Many hosting companies also offer database administration tools, such as phpMyAdmin. The more technical details depend on your expectation for the web site. A typical configuration for a medium-size web site use about 15GB/month for traffic; about 500MB of disk space for web site files, database space, emails, and so on; and at least one domain name.

A number of online resources can help you choose a hosting company, so take some time to read many of the hosting reviews available on the web. For example, PC Magazine's Hosting roundup is available at `http://www.pcmag.com/category2/0,1738,2269,00.asp`. You can also have a look at `http://www.web-hosting-top.com/`, which is an impartial list of good web hosting companies.

In the e-commerce web site you created in this book, you also used two external libraries: PEAR and Smarty. You might not find these modules included in hosting plans for several reasons. First of all, these libraries, which are written in PHP, can be easily installed manually by anyone by just copying the files to an appropriate server directory and then referencing their files in your project. Even if your hosting provider offers PEAR and Smarty, consider installing your own versions so you won't depend on the server's configuration.

You learned in Chapter 2 how to install Smarty and PEAR on your local web site. To install them on a remote web site, you just need to upload their files to the hosting server using FTP.

Creating the Database on the Hosting Server

The tool you'll use here is phpMyAdmin. After you have a phpMyAdmin working installation, you can use it to move the database from your machine to the server.

You'll first need to use phpMyAdmin on the development machine to export your database structures and data to an SQL script file, and then you'll use phpMyAdmin on the production server to execute the SQL script. Figure B-1 shows phpMyAdmin's export options.

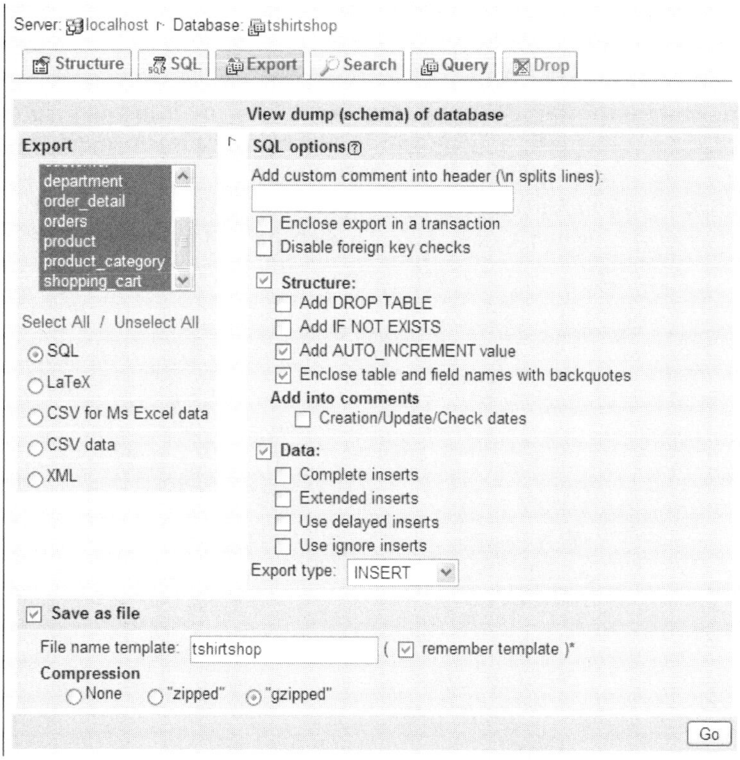

Figure B-1. *The phpMyAdmin database export page*

The steps to export your database from your development machine are

1. Select your database in phpMyAdmin and go to its Export page (shown in Figure B-1).

2. Click the **Select All** link under the **Export** list box.

3. Make sure the **Structure** and **Data** check boxes are checked.

4. Check the **"gzipped"** radio box and then supply a name of the file for export in the text box that now contains only _DB_ (for example, you can use tshirtshop for the name).

5. Press Enter or click the Go button.

6. Save the SQL script in your machine. You'll need to locate this file later, when you'll execute it on the production database.

After you have the SQL script, you'll need to create the database on the production server, and then execute this script into that database.

For creating the database, you'll use the administrative interfaces (usually based on a control panel) provided by your web hosting company. Most likely, if you use "tshirtshop" for the database name, your username on the hosting server will be automatically appended, so the name of the database will be something like *username_tshirtshop*.

After you have a database on the production server, use phpMyAdmin to open the database and execute the SQL script you created earlier. You must click the SQL link and you will see something similar to Figure B-2.

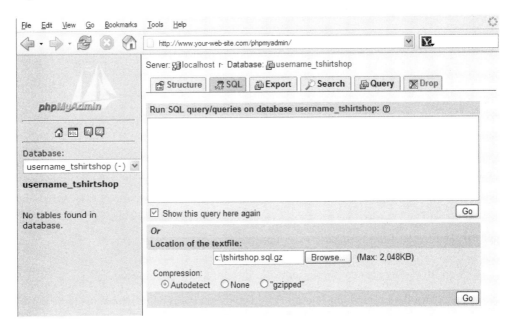

Figure B-2. *PhpMyAdmin SQL page on production*

Now you must browse to your SQL script file that you saved previously. Click the Go button to submit the form, and create your tables with all the data for the current database. After this step, you have completely restored your database from the development machine to the production server.

Copying the Application to the Production Server

After the database is ready on the server, it's time to copy the application itself. Usually you'll do this through FTP, or by using the file uploading tools offered by the hosting control panel. You have the best control over the process when using FTP.

Many good file managers are available that support FTP connections (such as Total Commander that you can download at `http://www.ghisler.com`). For a list of more FTP clients, visit `http://dmoz.org/Computers/Software/Internet/Clients/FTP/`.

Using your favorite file manager, copy all the files inside your `tshirtshop` folder to your folder on the production web server. After copying the files, you must modify your application's configuration file (`include/config.inc.php`) to update at least the database connection details (server, username, password, database). You get this data from your web hosting's server control panel.

While building TShirtShop, you have met more configuration options that you might need to change on the production machine (of course, for an advanced application you can create a mechanism that automatically uses different configuration options and database settings, depending on the location the application runs).

After copying all the files and configuring the database connection string, you should be all set to see your web site online. Good luck.

APPENDIX C

■ ■ ■

Project Management Considerations

It feels great to finish building a complete e-commerce store, doesn't it? For the purposes of this book, we dealt with many design issues on a chapter-by-chapter basis, while also covering the theory concepts. However, in real-world projects, many times you'll need to do the whole design work from the start. This appendix discusses how to manage building complete solutions in a professional manner.

Maybe it seems easier to just start coding without any up-front design, and with some luck, you might even create something that works the second day; however, when it comes to large projects, you'll face a lot of problems in the long term by doing that.

A project's life cycle includes more than simply coding away and building something ready to run—it should not be done hastily. For example, for almost any real-world software project, a critical part of its success is the database design, even if it only counts for a small part of the project's cycle. This makes perfect sense if you consider that e-commerce sites, web portals, search engines, and customer interfaces for service providers (banking, IT, insurance, and so on) are all basically interfaces to a backend database.

Of course, the way you display the data and the reports you present to the client also plays an important role in the success of the software. However, you can think of the database as the foundation of a house; if you make mistakes in the foundation, no matter how nice or trendy the house looks, it will still be torn down by the first wind.

Developing Software Solutions

In fact, the software solution's technical design is only a part of the software project's life cycle. To give you an idea of the steps involved in managing a complete software solution, imagine a real-world example, such as building an ERP (Enterprise Resource Planning) application for a clothing factory.

First of all, you need to know exactly what the client needs from the software, so you talk to the client about the goals of implementing such software in the network. This is the stage of gathering system requirements and software requirements for the application you need to build.

After you (as the project manager) fully understand the customer's requirements and discuss a budget allocation and a timeline for the project, a team of analysts works with the customer's commercial office to get information about the tasks performed in the factory, the work schedule, and the manufacturing equipment they have. Your analysts must be in touch with the region's economic regime, the employer's legal obligations, the import-export conditions, and so on—facts that are clarified with the commercial, economic, and personnel departments of the company. The analysts build the database, and describe the reports and the operations that the software must accomplish.

After adjustments (if necessary) by the customer, the analytical part ends by adding a written annex to the contract with all these features and a timeline that is agreed to by the customer. After this, any modifications in the database structure, the reports, or software functionality are charged extra.

Next, the design team creates a user-friendly, attractive interface that can be presented to the customer and changed to fit the customer's artistic taste. After this phase is completed, the coding part begins. This shouldn't take a long time because the programmers know exactly what they need to do. When they finish coding, the software is installed on a test platform at the customer site and the customer team simulates using the software for a definite period of time. During the testing period, the eventual programming and design bugs are revealed and fixed by the programmers. At the end of this phase, the customer should have a software application that runs by the agreed specifications, and deploys on the production machines. That's the end of the project; the final payments are made, and every modification the customer asks for in the future is billed.

That was a short version of a story about commercial software. Of course, the theory doesn't apply the same for all software projects. In the case of smaller projects, such as many e-commerce sites, several, if not all, the tasks can be performed by a single person.

Considering the Theory Behind Project Management

Many theories exist about how to manage the software development life cycle (SDLC). No model can be deemed the best, because choosing an SDLC model depends on the particularities of your project. You'll learn about the most popular project-management theories in the following pages.

The Waterfall (or Traditional) Method

The Waterfall method, also known as the traditional method, is the father of all methodologies. It consists of breaking the software project into six or seven phases that must be processed in sequential order to deliver the final product. The input of each phase consists of the output of the preceding phase (see Figure C-1).

Establishing the requirements is the first phase and can be divided in two as shown in Figure C-1. First, you must establish the system requirements of the project; at the end of this phase, you have a paper describing all the hardware needed for implementing, testing, and deploying the application. You also need the software platforms your application will be developed and tested on. The first two phases must include an opportunity study at the beginning and a feasibility study at the end. Basically, the first question is "Do we really need this from the business point of view?" After you establish the requirements, the feasibility study provides a high-level cost and benefit analysis so that a ROI (return on investment) can be estimated.

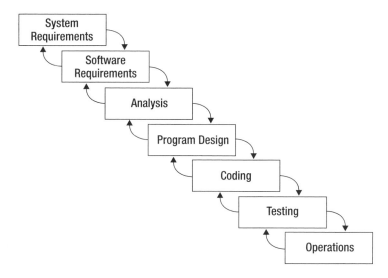

Figure C-1. *The Waterfall model*

In the Analysis phase, the analysts work with the customer to fully understand the customer needs. They have to spend time with the customer's staff to define the software functionalities, transcribing them in a professional analysis for the software engineers.

In the Program Design phase, the design team reads the specifications of the analysis and develops some prototypes that the customer must agree on. Usually, that is throwaway code.

In the Coding phase, programmers effectively code the application. This happens after the customer agrees on the software design delivered by the Program Design phase.

If a testing platform is provided, the programmers install the application there and test all the functionalities of the software. All the bugs discovered are corrected, and at the end of the testing phase, the software must be ready to go in production. If a testing platform is not provided, the programmers have to simulate or conduct the testing on the actual platform the software will run on; however, at the end of the testing phase, the programmers have to install a fresh copy of the bug-free software they created.

Everything is completed after deployment at the beginning of the Operations phase.

Note Every phase has a feedback to the preceding phase where new ideas can be added and errors are corrected.

Advantages of the Waterfall Method

The main advantages of the Waterfall method are its simplicity and the fact that everything is documented and agreed upon with the customer. This leads to some important benefits:

- Because everything is planned from the start, it's easy for the project manager to correctly estimate project costs and timelines.

- The rigorous initial planning makes the project goals clear.

- All requirements are analyzed and validated by the customer, so the customer can esti-mate the benefits incurred by the software application before it's actually implemented.

Disadvantages of the Waterfall Method

The disadvantages of the Waterfall method are

- The customer is not able to see the product until it's completely finished. At that stage, it can be very expensive to make any changes to the project.

- It has little flexibility for scope changes during the project's development.

- The architecture limitations are often not discovered until late in the development cycle.

- Because testing happens at the end of the coding phase, unexpected problems with the code might force developers to find quick fixes at the expense of the planned architecture.

- The Waterfall method doesn't work on projects whose requirements can't be rigorously planned from the start.

The Spiral Method

As a development of the Waterfall method, the Spiral method is more suitable for large, expen-sive, and complicated projects. Barry Boehm first described it in 1988 as an iterative waterfall in which every iteration provides increased software capability (see Figure C-2, which repre-sents the diagram created by Barry Boehm).

The diagram consists of a spiral divided into four quadrants. Each quadrant represents a management process: Identify, Design, Construct, and Evaluate. The system goes through four cycles of these four processes:

- *Proof-of-concept cycle*: Define the business goals, capture the requirements, develop a conceptual design, construct a "proof-of-concept," establish test plans, and conduct a risk analysis. Share results with user.

- *First-build cycle*: Derive system requirements, develop logic design, construct first build, and evaluate results. Share results with user.

- *Second-build cycle*: Derive subsystem requirements, produce physical design, construct second build, and evaluate results. Share results with user.

- *Final-build cycle*: Derive unit requirements, produce final design, construct final build, and test all levels. Seek user acceptance.

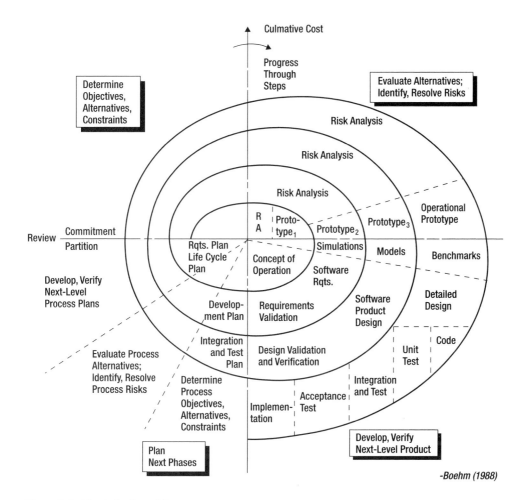

Figure C-2. *The Spiral model*

The main advantages of the Spiral method proposed by Boehm are

- The entire application is built on working with the client.

- Any gaps in the Requirement phase of the Waterfall method are identified as work progresses.

- The spiral representation conveys very clearly the cyclic nature of the project and the progression through its lifespan.

However, the Spiral method has some disadvantages as well:

- Requires serious discipline on the part of the client.

- Executive control can be difficult because in most projects, the client is not responsible for the schedule and budget.

■**Note** The Spiral method is more suitable for software in which the entire problem is well defined from the start, such as modeling and simulating software.

The Rapid Application Development (RAD) Method

RAD is another common project-management method that is, in essence, "try before you buy." Whereas in the Waterfall and even Spiral methods, the client was working with a lot of documentation, in the RAD approach, the client works with the software as it's being developed. The belief is that the client can produce better feedback when working with a live system as opposed to working strictly with documentation. When using RAD as a project-management method, customer rejection cases are significantly less when going in production.

The RAD method consists of the following phases:

- Business modeling

- Data modeling

- Process modeling

- Application generation

- Testing and turnover

The RAD approach allows rapid generation and change of UI features. The client works with the software just like in the production environment.

The main disadvantage of RAD is that the client will always want more enhancements to the software—not always important ones—and the developer must try to satisfy the client's needs. This can result in an unending cycle of requirements, going away from the main purpose of the project.

Extreme Programming (XP) Methodology

Extreme Programming (XP) is a very controversial method not only because it's the newest, but also because it eliminates a lot of phases from the traditional Waterfall methodology. XP is simple and based on communication, feedback, and courage.

The professional analysts are replaced with the client, who is very active in the process. The client writes a document named "User Stories," which is a simple description of the desired functionality of the software. The programmers read the document and give an estimated time frame for implementing every functionality. After receiving the time estimates, the customer chooses a group of functionalities to be developed first. This is called an **iteration**.

The developers use a **test-driven** design in the implementation phase, meaning that a testing method for the desired functionality is conceived before the code is actually written. Usually, every piece of code is written by a programmer under the supervision of another programmer who tests the functionality of the code.

After the code for the entire iteration is complete, it's then given an acceptance test with the customer, who approves (or disapproves) the iteration. The programmer keeps developing or improving code for that iteration until it passes the acceptance test.

The software is deployed in a number of **releases**, composed of one or more iterations; the software gets to the final release when all iterations that contain all the functionalities described in the User Stories document pass the acceptance test.

Picking a Method

More project management methods are available to you than the ones described so far. Because no single method is best, a good project manager must know in theory a little about all of them to choose the best one for the current project. Choosing the wrong tactic for a project might lead to failure, so the project manager needs to carefully consider all options before choosing how to deal with a particular project. A strategy like this will never work: "Okay, we have to build an e-commerce site. Let's do XP with this one, and maybe we'll spiral the next one!"

In many cases, it's best to use a mix of methods to suit your project. For example, if the client doesn't know for sure what she wants, you can use bits of XP and collaborate closely with the client during the development based on a User Stories document, add a few steps from the Waterfall method, and do some RAD on the way.

Anyway, it's very important to keep some of these procedures in mind for your next projects, because the way you manage your projects can save you time, money, and stress.

Understanding the E-Commerce Project Cycle

For most e-commerce projects, your best bet will be something with a Waterfall flavor, but with a bit of changes here or there.

If you have some knowledge about management and a good artistic spirit for web design, after you read this book, the e-commerce project can be a "one man show." First of all, you need to organize the tasks so that they take place in a logical, sequential order.

Understanding the customer needs should not be difficult. The customer wants an e-store where a range of products can be advertised and bought. You need to know the type of products the customer wants on the site and a little about future strategy (today the customer is only selling hardware components, but in the future, the customer might want to sell laptops). This is very important because the database and the whole architecture must be designed from the start to support future changes. You might also want to find out about how the shipping department is organized to optimize the handling and shipping process.

Most customers require artistic and functional design, so, in most cases, the next phase is **creating a web prototype**. Whether you do it yourself or hire a web designer, the prototype should be only a web site template—only HTML code with something like "Product name Here" instead of an actual product, without the need for any databases. Depending on the artistic taste of the customer, you might have to build several prototypes until you agree on a design.

Designing the database is, as I said, a critical phase of the project. The logical database design is developed from the Requirements gathering phase, and is agreed on with the customer. The database's logical design describes what data you need to store and the relationships between different entities of data (such as the relationship between products and departments), but doesn't include strict implementation details such as the associate table used to physically implement Many-to-Many relationships. If you're an advanced database designer, you'll create an optimal physical database structure yourself.

A number of tools (such as the ones presented at `http://www.infogoal.com/dmc/dmcdmd.htm`) enable you to design the database visually. (You can find even more useful links with a Google search on "data modeling.") These tools have very powerful features for designing relational database structures, and even generate the SQL code to turn them into real databases. Regardless of the database engine you're using, design your tables in a visual way (even with a pen and paper) rather than start by writing SQL queries.

Next, you **implement the data tier objects**. This is the place you start playing with your database, because you need to implement the data access logic that will support the other tiers in your application. In the process, you'll probably want to populate the database with some fictive examples to have a base for testing your queries. Before writing the queries as data tier objects, test them using a visual interface to the database engine that allows executing and debugging SQL queries. This will make your life easier when debugging the SQL code, because as all SQL developers know, the code doesn't always work as you expect it to the first time.

After the data tier is in place, you can continue by **building the middle tier** of your application. In this book, you learned some techniques about implementing the middle tier for various parts of the site, but you might want to choose other techniques for your particular project.

Building the user interface is obviously the next step. You already have a prototype that is usable only for design, because at the stage you created the prototypes, you didn't have a functional foundation. Usually, interface prototypes in software projects are throwaway code, but here you build the UI logic (preferably using Smarty or another templating engine) that generates the actual look of your web site with the design the customer agreed on.

A final testing phase is very important at the end of the project. The database will be populated with real records and a simulation is made to test the efficiency of the ordering process. Every process should be tested before production, so you must give your customer enough time to test every functionality of the site, to make some test orders, and to evaluate the shipping process. During this stage, any programming errors should be revealed for you to correct.

After the code is ready and tested on your local machine, the next step is to **find/provide a hosting solution**. Perhaps the best strategy is to host the project at a specialized provider, and if the site proves to be successful, the customer can invest in its own hosting solution.

Maintaining Relationships with Your Customers

In the ideal project, you include all the possible clauses in a contract; after you deliver the site and finish the project, you never want to hear from the customer again, except for developing new functionalities or changing the design, in which case, you charge the customer extra.

The most unwanted thing would be for the customer to ask you to make changes without paying for them, and that's possible if you are not careful with the contract and with the tools you provide the customer for administration.

For example, many e-commerce sites have poor catalog admin pages, which are nightmares for the programmers. Avoiding such a nightmare can be possible by providing proper tools and interfaces for the customer and, most importantly, describing how they work (eventually a user's manual). Many programmers don't take this detail seriously and prefer to bring the site up with an incomplete or hard to use catalog admin page, not knowing what's coming.

If the database is complicated, you must describe all the fields in a manual and how they must be completed; if an error occurs when the customer tries to submit a form to a database, you have to make the error page as eloquent as possible. Also, try to work with those who will use the tools you provide in the design stage and take a couple of hours to instruct them personally on how to use the tools. This will save you a lot of explanations over the phone or even going to the customer's office without being paid.

Index

∎H